TRANSLATION

OF A

COMPARATIVE VOCABULARY

OF THE

CHINESE, COREAN, AND JAPANESE

LANGUAGES:

TO WHICH IS ADDED

THE THOUSAND CHARACTER CLASSIC

In Chinese and Corean;

THE WHOLE ACCOMPANIED BY

COPIOUS INDEXES,

OF ALL THE CHINESE AND ENGLISH WORDS

OCCURRING IN THE WORK.

BY

PHILO SINENSIS.

BATAVIA:

PRINTED AT THE PARAPATTAN PRESS.

1835.

The following vocabulary appears to have been originally composed by a native of Corea, for the purpose of facilitating the acquisition of the Japanese language to those of his countrymen who should visit Japan: and as the Chinese language is common to both nations, he has made that the basis of the work. Thus the Chinese character is first written at the top of the page, then follows the sound of that character, expressed in Corean letters; after that comes the Corean word, both in the vernacular and learned idioms, and finally the Japanese, all expressed in Corean letters That which has been aimed at in the translation is, to give the meaning of each Chinese character at the top of the page, for the purpose of ascertaining which, the Chinese above has been compared with the Japanese below, and both referred to Chinese and Japanese Dictionaries. An attempt has also been made to express the sounds of the different Corean letters, by the help of a Japanese and Corean alphabet brought from Japan, and of an English and Corean alphabet which appeared in a periodical publication at Canton; in fixing these sounds regard has been had to the known sounds of the Chinese and Japanese words employed in the work, and though the translator has never yet seen or conversed with a Corean, yet he hopes he has not greatly erred in thus hazarding to elucidate their language. The Corean alphabet, with the scheme of orthography annexed, will, it is hoped, be sufficient to enable the student to decide on the power of the English letters employed: and the different indexes which follow will assist in the search for any given word. The English and Corean index will be found to contain almost every primitive or important English word, to which the vernacular Corean is joined, with figures of reference, the first shewing the page, and the second the line in which the given word is to be met with. The Chinese index is arranged according to the Chinese radicals, and is also provided with figures, pointing out the page and line, in which the character is to be found. The translator is induced to put forth the present work, merely as a help to those students who may wish to turn their attention to the Corean language, and who may not be possessed of better assistance. Should the least facility be hereby afforded for the attainment of a language of which hitherto little has been known, and should the advancement of knowledge and religion in those dark regions of the earth be in the smallest degree forwarded hereby, the translator's end will be abundantly answered.

DOUBLE INITIALS.

	Final		K as in kam. ㄱ	N as in nag. ㄴ	B as in bag.	PT as in Sarepta.	PS as in Psyche.	Z as in zany.	DZ as in adze.	SK as in skin.	ST as in stamp.	SP as in span.	SS as in massa.
SIMPLE FINALS.	A ㅏ	long as in cart.	ka 가	na 나	ba	pta	psa	za	dza	ska	sta	spa	ssa
	YA ㅑ	long as in yard.	kya 갸	nya 냐	bya	ptya	psya	zya	dzya	skya	stya	spya	ssya
	O ㅓ	long as in comb.	ko 거	no 너	bo	pto	pso	zo	dzo	sko	sto	spo	sso
	YO ㅕ	long as in yoke.	kyo 겨	nyo 녀	byo	ptyo	psyo	zyo	dzyo	skyo	styo	spyo	ssyo
	O ㅗ	short as in not.	ko 고	no 노	bo	pto	pso	zo	dzo	sko	sto	spo	sso
	YO ㅛ	short as in yon.	kyo 교	nyo 뇨	byo	ptyo	psyo	zyo	dzyo	skyo	styo	spyo	ssyo
	OO ㅜ	long as in boot.	koo 구	noo 누	boo	ptoo	psoo	zoo	dzoo	skoo	stoo	spoo	ssoo
	YOO ㅠ	long as in your.	kyoo 규	nyoo 뉴	byoo	ptyoo	psyoo	zyoo	dzyoo	skyoo	styoo	spyoo	ssyoo
	OO ㅡ	short as in good.	koo 그	noo 느	boo	ptoo	psoo	zoo	dzoo	skoo	stoo	spoo	ssoo
	I ㅣ	long as in shire.	ki 기	ni 니	bi	pti	psi	zi	dzi	ski	sti	spi	ssi
	A ㆍ	short as in hat.	ka ᄀᆞ	na ᄂᆞ	ba	pta	psa	za	dza	ska	sta	spa	ssa
DOUBLE FINALS.	E ㅔ	long as in ere.	ke 게	ne 네	be	pte	pse	ze	dze	ske	ste	spe	sse
	EY ㅖ	long as in whey.	key 계	ney 녜	bey	ptey	psey	zey	dzey	skey	stey	spey	ssey
	WA ㅘ	long as in quack.	kwa 과	nwa 놔	bwa	ptwa	pswa	zwa	dzwa	skwa	stwa	spwa	sswa
	WO ㅝ	long as in woke.	kwo 궈	nwo 눠	bwo	ptwo	pswo	zwo	dzwo	skwo	stwo	spwo	sswo
	OI ㅚ	short as in coin.	koi 괴	noi 뇌	boi	ptoi	psoi	zoi	dzoi	skoi	stoi	spoi	ssoi
	WI ㅢ	short as in quick.	kwi 긔	nwi 늬	bwi	ptwi	pswi	zwi	dzwi	skwi	stwi	spwi	sswi
	OOI ㅟ	long as in cooing.	kooi 귀	nooi 뉘	booi	ptooi	psooi	zooi	dzooi	skooi	stooi	spooi	ssooi
	YOOI ᆔ	long as in ewing.	kyooi ᄀᆔ	nyooi ᄂᆔ	byooi	ptyooi	psyooi	zyooi	dzyooi	skyooi	styooi	spyooi	ssyooi
	WE ㅞ	long as in way.	kwe 궤	nwe 눼	bwe	ptwe	pswe	zwe	dzwe	skwe	stwe	spwe	sswe
	WEY ᆒ	long as in weigh.	kwey ᄀᆒ	nwey ᄂᆒ	bwey	ptwey	pswey	zwey	dzwey	skwey	stwey	spwey	sswey
	WAI ㅙ	like English letter y	kwai 괘	nwai 놰	bwai	ptwai	pswai	zwai	dzwai	skwai	stwai	spwai	sswai
	AI ㅐ	like English letter i	kai 개	nai 내	bai	ptai	psai	zai	dzai	skai	stai	spai	ssai
	AI ㆎ	ditto but short	kai ᄀᆡ	nai ᄂᆡ	bai	ptai	psai	zai	dzai	skai	stai	spai	ssai
	IA ᆝ	long as in mania	kia ᄀᆝ	nia ᄂᆝ	bia	ptia	psia	zia	dzia	skia	stia	spia	ssia

To abandon, pa rir, 91 15
To abate, tor, 88 7
Abbot, tsyang lo, 53 4
Abdicate, mir pyo soor, 108 7
Abdomen, pai, 17 14
To abhor, won mang, 21 3
To abide, sar, 118 7
Abject, ts'hyon har, 88 13
Ability, tsar har, 109 12
Able, noong har, 22 13
Abode, sar, 34 10
Abolish, p'hey har, 91 16
Above, oos, 11 9, 112 3
To abound, man har, 87 15
Abouts, ko wi, 117 11
About to be, tsyang ts'hat, 26 16
Abroad, pas, 11 12, 110 6
Abrupt, tang tor, 24 3
Abundant, na oor, 90 6
Do. pooik pooik har, 93 4
Do. complete, ai ai, 105 16
Abyss, mot yon, 9 14, 111 6
Accept, pa toor, 92 4, 112 5
Accidentally, oo yon, 100 16
To accompany, po nair, 43 1
Do. moi sir, 114 15
Do. ham skwi, 97 10
To accomplish, ir or, 99 2
Do. tsi oor, 115 8
To accord, tso ts'har, 112 4
According to, pin ko, 98 8
On account of, mar mai, 110 10
To accumulate, yo ro, 92 11
Do. ssa hoor, 59 13, 110 9
Accurately, tsa sey, 120 14
To accuse, har so, 25 5

Acid, deeir, 48 12
Acorn, syang sir, 63 7
Acquiesce, ho har, 92 3
To acquire, o toor, 90 1
Acre, i rang, 58 13
Do. i rom, 117 5
Acrid, mai or, 48 12
To act, har, 27 12
Do. wi har, 96 4
Actor, hwi tsa, 15 8
To adapt, ma tsar, 119 10
To add, po ter, 88 9
Adder, tok sya, 82 6
Addicted, o ro, 28 11
Additional, to har, 88 7
Adequate, tsyok har, 98 6
Adjacent, kat ka or, 88 3
To adjust. tsor tsyor, 104 7
Do. (settle) ko rar, 107 8
Admiration, (note of) ip key, 122 10
To admire, syoong syang, 102 8
To admit, yong nap har, 95 14
To admonish, kyong key, 25 2
To adore, tsor, 29 11, 120 11
To adorn, skoo mir, 44 12
Do. (cultivate) tat koor, 95 16
To advance, na or, 29 6
Advantage, ni har, 121 9
56 1
Adversity, tsai hwa, 93 14
Adult, tsang tyong, 14 14, 115 12
Adze, tsa koi, 72 5
Afar, mor, 88 3

Affair, ir, 88 16
Affected, noot kir, 21 9
115 12
Affections, stoot tsyong, 22 2
Do. ptoot, 113 1
Affectionate, tsa pit, 112 13
Affinity, kyo rai, 13 11
Affliction, tsai hwa, 93 14
Affluent, nok nok har, 96 6
To affront, om syoo i no kir, 91 4
Aforetime, hyang tsya, 99 6
Afraid, nor nar, 21 8
After that, tsook tsai, 27 11
Afterwards, tooi, 11 8 122 9
Again, tto, 27 3
Do. too, 120 11
Again &again, kyom, 92 12
Do. tsyoong tsyoong, 104 16
Against the stream, yok syoo, 10 4
Age (generation), in kan, 115 1
To aged, noor koor, 19 15
To agitate, mooir, 113 2
Ago, ir tsook, 27 10
Agony, ar hoor, 50 1
To agree, ham har, 91 14
Agreeable, tsoor kir, 49 8
Agreement, maing sey, 25 14
Do. (written) syo key, 36 12
Ague, hak tsir, 50 6
Ah, ip key, 122 10
To aid, tsa roi, 110 1
Aim, stoot wi, 22 3, 113 4
Air (wind), pa ram, 1 10
To air, mor roi or, 6 11
Alarming, nor nar, 113 12

B

A babe, hai, 13 14
Bachelor (old), hor a pi, 15 14
The back, toong pai, 17 13 113 9
Back of the hand, syoo pai, 17 7
Do. of a sword, to pon, 40 7
Back again, to ro ñyor, 26 15
To backbite, ts'ham so, 26 5
Bad, mo tsir, 23 12, 110 9
A badger, o so ri, 79 10
A bag, poo tai, 71 8
A bait (for birds), tyo i, 78 6
Do. for fish, o i, 82 3
To bake, sar oor, 49 13
A balance, so oor stai, 115 6
A balcony, lan kan, 32 14
Baldness, tok too, 51 9
A ball (cannon), th'yor hwan 41 2
Do. hand, tsyook pang or, 76 3
do. t'han tsa, 121 5
Do. foot, tsyo ki, 76 3
A ballad, no rai, 42 13, 120 5
A bamboo, tai, 83 14
Do. shoots, tsyook syoon, 61 10. Do. tyoo, 120 4
Do. mat, sat, 69 1
To bamboo, th'ai tsyang, 54 1
A band, ko rom, 46 4
A bank, moor on tok, 7 16
Do. flat, moor ka tyong, 9 11
Do. mound, tey on, 58 14
Banner, took, 41 5
Banquet, tsan ts'hai, 42 4
A bar, sooi pi, 32 9
Barb of an arrow, sar mit, 40 13
Barbadoes millet, p'hi, 117 6, 50 7
Barbarians, southern, nam ban, 58 9
Do. northern, pook tyok, 58 10
Barbarous, tsan in, 24 4
Bare-shouldered, mer, 46 5
To bark, tsoo tsoor, 80 6
Barley, po ri, 60 8
Do. wild, i mo, 60 8
Barley shoots, maik a, 60 14
A barrel, th'ong, 70 14
A barren year, hyoong nyon, 3 7
A barrow, lyon, 75 5
To barter, pat kor, 55 16
Base, ts'hyon har, 88 14, 112 1
The base of a pillar, tsyoo ts'hyoo, 32 5
Basil, wild, ts'ha tso ki, 61 15
Basin, collection of water, kai ts'hyon, 9 15
A basin, bowl, ta ya, 70 10
To bask, mor roi ir, 6 11
A basket, kooey, 68 5
A bastard, or tsa, 13 9
To bastinado, mak tai, 54 1
A bat, p'hyon pok, 77 14
To bate, tor, 88 7
To bathe, mok yok, 44 7
Do. yak mak, 120 15
A batoon, hor, 45 6
Battle, field of, tsyon tsyang 39 2
Battle ax, poo wor, 40 15
A bay, moor koo pooi, 9 13
To be, wi har, 96 4
Do. i sir, 108 8, 109 1
A beach, moor ka pin, 9 12
A beadle, tsyoo wan, 36 1
A beak, poo ri, 78 1
A beam, toor spo, 32 3
Beans, tai too, 60 9
To bear, carry, mer, 30 8
Do. sustain, kyon tair, 98 3, 21 13
Do. young, nar, 41 16
A bear, kom, 79 2
Beard, na rot yom, 17 1
A beast, tsoong sing, 78 8, 113 13
To beat, ts'hir, 30 13
Do. with a bamboo, th'ai tsyang, 54 1
Do. to pound, moo ta rir, 59 8
A beaver, san tar, 79 9
Beautiful, a ram ta or, 19 6, 111 9
Beauty, ko oor, 86 7
Because, in har, 27 15
Do. in yon, 103 12
Do. tsi tsar, 110 9
To beckon, too roor, 30 3
To become, har, 27 12, 107 10
A bedroom, to tsang, 31 14
A bedstead, sang, 68 12, 120 4
Bedtime, in tyong, 5 9
A bee, por, 82 9
Bee's wax, mir lap, 64 5
A beetle, toong ik, 82 14
Before, arp, 11 8
Do. in time, mon tsyon, 96 9
To beg, ts'hyang har, 25 3
Do. intreat, koo har, 92 3, 118 9

To beget, nar, 41 16
A beggar, kor in, 15 16
To begin, pi ra sar, 117 5
Beginning, pi ro sar, 90 11
Do. pi roo soor, 108 5
In the beginning, tang ts'ho, 99 4
To begirt, moos skoor, 122 5
Begone! skoo tsi tsoor, 26 4
To beguile, so kir, 91 3
To behave, wi har, 96 4
To behead, pe har, 54 10
Do. po hir, 121 3
Behind, tooi, 11 8, 120 9
To behold, por, 30 1, 113 12
A belfry, tsyong loo, 34 13
To believe, sin th'yong, 102 14
A bell, soi pook, 43 8
A hanging bell, pang or, 72 13
Do. small, nyo lyong, 72 12
Bellows, p'hoong lo, 70 8
Do. small, syoo p'hoong lo, 70 8
The belly, pai pok, 17 14
Do. ai, 119 10
Belmetal, not, 64 9
To belong, poo rir, 99 1, 119 8; do. or koor, 110 3
Below, arai, 11 9, 112 3
A belt, yo tai, 45 14
To bemoan, oor, 52 9
A bench, soong sang, 68 12
To bend, koo poor, 29 13
Do. koo roon, 120 7
Do. a bow, hwar hyor, 40 11
Beneath, arai, 11 9, 112 3
Benefit, in har, 121 9, 66 1
Benevolence, k'hoor, 112 13
Benevolent, o tsir in, 22 5
Bent, kok tsyor, 103 4
Bent down, pa rir, 119 1
To bequeath, ki ts'hir, 95 8
To bereave, a soor, 92 2
Berlin blue, hwi hwi ts'hyong 67 11
To beseech, koo har, 92 3
To besiege, e oor, 39 7
To besmear, pa roor, 44 11
A besom, pwi, 71 15
To bestow, tsin hoor, 95 9
Do. pey p'hoor, 121 11
Better (rather), ts'har a ri, 27 6
Between, sai, 11 10
To beware, pang pi, 39 10
A bib, hyoong pai, 45 5
To bid, poon poo, 25 10
Big, k'hoon, 87 9, 109 6
Bignonia, o tong, 83 15
Do. mo kwi, 118 16
A bile, la lyok, 51 6
A bill (beak), poo ri, 78 1
A billet, for troops, pyong poo, 41 6
A billow, moors kyor, 10 5
To bind (tie), mait, 92 8, 107 10
To bind, kyor pak, 53 14
To bind on, moos skoor, 59 7, 122 5
Do. tie round, ssar, 88 10
Do. encircle, or koor, 92 7, 110 3
A birch tree, pot, 84 7
A bird, sai, 76 7, 108 4,
Do. divine, lan tyo, 76 7
Do. fabulous, pong hwang, 76 8, 109 1
A bit, of a bridle, ma ham, 73 8
To bite, no hoor, 49 4
Do. gnaw, kwi hoor, 101 14
Bitter, ssoor, 48 11
Black, ko moor, 67 13
Do. ka moor, 107 1, 108 13
A black spot, sya ma kwi, 51 5
Black lead, myon, 64 10
A bladder, pang kwang, 18 14
A blade (of a knife), nar, 40 7
Do. of corn, i sak, 59 2
Blame, ho moor, 53 12
Blind, syo kyong, 51 12
A blind, par, 33 5
Do. made of beads, tsyoo lyom, 33 5
Bliss, pok, 39 13, 110 10, 122 1
Blithe, sang k'hwai, 99 5
Blite, pi room, 61 9
Blood, p'hi, 18 15
To bloom, p'hooir, 86 4
A blossom, kot poo ri, 86 5
A blotch, sya ma kooi, 51 5
To blow, poor, 43 15, 114 2
To blow a flute, syoo p'ha ram, 43 11, 121 6
Do. a shell, ts'hyooi ra, 43 12
Do. the nose, haing pi th'ey, 20 12
Blue, tsok, 66 14, 120 4
Blunt, moo twir, 40 9
Do. weapons, kang p'hai, 40 16 3

Boa constrictor, koo roug i, 82 5
A board, p'han tsa, 32 15
To boast, tsya rang, 26 7, 122 5
A boat, syo syon, 73 16
Do. fast, k'hwai syon, 73 16
Do. flying, pi syon, 74 1
Do. trading, syang syon, 74 1
Do. fishing, o syon, 74 2
A boat hook, sa hwat tai, 74 6
The body, mom, 16 1, 108 15
A bog, mot, 9 6
To boil, sar moor, 48 2, 119 11
Do. rice pap tsi oor, 49 13
To boil to rags, moo ro nok oor, 48 6
Boiled water, syook syoo, 46 15
A boiler, si ro, 70 12
Bold, maing nyor, 22 14
A bolster, pyo kai, 46 7
A bolt, pit tsyang, 32 9
Bombasin, myon tsyoo, 65 16
A bond, myang moon, 56 4
A bondservant, tsyong, 15 13
A bone, spyo, 18 6, 120 15
A bonnet, kwan, 45 2
A book, ts'haik, 38 6
Do. koor wor, 114 10
A book press, syo tsin, 38 12
A boor, tyon poo, 14 16
A booth, ka ka, 32 1
Boots, hwo tsa, 46 8
Borax, poong sa, 65 1
A border, tsi kyong, 34 4
A bore, pi pwi, 72 7
To bore, ts'han tso, 73 2
To borrow, pir, 56 2, 116 1
Do. expressions, ka t'hak, 26 9
Borrowed, tsya tsya, 105 8
Bosom, ka sam, 17 12
Both, too, 118 5
A bother, man loi, 103 11
A bottle, soor tsoon, 69 12
Bottom, mit, 11 14
Boundary, han har, 95 5
Bounty, oon hey, 89 11
A bow, hwar, 40 9
Do. strong, kang koong, 40 10
A bow-string, si ooi, 40 10
Do. tso ar, 120 11
To bow, oop har, 29 11
To bow down, tsor, 29 11
Bowels, ai, 18 12
A bowl, tong hai, 70 12, 119 6
A box, syang tsa, 68 10
A boy, syo tong, 14 15
Do. a male child, sa na hai, 42 1
A bracelet, p'har soi, 44 14
To brag, tsya rang, 26 7
Brain, too syoo, 16 2, 18 7
Brake, fern, ko sa ri, 61 8
A bramble, ka swi, 84 11
Bran, kyo, 59 13, 119 12
A branch, ka tsi, 84 14, 112 10
To brand, stoom tsir, 52 3
Brass, tsyoo syok, 64 9
A brave man, yong oong, 14 7
Bravery, nar nair, 22 14
To bray, (in a mortar,) tsi hoor, 59 10
Brazil wood, so mok, 84 8
Bread, man too, 47 8
To break an agreement, pai yak, 102 15
To break in pieces, p'ha har, 39 14, do. pa a tsir, 97 16
To break in a horse, kir too rir, 80 6
To break off, mo kor, 94 8
Breakfast, tso pan, 46 13
A bream, kwor o, 81 3
Do. stone, ka key o, 80 16
The breast, ka sam, 17 12
A breast band, hyoong tai, 73 7
Breath, swir, 20 5
Breeches, pa tsi, 45 15
Breech-leather, ko tar kai, 73 10
To breed, nar, 41 16
A breeze, koop p'hoong, 2 1
Brethren, hyong tey, 12 12
A bribe, syon moor, 95 8
A bridge, ta ri, 34 3
Do. stone, tor ta ri, 34 4
A bridle, hyok, 73 8
Brief, kar ryok, 120-13
A brier, ka swi, 84-11
Bright, par koor, 6 4
Do. nam nyok, 113-15
Brightness, par kar, 114 6, 121-14
Brilliant, kyo kyo, 105 4
Brimstone, lyoo hwang, 65 3
Brine (pure), ts'hyong tsyang 47 9
To bring, it koor, 30 7
To bring up, ts'hir, 89 10
To bring forth, na hor, 41-16

To bring forth fruit, koor sir, 59 4
Brinjal, ka tsi, 61 6
A brink, moor ka, 9-12
Briny, stsar, 48-13
A broad brimmed hat, kat, 45 3
Broad, no roor, 87 11, 117 1
Do. no poor, 114 5
Brocade, pi tan, 65 7
To broil, koo oor, 48 4
Broken to pieces, tsan har, 92 10
A brook, si nai, 9 14
Brook stones, tsyok pyoi, 8 8
A broom, pwi, 71 15
Broth, kook, 46 15
Brother, elder, mat, 12 11, 112 9, 116 15, 117 9
Brother in law, elder brother's wife, hyong soo, 12 13
Brother, younger, a a, 12 12, 112 9
Younger brother's wife, tey soo, 12 14
Brothers in law, by marriage, tong syo, 13 6
Brow (forehead), ni ma, 16 4
The brow of a hill, tok san, 7 11
To brush away, poo tooi ts'hir, 94 12
A brute, tsoong sing, 78 8
To bubble, so sar, 10 10
Bubbling, hyoong hyoong, 106 7
Buck wheat, mo mir, 60 11
A bucket, syoo too, 70 15
A bud, ts'ho ri, 84 15
Do. kot poo ri, 86 5, 114 8
Buddha, poo ts'hyo, 53 2
To buffet, ts'hir, 30 13
A buffoon, kwang tai, 15 8
To build, sey oor, 95 12
Do. seyr, 110 5
Do. tsi oor, 115 8
Building, tsip, 107 13
A bullet, t'han tsa, 41 1, 121 5
A bundle, mook koor, 59 7, 122 5
Do. of clothes, po, 71 9
Do. of sticks, sooi mok, 85 3
To burn, poor poot t'hoor, 49 12
To burst, p'ha har, 39 14
To bury, moo toor, 52 10
A bush, p'ho ki, 87 7
Business, ir, 88 16
Do. pyo sar, 36 5, 111 13, 111 14
Busy, pat poor, 96 13
But, ta man, 27 4
Do. (however), koo ror, 27 16
Butt, t'hong, 70 13
A butterfly, na pooi, 82 7
The buttocks, por ki, 17 16
A button, tar mak i, 46 4
To buy, sar, 55 12
A buzzard, song kor mai, 77 1
By (with), pso. 26 13
A by place, pyon pang, 34 8

C.

A cabbage, ko lyo ts'hai, 58 5, 60 8
A cabin, ts'hang pang, 74 8
A cabinet, ts'hoong ham, 68 7
A cable, tyong lam, 74 7
A cage, and pitfall, ham ts'hoong, 104 5
To cajole, a tang har, 26 5
A caitiff, syo in, 14 9
A cake, stok, 47 5
A calabash, ho ho, 61 6
Do. dried, pak, 70 15
Calamity, tsai hwa, 93 14
To calculate, heym, 54 12
Do. beforehand, ey t'hak, 104 2
A caldron, ka ma, 70 4
A calendar, lyok syo, 38 4
A calf, syo i ya tsi, 78 16, 121 1
Calico, yoon p'ho, 66 1
To call, poo roor, 20 16, 118 12
Callous, ser, 92 9
Calm, ko yo, 29 14, 113 1
A calm, p'hong tsi, 2 2
To calumniate, ts'ham so, 26 5
The calyx, hwa t'hey, 86 6
A camel, yak tai, 78 15
Camlet, kyo tsik, 65 16
A campaign, p'hyong ti, 7 9
Can (to be able), or har, 28 9
Candied orange, kyoor pyong, 48 1
Do. peel, toong tyong, 48 14

yop hwa, 86-2
A centipede, o kong, 82-2.
The centre, ka ou tai, 11-10
To centre, mat ts'hir, 40-15
A ceremonial card, ley tan, 36-13
Ceremonial presents, ley moor, 36-14
Ceremony, ley to, 22-6, 112-2
Certain(real), hwak sir, 24-1
Do. sure, tyok tang, 102-16
A certain person, a mo, 89-3
Certainly, tsa yon, 100-16
Do. soo soo ri, 113-6
Do. ir tyong, 103-12, 111-8
Ceruse, poon, 67-9
Cerulean, p'hoo roor, 67-8
Cessation of wind, p'hoong tsi, 2-2
Chaff, kyo, 119-12
Chagrin, oor oor, 105-6
A chair, kyo ooi, 63-13
Do. sedan, kyo tsa, 75-6
Do. small, syo kyo, 75-6
A chalice, sor tsoon, 69-12
To challenge, to tsyou, 39-4
A chamber(side), haingnang, 122-4, 31-16
Do.(upper), ta rak, 31-12, 113-12
Do. room, koo toor, 31-13
Do. pang, 119-16
To change, pyon har, 92-15
Do. thoroughly, pyon t'hong, 104-8
To chant, oor p'hoor, 37-12
Do. oo p'hoor, 111-16

Chapter, koor wor, 108-12
A character, (letter), koor wor, 108-5
Charcoal, soor, 40-11
To charge, tyong nyong, 103-2
Do. poo ts'hyok, 103-2
To take charge, tsa poor, 111-14
A charger, tsyoon ma, 98-11
Chariot (Imperial), nyon, 75-5, 114-15
Charitable, no roor, 23-4
Charity, o tsir, 22-5
Charming, ko or, 19 6
To chase, san haing, 94-6
Chaste, ko toor, 22-11, 109-9
To chastise, tsoi tsoor, 53-13
To chat, mar sam, 109-13
A chattering sparrow, tsyak tso, 77-15
Cheap, tsyon har, 88-14
To cheat, so kir, 91 13
The cheek, spyam, 16-5
The cheek-bones, po tsyo kai, 16-5
Cheerful, k'hwai har, 21-8
Do. hearty, sang k'hwai, 99-13
Chenopodium, to t'hars, 61-14
A cherry, aing to, 63-1
Chess, pa tok, 75-13
Do. ancient, tsyang kooi, 75-15
Chess board, p'han, 75-13
Chess men, kooi tsa, 75-14

A chest, kooey, 68-5
A chest of drawers, ts'hoong ham, 68-7
A chestnut, pam, 63-5
Do. yellow, hwang ryoor, 63-5
To chew, kwi hoor, 101-14
To chide, skoo tsi tsoor, 26-4
Chief, nim koon, 116-12
Chief minister, tsai syang, 35-9
A chief, koi syoo, 96-1
A child, hai a, 13-14
Do. a hai a, 112-8
Childless, ho or, 15-15
Chill, so noor, 6-8
A chimney, koor tok, 33-1
Do. of bamboo, you tsyook, 69-6
The chin, t'har, 17-3
China grass, hwon ts'ho, 86-10
The chine, toong mara, 17-18
Chisel, skoor, 72-6
Chit chat, han tam, 25-15
Cholera, kwak ran, 50-4
To choose, kar hir, 93-9
To chop, skak koor, 73-2
A chopping knife, tsak to, 72-14
Chop sticks, tsyo, 70-3
Chronicle, sa kwi, 117-10
Chrysanthimum, kook hwa, 85-7
A cicatrice, to te, 51-8
Cinnabar, tsyoo sa, 64-16
Cinnamon, key syoo, 83-13
A cipher, koor wor, 108-5 5

Cool, ts'hyo lyang, 102-5
To cool, sik oor, 48-7, 111-2
A coop, ham tsyong, 104-5
Copper, koo li, 64-8
Do. black, o tong, 64-11
Do. native, saing tong, 64-12
Do. smelted, syook tong, 64-12
Do. in bars, ts'hyok tong, 64-13
A copy, pat t'hyop, 38-3
Coral, san ho, 64-4
A cord, no, 71-12, 118-7
Cordwood, swi mok, 85-3
Corea, tsyo syon, 58-3
Do. ka lyo, 58-5
Coriander, syoo yoo, 85-16
A cormorant (fishing), lo tsa, 76-14
Corn, pyo, 60-4
Corn field, pat, 58-12
Cornelian, ma no, 64-5
A corner, soo rong i, 11-15
Do. (edge), mo, 95-6
Corolla, yo hai, 86-5
A corpse, tsook om, 52 7
Corpulent, sar tsir, 19-10
To correct, ts'hir, 39-5
Correct, tan tsyong, 23-2
Do. tsyong har, 110-6, 117-12
Do. writing, tsyong syo, 38-1
Do. koor si, 114-9
To correspond, poo tsak, 101-11
Corresponding, pok pok, 28-3
Do. suitable, wi yon, 100-15
Corrupt, mang tong toi, 90-8
Coat, kap, 55-13
Costly, kwi har, 88-14
A cottage, mo ok, 31-16
Cotton, so om, 66-5
Cotton silk, myon tsoo, 65-16
A cotton screw, ap ko, 66-5
To couch, tsoot koo rir, 31-2
A couch, sang, 68-12, 120-4
A cove, kai, 9-9
A covenant, on yak, 25-14, 116-3
A cover, too e, 70-6
To cover, kai tsi, 70-7
Do. (hide), ka ri oor, 94-11
A coverlet, ni poor, 46-6, 109-3
To covet,— } t'ham har, 23-10
Covetousness, }
To count, heym, 54-12
The countenance, nat an, 16-4
Do. color of, pis, 117-14
Country, various, see 57-9, to 58-3
A country house, nong so, 59-16
To couple, staak, 41-13
Courageous, maing nyor, 22-14
A courier, pi kak, 15-7
A court, stoor, 33-7, 116-16
The court, tyo tyong, 35-8
Do. a ts'ham, 108-11
Do. of a mandarine, koo ooi, 33-15
To courtesy (bow), oop har, 29-11
A courtezan, nyo ki, 15-11
Cousins, tsyong hyong tey, 13-5
Do. distant, tsai tsyong, 13-5
A cow, syo, 78-16, 121-1
Cow's milk, t'ha lak, 47-9
A crab, kai, 82-1
Do. to ts'hyoong, 81-13
A craftsman, tsyang in, 15-2
Crafty, oi ram, 91-5
A crag, pa hai, 7-13
A cramp (staple), tsir tyong, 72-8
A crane, paik lo, 76-12
Crape, tsoo sa, 65-13
A crape cap, sa mo, 45-1
To crave, koo har, 92-3
To crawl, koo moo ko rir, 83-9
A creek, kai, 9-9
Crescent (of the moon), tik, 121-16
A crew, sa kong, 72-10
A cricket, sair sor, 82-12
A crime, ho moor, 53-11, 108-9
Crimson, tai hong, 66-12
A cripple, ts'hyook kak, 51-15
Crockery, tsir kot, 70-11
A crocodile, kyo lyong, 80-10
To croak, koo poor, 29-11, 115-7
Crooked, koo peor, 90-4
Do. kok tsyor, 103-4

7

A crooked road, man lo, 8-4
To crop, pooir, 59-6
Cross practices, hoing haing, 104-4
A cross beam, to ri, 32-3
Crosswise, pis skir, 115-16, 93-1
To crow, oor, 78-3, 109-1
A crow, ka ma koi, 77-12
Crow's fan, sya kan, 86-13
Crown of the head, tyong pa ki, 16-3
Cruel, tsan in, 24-4
A crumb, ka ra, 47-13
A crump leg, ts'hyook kak, 51-15
To cry, oor, 52-9
Crystal, syoi tsyang, 64-7
A cubit, tsa, 55-8, 110-11
A cuckoo, too kyon, 77-4
Cuckoo flower, too kyon hwa, 85-10
A cucumber, hwang kwa, 61-5
To cudgel, mak tai, 54-1
To cultivate, tat koor, 95-16, 122-1
Cunning, oi ram, 91-5
A cup, tsi wan, 69-16
Do. (wine), tsan, 69-14, 120-6
A cur, kai, 79-15
A curb, koor e, 73-7
To cure, koo pyong, 52-1
A curtain, tsyang, 69-4, 113-16, 119-16
Do. musquito, moon tsyang, 69-4
To curve, top ko ts'hoor, 113-11
A cushion, pyo kai, 46-7
To cut, sa kir, 98-14
To cut with shears, kar kir, 98-13
To cut out clothes, ma rar, 45-16
To cut off, skoon hoor, 92-6
To cut short, i tsoo ro tsir, 92-14, 112-16
To cut a figure, saing kwang, 99-12
A cuttle fish, o tsok o, 81-4
Cycle (characters of), see 6-13, to 7-7
Cymbals, paik, 43-15
A cypress, tsat, 83-15

D.

A dagger, k'har, 40-6
To damage, hai har, 91-7
Damask, tsang tan, 65-8
To damp, tso tsoor, 10-14
A damsel, key tsip, 105-9
A damson, oi at, 63-2
Do. oi yas, 107-15
To dance, stooir, 31-1, 121-2
Dangerous, ooi ts'hoi, 89-16
Do. hom har, 97-6
A dappled horse, ts'hong ma, 78-12
To dare, kam hi, 27-14
Do. koo t'hir, 109-8
Dark, a took har, 6-5, 117-2
Do. gloomy, myong myong, 105-5
A date fruit, tai ts'hyo, 63-4
To daub, to ts'hir, 67-16
Daughter, nyo sik, 13-1
Daughter in law, myo na ri, 13-1
Dawn, p'hyong myong, 5-4
A day, nar ir, 4-12
Day time, nat tsyoo, 5-2, 120-3
Day light, sa pey, 5-6
This day, koom ir, 4-11
Next day, ik ir, 4-12
This very day, tsook ir, 4-14
Day before yesterday, tsai tsak ir, 4-15
Future day, myong hoo ir, 4-15
What day, ha ir, 4-16
All day long, tsyong ir, 5-3
How many days, kooi ir, 5-1
Deafness, kooi mok oor 51-9
To deal, hoong p'han, 55-16
A dealer, syang ko, 56-10
Dear, kwi har, 88-14
Death, tsoor oor, 52-6
To debase, hor, 26-6, 109-8
To debate, kong lon, 25-6
Debauched, oom tan, 24-14
A debt, pit, 56-3
A decade, yor hoor, 4-2
To decapitate, pe hir, 54-10
Decaying, soi har, 89-15
Deceitful, koo root har, 90-8
Do. (clandestine), koo ook, 98-11
To deceive, so kir, 91-3
To decide, kyor tan, 54-5
To deck, skoo mir, 44-12

To declare, sar or, 25-4
To decline, sya ley, 96-3, 118-12
To decline eating, syon t'hoi, 42-15
Declining, ki oor, 107-3
To decoct, tar hir, 48-5
To decorate, skoo mir, 44-12
To decoy, tar nair, 26-4
To decrease, tor, 88-7
A decree, lyong har, 36-8
Decrepid, soi har, 89-15
Deeds, haing sir, 22-7
Deep, kip hor, 10-8
Do. ki kor, 111-1
A deer, sa sam, 79-4
To defame, ts'ham so, 26-5
A defeat, p'hai har, 39-14
Defective, kyor yon, 101-1
To defend, pang pi, 39-10
To defend one's self, har so, 25-5
To defend the borders, syoo sa ri, 39-10
Do. (guard), koo bo, 89-9
To defer, ts'hyon yon, 101-5
Deficient, son har, 88-8; do. inadequate, yong ryoi 90-6
To defile, moor toor, 110-1, 67-2
To define, han har, 95-5
Deformed, to ro oor, 19-12
To defraud, so kir, 91-3
To defy, to tsyon, 38-4
To degrade from office, nai ts'hir, 54-7
A degree of nobility, pyo sar, 113-6

Dejection, syo syo, 104-15
To delay, ts'hyon yon, 101-5
Delaying, tsi ts'hey, 100-6
To deliberate, ooi lon, 25-6, 118-9
Delicate, myo har, 19-8, 121-10
Do. feeble, nyo nyo, 105-15
Delight, tsoor kir, 23-8, 118-12, 120-8
A delineation, koo rim, 113-13
Delirium, mi ts'hir, 50-12
To deliver, kon tsir, 30-16
Do. (rescue), koo won, 39-9
Do. to give, mat tsir, 92-4
A dell, mois spoo ti, 117-2
Demeanour, koo ts'hir 111-7
A demigod, po sar, 53-3
A demon, ya ts'ha, 53-8
A den, koor, 8-14
A dentist (female), a p'ha, 15-11
To depart, kar, 29-4, 111-16
To depend on, him ni poor, 97-8, 109-4
Depraved, p'hyon pyok, 24-5
To deprive of, a soor, 92-2
A deputy, po koom, 96-2
To derange, lam tsap, 102-10
To deride, hyo ts'har, 20-11
To descend, ma rir, 29-10
A description, soor, 113-13
To desert, pai pan, 40-1
A desert, toor ya, 8-1, 116-15
Do. a tak har, 116-7

Deserted, lyo lyo, 105-9
A deserter, op soor, 121-4
A designation, tsa, 13-16
Design, stoot, 22-3
To desire, won har, 28-9
Desire, ha ko tsyo har, 96-8, 109-16
To desire ardently, sa mo, 109-9
To desist, tyong tsi, 104-3
A desk, syo an, 38-11
Desolate, lyo lyo, 105-9
A despatch, kyok syo, 95-11
To despoil, no lvak, 39-6
A despot, oos toom, 115-15
Destitute, koong har, 95-9
Do. oi ro or, 15-15, 122 7
To destroy, myor har, 39-15
To detain, mo moor, 29-14
To determine, kyor tan, 54-5
To detest, won mang, 21-3
Detriment, son har, 88-8
A devil, kwi sin, 53-8
To devise, to mo, 101-12
Devotedly, o ro, 28-11
Devont, tsot sa or, 91-6
Deuterogamy, hoo sir, 12-10
Dew, o sor, 2-12
Do. i sar, 107-10
Diarrhoea, li tsir, 50-6
A diary, ir kooi, 38-4
Dice, ssang lyook, 75 16
To die, tsook oor, 52-6
To differ, ta na, 112-1, 112-2
Different, ta roor, 23-13 8

Do not, poor ka, 103 15
Do. op soor, 109-13
Do. a nir, 109-14, 112-16
Duck, an herb, so ro tsyang i, 62-1
A doctor, ooi won, 36-2
Doctrine, to li, 108-11
A document, moon tsyok, 37-3
Do. (a despatch), kyok syo, 95-11
A dog, kai, 79-15
Do. shaggy, to p'hor key, 79-15
Do. (wild), soong rang i, 79-3
Dog days, first of, ts'ho pok, 4-6
Do. middle of, tsyoong pok, 4-7
Do. close of, mar pok, 4-7
The dog teeth, o ts'hi, 16-15
Doings, haing sir, 22-7
To dole, pan p'ho, 95-7
Dolour, min mang, 21-2
Dolychos hirsutus, ts'hoork, 87-1
Dolychos polystachios, toong, 84-9
To domineer, oos toom, 115 15
Done, ir tsook, 27-10
A door, moon, 32-8
Do. o t'he, 116-13
Do. (inner), tsi ke, 32-12
A door-blind, par, 33-5
A dot, tyom, 37-16
Double, kap tsyor, 56-6
Do. ssang, 89-6
To doubt, ooi sim 91-3, 114-4
A dove, pi toor, 77-11
Down, a rai, 11-9
Downright, ko toor, 90-4
To doze, tso ar, 31-7
To drag, it koor, 75-10
Do. or koor, 94-11
A dragon, mi roo, 80-10, 108-3
Dragon boat festival, tan o, 4-6
Dragon's eyes (a fruit), lyong an, 62-9
A dragon fly, tsan tsa ri, 82-10
A dram, (Chin.), ton, 55-5
Drama, no rat, 75 12
To draw (pull), koor oor, 75-10
To draw water, ki roor, 10-15
To draw up soldiers, tsin ts'hir, 38-16
To draw out, spa kir, 39-13, 118-14
To draw down, i koor, 97-14
A drawer, ham, 68-7
Do. chest of, ts'hoong ham, 68-7
A drawing, koo rim, 38-5
Dread, too rir, 21-7, 120-12
Do. tsyo har, 119-7
To dream, skoom, 31-8
Dregs, ko roor, 47-4
Do. of wine, tso pak, 102-9
Do. tsai kang, 119-12
To dress, nip oor, 46-11
Do. ni poor, 108-6
To dress food, poor tsi toor, 49-12
Drifting snow, pi pi, 106-1
To drink, ma sir, 42-10
To drip, too roor, 10-12
Do. ma tsar, 118-14
To drive, mor, 80-8, 114-10
To drive out, stso ts'har, 29-12, 113-4
To drive a carriage, c ko, 96-7
Drizzling, mong mong, 106-5
Drizzling rain, sey oo, 2-6
To droop, i oor, 86-8
To drop, to fall, tsir, 86-4
Dropsical swelling, ts'hyang man, 50-14
A drove, moor, 98-5
Drought, kam oor, 2 7
To drown, spa tsir, 10-11
To drum, kas pook, 114-2
A drum, pook, 43-8
Long do. tsyang ko, 43-9
To be drunk, ts'hooi har, 42-12
To dry in the sun, mor roi ir, 6-11
Dry (withered), ta roor, 86-9
Do. mak mak, 105-16
Dry, ma ror, 97-6
A duck, o ri, 77-13
Duckweed, p'hyong ts'ho, 87-5
To duck, moo tsa mi, 75-3
A duke, koo wi, 88-15, 115-9

Exceedingly, t'hai kwa, 103-4; do. koo moo, 112-9
An excellency, kin, 109-14
Excellent, a ram ta or, 117-15, 121-10
Excellent scholars, lyor sa, 14 5
Excelling, nar oor, 90-6, 111-13
Excessive, ir tsyor, 96-14
Do. t'hai kwa, 103-4
To exchange, sa p'hir, 95-13, 112-11
To excite, ptor, 30-14
Excrement, stong, 18-16
Excursion season, tsyoong yong, 4-10
To excuse, tsyop oor, 54-5
Exertion, no p'har, 122-2
To exhaust, ta har, 93-7, 110 15, 110-16
Do. koong koo har, 98-8
To be exhausted, it poor, 21-15, 115-16
Exhausted, kyoong koor, 101-4
To exhort, kwon har, 25-13 117-8
To exist, i sir, 108-3
To expand, pe p'hoor, 69-5
Expanded, as water, myo myo, 105-10
Expansive, kap, 113-16
To expect (hope), pa rar, 29-15
Expedient, mat tang, 27-13
To expel, stso ts'hor, 29-12, 113-4

To expend, ho pi, 96-6
To expire, kwi tsyor, 51-16
To explain, tsoo nair, 37-13
Explore, koo har, 118-9
An express, ts'hik sa, 35-13
Expressions, mar sam sa, 24-16, 111-8
To extend to, mi ts'har, 93-11, 109-4
Extended, tsyang tai, 100-5
Do. tai kwang, 108-8
Do. spread out, yang yang, 105-7
Eterior, pat, 110-6
To exterminate, myor har, 39-15; do. psor, 116-1
Do. cut off, skoon hoor, 92-6
To extinguish, poor sko tsir, 49 15
Do. a lamp, myor toong, 71-5
To extol, ir k'ha roor, 96-3 107 14
Extraordinary, pi syang 103-7
Extravagant, sya ts'hi, 23-15, 115-1
Extreme, kook har, 28-8
Do. ka skai, 118-2
Extremity, skoot, 90-12
Exuberant, ts'hyo ts'hyo, 105 12, do. syong har, 111-4
The eye, noon, 16-7, 119-5
Pupil of do. noon poo ts'hya, 16-8
White of do. paik tsyong, 16-7
The eye ball, noon mang or, 16-8

The eye brows, noon sop, 16-6
The eye lash, noon too ai, 16-9

F.

Fabulous bird, sai, 76-11, 119-3
The face, nat, 19-3, 113-6
Fact, haing sir, 22-7
To fade, i oor, 86-8
A faggot, swi mok, 85-3
To fail, koip tsir har, 92-5
Fair, beautiful, a ram ta or, 19-6
Do. just, kong tsyong, 24-5
A fair wind, syoon p'hoong, 1-15
Fair weather, kair, 2-9
A fairy, syon in, 14-4, 113-14
A fairy stone, koi syok, 8-7
Faithfulness, mi toor, 22-9
A faithful minister, ts'hyoong sin, 14-4
A falcon, mai, 76-10
A falconer, oong sa, 15-4
To fall, tsir, 86-4, 119-2
To fall down, op to tsir, 29-9 112-16
Fall of the leaf, pnyop ro tir, 118-16
Fallacious, koo root har, 90-8
Fallen, ki oor, 115-10, 92-13
Falling to ruin, lak lak, 105-12
False, ko tsoot, 90-7
False hair, tar ai, 44-2
Do. ornaments, spoo rir, 44-11
A family, tsi key, 114-13

A family connected by marriage, hon ka, 13-12
A family name, kak si, 14-1
Famished, soor hoor ey, 49-9
Fame, myong syong, 99.15
Do. so rai, 110-7
Famous women, ryor nyo, 14-6
A fan, poo ts'ha, 69-6, 120-1
Far, distant, mor, 88-3
Far apart, song kwir, 88-4
A farce, no rat, 75-12
Farmer, nyo room tsi oor, 58-14
Fashion, ko tong, 19-14
Fast, quick, k'hwai k'hwai, 106-8
Do. spa rar, 90-13
A fast boat, k'hwai syon. 73-16
A fastening, kor sai, 32-13
Fasting, tsai key, 52-14
Fat, sar tsir, 19-10, 115-2
Father, api, 12-4, 110-13
Father's elder brother, mat; and younger, do. a tsa pi, 112-7
Father and mother, ko pi, 12-5
Father in law, husband's father, sooi a pi, 12-8
Wife's father, oi koo, 12-9
Fatherless, oi ro ar, 122-7
To fathom, to toom oor, 94-7
Fatigued, kas par, 113-2
A fault, ho moor, 53-12
Do. tsi nar, 96-10
Do. ti nar, 109-11
Favour, ko ir, 69-11, 118-2
Do. oon hey, 115-11
Fear, nor nar, 21-8, 113-12
Do. tso hoor, 120-11
To feast, mok ir, 48-10
A feast, tsan ts'hai, 42-4
Do. on embarkation, ha syon yon, 42-4
Do. on disembarkation, syang syon yon, 42-6
A feather, tsit, 77-16, 108-2
Fed to the full, pai poo rar, 119-11
Feeble, nyo nyo, 105-15
To feed, mo koor, 48-9, 109-2
To feel, man tsir, 30-11, 119-4
Feeling, soor hoor, 112-13
To feign, so kir, 91-3
Felicity, pok, 89-13
A female, key tsip, 42-1, 109-9
Female, of beasts, am, 79-16
A fen, mot, 9-6
A fence, oor sop, 33-11
To ferment, pi tsoor, 47-1
Fern, ko sa ri, 61-8
Ferocious, maing nyor, 20-14
A ferry, na ra, 9-15
Fertile, yot mar, 115-3
A fertile year, p'hoong nyon, 3-7
Fervent, to oor, 120-16
Festival of spring, lip ts'hyoon, 4-5
Do. of the dragon boat, tan o, 4-6
Do. of the 7th evening, ts'hir syok, 4-8
Do. of the tombs, ham sik, 4-5
Fetid, poo ts'hyooi, 49-1
Fetters, kwi key, 41-9
Fever and ague, hak tsir, 50-6
Few, tsya koor, 87-15, 122-7
Ficus erecta, pyok lyo, 86-14
A fiddle string, tsoor, 43-6
Do. si oor, 120-5
Fidelity, ts'hyoong syong, 22-8, 110-16
A field, pat, 58-12, 109-3, 116-14
Field of battle, tsyon tsyang, 39-2
A field path, pat ko ri, 58-13
A fiend, kwi sin, 53-8
Fierce, maing nyor, 22-14
A fierce wind, p'ho p'hoong, 2-1
A fife, p'hi ri, 43-13
A fig (Chin.), kam, 62-14
Do. (dried), kan si, 62-14
To fight, ssa hor, 39-4
Figure (shape), t'hai to, 19-9
A file, string, kot ts'hi, 71-16
Do. for filing, tsoor, 72-4
A filial child, hyo tsa, 14-5
Filial piety, hyo to, 22-8, 110-15
To fill, ts'har, 88-5, 119-10
To fillip, t'har, 43-7
Filthy, to ro oor, 19-11
Finally, ma ts'ham nai, 27-15, 111-12

A flying ant, poo yoo, 82-11
Foam, kop p'hoom, 10-10
A foe, won syoo, 76-7
Fog, an kai, 2-12
Foggy, mong mong, 106-5
A fold, tsoo room, 46-2
To fold the hands, ko tsar, 108-12
A folded garment, t'hyop ooi, 45-10
Foliage, nip, 84-15
Folk, paik syong, 14-13
To follow, ko na rir, 89-7
To follow (comply), sta roor, 29-12
To follow after, sta rar, 93-11
Fond, tsoor kir, 91-8, 119-5
Food, pan ts'han, 46-16
Do. ts'ha pan, 119-9
Foolish, o rir, 24-12
The foot, par, 13-4, 120-7
Sole of do. tsyok tsyang, 18-5
The foot of a hill, san lok, 7-11
A foot path, kyong lo, 8-5
A foot step, tsa ts'hoi, 20-2
For (because), too p'hoor, 109-5
To forage, no lyak, 39-6
To forbear, ts'ham oor, 21-14
To forbid, mar, 98-1, 115-13
Force, him, 20-4, 110-15
Forcible, kang ing har, 97-7
A ford, na ra, 9-15
To ford, kon nor, 74-16
The fore finger, tsi in tsi, 17-9
The forehead, ni ma, 16-4, 120-11
Foreign parts, oi pang, 34-8
A forest, soo p'hoor, 85-2, 118-4
To forfeit a bond, pai yak, 102-15
A forge, p'hoor moo, 72-2
To forget, ni tsoor, 21-12, 109-12
To forgive, sya har, 54-6
The form, or koor, 19-3, 110-6
Formerly, mon tsyon, 96-9
Forthwith, too tooir, 28-1
A fortune teller, pok tsya, 15-1
Foster child, yang tsa, 12-19
Foster father, yang poo, 12-6
Do. mother, yang mo, 12-5
Foul wind, pang kooi, 19-1
To found, tsi oor, 64-14
A foundation, t'ho, 33-6, 111-11
A founder, tsyoo tsyang, 15-3
To founder, p'ha syon, 75-2
A fountain, saim, 9-7
Four, nok, 54-14, 109-6
The four quarters, sa pang, 11-15
A fowl (domestic), tark, 77-11, 116-14
A fowling piece, tyo ts'hyong, 41-2
A fox, yo oo, 79-6
Do. arctic, sark, 79-7
A fragment, tong i, 88-1
Fragrant, hyang kooi, 48-14
Fragrance, kot ta or, 86-7, 111-3
A frame, (a stand), si rong, 33-4
Frantic, mi ts'hir, 50-12
A freckle, stam stooi, 51-3
To freeze, or tong, 11-1
Do. o rar, 119-4
Frequent, tot tot, 95-15
Fresh, sai, 90-10
Do. not saltish, mar kar, 108-1
To fret, tap tap har, 21-6
A friar, sa mi, 53-6
A friend, poong oo, 13-13
Do. pot, 112-11
Do. old, ts'hin koo, 13-14
Friendly enquiry, moon tsyang, 36-15
Frigid, so noor, 6-8, 120-16
Do. lyong lyong, 106-6
Fringe, in skin, 95-3, 118-6
To frisk, ts'hoom ts'hoom, 42-14
A frog, kai koo ri, 83-7
From (out of), poo t'hoor, 28-9
From, mar mai, 96-15
In front, pat, 11-12, 110-6
Do. tsai tsyon, 99-7
The front teeth, moon ts'hi, 16-15
A front room, tsip t'ho, 31-15
Froth, kop p'hoom, 10-10 12

Frugal, kom so, 23-15
Fruit, kwa sir, 62-8
Do. yo room, 107-15
Fruit (to bring forth), kyor sir, 59-4
Fruitless, poor sir, 59-4
Fruitful, yat mar, 115-3
To fry, pok koor, 48-3
A frying pan, tsyon t'hyor, 70-5
Fuel, som, 85-3, 122-1
To fulfil, hyo him, 91-12
Full, ts'har, 88-5, 107-3, 119-10
To be full, pai poo roor, 49-8
Full-grown, tsyang syong, 19-15
Full moon, po rom, 4-2
A full year, kooi nyon, 3-6
To fumigate a vessel, yon hoon, 75-4
A funeral, sing sa, 52-6
A fungus (stone), syak i, 61-11
Do. (wood), syong i, 61-12
A fur dress, kat ot, 45-9
A furnace, hwa ro, 70-7
Furniture, koo root, 68-4
To fuse, ni kir, 64-15
In future, tsyang lai, 100-12
A future day, myong hoo ir 4-15

G

Gaiety, pan hwa, 99-16
Gain, li har, 56-1
Gaiters, haing tsyong, 46-7
A gale, p'ho p'hoong, 2-1
The gall bladder, ssoor kai, 18-13
A gallery, mar roo, 32-15
Do. ta rak, 31-12, 113-12
To gallop, tar nir, 80-8, 116-8
Gamboge, syok ong hwong, 67-7
To gambol, ts'hoom ts'hoor, 42-14
Gaming, na ki, 76-1
The gamut, pop ts'hook, 107-8
A gantang, (a peck), mar, 55-6
A gaol, ok, 53-16
A garden, tong san, 33-7, 118-14
A garden balsem, pong syon hwa, 85-12
To gargle, yang ts'hi tsir ha, soo, 44-8
Garlick, ma nar, 61-3
Do. small, tar, 87-2
Garments, ts'hi ma, 45-13, 108-6
A garment (single), tan ooi, 45-9
Do. (folded), t'hop ooi, 45-10
The gate of a village, lyo yom, 34-12
To gather, tsoo oor, 30 14
A gathering, hok, 51-5
To gather in fruits, ko toor, 59-14, 107-6, 117-4
A gauntlet, tsyang kap, 41-8
Gauze, kim, 65-15
Gauze (puckered), tsoo sa. 65-13
To gaze, to ra por, 29-15
Do. tor poor, 120-14
A gelding, syon ma, 78-14
A gem, ok, 64-3
Do. koo soor, 107-12, 110-11
A general, tai tsyang, 35-10
Do. tsyang syoo, 114-11
General (universal), mo tor, 28-12
Generally speaking, tai kai, 99-4
A generation, in kan, 115-1
Generous, kang kai, 100-2
Genial showers, kooi oo, 2-8
Genial warmth, hwon hwa, 6-6
Genius of the hills, syon in, 14-11, 113-14
A gentleman, lyang pan, 14-12
Gently flowing, yong yong, 106-4
To get, si ro kom, 27-7
Do. obtain, o toor, 90-1, 109-12
To get again, hoong li, 56-1
To get one's bread, kyong yong, 104-12
A ghost, kooi sin, 53-8
Ginger, saing kang, 61-2, 107-16
Ginseng, in som, 86-11
To gird, moos skoor, 59-7, 122-5
A girdle, tooi, 45-13
Do. stooi, 122-5
A girl, key tsip, 42-1, 109-9

A girth, too tai, 73-5
To give, ta mor, 28-6
To give to, tsoor, 92-2, 114-14
Do. (to deliver over), mat tsir, 92-4
Glad, kit koor, 23-7, 118-11
Glass, lyoo li, 64-6
A glass, tsyong tsa, 70-2
To glitter, hooi hwang, 99-16
Gloomy, myong myong, 105-5
Glory, yong hwa, 89-12, 111-11
Glue, a kyo, 65-5
Do. (fish), poo re, 81-11
Glutinous rice, ts'hap psar, 60-6
A glutton, tam pooi, 79-10
A gnat, mo kooi, 82-14
To gnaw, moors, 80-5
Do. kwi hoor, 101-14
To go, kar, 29-4, 107-5, 111-16
To go out, nar, 29-7, 107-12
To go in, toor, 29-7
To go through, sa ma ts'har, 98-4, 114-5
To go down, na rir, 29-10
To go up, o roor, 29-10
To go to rest, tsar, 31-7
To go to, ni ra, 96-11
To go and walk, ts'hyoor hing, 100-8
A goat, yang, 79-9
A god, (idol), po sar, 53-3
Gold, soi, 63-15, 107-11
Gold ore, ni koom, 63-16
Gold thread, koom syon, 65-10
A gong, tsaing, 41-4
Gongmetal, not, 64-9
Good, tsyo hoor, 19-7, 113-6
Do. tsar har, 23-12
A good appearance, ho yang, 101-11
Goods, moor hwa, 55-13
Goodness, o tir, 109-10, 110-10
A goose, ke yoo, 77-7
Goose foot (a plant), to t'hars, 61-14
To gore, tsi roor, 80-6
To govern, ta sa rir, 53-11, 117-3
Government business, tsyong sa, 36-8, 111-14
Government office, ma ar, 33-15
A gourd, tsyo kwa, 63-12
Do. dried, ho lo, 70-16
A gown, tsyang sam, 53-7
Grace, oon hey, 89-11, 115-11
Graceful, pis nar, 107-11
Gradually, tsyom tsyom, 106-2
Grain, kok sik, 60-4
Grains of liquor, ko roor, 47-4
A granary, kos tsip ts'hang, 34-13
Grand, k'hoom, 87-9
Grand father, tso poo, 12-3
Grand mother, tso mo, 12-3
Grand son, son tsa, 13-4
To grant, tsyoon har, 98-12
A grape, p'ho to, 63-7
Do. wild, san to, 63-8
To grasp, tsap oor, 30-4, 113-5, 117-10
Do. tsa par, 120-16
Do. in the claws, to ooi ts'hir, 78-4
Grass, p'hoor, 86-9, 109-5, 118-14
Do. China, hwon ts'ho, 86-10
Do. coarse, stooi, 87-3
Do. common, skor, 87-4
Grass cloth, tsya p'ho, 66-2
Grass green, ts'ho lok, 66-14
A grasshopper, mautes, tang lang, 82-11
To gratify, im wa, 104-8
A grating, tyoong kit, 32-16
Grave (sedate), ts'ham toir, 122-5
A grave, moo tom, 52-11, 114-7
Gravel, moong o ri tor, 8-7
To graze, mo koor, 109-2
Grease, ki room, 47-12
Great, k'hoon, 87-9, 109-6
Do. k'hoor, 107-13
Great heat, koo yor, 6-7
Great grand father, tsoong tso poo, 12-2
Do. mother, tsoong tso bo, 12-2
Great grand son, tsoong son, 13-4

Great keeper, syoo lyong, 35-11
Green, p'ha roor, 67-14
Do. p'hoo noor, 118-15
Green, (grass), ts'ho lok, 66-14
Do. (dark), a ts'hang, 66-15
A green gage, a ka oi, 63-6
A green shell, la tyon, 64-7
A green duck, pi ts'hyooi, 76-10
Grief, koon sim oo, 21-2
Grieved, ts'hik ts'hik, 106-10
To grind, kar, 59-11, 112-12
A grind stone, mai, 59-11
Do. soot tor, 73-1
A groom, li ma, 15-3
A grot, kor, 8-2
A grove, soo p'hoor, 85-2
The ground, tta, 7-9
A group, man oor, 98-6
To grow, nar, 41-16
A grub worm, poi stsang i, 82-12
Do. koom pong i, 83-9
Gruel, tsyook, 46-16
Guaicum, hwi hwa, 84-6
To guard, pang pi, 39-10
Do. (defend), koo ho, 89-9
To guess, swi kwi, 91-1
A guest son, 42-7, 108-16
Do. stranger, na koo nai, 96-5
Guilt, ho moor, 53-11
A guitar, pi p'ha, 43-5
Do. pi hwa, 114-2
A gulf, moor koo pooi, 9-13
To gulp, sam k'hir, 49-2
The gums, kis moo oom, 16-13
A gun, tyo ts'hyong, 41-2
Gunpowder, hwa yak, 41-3
A gust of wind, sap sap, 106-3
Guts, ai, 18-12, 119-10

H

Hail, moo rooi, 2-11
Hair, t'ho rok, 17-2, 80-3, 109-5, 121-11
A hair pin, pin hyo, 44-13
Hair cloth, ts'hyang ooi, 45-8
Half, pan, 87-16
A hall, tsip tyon, 31-11, 110-8, 113-10
Halo (of the sun), ir oon, 1-5
Do. (moon), wor oon, 1-9
A hamlet, ma ar, 34-10
A hammer, (sledge), soi ma ts'hi, 72-2
Do. iron, t'hyor t'hoi, 72-3
A hamper, sork, 71-6
The hand, son, 17-6, 120-7
Back of do. syoo pai, 17-7
Palm of do. son pa tang, 17-7
To hand down, tsyon har, 92-1
Do. om kir, 110-7
Do. tsoor, 117-15
A hand carriage, lyon, 75-5
Hand cuffs, kooi key, 41-9
A handful, ir ak, 55-9
Handsome, tsa t'hai, 19-8
A handle, tsa ro, 73-1
Do. ing tsa, 121-11
To hang, kor, 94-10
To hang down, too ri oor, 93-2
To hang up by the heels, to hyon, 104-1
Hanging, tar, 88-12, 121-15, 108-12
A hanging board, hyon p'han, 33-3
To hanker, koo rir, 21-11
To happen, ma tsam, 28-1
Do. ma ts'har, 119-10
Happiness, pok, 89-13, 110-10, 122-1
Happy, yoo pok, 101-2
Harassed, oor oor, 105-6
Do. kas par, 113-2
To harbour (mentally), p'hoom oor, 21-12, 112-9
Hard, koot ser, 23-5
Do. difficult, o ryo or, 90-15
Do. not soft, ser, 92-9
A hare, t'hot ki, 79-13
Hare lip, kyoor syoon, 51-13
A harlot, nyo ki, 15-11
Harm, hai har, 91-7
Harmonious, ko ror, 23-3
Do. hwa mok, 89-10, 112-3
Do. amicable, hwa mok, 89-10
A harp, ko moon ko, 43-4, 121-6
Do. hai koom, 43-5, 121-6
Harvest, ko toor, 59-14
In haste, ts'hang tsor, 102-12
Hastily, hoor hoor, 105-2
Hasty, tso har, 24-9
Do. swift, koop har, 90-16

A hat, kwan, 45-1
Do. ko kar, 114-15
Do. broad-brimmed hat, 45-3
A hatchet, to ts'hai, 72-6
To hate, han har, 21-3
Hatred, mooi or, 23-9
To have, i sir, 90-2, 108-8
Haughty, ko man, 24-2
To haul, skoor oor, 75-10
A hawk, song kor mai, 77-7
Hazardous, ooi t'hai, 89-16
Do. om har, 97-6
A hazelnut, kai am, 63-4
He, tso, 89-4, 115-5
The head, ma ri, 16-1, 108-13
A head (chief), kwi syoo, 96-1
Do. of an arrow, sar mit, 40-13
A headkerchief, too kin, 45-4
Head-ache, too t'hong, 50-8
To heal, am koor, 51-8
To heap up, ssa hoor, 59-15
Do. p'ho p'hir, 92-11
To hear, toor nir, 25-4
Do. too roor, 94-3, 110-8, 122-7
The heart, nyom t'hong, 18-9
Do. ma am, 113-2
Heart, sang k'hwai, 99 13
Heat, to oor, 6-7, 107-5
Heat, steady, ts'hyo syo, 4-8
Heat, great, koo yor, 6-7
A heater, (iron), lak t'hyor, 72-15

To heave, toor, 30-12
Heaven, ho nar, 1-3
Do. 107-10, 119-4
Heavy, moo ko or, 87-10, 107-16
Hedge, oor sop, 33-11
A hedgehog, ko som tot, 79-13
Heed, syo sim, 23-2
The heel, par tooi ts'hook, 18-6
Heir apparent, t'hai tsa,
Do. princess, tong koong, 35-3
A helmet, t'hoo koo, 40-4
Help, to or, 96-4; ta ar, 122-9
Do. p'hi tir, 115-10
Hemp, sam, 86-16
A hen, sat ki, 77-15
Herbs, na mar, 60-16
A herd, moor, 98-5
A hero, ho kor, 14-8
A heron, han sai, 76-14
To hesitate, ham ooi, 91-1
Hibiscus, koon hwa, 85-15
To hide, ka ri oor, 94-11
Hidden, koo ook, 93-15
High, no p'hoor, 88-14, 114-15
High, a a, 105-15
A high island, tsyor to, 9-5
High water, tsyo syoo, 10-3
Hilarity, sooi hwon har, 21-7
A hill, mo. ,an, 7-10
Do. mois poor ri, 107-12
Do. rugged, ko kai, 7-13
A hillock, spe tsyok, 8-16

Hilt (of a sword), pa ki, 40-8
To hinder, lan ts'hyoor, 101-8
A hinge, tsi to ri, 32-12
The hip, swin ta ri, 18-2
To hire a horse, ko ma, 73-13
A hired servant, ko kong, 15-13
His, koo, 117-15
History, sa kwi, 117-10
To hit the centre, mat ts'hir, 40-15
To hoard, kar mar, 107-6
Hoar frost, so ri, 2-11, 107-10
A hoe, ho mai, 58-16
Do. sarp, 72-9
Do. small, ka rai, 72-10
To hoe, ki oom air, 59-3
A hog (wild), san tsey, 79-14
To hoist sail, kwai pong, 74-13
To hold fast, ka tsir, 30-4, 113-5
Do. with both hands, oo hooir, 30-5
Do. under the arm, skir, 30-6
Do. in the mouth, mok oom oor, 49-5
A hole, mey or, 8-18
A holiday, myong ir, 4-4
A hollow, o mok, 3-16
Holy, syong in, 22-4
At home, toor, 112-6, 29-7

Honest, syoon pak, 23-1
Honey, skoor, 47-13
Honey fruits, mir kwa, 47-15
To honour, ma ra, 116-11
Honourable, no p'hoor, 88-13, 112-2, 114-15
A hoof, koop, 80-3
A hook, kar koo ri, 72-11
A hoop, t'he, 70-14
To hope for, pa rar, 29-15
Horary characters, from 6-10 to 7-7
A horn (to play on), tsyoo ra, 43-10
A horn (of a beast), spoor, 80-2
A horned owl, hyoo lyoo, 77-3
A horse, mar, 78-11
A fine horse, tsyo ma, 78-11
A dappled do. t'hong ma, 78-12
A piebald horse, pak ma, 78-14
A red do. tsyok ma, 78-12
A spotted horse, ts'hyoo ma, 78-13
A white do. paik ma, 78-13
A horse-load, pok moor, 73-11
A host (an entertainer), tsyoo in, 42-7
Hot, to oor, 6-7, 107-5, 120-16
Hot water, syook syoo, 46-15
4 Hot wine, syo tsyoo, 47-2

A hot well, on tsyong, 9-16
A hound, to p'hor ke, 79-15
An hour, stai si, 5-11
Hours of the day, 5-13 to 6-2
Hourglass done, p'ha loo, 5-9
That hour, ka si, 5-11
This hour, ts'ha si, 5-12
What hour, ha si, 5-12
A house, tsip ka, 31-13
Household, ir ka, 13-11
House rent, ka sey, 56-8
How, ko ooi, 27-8
How, yo ha, 103-13
How? os styo, 109-7
Do. ip key, 122-7
How many days, kooi ir, 5-1
How much, kwi ha, 104-11
However, koo ror, 27-16
Hovenia, raing tsa, 84-10
To hug, am oor, 20-6
Human, sa ram, 108-4
Humble, kyom son, 22-10, 117-12
Humpbacked, kooi pai, 51-13
A hundred, ir paik, 55-2
Do. on paik, 116-10
A hundred weight, syom, 55-6,
To hunger, tsoo rir, 49-10, 119-12
To hunt, san haing, 94-6
A huntsman, lyop ho, 15-4
Hurried, pat poor, 96-13
Do. ts'hong ts'hong, 105-2

Do. precipitate, hwang hwang, 105-14
In a hurry, ts'hang tsor, 102-12
To hurt, hai har, 91-7
Husband, tsi a pi, 12-9
Do. tsis a pi, 112-4
Do. father, sooi a pi, 12-8
Do. mother, sooi o mi, 12-8
Husband and wife, poo poo, 12-13
Husbandman, nyo room tsi oor, 58-14, 117-3
Husk of grain, pyo kop p'hoor, 59-13

I

I, myself, na, 89-1, 117-6
A jacket, tsyok sam, 45-10
Jail, ok, 53-16
Japan, it'h pon, 58-7
A jar, tok, 70-11
Jaundice, hwang tar, 50-11
To jaunt, nor, 52-14
Ice, o room, 11-1
An icicle, syoo lyong, 10-2
Idea, stoot, 22-3
Idle, ke o roor, 24-6
Idol, po sar, 53-1
Jealous, roo kwi, 91-7
To jeer, pi oo soor, 26-6
Jelly, (of pulse), too poo, 47-8
To jest, tsyo long, 25-16
A jewel, ok, 64-3
If, man ir, 27-10
Ignominy, yok har, 39-12
Ill, bad, mo tsir, 23-12
To illuminate, pi ts'hoir, 6-10

To imagine, saing kak, 21-10
To imitate, pon pa toor, 91-12
Do. pon por, 109-10
Do. exactly, tsook hyo, 104-7
Imitated, tsya tsya, 105-8
Immediately, tsook koom, 99-8
To impede, ts'hyor tsyoo, 101-16
Impediment in walking, tsa tsyo, 100-7
Imperial household, tsong sir, 35-6
To implore, koo har, 92-3
Important, weighty, moo ko oor, 107-16
Important, pi kyong, 103-7
Do. tsoong yo, 120-13
Importunate, ts'hoi ts'hok, 103-16
Impost, kong sey, 60-1
Impoverished, kyoong koor, 101-4
To imprison, ka tor, 53-15
In (at), noor, 20-14, 117-3
In order to, pso, 26-13, 111-15
In vain, syok tsyar op sar, 28-10
Inadequate, yong ryor, 90-6
Inauspicious, hyoong har, 89-14
An incense pot, hyang hap, 70-10
Incessant, tong tong, 105-13
An inch, ts'hi, 55-8
Do. ma tai, 110-12
To incite a quarrel, ts'hyo kir, 26-2
To incline, ki oo ro tsir, 92-13 115-10
Incoherent, so o, 100-3
Income, lyang sik, 60-2
Increased, to har, 88-7, 118-2
To inculcate, tyong nyong, 103-2
Do. o tir, 111-10
Indeed, kwa yon, 100-14
Indeed! ip key, 122-10
Index, (to a book), mok lok, 37-2
To indicate, ka rat ts'hir, 30-3
Indigent, ka nan har, 56-12
Indignant, poon har, 21-4
Indignation, ai to ror, 21-4
Indistinct, hong hong, 100-1
Do. (dull), ai tai, 101-15
An individual, ir ts'hyok, 55-10
Indolent, ke o roor, 24-6
To induce, ta rir, 108-16
To indulge one's self, im wa, 104-8
Industrious, poo tsoo ron har, 24-6
To inebriate, ts'hyooi har, 42-12
Inexhaustible, moo koong. 104-13
An infant, hai, 13-14
Infinite, moo koong, 104-13
Infirmity, yak har, 115-10
An inflammation, tsyoong p'hoong, 50-7
Do. in the head, too p'hoong, 50-7
To inflict, tsoi tsoor, 53-13
Influence, kwon sey, 93-13
To influence, noot kir, 115-12
To inform, ko har, 25-4
Ingathering, kok sik ko toor, 117-4, 59-14, 107-6
Ingenious, soor kooi, 22-15
Do. clever, kong kyo, 24-10, 121-8
To inhabit, sar, 118-7
To inherit, ni or, 120-9
An injunction, ko tong, 112-6
To injure, syor oor, 21-5
Do. hurt, hai har, 91-7
Injured, son har, 88-8
To do an injury, i tsoo ro tsir, 92-14, 112-16
Injury done by insects, ts'hyoong son, 83-11
Ink (indian), mok, 38-9, 110-1
Ink (liquid), syeo mook, 38-6
An ink stone, pyo lo, 38-10
Do. portable, kwai yon, 68-9
Do. box, yon syang, 38-10
Do. dripper, yon tyok, 38-11
An inlet, kai, 9-9
An inn, soot mak, 34-15
An inner door, tsi ke, 32-12, 114-13

To inquire, moo roor, 25-1
Do. moo rar, 108-11
Do. minutely, tsa sey, 23-6, 120-14
Insane, mi ts'hir, 50-12
An insect, pai rai, 82-5
Do. small, kooir, 83-10
Do. at the bottom of vessels, so rir, 83-10
Inside, sok, 11-12
Insipid, soong ko oor, 48-13
Do. thin, tam pak, 102-1
Insolent, om syoo i no kar, 91-4
To inspect, ko moor, 117-14
Inspiration, ho hoop, 20-7
An instant, kyong kak, 99-9
The instep, tsyok pai, 18-5
To institute, syor, 29-1, 110-5
To instruct, ka ra ts'hir hoon, 37-9, 112-5
Do. inform, poir, 93-12
An instructor, hoon to, 35-16
An instrument, koo root, 68-4
To insult, om syoo i no kir, 91-4
Integral, oon tsyon, 87-16
Integrity, tan tsyong, 23-2
Intelligent, ts'hang myong, 22-16
Intelligible, myong paik, 99-13
Intense, ir tsyor, 96-14
Intention, stoot ooi, 22-3, 113-4
To inter, moo toor, 52-19
Intercalary, poo rar, 107-7
Intercouse, sa p'hir, 95-13
To interdict, mor har, 98-2
Interest, li har, 56-1
Interim, sa i, 11-10
Interior, an, 11-11, 114-5
Interpret, tsoo nair, 37-13
An interpreter, t'hong sa, 36-4
Interrogation (note of), on, 122-10
To interrogate, hir nan har, 26-3
Do. (examine), tsyo tsoor, 54-2
The intestines, ai tsyang, 18-12, 119-10
Intimate, ts'hin har, 13-10
Into, toor, 29-7, 112-6
To be intoxicated, ts'hyooi har, 42-12
To invade, ts'him no, 39-6
To investigate, sa haik, 54-3
An invisible being, sin lyang, 53-3
To invite, ts'hyang har, 42-12
To invoke, pir, 53-4
To involve, to ro ir, 118-11
Inward, an, 11-11
Job's tears, coi i, 60-14
To join, lyon har, 92-6
Do. in succession, na cor, 92-7, 112-10, 120 9
A joint, ma tai, 95-12, 112-15
To joke, tsyo long, 25 16
A journal, ir kwi, 38-4
A journey, ko tsyong, 101-7
Joy, kit koor, 23-7, 118-11
Iron, soi, 64-11
An iron ball, t'hyor hwan, 41-2
An iron hammer, t'hyor t'hoi, 72-3
An iron rake, t'hyor p'ha, 72-10
An iron heater, lak t'hyor, 72-15
An iron (smoothing), oor too, 72-16
Irregular, so o, 100-3
Irresolute, tsyoo tsyo, 100-7
Is it so ? on, 122-10
Isinglass, poo re, 81-11
An island, syom to, 9-5
Do. high, tsyor to, 9-5
An isle, moor ka tsyoo, 9-11
An islet, moor ka tsyo, 9-12
To issue forth, pai p'hoor, 108-9, 121-11
It, kar, 111-5
It is, i , 28-4
Do. is, 110-12, 111-3
Do. ip key, 122-10
Do. right, or hoor, 90-3
It is not, koo roor, 90-3
The itch, ka ryo or, 51-7
A jug, hang, 70-13
To judge of, sar p'hir, 120-14
A juggler, hwan syoor, 15-9
A jujube, tai ts'hyo, 63-4
To jump, stoo ir, 31-1, 121-2
A junk, tai syon, 73-7

Maize, ok syo, 60-12
To make (do), tsi oor, 96-5, 108-5, 110-4, 112-14
To make (cause), ha ya kom, 28 6
To make a bow, oop har, 29-11
To make ready, tsyang man har, 42-9
To make up, ki or, 88-9
A male child, sa na hai, 42-1
Male of beasts, soo, 80-1
The male principle, pyot, 6-3, 107-8
Mallows, a ok, 61-7
Do. marsh, poo yong, 85-15
Do. Syrian, koon hwa, 85 1
A man, saram, 14-3, 108-5
Do. a male, a mar, 109-10
A man of talent, mai or, 115-13
Manacles, kooi key, 41-9
To manage, ka oom ar, 36-7
A mandarine's court, koo ooi, 33-15
A mandarine duck, won ang, 76-10
A mane, kar ki, 80-1
A mangle, yon, 71-14
Manifest, nam ra nar, 90-5
A manner, mo yang, 19-4
A mansion, ma ar, 33-15, 114-11
A mantle, p'hyo ooi, 45-7
Do. (rain), oo tsang, 45-12
Manure, stong, 13-16
7 A manuscript, syoo pon, 36-16
Many, man hoor, 87-15
Do. man oor, 98-6
Do. kar, 115-14
A map, ti to, 101-7
A marigold, kook hwa, 85-7
A marine, kyok koon, 74-10
A mark (to shoot at), sor, 40-14
A market, tsyo tse, 34-14, 119-5
Market price, si tsik, 55-14
Marriage, hon in, 41-11
Marrow, kor syoo, 18-7
To marry out a daughter, syo pang ma tsir, 41-13
To marry a wife, tsyang ka too rir, 41-14
A marsh, mot t'haik, 9-6
A marsh fever, tsyang kooi, 11-3
Marsh mallows, poo yong, 85-15
A mast, tot tai, 74-5
Master (teacher), soo song, 14-10
Do. (lord), nim koon, 116-12
A mat, tot, 68-15, 114-1
Do. floor, t'hyop syok, 68-15
Do. thin, ti ooi, 68-16, 114-1
Do. of bamboo, sat, 69-1
A match (fire), hwa soong, 41-3
To match, stsak, 41-13
A match maker, tsyong mai, 41-11
Material, tsai mok, 84-16
Matter (business), ir, 88-16
A mattress, yo, 46-6
Do. square, pang syok, 68-16
Mature, ni koor, 117-7
May or can, or har, 28-8
May be, kam hi, 27-14
Meadow, pat, 58-12
Meagre, ts'hyo ts'hyooey, 19-14
A meal, pap, 46-13, 119-9, 112-2
Mean, na tsar, 88-13
To measure, hey a rir, 94-4, 109-16
A measure of 10 feet, kir, 95-1
Meat, ko ki, 47-4
Do. (minced), hoi, 47-6
Measles, ma tsin, 51-1
A mechanic, tsyang in, 15-2
A mediator (in marriages), tsyoong mai, 41-11
Medicine, yak, 52-2
To meditate, tsam tsam, 26-8, 118-9
The medium, ka on tai, 117-11, 11-10
To meet, ma tsoor, 42-8
Do. man nar, 97-2
Do. assemble, mo toor, 91-14
Do. accidentally, hai hoo, 100-8
Melancholy, syo syo, 104-15
A melon, oi, 61-4

Do. (true), tsin kwa, 63-12
To melt, sa ra tsir, 11-2
Do. (metals), no kir, 64-14
A memorandum, kon kooi, 37-2
To mend (to repair), sew li, 33-11
The menses, kyong syoo, 41-14
Merchandize, moor hwa, 55-13
A merchant, syang ko, 56-10
Merciful, ka lyon, 103-7
Merily, a tsik, 27-7
Merit, kong myong, 36-10
Do. kong, 94-2, 115-3
Do. kong op, 102-8
Mespilus Japonica, na mo, 118-15
A messenger, sa sin, 35-12
Do. (one sent), poo rir, 93-10
Do. special, ts'hik sa, 35-13
Do. faithful, sin sa, 35-13
Do. ready, ts'hai pi kwan, 36-1
Met together, hwa hwa, 100-9
Metal, plate, so koor, 115-4
Metropolis, mo tor, 113-7
Mid autumn, ts'yoo syok 4 9
Middle, ka on kai, 11-10, 117-11
The middle finger, tsyang tsi, 17-10
A mids-man, tong bo, 56-11
Might (power), hyong sey, 93-13
A military officer, koon kwan, 36-3
Military affairs, ho pan, 38-14
Milk, t'ha lak, 47-9
The milky way, oon ha, 1-10
Millett, ki tsang, 60-7, 117-6
Do. Barbadoes, p'hi, 60-7, 117-6
A minaret, t'hap, 53-1
To mind, tso ts'har, 111-14
The mind, ma am, 113-2
To mingle, sot kir, 97-13
A minister, sin ha, 35-8, 108-14
Do. prime, soong syang, 35-9
Do. chief, tsai syang, 35-9
Do. saing loo, 114-11
Mint (a plant), kam kwak, 62-4
Minute (recondite), oon oon, 105-3
Mire, ni nyong, 8-12
Mirror, koo oor, 44-15
Miserable, kwa ro or, 91-9
Do. ka lyon, 103-6
Do. wretched, sin ko, 102-12
Misery, tsai hwa, 89-13
Misfortune, tsai hwa, 93 14
To mislead, hok har, 24-1
Do. tar nair, 26-4
To miss, ir hoor, 90-1
M st, no oor, 2-13
To mistake, a took har, 24-8
Mistrust, wi sim, 91-3
A mite, kooi to ki, 83-8
To mix, ts'ham ey, 94-15
Do. sot kir, 97-13
To moan, oor, 52-9
Mode, mo yang, 19-4
Modern, i tsai, 90-9
Modesty, ko tar, 22-11, 109-9
To moisten, tso tsoor, 10-14
Moisture (of the body), tsin aik, 20-6
A mole (a beast), too to tsooi, 79-11
Momentous, moo ko oor, 107-16
Monarch, nim koom, 35-5
A monastery, am tsa, 53-1
Money, ton, 64-1
Mongolia, mong ko, 58-8
A monk, sa mi, 53-6
A monkey, tsain nap i, 79-6
A month, tar wor, 3-8
1st month, tsyong wor, 3-8
2nd do. i wor, 3-9
3rd do. sam wor, 3-9
4th do. sa wor, 3-10
5th do. o wor, 3-10
6th do. lyook wor, 3-11
7th do. ts'hir wor, 3-11
8th do. p'har wor, 3-12
9th do. koo wor, 3-12
10th do. sip wor, 3-13
11th do. sip ir wor, 3-13
12th do. sip i wor, 3-14
Intercalary do. yoon wor, 2-14
This month, koom wor, 3-15

That month, tang wor, 3-15
Last month, ko wor, 3-16
Next month, lai wor, 3-16
Monument, pi syak, 52-11
Moon, tar wor, 1-4, 107-3
Do. full, po rom, 4-2
Do. wane, koom oom, 4-3
Do. new, ts'ho ha ra, 4-3
Moonlight night, wor ya, 5-8
To moor, poo t'hoor, 74-16
More, ta si, 27-3
Do. additional, to har, 88-7, 111-16
More and more, katak, 92-12
Moreover, ha moor myo, 28-2
Morning, a ts'ham, 5-5, 108-11, 115-8
A morsel, ka ra, 47-13
A mortar, hwak, 59-9
Moss, sweet, kam t'hai, 62-5
Do. common, it ki, 87-5
Mother, o mi, 12-5, 112-6
Mother in law, husband's mother, soor o mi, 12-8
A motto, koor tey, 37-13
To move, oom tsook ir, 29-3
Do. mooir, 113-2
Do. abruptly, tsir oor, 93-6
To be moved (mentally), soor p'hoor, 118-12
Mould, earth, hark, 8-8, 116-2
A mound, too ton, 7-15, 115-7, 118-4
Do. (bank), tey on, 58-14
Do. a cemetery, tsyang
8 soong, 34-16

To mount, o roor, 29-10, 111-13
Do. on horseback, t'har, 75-9
A mountain, mois moo ni, 116-11
Mountain top, sai, 7-12
Do. vapour, am kooi, 9-1
To mourn, oor, 52-9
Mourning dress, nip oor, 52-8
A mouse, tsooi, 79-12
A mouse deer, no ro, 79-5
A moutan flower, mok tan, 85-6
Mouth, ip koo, 16-12, 119-10
To mow, pooir, 59-6
Must, man hoor, 87-15, 98-6
Mud, tsoon hark, 8-11
A mud eel, ts'hyoo o, 81-8
Muddy, hoor ir, 10 7
Mugwort, ssook, 87-3
A mulberry, spong na mo, 83-16
A mule, no sai, 79-1, 121-1
A mullet, ts'hooi o, 80-12
A muscle (shell fish), hong hap, 81-14
The muscles, sar, 18-8
A mushroom, po soot, 61-10
Do. fragrant, hyang sin, 61-11
Music, p'hong lyoi, 43-3, 112-1
A musical stone, syok kyong, 43-9

A musk deer, sa hyang no, ro, 79-5
Musket, tyo ts'hyong, 41-2
A musquito, mo ko oi, 82-14
Musquito curtains, moon tsyang, 69-4
Must, pan toot, 28-7
Do. pan took, 109-11
Mustaches, na rot syoo, 17-1
Do. grey, paik par, 17-3
Mustard plant, key tsa, 61-2, 107-16
Mutually, so ra, 97-9
A myriad, ir man, 55-3, 109-4
Myself, na, 89-1
Mysterious, soom kir, 91-10

N

A nag, mai ya tsi, 78-15
A nail (a spike), mot, 72-8
The nails of the fingers, son t'hop, 17-11
Naked-shouldered, mer, 46-5
Name, ir hom, 13-16, 110-5
Napkin, syoo kon, 46-5, 119-16
Narrow, tsop oor, 87-11
A nation, na ra, 33-13
National altars, sya tsik, 33-14
A native village, ko hyang, 34-9
Nature, t'hyon syong, 22-2
Do. syong, 113 1
The navel, pai skop, 17-15
Navigable, noo toor, 113-9
Near, kat ka or, 88-3

Do. kas ska oor, 108-15, 118-3
Do. ts'hin i har, 98-11, 119-13
Nearabouts, koon kan, 99-1
Do. kwi kai, 104-2
Neat, pin pin, 105-7
Necessary, mo ro mi, 26-15
The neck, mok, 17-4
Do. kis, 122-3
Need, tsyong yo, 28-14
A needle, pa nar, 72-15
Needy, ka nan har, 56-12
Nature, mar, 98 1
Neigh, oor, 80 4
A neighbourhood, i oot, 34-11
Nephew, tsok ha, 13-2
A nest, kit too rir, 78-5
A net, ko poor, 71-10
A net-string, pyo ri, 71-10
Nevertheless, pi rok, 28-7
New, (modern), i tsai, 90-9
New, (fresh), sai, 90-10, 117-7
New moon, ts'ho ha ra, 4-3
News, (tidings), syo sik, 103-5
New year's eve, tse syok, 4-11
Next day, ik ir, 4-13
Next month, lai wor, 3-16
Next year, myong nyon, 3-4
Next in order, po koom, 98-10
Niece, brother's child, tsir nyo, 13-3
Do. sister's child, saing tsir, 13-3
Do. wife's sister's child, ts'hyo nam, 13-6
Niggardly, lin har, 23-11
Nigh, kat ka or, 88-3
Night time, pam ya, 5-2, 107-14
A nightingale, koit ko ri, 77-6
Nine, a hop, 55-1, 116-9
Nipples, tsyot, 17-18
A nit, hyo, 83-4
Nitre, yom ts'hyo, 65-3
No, mot har, 98-1
Nobility, sey tsa, 35-4
A noble, pyo soor, 114-12
Noble, kooi har, 88-14
Do. koo har, 112-1
A noise, soot too o rir, 21-1
None, op sar, 90-2
The north, pook nyok, 11-5
The north wind, pook p'hoong, 1-12
North-west do. syo pook p'hoong, 1-14
North-east do. tong pook p'hoong, 1-14
The nose, k'ho, 16-10
Bridge of do. pi lyang, 16-10
Dimple under do. in tsyoong, 16-11
The nostril, pi kong, 16-11
Not, op sar, 90-2
Not yet, a nir, 98-2, 110-11, 111-5
A note, tan tsa, 37-1
Do. in music, pop ts'hook, 107-8
Notion, stoot, 22-3
Notwithstanding, pi rok, 28-7
To nourish, ts'hir, 89-10, 108-13, 109-7
Now (at present), tsook koom, 99-8
Now (this time), ts'ha si, 5-12
Now and then, ma tsam, 28-1
A number, heym, 54-12
Numbness, ma mok, 50-15
Do. of the legs, kak ma, 50-13
Do. of the feet, tsyok ma, 50-16
Numerous, man hoor, 87-15
A nun, song, 5-35
Nuptials, hon in, 41-11
A nurse (wet), yoo mo, 13-8

O

An oak, to t'ho ri, 84-4
Do. large kind, ka rai, 84-4
An oar (large), no, 74-6
An oath, maing sey, 25-14
Obedient, syoon har, 23-3
Obeisance, tsor, 29-11
To obey, syoon har, 23-3
To oblige (compel), pan toot, 28-7
Oblique, pit kir, 93-1
Obscene, oom lan, 24-14
Obscure, hon hon, 105-5
To observe, por, 31-1, 113-12, 118-13

Obstruction, ma koor, 116-13
To obtain, si ro kom, 27-7
Do. (get), o toor, 90-1, 109-12, 121-4
Obtuse, moo twir, 40-9
To occasion, na roo ir, 95-10
Do. mir oo ir, 107-9
Occult, koo ook, 93-15
The ocean, syoo tsong, 10-2
Ochre, syok tsa hwang, 67-7
An ode, koor wor, 110-2
Odour, kot ta or, 86-7
Of, kar, 111-4
Offence, ho moor, 53-12
To offend, pom har, 53-12
To offer up, i pa tsi, 42-9
Do. (to present) pat toor, 89-8
Do. in sacrifice, tsey sa, 120-10
Office (rank), koo wi, 108-4
An office (employment), pyo sar tsik, 36-5, 111-13, 111-14, 113-6, 114-12
Office of government, ma ar, 33-15, 114-11
An officer, kwan won, 35-15
Offspring (son), a too, 12-16
Often, tot tot, 95-15
Oil, ki room, 47-12
An oilskin dress, yoo sem, 45-11
Oil cloth, hok ma p'ho, 66-3
Oil green, yoo lok, 66-13

Old (ancient), te, 90-9
Old (not new), te, 90-10, 119-13
Old (aged), noor koor, 19-15, 119-13, 119-14
Old corn, mook oor, 59-5
An old man, ha ra, 89-5
An old woman, har mi, 89-5
Omen, tsyo tsin, 101-10
On all sides, sa myon, 11-16
Of one sort, ir yang, 102-3
On one side, kas, 11-13
One, har, 94-13, 108-15
One and the same, ir pan, 102-3
One-eyed, ir mok, 51-11
One's-self, soo soo ro, 27-2
One thing, ar ts'hyok, 55-10
One head of cattle, ir t'hai, 55-10
An onion, p'ha, 61-3
Do. wild, ya ts'hoong, 61-16
Do. red, tsa ts'hoong, 61-16
Only, o tsik, 27-5, 109-7
Do. han kat, 27-6
To ooze out, sam loo, 102-6
To open, yor, 32-10, 113-15
Do. as a flower, p'hooir, 86-4
Open country, on tok, 7-15
To open one's mouth, kai koo, 25-7
To open a seam, t'ho tsir, 93-5
To operate, wi har, 96-4
Opinion, stoot, 22-3
An opponent, tai tyok, 39-3

Opportunity, kwi hoi, 100-5
To oppose, o kwir, 91-13
Opposite, tai har, 95-14, 113-16
To oppress, ok t'hook, 101-14
Or, hok, 27-9
Orange (sweet), kyoor kyoor, 62-10
Do. (common), kan tsa, 62-10
Do. (small), kyoor kan, 62-11
Do. honied, mir kam, 62-11
To ordain, syor, 29-1
An order, lyong har, 36-8
Do. series, toor room, 95-1
To order, poon poo, 25-10
Do. poo rir, 93-10, 109-15
Next in order, po koom, 98-10
Ordinary, tot tot, 95-15
Ordure, sto, 18-16
Origin, pi ro sar, 90-11
Original, hir, 117-9
Do. head, oot stoom, 96-1
Originally, won lai, 100-12
Orion (a star), sam syong, 1-9
An ornament, ts'hai saik, 67-4, 113-14
Ornamented silk, tsan tan, 65-8
Ornamental, moon ts'hai, 99-14
An orphan, oi ro or, 15-15, 122-7
An ostler, li ma, 15-3

Other, ta roor, 28-13
An otter (land), san' tar, 79-9
Do. river, syoo tar, 79-9
Over (above), oos, 11-9
Over and above, nam oor, 88-6
Over against, hyang har, 97-3
Overbearing, kang in, 101-13
Overcome, i kwir, 110-4
Overflowing, nam oor, 88-6
Overplus, nam oor, 88-6
An overseer, kam sa, 35-10
To overset, op to tsir, 29-9
To overspread, ni poor, 109-3
To overthrow, op to tir, 112-16
Overwhelming, ts'hang ts'hang, 105-10
Ought, mat tang, 27-13
Do. pas stang, 110-15
Do. mas stang, 111-10
An ounce, lyang, 55-4
Out of, poo t'hoor, 28-9
Outrageous, kang har, 23-14
Outside, pat, 11-12, 110-6, pas, 112-5
Outstretched, no roor, 117-1
Outward, pat, 11-11
An owl, ot pa mi, 77-8
Own, mom, 109-14
Ox, syo, 78-16

P

Pace (step), ko room, 29-1
A pack, po, 71-9
To paddle, tso oor, 74-15
Paddy, tso, 60-11
Do. early, pyo, 60-5
Pæony, tsyak yak, 85-6
A pagoda, tsyor, 52-16
A pail, syoo t'hong, 70-14
Pain, ar hoor, 50-1
Do. in the thorax, hyoong t'hong, 50-7
Do. in the belly, pok t'hong, 50-9
To paint, koo rim, 113-14
A painter, hwa won, 36-2
A pair, ssang, 89-6
To pair, stsak, 41-13
A palace, tsip koong, 31-10, 113-10
Do. precincts of, tsip kwor, 31-10
Palisade, oor sop, 33-11
A palm (tree), tsong lyo, 84-1
Palm of the hand, son pe tang, 17-7
Palma Christi, p'hi ma tsa, 86-14
Palsy, ma mok, 50-15
A pan (iron), sot, 70-4
Do. small, no ko, 70-5
A pan (earthen), pyong, 69-11
A pan-pipe, saing hwang, 43-7 Do. tyo, 114-2
A pannier, t'hai an, 73-4
To pant, ts'yon man, 50-13
Pantaloons, pa tsi, 45-15
A papaya, mok kwa, 63-3
Paper, tsyo hooi, 38-7, 121-7
Do. variegated, moon tsi, 38-8
Do. coloured, saik tsi, 38-8
The paper tree, tak, 84-5
Parallel, p'hyong har, 93-1
Paralysis, ma mot, 50-15
Paramount, koi syoo, 96-1
A parapet, syong kak hoi, 34-1
A parasite, kooi saing, 64-12
A parasol, ir san, 69-2
A parcel, po, 71-9
To pardon, sya har, 54-6
A parent, o pi i, 12-4
A parental tablet, sin tsyoo, 52-12
A parish, sya tan, 34-12
A parlour, sya lang, 31-14
A parrot, aing moo, 76-11
Parsimonious, lin har, 23-11
Parsley, mi na ri, 62-2
Part (share), nan hor, 108-12
Part (not the whole), pan, 87-16
To part (divide), poon kan, 102-9
Partial (private), p'hyon pyok, 24-5
Particular, sa sa, 88-15
A partition, pa ram, 32-6
A partridge, tsya ko, 77-3
Patrimony, op, 94-1
Party colored, o rok, 68-2
A pass, an entrance, mo kai, 34-2
Do. a warrant, p'hyo sin, 41-7

To pass by, tsi nar, 96-10, 118-13
To pass through, sa ma ts'ha, 98-4, 114-5, 114-6
Passed (done), ir tsook, 27-10
Passion, stoot, 22-2
Passport, p'yo sin, 40-7
Paste, kook syoo, 47-7
Pasturage, mok tsyang, 34-16
To pasture, ts'hir, 116-5
A path, kyong lo, 8-5
To be patient, kyor tair, 21-13
Patrimony, op, 94-1, 111-11
A pattern, pop, 53-10
A pavilion, tyong tsa, 31-12, 116-12
To pause, koo ts'hir, 96-12
A paw, ts'har, 80-4
To pawn, tyon tang, 56-3
To pay down, ka p'hoor, 56-7
A pea, syo too, 60-10
Pea green, too lok, 66-13
A peach, pok syong hwa, 62-16
Peach colour, to hong, 66-12
Peaceful, p'hyong an, 89-15, 111-8
A peacock, kong tsyak, 76-9
A peak, mois pong o ri, 7-12
A pear, pai, 62-13
Do. sweet, a ka oi, 63-6, 111-15
A peasant, tyon poo, 14-16
A pearl, koo sar, 64-2, 107-14
Do. (rock), tsin tsyoo, 64-2
Do. (perfect), moo kong tsyoo, 64-3
Pebbles, moong ori tor, 8-7
A peck (a gantang), mar, 55-6
To peck, tso oor, 78-4
A pecul (1cwt. Ch.), syom,
To peep, yot por, 29-16
A peer, pyo soor, 114-12
A pellet, t'han tsa, 41-1, 121-5
A pencil (hair), poot, 38-9, 121-7
Penetration, yo o, 22-16
A penman, noong p'hir, 38-2
A penny, ton, 64-1
A penthouse, ooi pak, 32-6
The people, paik syong, 14-13
Pepper, ho ts'hyo, 63-10
Do. (water), ts'hyon ts'hyo, 63-11
Do. (wild), san ts'hyo, 63-11
To perceive, skai ts'hir, 21-13
A perch, poo o, 81-1
To perch, kit too rir, 78-5
Perfect, oon tsyon, 87-16
To perforate, skooer, 93-6
Do. (to string), ni koor, 98-4
To perform, ir or, 99-2
Perfume, kot ta or, 86-8
Perhaps, hok, 27-9
Perilous, ooi t'hai, 89-16
A period, si tsor, 4-4, 115-6
A periodical sickness, si pyong, 50-3
To perish, mang hor, 39-15
To permit, tsyoon har, 98-12
Perpetual, myon myon, 105-15
Perplexed, tsyoo tsyo, 100-7
A person, mom, 118-1
Perspicuous, myong paik, 99-13
Perspiration, stam, 20-8
To persuade, ni nar, 115-11
To pervade, sa ma ts'har, 98-4, 114-5
Pervading, too ro, 97-8
Perverse, p'hyak har, 24-12
Do. pis skin, 115-16
To peruse, nir koor, 37-12
A pestle, kong i, 59-10
Do. stone, pang ha, 59-9
Petal, yo hai, 86-5
To petition, koo har, 92-3
Petticoats, ko ooi, 45-15
Petty, koo koo, 106-9
Pewter, nap, 64-10
A pheasant, skwong, 77-10
A philosopher, syong in, 14-3
Phlegm, tam, 50-13
A phlegmatic disease, tam pyong, 50-4
Phoenix, pong hwang, 76-8, 109-1

Physic, yak, 52-2
A physician, ooi won, 36-2
To pick, k'hair, 94-8
Do. (pluck), star, 98-16
To pick up, tsoo oor, 30-14
Pickle (clear), ts'hyong tsyang, 47-9
Do. (sweet), kam tsyang, 47-10
Pickled meat, tsot, 47-11
A picture, koo rim, 36-5
Piebald, o rok, 68-2
Do. pan pak, 102-7
A piebald horse, pak ma, 78-14
A piece (of cloth), p'hir, 55-7
A piece (fragment), tong i, 88-1
To pierce, ts'han tso, 73-2
Piety (filial), hyo to, 22-8
A pig, tot, 79-14
A pigeon, pi toor, 77-11
To pile up, yo ro, 92-11
Do. on one another, t'hyop t'hyop, 105-1
A pill, t'han tsa, 121-5
To pillage, no lyak, 39-6
A pillar, ki tong, 32-5, 113-16
Base of do. tsyoo ts'hyoo, 32-5
A pillow, pyo kai, 46-7
Pincers, tsip ke, 72-3
A pinch, ir ts'hwar, 55-9
A pine, sor, 83-14, 111-4
Pine fruit, syong tsa, 84-11
A pint, toi, 55-7
A pink, syok ts'hyook hwa, 85-14
Pious, tsot sa or, 91-6
A pipe for playing, t'sho kim, 43-14
Do. (long), tsyoo ra, 43-10
A pipe (tobacco), yon tsyook, 69-16
A pipe (tube), hong, 72-1
To pipe, syoo p'ha ram, 43-11
Piss, o rom, 18-6
Pistachio nut, pi tsa, 62-10
A pit, koor hong, 8-12
Do. (to take in), moot tsi roor, 39-16
A pitfall, sko tsir, 8-13
A pitcher, pyong, 69-11
Do. flowe.ed, hwa pyong, 69.11
Pitiable, ka syok, 103-6
To pity, [illegible] yot poor, 21-5
A pivot, tsi to ri, 32-12
To place, toor, 91-16
A place, kot, 97-4, 118-7
A plaice, pang o, 80-13
Plain (level), ko roor, 93 8
A plain (desert), toor ya, 8-1
A plain country, p'hyong ti, 7-9
A plait, tsoo room, 46-2
To plan, skoi, 22-15, 117-15
A plane, tai p'ha, 72 5
To plant, tsai sik, 59-1
Do. si mar, 117-16
A plantation, non, 58-12
A plank, nor, 84-16
Plantain, p'ha ts'hyo, 66-11
Plate, pan, 65-15
A platter, tyop si, 70-2
A play, no rat, 75-12
To play (sport), koo kyong, 91-11, 119-5
To play (on the harp), t'har, 43-7
Do. (gently), t'hai p'hyong, 43-11
To play at chess, ts'hyak kooi, 75-15
To play on a pipe, tong syo, 43-12
A player, kyong tsai in, 15-7
Playful talk, long tam, 25-16
To plead. syong sa, 26-2
To be pleased, kit koor, 21-6, 118-11, 120-8
A pledge, por mo, 56-4
To pledge (pawn), tyon tang, 56-3
Do. tsi tang, 103-1
To pledge in drinking, syoo tsyak, 25-8
Plentiful, syong har, 89-15
Pliant, poo too roor, 23-4
To plot, mo hai, 101-12
To plough, pat kar, 58-15
A plough, po sip, 58-15
A plough share, sta pooi, 58-16
To pluck, k'hir, 94-8
Do. pick, star, 98-16
A plum, mai sir, 63-6
Plum color, ts'him hang saik, 66-10

2

A plum blossom, mai hwa, 85-7
A plum (sour), ot, 63-3, 107-15
To plume the feathers, swoi oo, 78-2
To plunder, no lyak, 39-6
Do. kop hor, 39-12
To plunge, tsam kir, 108-2
Pock marked, myon ma, 19-13
Poem, koor wor, 110-2
To point, ka rat ts'hir, 30-3, 122-1
The 8 points, p'har pang, 11-16
Pointed, spo tsyok, 88-2
Poisonous snake, tok sya, 82-6
A pole (for a boat), sa hwat tai, 74-6
Politeness, ley to, 22-6, 112-2
Pomatum, lap yoo, 44-10
A pomegranate, syok lyoo, 62-15
A pomfret (fish), pyong o, 81-6
A pool, mot tsi, 9-10, 116-15
Poor, ka nan har, 56-12
Do. destitute, koong har, 95-9
Populace, paik syong, 14-13
Porcelain, tsir kop, 70-11
Do. tir kos, 108-8
A porcupine, ko som tot, 79-13
A porpoise, yoo o, 81-2
Do. river, ha ton, 81-6
Porridge, kook, 46-15
A portable inkstone, kwai yon, 68-9
A portable stone, sin syon lo, 70-9
Potion, nan hor, 112-11
A portmanteau, p'hi long, 68-6
A position, mo, 11-14
To possess, i sir, 90-2
Possessions, tsai san, 56-9
Possible, or har, 28-8
A post (pillar), ma ra, 32-4
Do. a prop, mar stok, 71-16
A post (a courier), ok, 34-7
Pot, pa ri, 70-1
Do. earthen, sa par, 70-1
Potatoes, ma, 61-12
A potter, tir kos, 108-8
A pound (Chin.), koon, 55-4
To pound (in a mortar), ssi hoor, 59-10
To pour out wine, tsyak tsyoo, 42-11
Powder, hwa yak, 41-3
Power, hyong sey, 93-13
Powerful, noong har, 22-18
Practice, hai sir, 22-7
To practice, haing har, 95-16
To praise, ki rir, 25-13, 110-2, 116-8
Do. one's self, tsa ts'hing, 26-10
To praise and blame, p'ho p'hyom, 36-9
A prawn, sai o, 82-2
Prayer, pir, 53-4
To preach, kang har, 57-11
To prate, mar sam, 109-13
Preceptor, soo soong, 14-10
Precincts of a palace, tsip kwor, 31-10
Precious, po pai, 107-15, 110-11
Precious things, po pai, 63-15
A precious sword, po kom, 40-5
A precious stone, koo soor, 110-11
Precipitate, hwang hwang, 105-14
A precipitous hill, pa hoi, 7-13, 117-2
Precise, tsa sey, 23-6
To prefer (exalt), tsyon ko, 36-9
To be pregnant, pair, 41-14
To premeditate, ey t'hak, 104-2
Premier, tsai syang, 35-9
Preparation, kwi ri, 96-9
To prepare, tsyang man har, 42-9
To be present, i sir, 109-1
Present (now), tsook koom, 99-8
To present, po noir, 43-1
To present up, pat toor, 89-8
Do. tyong har, 96-16
A present at parting, tsyon song, 42-16
To preserve, i sir, 111-15

To press down, noo roor, 97-16
To press upon one, kas syool moor, 113-6
Pressing, tsa tsoor, 86-11
To press on, poi ar, 121-13
Do. tsyor pak, 102-13
To presume on, mi tar, 109-14
To pretend, ka t'hak, 26-9
Pretty, ko or, 19-6, 121-12
Previously, hyang tsya, 99-6
A price, kap, 55-13
To prick, tsi roor, 54-8
Pride, kyo man, 91-4
A priest of Buddha, tsyoong, 53-5
A priest of the sect Taou, to sa, 14-11
A priest's cap, soong mo, 53-6
Priest's garments, saing p'ho, 66-4
Prime minister, soong syang, 35-9
A prince, nim koom, 110-13
A prince of the Empire, tsey hoo, 35-5
A princess, kong tsyoo, 35-7
Do's husband, poo ma, 35-7
A principal, pa ror, 96-2
Principal [chief], nim koon, 116-12
Principal wife, tyok sir, 13-7, 120-9
A principle, to sa rir, 117-14

A print, in, 37 5
A prior, syang lo, 53-4
A prison, ok, 53-16
Private, sa sa, 88-15
A private seal, to syo, 37-6
A privy, tooi skar, 32-2
To probe, kyong key, 112-12
To proceed, na or, 29-6
To proclaim, ko har, 25-5
Do. pai p'hoor, 116-7
To procrastinate, ts'hyon yon, 101-5
To procure, si ro kom, 27-7
To produce, nar, 41-16, 107-11
Production, yor moi, 62-8
Profession, calling, op, 94-1
Profit, li har, 56-1, 121-9
Profitable, yoo ik, 102-2
Profligate, pang tsa, 24 11
Profound, kip hor, 10-8
To prohibit, mar, 98-1
Prolapsus ani, tai ha, 50-11
To promise, ho har, 92-3
To promote to office, pong har, 114-13
Proof, ping ko, 98-8
To prop, koi or, 30-12
A prop, mar stok, 71-16
Proper, mat tang, 27-13
Propriety, ley to, 22-6, 112-2
A prospect, pyot, 97-4
Prosperous, hoong mi, 21-9
A prostitute, nyo ki, 15-11
Prostrate, tsyot pa tsir, 29-9, 112-16

To protect, koo ho, 89-9
To protract, ts'hyon yon, 101-5
To be proud, tsya rang, 29-7
Do. kyo mar, 19-4
To prove (try), si hom, 91-11
To provide, ka ts'har, 96-16, 119-9
A proverb, on moon, 38-5
A province, ko ar, 116-9
Provisions, lyang sik, 60-2, 119-14
Provisionally, kwon to, 103-13
To provoke, i koor, 97-14
A prow (ship's head), syon too, 74-3
Prudent, syo sim, 23-2
To pry, yot por, 29-16
A psaltery, tsaing, 43-6
Public, koo ooi, 88-15, 115-9
Public (to make), syok kong, 54-4
Publicly, kong yon, 101-1
To publish, sar or, 25-4
To pull, tar ooir, 30-11
Do. haul, skoor oor, 75-10
To pull out, spa hir, 32-13
The pulse, maik, 18-15
Pulse (beans), tai too, 60-9
Pulse, jelly, too poo, 47-8
Pumelo, yoo tsa, 62-12
Punctual, koot, 110-6
To puncture, ts'him, 52-2
To punish, tsoi tsoor, 53 13

Do. pai hir, 108-9, po hir, 121-3

Punishment, hyong por, 53-10, 116-4

A pupil, syon pai, 14-6

Pungent, mai or, 48-12

A puppet, kwang tai, 15-8

To purchase, sar, 55-12

Pure (clear), mar koor, 10-7, 121-11

Do. (upright), ts'hong lyom, 12-11

Purity, tsyong lyom, 112-15

A purging, syor sya, 50-5

Purple, tsa tsi, 66-15

Do. sam ts'hyong, 67-11

A purpose, tsa par, 113-5

Pursa pastori, nang i, 61-7

To pursue, sta rar, 93-11

Pus, nong tsoop, 51-7

To push, mir, 30-10, 108-7

To push a boat, t'hang tsyoo, 74-15

To put, place, toor, 91-16

To put off, po soor, 46-10

Do. ts'hyoo i, 56-9

To put on, nip oor, 46-11

To put out, poor sko tsir, 49-15

To put in order, ta sa rir, 53-11, 117-3

Do. po rir, 98-9

Putrid, poo ts'hyoo:, 49-1

Q

A quadrant, koo soon, 121-15

A quadruped, tsoong sing, 78-8

A quail, mot ts'ha ra ki, 77-13

To quarrel, ta t'hor, 26-3

To incite to quarrel, ts'hyo kir, 26-2

Quarter of the moon, first, syang hyon, 4-1

Do. last, ha hyon, 4-1

Quarter of the heavens, (the four), sa pang, 11-15

A quarter, place, mo, 109-4

A quay, na ra, 9-15

Queen's metal, ham syok, 64-12

Queer, koi i har, 91-10

To qnench, poor sko tsir, 49-14

To question, moo roor, 25-1

Quick, spa rar, 90-13

Do. k'hwai k'hwai, 106-8

Quicksilver, syoo oon, 64-1

Quiet, p'hyong an, 89-16, 122-2

To be quiet, ko yo, 29-14

A quilt, ni poor, 46-6

Quinsy, hoo pi, 50-10

To quit, leave, li pyor, 100-9

Quite, oom tsyon, 87-16

R

A rabbit, t'hot ki, 79-13

Radish (turnip), lo pok, 61-1

A raft, ste, 74-2

Do. of wood, toong kor, 65-1

A rafter, syo, 32-6

Rage, no har, 23-7

A railing, lan kan, 32-14

Rain, pi oo, 2-5, 107-9

Do. sudden. koop oo, 2-5

Do. drizzling, sey oo, 2-6

Do. constant, lim oo, 2-7

Rainbow, moo tsi ke, 2-9

Rain water, pis moor, 10-1

A rain mantle, oo tsang, 45-12

Do. hat, sa lip, 45-13

Do. dress, sa ooi, 45-14

Rainy, p'hai yon, 109-14

To raise, toon, 120-6

To raise troops, kooi pyong, 38-15

A rake (iron), t'hyor p'ha, 72-10

To ramble, nor, 42-14

Do. no nir, 119-3

Rank (dignity), ts'ha rey, 36-6; pyo sar, 113-3

Rank, rancid, no rir, 48-16

Rape (turnip), swir moo oo, 61-1

A rapid, yo hoor, 9-9

Rapidly, hoor hoor, 105-2

Rare, kwi t'hook, 101-3

A rash, o roo or ki, 51-4

Rashly, a tsya, 99-6

A rat, tsooi, 79-12

Rather (better), ts'har a ri, 27-6

Rather much, tsa mot, 26-16

A raven, ka ma koi, 77-12

A ravine, koor hong, 7-16

Raw, nar kop, 48-7

Do. unacquainted, sing so, 104-9

A raw smell, pi rir, 48-15

Raw silk, sir hyor, 66-7

12

To reach to, mi ts'hoor, 93-11, 109-4
To reach forth, hyor, 122-8
To read, nir koor, 37-12, 119-5
Ready, in p'hyon, 97-1
Real, hwak sir, 24-1
Really, tsyong syong, 111-9
To reap, pooir, 59-6
A reap hook, nat, 59-6
Reason, to sa rir, 117-13
A reason, yon ko, 103-3
To rebel, pan har, 39-16
A rebel, pai pan, 121-4
Rebuke, skoo tsi tsoor, 26-4
A receipt, tan tsa, 37-1, 114-3
To receive, too rir, 59-14
Do. pa toor, 92-4, 112-5, 112-6
Do. (to connect), poo ts'hir, 96-12
Do. poo roor, 120-5
To receive an order, tang po, 23-9
Do. a gift, ni oor, 92-5, 114-6
To receive with reverence, pat toor, 112-6
Recent, sai, 90-10
To recite, oi or, 37-10
To reckon, heym, 54-12
To recline, wi tsi har, 97-5
To recollect, kwi lok, 37-3
To recommend and exalt, ts'hyon ko, 36-9
To recompense, kap hoor, 96-8

To be reconciled, hwa ts'hin, 40-2
Recondite, oon oon, 105-3
A record, kooi lok, 37-3
Do. pip, 114-7
A recorder, lok sa, 36-3
To recover, koo won, 39-9
To rectify, ko ir, 115 9
Red, poor koor, 67-5, 116-8, 116-13, 119-4
A red horse, tsyok ma, 78-12
To reduce, koos spoor, 108-14
Reeds (young), to tok, 61-13
Reflection, pi ts'hoir, 6-10, 111-6
Reform, to ir, 109-3
To refrain, ts'ham oor, 21-14
A region, mo, 109-4
A register, koor wor, 111-12
Regretting, oor oor, 105-6
To regulate, tyo li, 52-4
To reject, pa rir, 91-15
Do. o tir, 115-13
To reject from favour, sya ley, 118-12
A rein, tsyoo ri oor, 93-9
To rejoice, kis skoor, 118-11
Reiterated, loo loo, 105-1
Relation of life, moon, 121-7
A relation by blood, ts'hin har, 13-10, 119-13
Do. by marriage, kyo rai ts'hyok, 13-4
Do. a am, 119-13

A relative (near), o poi, 12-4
To release, no hoor, 54-6
To relieve, p'hi tir, 115-10
To relinquish, yo hwir, 112-14
To relish, tsoor kir, 49-8
To rely on, wi tsi har, 97-5
To remain, mo moor, 39-14
Remedy (vital), myong yak, 52-1
Remiss, too moor, 88-11
To remit, sya har, 54-6
Do. mor, 117-1, 121-5
Remote, mak hir, 88-12
Do. yoo yoo, 105-9
Do. hyong yon, 100-13
To remove, om kir, 92-16 113-4, 119-3
To remunerate, syang ts'hoor, 95-7
To rend, stswir, 93-5
To render, poo rar, 93-10 109-15
Rent, kong sey, 61-1
Do. nak, 117-7
To repair, syoo li, 33-11
Do. (make up), ki or, 88-9
Do. a vessel, syoo tsoop, 75-4
A repast, pap, 46-13
To repay, ka p'hoor, 56-7
To repeat, kyom, 92-12
Repeatedly, ni kir, 110-8
Repeated, tsyoong tsyoong, 104.16
To repent, nooi oot ts'hoor, 21-14

23

A rippling sound, p'hoong p'hoong, 106-7
To rise /(as the tide), no moor, 10-6
To rise up, nir, 28-16, 111-2, 118-5
Rite, ley to, 22-6
A river, ha syoo, 9-4
Do. ka ram, 108-1
Do. large, moor kang, 9-3
A rivulet, si nai key, 9-14, 115-5
A road, kin, 8-3, 114-12, 116-1
Do. crooked, man lo, 8-4
Do. slanting, sya lo, 8-4
To roam, nor, 42-14
To roar, oor, 80-4
To roast, koo oor, 48-4
Do. (burn), sar oor, 49-13
To rob, to tsok tsir har, 53-13
A robber, kang to, 15-16
A robe, tsyang sam, 53-7
Do. to tsok, 39-3, 121-3
Robust, kon tsang, 23-13
A rock, pa hoi, 7-12
Do. tor, 116-15
A rocky precipice, syok pyok, 7-13
A rock pearl, tsin tsyoo, 64-2
A rock swallow, ho yon, 77-9
A rock sucker, saing pok, 81-15
Do. dried, tsyon pok, 81-16
A rod, mak tai, 54-1
Rogue, syo in, 14-9
A roll (volume), kwon, 38-7
To roll up, ko toor, 30-15
The roll of a carriage, lin lin, 105-13
A roof, ki soo ri, 32-7
A room, koo toor, 31-13
To roost, kit too rir, 78-5
A root, poor hooi, 84-13, 119-1
A rope, no, 71-14
A rose, tsang mi, 85-9
Rotten, sok koor, 48-16
Rotten wood, so koor, 85-1
To rove, no nir, 119-3
Rouge, yon tsi, 44-10
Rough speaking, o sap, 26-10
To round off, pop sik, 112-12
Round, toong koor, 88-2
Do. moo lyot, 120-1
A round collar, tan lyong, 45-5
To rouse, ptor, 30 14
To row, tar ooir, 30-11
A row, tsoor, 98-9
To rub (in the hand), pya pooir, 30-9
A rudder, ts'hi, 74-4
A rug, tam, 69-1
A rugged hill, ko kai, 7-13
To ruin, ha ya tsir, 92-13, 116-4
Ruiued, lang tsya, 99-15
Do. lang p'hai, 101-16
A rule, pop, 53-10
Do. ko tong, 112-6
To rule, ta sa rir, 53-11
Rump, por ki, 17-16
To run, tar oor, 29-2, 121-2
To run away, poon tsoo, 100-4
A runner, po haing, 15-6
Do. special, pyor ts'hai, 35-16
Running hand, ts'ho syo, 38-1
Do. tip, 114-9
A rush, ta pok ssook, 87-2
A rusty colour, saing koo, 67-16
Rye, ts'hyok ts'hyok, 60-12

S

A sabre, hwan to, 40-5
A sack, tsoo mo mi, 71-8
Do. ta mas, 119-6
A sackbut, saing hwang, 43-7
A sacred place, t'ho tas koor, 116.12
A sacrifice, tsey sa, 52-13, 120-10
A sacrificial temple, sa tang, 52-12
A sacrificial vessel, to ma, 70-16
Sad, syo syo, 104-15
A saddle, ki roo ma, 73-4
Covering for do. an kap, 73-5
Saddle ornaments, ta rai, 73-6
Saddle cloth, on ts'hi, 73-9
Saddle band, ki roo ma tsi oor, 73-11

2

A safe, ts'hyon an tsyoo, 68-8
Do. secure, p'hon har, 115-14
Saffron (bastard), hong hwa, 85-13
A sage, syong in, 14-3, 110-4
A sail, tot, 74-5
To hoist sail, kwi pong, 74-13
To take in do. sya pong, 74-13
A sailor, sa kong, 74-10
Saint, syong in, 14-3
Salad, poo roo, 61-8
Saliva, ts'hoom, 20-9
A salmon, lyon o, 80-13
Salmon trout, syong o, 81-5
Salt, so kom, 47-11
Saltish, stsar, 48-13
Do. pts'har, 108-1
Saltpetre, yom ts'hyo, 65-3
To salute, ts'hyang har, 25-3
The same, han ka tsi, 90-5
Do. ir yang, 102-3
Sand, more, 8-9, 116-7
Do. fine, sey sa, 8-9
Sandal wood, pak tan, 84-7
Sarcenet, o roo noo koor, 65-11
A sash, tooi, 45-13, stooi, 122-5
Satin, pi tan, 65-8
To be satisfied, soor har, 119-12
Satisfied, pai poo roor, 49-8
To save, koo won, 39-9
To saunter, po toor, 97-15
Sauntering, no nir, 118-10, 119-2
Savoury food, an tsyoo, 47-3
A saw, lop, 72-4
To say, ni rar, 28-5, 116-12, 115-12, 122-9
A scab, te te, 51-8
A scabbard, kom p'hoor, 40-8
A scaffold, ka ka, 32-1
To scald, skoor oor, 48-5, 108-10
A scale, pi nor, 81-10, 108-2
Scales (steelyard), tso ar, 69-9
Scallions, poo ts'hai, 61-4
To scape, myon har, 97-7
Scarce, hwi han, 102-4
Scarcely, kyo yo, 98-7
Scarlet, tsin hong, 66-11
Scarred, ho moor, 19-13
To scatter, hoot roor, 92-16, 118-10
Scent, kot ta or, 86-8
To scheme, to mo, 101-12
Scheming, skoi, 22-15
A scholar, syon pai, 14-6, 115-14
Scissors, tsyon tsa, 72-14
A scoop, p'ha rai, 74-9
To scoop out, p'hair, 94-7
To scour with sand, sa t'hai, 104-1
To scourge, t'hai tsyang, 54-1
To scratch, koor koor, 30-5
To screen, ka ri oor, 93-2
Do. ka rir, 119-1
A screen, tsyang tsa, 32-14
Do. for the light, ts'hya yang, 33-2
Do. for the face, ts'hya myon, 33-2
Do. for the wind, pyong p'hoong, 68-14
Do. for the sun, ts'hya ir, 69-3
A scribe, sya li, 36-4
To scrub, sa t'hai, 104-1
To scruple, wi sim, 91-3
To scrutinize, tsyo tsoor, 54-2
To scuffle, ssa hor, 39-5
A scull (oar), no, 74-6
Scurf, po tsoom, 51-3
Scurfy, stai, 19-14
Do. ptai, 120-15
The sea, pa ta, 7-3, 108-1
A sea blubber, kyom o, 81-7
A sea snail, kan ko o, 81-9
A seal (a stamp), in, 37-5
Do. private, to syo, 37-6
The seal character, tsyon tsa, 37-15
A seam, hor, 46-2
Sea moss, hai ooi, 62-5
A sea spider, p'har ts'hyo o, 80-14
Do. small, syo p'har ts'hyo, 81-10
To search to the bottom, ts'hyoo swai, 54-3
Seasons, the four, see 2-16
Seasonable, ma ts'hi, 97-12
A seat (chair), kyo wi, 68-13

Seaweed, syok hwa, 82-2
Second wife, hoo sir, 12-10
A second (in office), po koom, 96-2
Secret, pwik pwik, 88-4, 115-13
A secretary, sya li, 36-4
To secure, po toor, 56-5
A security (bond), myang moon, 56-4
A sedan chair, kyo tsa, 76-6
Sedate, ts'ham toir, 122-5
A sedge, yo hang, 86-15
Sediment, tsoo ooi, 47-5
To seduce, tar nair, 26-4
Sedulous, oon koon, 100-3
To see, por, 30-1, 113-12
Do. poor, 118-5
A seed, ssi, 59-1
Seedtime, paik tsyong, 4-9
To seek, no, 118-7
Seemingly, wi hwi, 99-11
To seeth, tsi tsir, 48-4
To seize, tsa pa too rir, 53-14
To select, kar hir, 93-9
Self, soo soo ro, 27-2, 113-6
Do. mom, 109-14, 118-1
Self-willed, p'hyak har, 24-12
To sell, p'har, 55-12
To send, po nair, 118-11
To send on a message, ts'hai song, 93-9
To send up a statement, pong ts'hyo, 54-2
A senior, mat, 117-9
To separate, tsi li, 101-5
Separated, mak hir, 88-12
Do. to a distance, li pyor, 100-9
A separate document, pyor pok, 36-12
Separated (divided), poon kan, 102-9
Separation, li i, 42-2
A sepulchre, moo tom, 52-11
Sequel, ma ts'ham, 90-11
Serene, ko yo, 29-14
A series, kwa ki, 94-2
Do. ts'ha rey, 98-10
Do. rank, too room, 95-1
Serious, pi kyong, 103-7
A serpent, pai yam, 82-6
A servant, tsyong pok, 15-12
Do. female, tsyong pi, 15-13
Do. hired, ko kong, 15-13
To serve, syom kir, 89-8, 110-13
To serve in an office, pyo sar sa, 36-5
To serve up (a dinner), tam oor, 48-8
Service, yok sa, 94-1
Sesame, tsin im, 60-13
To set, pe p'hoor, 97-15, 114-1
To set in order, tsyong tsey, 38-16
To set a price, kang ka, 55-15
To set up, toor, 91-16
To set against, ta ta roor, 96-10
To settle to clearness, mar kar, 111-6
Settled, tyong tang, 102-16
Do. ir tyong, 111-8
Seven, nir kop, 54-16
The seven stars, ts'hir syong, 1-8
To sever, tsi li, 101-5
Several, ko wi, 27-8
Severe, rigid, om syook, 103-15
Severe, cold, ts'har han, 6-9
Do. ts'ham toir, 122-5
Severity (strictness), om har, 39-1
To sew, hor, 46-2
Shade, koo roor, 6-3
Do. koo noor, 110-12
A shade, tsok tsa, 68-14
Do. of the sun, ir yong, 6-9
A shadow, ko rim tsa, 20-2
The shaft of an arrow, ko to ri, 40-13
A shaggy dog, to p'hor ke, 79-15
To shake, hoor toor, 30-10
Do. (rouse), ptor, 30-14, 114-15
Shall, tsyang ts'hat, 26-16
Shallow, yot t'hoor, 10-8
Shame, poos koo rir, 118-3, 21-15
Shape, or koor, 19-3
A share, nan hor, 112-11
A shark, sa o, 80-12
Sharp, li har, 56-1
Sharp-pointed, spo tsyok, 88-2

2

Soft, poo too ro or, 23-4
Do. pliable, yon har, 92-9
Soft cloth, yoon p'ho, 66-1
Soil (earth), hark, 8-8
To solace, wi ro, 89-9
A soldier, koon sa, 38-14
Do. pyong ma, 114-14
To raise soldiers, kooi pyong, 38-15
The sole of the foot, tsyok tsyang, 18-5
Solitary, (alone), oi ro ar, 122-7, 15-15
Solitary, lyo lyo, 1905-
Solitude, koi o, 118-9
Sombre, am am, 106-9
Do. a tak har, 117-2
Some, hok, 27-8
Son, a toor, 12-16, 112-9
Son-in-law, sa hoi, 13-2
Son's wife, myo na ri, 13-1
A song, no rai, 42-13, 120-5
Soon (early), ir oor, 5-7
A sorcerer, moo tang, 15-10
A sore, om, 51-2
Sorrel, san tsyang, 62-1
Sorrow, min mang, 21-2
Do. soor p'hoor, 23-8
To sort, kom ts'har, 98-12
A sort, kar or, 122-8
A sovereign, nim koom, 35-5, 108-4, 110-13
Do. great, tai koon, 35-6
The soul, hon paik, 52-7
A sound, so rai oom, 20-10, 110-7, 117-13
To sound, oor i ir, 20-16
Sour, sooir, 48-12

Source, koon won, 9-7
The south, nam nyok, 11-6
Do. arp, 117-5
The south wind, nam p'hoong, 1-12
The south east do. tong nam p'hoong, 1-13
The south west do. sya nam p'hoong, 1-13
To sow, ssi, 59-1
Sowing, kok sik si moot, 117-4
A space (open), t'ho, 34-15
A spade, kwang i, 72-9
Sparing, at kir, 23-11
A sparrow, ts'ham sai, 77-14
A sparrow hawk, sai mai, 77-1
To speak, kar, 28-5
Do. ni nar, 116-12, 122-9
To speak of, ir k'ha roor, 96-3
To speak roughly, o sap, 26-19
Do. disorderly, mang par, 26-11
A spear, ts'hang, 40-16
Special, kwi t'hook, 101-3,
A speck on the eye, no yook, 51-10
Spectacles, an kyong, 69-9
Speedy, spa rar, 90-13
To spend, ho pi, 96-6
To spew out, spoon oor, 49-6
A spider, ko mooi, 83-2
To spin, tsir sam, 66-9, 119-15
A spindle tree, too ts'hyoong, 84-2

The spine, toong ma ra, 17-14
A spinning wheel, pang ko, 66-6
A spinster, ts'hyo nyo, 41-12
A spiral shellfish, syo ra, 81-13
A spirit (soul), hon paik, 52-7
Spirit (breath), kooi oom, 20-4, 112-10
Spirits, (animal), tsyong sin, 20-6
Do. sin lyong, 113-2
Do. hyong har, 113-14
To spit, ts'hoom pat t'hoor, 20-10
Spittle, ts'hoom, 20-9
Splendid, nam nyok, 113-15
To split, koo ts'hoor, 112-12
To spoil (plunder), no lyak, 39-6
A spoon, soor, 70-3
To sport, koo kyong, 91-11, 119-5
Do. or koor, 94-11
Do. hoi long, 103-9
A spot, ki mooi, 51-4
A spotted horse, ts'hyoo ma, 78-13
A spouse, wife, an hai, 12-10
To spread out, pe p'hoor, 69-5, 107-4, 114-1
Spread abroad, too ro, 97-8
Do. moo koor, 119-1
Spread out, yang yang, 105-7
A spring of water, koon won, 9-7
Spring season, pom, 2-16

Spring festival, lip ts'hyoon, 4-5
A spring, in machinery, t'hoor 66-8, 118-5
To sprinkle, spoo rir, 10-13
To spurt out, spoom oor, 46-6
To spy, por, 30-1
A spy glass, ts'hyon li kyong, 69-8
A square, mo nar, 122-3
To squat, koro an tsoo, 31-2
To squeeze under the arms, skir, 94-9
To squint, hoor kooir, 29-16
A squinting eye, sya an, 51-11
A squire, lyang pan, 14-12
A squirrel, ton p'hi, 79-8
Do. flying, ta ram i, 79-11
To stab, tsi roor 54-8
Stable (firm), koo toor, 92-10
A stable, oi yang, 32-1
A staff, mak tai, 54-1
A stag, sa sam, 79-4
A stage, ka ka, 32-1
Stairs, som, 33-8, 114-3
A stalk, skok tsi, 63-13
A stalk, tsoor ki, 87-6
A stall, tsang, 68-5
To stammer, mar koo toor, ts'ham, 26-8
A stamp, in, 37-5
A stanchion, tai kong, 32-4
To stand, syor, 29 1, 110-5
A stand (frame), si rong, 33-4
A stand (a stopping place), 34-7

To stand on tip toe, tsyo ki too tooir, 96-11
A standard, took, 41 5
A staple, tsir tyong, 72-8
Star, pyor, 1-6, 107-4, 114-4
Starving, soor hoor ey, 49-9
State, tsoo oom, 95-5
A statement (to send up), pong ts'hyo, 54-2
A station, pyo sar ooi, 36-6
Do. pyo soor, 108-7
To stay, poo t'hor, 119-6
Steady heat, ts'hyo syo, 4-8
To steal, to tsok tsir har, 53-13
To steam, pap tsi oor, 49-13
Steelyards, tso ar, 69-9
A steep place, kooi koo, 8-15
To steep (in water), tsam kir, 10-11
A stem (prow), syon too, 74-5
To step, ko room, 122-3, 29-1
Do. over, nom oor, 31-5
Steps, sa ta ri, 33-6
Do. ta ri, 114-3
A stern, syon ts'hyo, 74-4
Stern (rigid), loom loom, 106-10
Do. swik swik har, 19-5, 110-14
To stew, stir, 48-3
Do. ptir, 120-10
To stick (stab), tsi roor, 54-8
To stick the head on a pole, hyo si, 54-10

Stiff, koot ser, 23-5
Do. (as wood), mok king, 24-1
Do. (firm), koo toor, 92-10
To be still, ko yo, 29-14, 113-1
Still yet, to ook, 27-2
Do. o hi ryo, 27-5
Do. (silent), tsyok mak, 103-11
Do. tsyok tsyok, 105-8
Stillness, koi o, 118-8
To stink, mat t'hoor, 49-2
Stinking, nai, 48-14
A stinking insect, ts'hyooi ts'hyoong, 82-3
To stir, oom tsook ir, 29-3
Stirrup, toong tsa, 73-6
To stitch, hor, 46-2
A stock of a tree, mat 84-13
Stock fish, tai koo o, 80-15
Stockings, po syon, 46-8
The stomach, yang, 18-13
Coats of do. man ha, 18-10
A stone, tor syok, 8-6, 115-5, 116-15
Do. fairy, koi syok, 8-7
Do. of a brook, tsyak pyor, 8-8
A stone tablet, pis, 115-4
A stone bream, ka key o, 80-16
A stone fish, syok o, 81-8
A stone wall, psar, 33-10
A stone bridge, tor tari, 34-4
A stone pestle, pang ha, 59-9 2

A stone fungus, syok i, 61-11
To stop, koo ts'hir, 96-12, 111-7
Do. (cease), tyong tsi, 104-3
To stop up, ma koor, 116-13
A stoppage in the throat, in saik, 49-7
To store up, kam ts'hoor, 59-16
A storehouse, kos tsip ko, 34-14
A stork, hwa, 76-9
A storm, tsan p'hoong, 2-2
A stone (portable), sin syon lo, 70-9
Stout, kon tsang, 23-13
To straddle, t'har, 80-7
Straight, ko toor, 90-4
Straight forward, ko tan, 117-10
To straighten, p'hyor, 29-13
To straiten (distress), p'hip pak, 39-8
Straits (distress), tsai aik, 93-14
A strainer, tsyo rai, 71-2
A strand, moor ka pin, 9-12
Strange, koi i har, 91-10
A stranger, na koo mi, 96-5
To strangle, kyo har, 54-9
Stratagem, to mo, 101-12
Straw, tip, 59-7
Straw shoes, ts'ho hey, 46-9
A straw basket, sam rai, 71-15
A strawberry, sta ar ki, 63-8
7 To stray, no nir, 119-3

A stream, nai, 9-6, 111-5
Do. (in a valley), si nai kan, 9-14
A streamlet, moor ka rai, 9-13
Against the stream, yok syoo, 10-4
With the stream, syoon lyoo, 10-4
A street, kori, 8-3
Strength, him, 20-4
Do. sim, 110-15
To stretch out, p'hyor, 29-13
Do. toor, 120-7
To strew, hoot roor, 92 16
To strike, too ta rir, 30-8
Do. the harp, t'har, 43-7
Strictness, om har, 39-1
Do. swik swik, 110-14, 19-5
To strip, po soor, 46-10
To strip off, koo rar, 118-8
A string, no, 71 12, 118-7
A stringed instrument, si oor, 120-6
To strive, ta t'hor, 26-3
A stroke (in writing), koo oor, 37-16
To stroll, nor, 42-14
Do. no nir, 119-3
Strong (firm), swik swik har, 19-5
Do. (violent), kang har, 22-14
To struggle, ta t'hor, 26-4
Stubborn, ko tsip, 23-16
To study, ni kir, 37-11, 110-8
To stumble, ko ts'hir, 31-3

Do. (slip), ts'ha t'ha, 101-4
Stupid, o rir, 24-7, 122-8
A sturgeon, min o, 80-16
To subdue, i kwir, 110-4
A subject, sin ha, 108-14
To submit, hang pok, 39-13
Subsequently tooi, 11-8
Substance, (body), mom, 16-2, 108-15
Subtile (fine), tsyong har, 98-5, 116-6
To subvert, ki oor, 115-10
Suburbs, pat syong, 33-16
To succeed (prosper), hoong mi, 21-9
To succeed to, ni oor, 92-5, 120-9
To succour, to or, 96-4
Such like, nom, 122-9
To suck, spar, 49-3
A sudden wind, koop p'hoong, 2-1
A sudden rain, koop oo, 2-5
Suddenly, moon took, 28-10
Do. (rashly), a tsya, 99-6
Do. (accidentally), oo yon, 100-16
To suffer, tang har, 98-3
Sufficient, tsyok har, 98-6
Sugar (brown), sa tang, 47-15
Do. white, syor tang, 47-16
Sugar candy, ping tang, 47-16
To suit, ma ts'har, 119-10
Suitable, mat tang, 27-13
Do. corresponding, wi yon, 100-15
Sulphur, lyoo hwang, 65-3

Sultry, koo yor, 6-7
Sum, heym, 64-12
Sumach, syoo yoo, 85-16
Summer, nyo room, 2-16, 113-7
Summit, tyong pa ki, 16-3
The sun, nar, 1-3, 107-2
Sunk, kor mor, 100-4
Sunshine, pyot, 6-3
A sun flower, kyoo hwa, 85-8
Superabundant, nam oor, 88-6
Superfluity, na mar, 107-7
A superior, tsyang tsya, 14-8
Do. oos, 112-3
The superior principle of nature, pyot, 107-8
Supper, syok pan, 46-14
Supple, poo too ra or, 23-4
To supplicate, koo har, 92-3
To supply, i pa tsi, 42-9
A support, him ni poor, 109-4
To support, koi or, 30-12
To suppose, pe p'hoor, 97-15
Do. wi sim, 114-4
To suppress, noo roor, 97-16
Sure, tyok tang, 102-16
Surety, tsi tang, 103-1
Surface, nat, 19-3
To surfeit, soor wir, 119-11
To surmount, i kwir, 76-4
Surname, syong, 13-14
A surplice, noo to ki, 46-3
Surplus, na mar, 107-7
To surprise, om soop har, 39-8
Surprising, koi i har, 91-10
To surrender, hang pok, 39-13
To surround, e oor, 39-7
To suspect, wi sim, 91-3
To suspend, kor, 94-10
Suspended, tar, 88-12, 121-16
Suspicious, wi sim, 91-3
To sustain, tang har, 98-3
To sustain an office, mat toor, 36-7, 121-8
Swaddling cloth, kang po, 42-2
A swallow, tsyo pi, 77-9
Do. rock, ho yon, 77-9
To swallow, sam k'hir, 49-2
A swan, ko he, 76-13
A swarm, moor, 98-5
Sweat, stam, 20-8
To sweep, ssoor, 30-15
Do. too ir, 98-15
Sweet, tar, 48-11, 111-15
Sweet pickle, kam tsyang, 47-10
Sweet moss, kam t'hai, 62-5,
Sweet meats, mir kwa, 47-14
To swell, poo oor, 50-14
To swerve, ki oor, 97-5, 115-10
To swim, he oom, 75-3
Swift, koop har, 90-16
A swing, ts'hyoo ts'hyon, 76-4
A sword, hwan to, 40-5
Do. kar, 107-13
Do. precious, po kom, 40-5
Do. sharp, li to, 40-6
Sycamore tree, sin na mo, 84-8
Do. red, tan p'hoong, 84-12
Syrian mallows, koou hwa, 85-15

T

A table, t t'hak tsa, 33-4
Do. ts'ha ik sang, 68-13
Table lan d, on tok, 7-15
To tack s hip, tsi pong, 74-12
A tadpol e, kwa too, 83-7
Taffeta, tip, 65-14
A tail, sh o ri, 80-2
To take, ts'hyooi har, 91-15
Do. a ar, 111-6
To take (catch), tsa pa too ri, 53-1 14; tsi poor, 121-4
To take le ave, ha tsik, 42-16
To take u p, tey kooi, 25-9
Do. priso ner, sa ro tsap oor, 39-12
Do. (as a loan), sey nair, 56-7
Do. in sai l, sya pong, 74-13
Do. hold of, tsap oor, 94-14
Do. char ge of, tsa poor, 111-14
Talent, t ai tso, 22-13, 109-10
A talented man, kos spoo ri, 86-5, 11 4-8
To talk, ke ng har, 37-11
Talk (leis ure), han tam, 25-15
Tall, no p'h oor, 114-15
A talon, my narit'hop, 78-1
A taper, ts' yo, 71-3
Tardy, nak oor, 90-16

A target, kwan hyok, 40-14
Taro (a vegetable), t'ho ran, 61.15
To tarry, ki ta rir, 94-16
Tartars, (wild), orang kai, 58-10
Tartary, tar tsa, 58-9
To tattoo, tsa tsai, 54-8
A tassel, skin, 46-3
Do. kin, 114-16
To taste, mat por, 48-9, 120-10
A taste, mat, 48-10
Tasteless, soong ko oor, 48-13
A tax, kong sey, 60-1
Tea, ts'ha, 42-10
Tea color, ta saik, 66-16
To teach, ka ra ts'hir kyo, 37-9
A teacher, soo soong, 14-10, 108-3, 112-5
To tell, sar or, 25-4
To tear, stsooir, 93-5
Tears, noon moor, 20-8
The teeth, ni, 16-14
Do. front, moon ts'hi, 16-15
Do. dog, o ts'hi, 16-15
Do. to shed, t'hyo ts'hyoon, 16-16
A telescope, ts'hyon li kyong, 69-8
To tell, ko har, 25-5
Temper, stoot, 22-2
Tempest, p'ho p'hoong, 2-1
A temple (ancestorial), tsong myo, 122-4, 33-14
Temple, tsyor, 52-10
The temples, kwi mit, 16-6
To tempt, tar nair, 26-4
Ten, yor, 55-1
Tenderness, tsa pit, 112-13
Tendon, ham stsor, 18-8
A tendril, no ts'hoor, 87-6
A tent, tsyang mak, 69-3
Termination, skoot, 90-12
A terrace, tai, 33-8
To terrify, tso hir, 91-6
A territory, tsin tsyong, 34-6
Testimony, tsoong in, 56-5
Than, kyon tsor, 97-11
To thank, sya rey, 96-3, 118-12
That, koo, 27-1, 117-16
That month, tang wor, 3-15
That year, tang nyon, 3-3
That person, tso, 89-2
Do. na han, 100-11
That which, nom, 122-9
A thatch, stoom, 71-7
To thaw, song ai, 10-16
A theme, koor tey, 37-13
Then, sa, 108-16
Do. pop ts'hook, 110-16
Do. mar ri oor, 111-16
Then (in consequence), pa ya hoo ro, 27-9
Do. (after that), tsook tsai, 27-11, 118 4
Therefore, tsim tsoot, 27-16
Thereupon, po ya hoo ro, 27-9
They, koo, 117-16, 27-1
Thick (not thin), toot ro or, 87-13
Do. too t'ho oor, 117-9
Thick set, paik paik har, 88-4, 115-13
A thicket, tom p'hor, 65-2
Thief, to tsak, 121-3, 39-3
The thigh, soo in ta ri, 18-2
A thimble for sewing, stair, 72-16
A thimble for archers, kak tsi, 41-8
Thin, yo oir, 19-10
Thin (not thick), yor oor, 87-13, 111-1
Thin, insipid, tam pok, 102-1
A thing, kot, 88-16, 113-4
To think, saing kak, 21-10
Do. sa raing, 111-7
Do. soo ts'hir, 122-15
To thirst, kar har, 49-10
This, i, 28-4, 109-5, 117-4
This day, koom ir, 4-12,
This very day, tsook ir, 4-14
This evening, koom syok, 5-10
This month, koom wor, 3-15
This year, koom nyon, 3-3
This hour, ts'ha si, 5-12
This person, tsyo han, 100-11
A thorn bush, ka sooi, 84-11
Thou, no, 89-1
Though, pi rok, 28-7
Thought, nyom har, 110-4
Do. anxious, sa nyom, 118-10
A thousand, ir ts'hyon, 55-2, 114-14
A thousand leafed flower, ts'hyon yop hwa, 86-2

Thread, sir, 66-7
To thread, skwer, 93-6
To threaten, tso hir, 91-6
Three, sok, 54-14
Thrifty, at kir, 23-11
To thrive, hoong mi, 21-5
The throat, in hoo, 16-16
Do. (stoppage in), in saik, 49-7
Do. (dryness in), hoo kan, 49-7
Throng, moor, 98-5
Through, sa ma ts'har, 98-4
To throw, to tsir, 04-10, 112-11
To throw up earth, poot to toor, 59-3
The thumb, mo tsi, 17-9
To thump, moo ta rir, 59-8
Thunder, oo loi, 2-3
Thus, yo sa, 99-5
Thus only, i i, 99-5
Thwart, pis skir, 115-16, 93-1
A tick, tsin tooi, 83-8
Ticket (soldier's), p'yong poo, 41-6
Tide, tsyo syoo, 10-3
Tidings, syo sik, 103-5
Tidy, tso hor, 19-7
To tie, p'hoor, 92-8
To tie up, kyor pak, 53-14
To tie round, ssar, 88-10
Tiger, pons, 78-10
A tile, tsi sai, 32-8
To till the ground, pat kar, 58-15
Timber, tsai mok, 84-16

A time, si tsyor, 4-4, 115-6
Do. koo noor, 110-12
Timorous, nor nar, 21-8
Tin, tsyoo syok, 64-9
Tinkling, lyong long, 100-1
Tipsy, ts'hyooi har, 42-12
Tired, kas par, 113-2
Tissue, kip, 65-7
To (up to), ni ra, 96-11
A toad, ha ma, 83-5
Do. large, syom yo, 83-6
A toadstool, po soot, 61-10
To day, koom ir, 4-12
Together with, ha or, 28-13, 116-10: ka oor, 121-10
Do. to poor, 95-13, 110-14
To toil, syoo ko ro oor, 21-16
A toilet, tan tsang har, 44-12
A token, p'hyo har, 95-10
Toll, kong sey, 60-1
A tomb, moo tom, 52-11
Tombs, feast of, han sik, 4-5
A tombstone, pi syak, 52-11
To morrow, myong ir, 4-14
Tongue, hyo, 16-13
A tool, koo root, 68-4
A tooth, ni, 16-14
A tooth-stick, soo mok, 44-9
Top (summit), tyong pa ki, 16-3
A torch, hwai, 71-14
A torrent, p'hok p'ho, 9-8
Torrid, koo yor, 6-7
Tortoise, ko pok, 81-12
Do. land, tsya ra, 81-12
Tortoise shell, tai mo, 64-6
Torture, hyong por, 53-10

To tally, tsyon yon, 100-13
Tottering, moon ho tsir, 92-13
To touch, mar tsir, 30-11
Tour, nor, 42-14
Tow, hemp, sam, 86-16
Towards, hyang har, 97-3
Towel, syoo kon, 46-5, 119-16
A tower, t'hap, 53-1
A town, ko os oop, 34-5, 113-7
A trace, tsa ts'hoi, 20-2, 116-9
To trade, hoong p'han, 55-16
A trader, syang ko, 56-10
A trading boat, syang syon, 74-1
To train a dog, po root, 80-7
Traitor, pai pan, 121-4
To trample, parp oor, 31-4, 111-1, 116-2
Tranquil, na ro yo, 97-3
Do. an tsyong, 121-7
To tranquillize, p'hyong har, 108-12
Do. p'hyon, 122-2
A transcript, pot kir, 37-4
To transform, pyon t'hong, 104-8
To transgress, pom har, 53-12
Do. tsi nar, 96-10, 109-11
Transient, tsam sen, 90-14
To transmit, kar, 92-1
To transmit a message, tsyan kar, 25-10 29

V. U.

Vegetables, na mar, 60-16, 107-16
Verbose, syom o, 26-1
Verdigrease, tong lok, 67-14
On the verge of, pa too ra or, 118-3
Verily, kwa yon, 100-14
Vermacelli, to myon, 47-7
Vermilion, tsyoo hong, 67-5
Verse, koor wer, 110-2
Very (exceeding), ka tsang, 27-5, 116-6
Do. koo moo, 112-9
Do. sim har, 96-13, 111-12
A vessel (utensil), koo root, 68-4
Do. koo roos, 109-16
A vessel (ship), pai, 73-15
A vest, ts'hi ma, 45-14
Vexed, oor oor, 105-6
Ugly, to ro oor, 19-12
Viands, an tsyoo, 47-2
Vice, mo tir, 23-12, 110-9
Vicious, mo tsir, 23-12
Victuals, pan ts'han, 46-8
To view, por, 30-1, 113-12
Vigour, him, 20.4
Vile, ts'hyon har, 88-14, 112-1
To vilify, hor, 26-6, 109-8
A village, sooi kor, 34-9
Do. small, ma ar, 34-11
Vine (grape) p'ho t'ho, 63-7
Vinegar, ts'ho, 47-12
Violent, kang ing har, 97-7
Do. overbearing, kang in, 101-13
A viper, tok sya, 82-5
Virgin, nyo sik, 13-1
Virtue, k'hoon, 22-7, 110-5
Virtuous appearance, tok saik, 99-12
Visage, nat, 19-3
The viscera, o tsang, 18-9
To visit, por, 30-1
A vital remedy, myong yak, 52-1
An ulcer, ts'hang tsir, 51-2
A umbrella, oo san, 69-2
Unacquainted, sing so, 104-9
Unawares, oo yon, 100-16
Uncertain, ts'hang mang, 99-10
Uncle, syook poo, 12-7
Do. father's elder brother, mat, 112-7
Do. younger brother, a tsa pi, 112-7
Uncommon, pi syang, 103-7
Unconstrained, tsyong yong, 102-5
Undecided, yoo ey, 104-3
Under, a rai, 11-9
To undergo, tang har, 98-3
To understand (know), ar, 94-3, 109-11
Do. thoroughly, sa ma ti'har, 98-4
Underwood, tom p'hor, 85-2
Undeterminate, tsyoo tsyo, 100-7
To undress, po soor, 46-10
Uneasy, mi an, 102-13
Uneven, ts'ham ts'hi, 102-7
Unhappy, poor haing, 104-5
An unicorn, kooi lin, 78-8
Uniform, ir yang, 102-3
Uninterrupted, myon myon, 105-14
Unit, han, 54-13
To unite, ham har, 91-14
United, hwa hwa, 100-9
To unite in one, mo tar, 115-9, 91-14, 114-7
Do. comprize, kyom har, 94-15
Universal, mo tor, 28-12
To unload, poo ri oor, 73-12
Unlucky, hyoong har, 89-14
Do. poor haing, 134-5
Unprofitable, moo ik, 102-2
To unravel, ko rar, 121-9
Do. indistinct, hong hor, 100-1
Unsettled, pom lam, 24-3
Do. incessant, tong tong, 105-13
To unsew, t'ho tsir, 93-5
Unskilful, tsor har, 24-7
An unsteady wind, p'hyo, p'hoong, 75-1
Do. anchorage, p'hyo pak, 75-1
To untie, p'hoor, 92-8
Until, mi ts'hoor, 93-11
Untrue, ko tsoot, 90-7
Unusual, pi syang, 103-7
A voice, so rai syong, 20-15, 110-7
Void, pooir, 88-5
A void, t'hoom, 95-6
A volume, kwon, 38-7
To vomit, t'ho har, 49-6
A vomiting, koo ngyok, 50-5

Voyage, syoo lo, 8-6

To uphold, poot toor, 30-7, 115-10

Upon, oos, 11-9

Upright, syoon tsik, 23-1

Do. (just), kong tsyong, 24-5

To upset, op to tsir, 29-9, 112-16

Do. throw down, kot ko ro tsir, 31-5

Upset, moon, ho tsir, 92-13

To urge, kwon har, 25-18, 117-8

To urge to drink, sa tsyoo, 42-11

Do. to eat, kwon sik, 42-15

Urgent, tsa tsoor, 88-11

Do. kin har, 96-14

Do. tsyor pak, 102-13

Urine, o tsom, 18-16

Urinous smell, nyo ts'hooi, 49-1

To use, pso, 98-7, 116-6

Usual, sim syang, 103-3

Usurping, ts'ham ram, 97-13

A utensil, koo root, 68-4

Utmost, ta ar, 110-16

To utter, ni oar, 116-12, 122-9

Vulgar, to ro oor, 19-11, 122-7

Do. common, ya syok, 101-13

Vulgar people, ha in, 14-13

W

Wadded clothes, ha tot, 15-8

A wagtail, ts'hyok lyong, 77-5

Waggon, soor rooi, 75-5

To wail, oor, 52-9

A wainscot, pa ram, 32-16, 114-10

The waist, ho ri, 17-15

To wait upon, moi sir, 89-7, 119-15

To wait, moo ri, 94-16

To wake, skair, 42-12

To walk, neyr, 29-2, 110-3

Do. up and down, pai hoi, 29-3

Do. mo moor, 122-6

A wall, tam, 33-10, 119-8

Stone do. psar, 33-10

A wallet, po, 71-2

A walnut, ho to, 63-1

Wander, nor, 42-14

Wane of the moon, koom oom, 4-3, 121-16

Want, (need), tsong yo, 28-14, 120-13

To want, koip tsir har, 92-5

Wanton, kan ak, 24-4

Wanes, moor hwa, 55-12

A warm cap, nan mo, 45-4

Warmth, ta sar, 6-6, 111-2

To warm, kyong keys, 118-1

The warp, nar, 66-10

A warrant, p'hyo sin, 41-7

Warrior, koon sa, 38-14

A wart, ki mooi, 51-4

To wash, cleanse, ir to, 10-13

Do. to bathe, sai soor, 44-7

A washing tub, nat sei soor, 44-8

A washing block, ta to mi, 71-13

Wash balls, i tsa, 44-9

Waste land, toor kyo, 8-1

Do. ground, ko ts'hoor, 59-5, 107-2

To waste, ho pi, 96-6

A wasting wind, tsan p'hoong, 2-2

Water, moor syoo, 10-1, 107-11

Rain water, pis moor, 10-1

High water, tsyo syoo, 10-3

Low water, syok syoo, 10-3

A water fall, p'hok p'ho, 9-8

Water travelling, syoo lo, 8-6

A waterman, p'ho han, 15-5

Water nut, mor am, 62-3

Water melon, syo kwa, 63-12

A water fowl, pa ram ka pi, 77-2

A water lily, lyon hwa, 85-5, 118-13

A wave, moor kyor, 10-5

Way (road), kir, 8-8

Way (the right), to li 108-11

Wax, mir lap, 65-4

Wax of the moon, tik, 121-16

Do. vegetable, paik lap, 65-4

We, a toong, 100-10

Weak, yak har, 23-14, 115-10

Weal, pok, 89-13

Wealth, tsai san, 50-9

Weapon, see 40-3

To wear, nip oor, 46-11
Do. ni poor, 108-6
To be weary, kas par, 11-32,
A weasel, tsyok tsyop i, 79-12
To weave, stsar, 66-10
To wed, tsyang ka too rir, 41-14
To weep, oor, 52-9
To weigh, tso ar, 69-9
To weigh anchor, par tyong, 74-14
A weight, ta rim, 69-0
Weighty, moo ko oor, 87-10, 107-15, 121-8
Do. tsoong yo, 120-13
A weighing basket, sa soor, 69-10
A well, oo moor, 9-16
Do. hot, on tsyong, 9-16
Well (good), tsyo hoor, 19-7
Well adjusted, pin pin, 105-1
The west, syos nyok, 10-5, 113-3
The west wind, syo p'hoong, 1-11
A whale, ko rai, 81-11
Wet, tso tsoor, 16-14
A wet nurse, yoo mo, 13-8
What? ot tsi, 27-8, 116-3
What day? ha ir, 4.16
What hour? ha si, 5-12
What place? ha ts'hyo, 104-4
Wheat, mir, 60-9
A wheel, pak hoi, 75-7
When? ha si, 5-12
Whether, hok, 27-9

A whet-stone, mai, 59-11
Which, pa, 27-1, 111-11, 119-7
A whip, ts'hai, 73 10
To whirl, koo oor, 75-8
A whirl wind, syon p'hoong, 1-16
A whirl pool, so, 9-8
Whisker, look syoo, 17-2
A whisper, poo i o, 26-1
Do. hain, 109-2
White, hwin, 67-9
Do. (clean), ho ho, 105-4
White lead, poon, 67-9
White goose foot, to t'hars, 61-14
A white horse, paik ma, 78-13
Who? moo koo, 89-3, 115-8, 118-6
Whole (perfect), oon tsyon, 87-16
A whole year, tsyoo nyon, 3-6
Whole, tsyon zyon, 100-13
Wickedness, mo tsir, 23-12, 110-9
Wide, t'hoop, 116-15
Wide apart, song kwir, 88-4
Do. so t'hong ba, 118-5
Widely spread, moo koor, 119-1
A widow, hor o mi, 15-14
A widower, hor o pi, 15-14
Wife, an hai, 12-10
Principal wife, tyok sir, 13-7
An inferior wife, syo or, 43-8

Second wife, hoo sir, 12-10
Son's wife, myo na ri, 13-1, 112-1
Wife's father, oi koo, 12-10
Wild goose, ko he, 76-13
Do. ki ro ki, 76-16, 116-13
Wild duck, ta wa ki, 76-13
Do. mar myo ki, 76-15
A wild dog, soong rang i, 79-3
A wild hog, san tsey, 79-14
Will, tsyang ts'hat, 26-16
The will, stoot tsi, 22-3
Do. ptoot tsi, 113-3
A willow, po toor, 34-2
Do. blossoms, lyoo syo, 85-16
To win, i kwir, 76-4
The wind, pa ram, 1-10
Wind in the stomach, pok myong, 20-12
Do. from various quarters, see 11-1, to 11-14
Winding, so rir, 113-11
A window, ts'hang, 32-11
Window grating, ts'hang yon, 3-11
Wine, soor, 47-1
Do. koor, 120-5
Do. clear, ts'hyong tsyoo, 47-
Do. thick, t'hak tsyoo, 47-2
Do. hot, syo tsyoo, 47-2
A wine press, tsyoo tsa, 69-13
A wine boiler, tsyoo tsyon tsa, 69-1
A wine cup, tsan, 39-14, 120-3

A wing, nar kai, 77-16
Winter, kyo oo, 3-1, 107-6
Do. solstice, tong tsi, 4-10
Winter melon, tong kwa, 61-5
Do. cherry, hoong ko lang, 63-9
Winter fir, tong paik, 86-1
To wipe, ssoo soor, 30-13
To wipe dust, ptor ts'hir, 30-9
To wipe off a reproach, syor ts'hi, 16-9
Wisdom, tsi hey, 18-9
To wish, wan har, 120-16
The wishes, ptoot tsi, 22-3, 113-3
With (by), pso, 26-13
With (together), 95-13, 110-14
With the stream, syoon lyoo, 10-4
Within, an, 11-11, 114-5
To wither, ta roor, 86-9
Without, pat, 11-11
To be without, op sar, 90-2, 111-12
A witness, tsoong in, 56-5
A wizard, hwa rang i, 15-10
A wolf, ir hi, 79-4
Do. myo har, 121-10
A woman, key tsip, 42-1, 109-9
The womb, t'bai, 41-15
Wonderful, koi i har, 91-10
Wonderful, myo har, 19-8
Do. doctrine, myo li, 104-9
A wood, soo p'hoor, 85-2, 118-4
A woodman, tsyo poo, 15-6
A woodpecker, tat tyo koo ri, 77-10
The woof, psi, 66-11
A word, mar sam on, 24-16, 111-8, 122-9
Do. of command, ho lyong, 39-1
Work, kong poo, 37-10
Do. pa ts'hi, 121-12
A worm, koo in, 83-1
The world, in kan, 115-1
To worship, tsor, 29-11, 120-11
A worthless man, syo in, 14-9
A worthy man, koon tsa, 14-4
Wounded, ts'hik ts'hik, 106-10
To wrangle, ssa hor, 39-5
Wreck, p'ha syon, 75-2
A wren, ts'hoo lyo, 77-5
Wretched, kwa ro or, 91-9
Do. sin ko, 102-12
Wrinkled, tsing kwir, 19-12
The wrist, syoo wan, 17-8
To write, ssoor, 37-15
A writing table, syo an, 38-11
A written agreement, syo key, 36-12
Wrong, koo roor, 90-3
Do. ts'ha ts'hak, 103-16

Y

A yam, ma, 61 12
Yawning, ka hoom, 20-7
Ye, yo tong, 100-10
A year, han hais, 3-2, 107-7, 121-13
Different kinds of years, see 3-2, to 3-7
Yellow, noo roor, 67-6, 107-1
Do. ochre, syok tsa hwang, 67-7
Do. powder, hwang tan, 67-8
Do. varnish, hwang tsir, 67-8
Yes, i, 28-4
Yesterday, tsak ir, 4-13
Do. and to day, tsak koom, 99-8
Do. day before, tsai tsak ir, 4-15
Yesterday evening, tsak syok, 5-10
Yet, still, to ook, 27-2
Yielding, sa yang, 22-10
To yield, hang pok, 39-13
Young, orir, 19-16, 108-7
Young (small), tsyo moon, 19-16, 119-14
A young person, a hai, 14-14
You, no, 89-1
A young woman, key tsip, 109 9
Younger brother, a a, 12-12
Do's wife, tey soe, 12-14
Younger sister, a a noo si, 12-15
A youth, yoo a, 13-15

朝鮮偉國字彙

「朝鮮偉國字彙」

이책은 西洋人들의 韓國語 敎育을 위하여 만든 語彙集으로 李朝朝의 司譯院 倭學書였던 「倭語類解」에 漢字敎習書인 「千字文」을 添加하여 英語로 번역하고 그에 대한 索引을 붙인 것이다。「朝鮮偉國字彙」의 偉國은 倭國의 잘못이거나 倭國이란 말을 피하고자 한 것으로 보이며 「偉國字彙」는 「倭語類解」를 指稱한 것으로 생각된다。

本書의 編者는 英國人 宣敎師 Walter Henry Medhurst (筆名 Philo Sinensis, 中國名 麥都思)로서、그는 1786年 英國 런던에서 태어나 1819年 宣敎師에 任命되었고、그후 바타비아、페낭 싱가폴、보르네오、발리島 等地에서 布敎活動을 하였다。1835年 中國에 건너가 廣東、上海를 轉轉하다가 1856年 英國에 돌아가 그 이듬해에 死亡하였다。그는 말레이語와 中國語에 能通하였으며 많은 著述을 남겼는데 그의 冊은 주로 本書와 같은 語彙集이 많으며 말래카(Malacca)、바타비아、上海、廣東、마카오 等地에서 出版되었다。

「朝鮮偉國字彙」도 바타비아 (지금의 자카르타)에서 1835年에 刊行되었으며 바타비아는 그가 가장 오래 滯在하였고 또 가장 활약을 많이 한 곳이다。

編者 자신이 쓴 것으로 믿어지는 이冊의 英文 序文에 의하면 그는 韓國人을 만난 일도 없고 韓國語를 사용한 일도 없었던 것으로 보이는데 그럼에도 불구하고 그가 이 冊을 編撰하게 된 것은 「倭語類解」와 「千字文」의 中國語와 日本語를 기계적으로 번역하고 韓國語를 로마字로 轉寫함으로써 可能했던 것으로、그로 인하여 이 책에는 飜譯上의 誤謬가 많이 보이고 있다。

이 책의 體制는 「朝鮮偉國字彙」라는 書名이 붙어 있는 右便으로부터 「倭語類解」와 「千字文」이 英語로 번역되고 韓國語와 日本語의 發音이 로마字로 轉寫되어 한글과 함께 記載되어 있다。「千字文」 다음에 이 두 책에 收錄된 漢字語彙의 總目錄인 「全本漢字依部目錄」이 실려 있는데、이 目錄은 「倭語類解」와 「千字文」에 收錄된 漢字語彙를 部首와 劃數에 의하여 찾을 수 있도록 한 것이다。이 目錄에 登載된 語彙는 그 바로 밑에 그것이 收錄된 페이지數와 行數가 표시되어 있으며 특이하게도 다른 部分과 달리 蘇州碼字(蘇州商人들이 交易 帳簿記入用으로 쓰던 數字)를 사용하였다。

이와 반대로 이 책의 左便으로부터는 「TRANSLATION OF A COMPARATIVE VOCABULARY OF THE CHINESE, COREAN AND FAPANESE LANGUAGES : To which is added The Thousand Character classic, in Chinese and Corean, The Whole Accompanied by Copious Indexes, of all the Chinese and English Words Occuring in the Work」라는 긴 題目으로 된 表紙가 있고 그 다음에는 Medhurst가 쓴 것으로 보이는 序文과 Corean Alphabet이라 하여 한글 하나 하나에 대하여 로마字를 對應시킨 한글 轉寫 早見表가 있으며 이어서 「倭語類解」、「千字文」의 번역에 나타난 英語 語彙를 알파벳順으로 나열하고 그에 해당하는 韓國語를 로마字로 轉寫하여 記錄하고、그 語彙가 收錄된 面數와 行數를 표시한 「英韓比較語彙集」이 30葉에 걸쳐 실려있다。이 영문 語彙集은 左便에서 右便으로 面數가 계속되어 반대편에서 시작한「倭語類解」와는 「全本漢字依部目録」의 끝부분에서 마주치게 되었다。

이 책에서 번역된 「倭語類解」를 司譯院에서 刊行한 「倭語類解」와 比較해보면 대체로 충실하게 原本을 따른 것으로 보이며 部分的으로 韓國語나 日本語를 取捨選擇한 것도 있고、「千字文」은 「石峰千字文」을 藍本으로 하였다。

이 冊은 當時 西洋人이 韓國語를 學習하는데 사용할 수 있는 唯一한 語彙集으로 西洋人의 손으로 著作된 最初의 것이다。그러므로 韓國語를 硏究하려는 西洋人에게는 상당한 愛好를 받은 것으로 보이며 많은 韓國語 硏究者의 著書속에 이 책의 이름이 보인다。

이 책은 서울大學校 中央圖書館、日本天理大學 附屬圖書館、東洋文庫、美國 Harvard 大學、燕京學會圖書館 그리고 몇몇 個人에 의해서 所藏되고 있으며 日本 雄松堂書店의 新田勇次氏가 所藏한 것을 影印하여 藤本幸夫 敎授의 解題를 붙여 刊行한 것도 있다。

이 影印本은 燕京學會本을 底本으로 시작하였으나 서울大學校 中央圖書館本과 比較한 結果 印刷上의 問題點이 있어서 日本의 影印本을 再影印한 것이다。

鄭 光

Orion	Argo	Halo of the moon	Eclipse of the moon	The Moon	Heaven	天文	倭語類解 上
參星	老人星	月暈	月蝕	月	天	Celestial objects.	Japanese words assorted and explained Vol. I.
		계쯔운 kĕytś oōn	계쯔쇼구 kĕytś syŏk'	계쯔 kĕytś	텐 tĕn		
삼셩 săm syŏng	로인셩 lŏ īn syŏng	월운 wŏr' oōn	월식 wŏr sik	돌월 tăr wŏr	하놀텬 hā năr' thyŏn		
신세이 sīn sēy ī	로우ᅀᅵᆫ세이 lŏ oō zīn sēy ī	즈기노가사 tsoŏ kī nŏ kā sā	괃쇼구 kwăt syŏk'	즈기 tsoŏ kī	소라아메 sŏ rā ā mēy		

The seven stars	Asterion	A star	Halo of the sun	Eclipse of the sun	The Sun
七星	三台星	星	日暈	日蝕	日
		세이 sēy ī	ᅀᅵ쯔운 zits oōn	ᅀᅵ쯔쇼구 zits syŏk'	ᅀᅵ쯔 zits
칠셩 ts'hir syŏng	삼틔셩 săm thăi syŏng	별셩 pyŏr syŏng	일운 ir oōn	일식 ir sik	날일 năr ir
시찌세이 sī tsī sēy ī	산다이세이 sān tā ī sēy ī	호시 hŏ sī	히노가사 hī nō kā sā	닛쇼구 nit syŏk'	히 hī

A whirl-wind	A fair wind	The north east wind	The south east wind	The south wind	The east wind	The milky way	Capricorn
風旋	風順	風北東	風南東	風南	風東	河銀	星牛牵
셴 sēyn 후 hōō 우 ōō	쥰 zyōōn 후 hoo 우 ōō	도 tŏ 우 ōō 혹 hŏk' 후 hoō 우 oō	도 tŏ 우 oō 난 nān 후 hoō 우 oō	난 nān 후 hoō 우 oō	도 tŏ 우 oō 후 hoō 우 oō	긴 gīn 가 kā	견 keyn 규 gyoō 우 oō 셰 sēy 이 ī
션 syōn 풍 phcōng	슌 syoōn 풍 phōong	동 tŏng 북 pook 풍 phōong	동 tŏng 남 nām 풍 phōong	남 nām 풍 phōong	동 tŏng 풍 phoōng	은 oōn 하 hā	견 kyōn 우 oō 셩 syōng
즈 tsoō 지 tsī 가 kā 셰 zēy	쥰 zyoōn 뿌 boō 우 oō — 오 ŏ 이 ī 가 kā 셰 zēy	기 kī 다 tā 꼬 gŏ 지 tsī	하 ha 예 ēy 고 kŏ 지 tsī	하 hā 예 ēy 가 kā 셰 zēy	고 kŏ 지 tsī 가 kā 셰 zēy	아 ā 마 mā 노 nŏ 가 gā 와 wā	이 ī 누 noō 가 kā 이 ī 호 hŏ 시 sī

A flowing wind	A contrary wind	The north west wind	The south west wind	The north wind	The west wind	The wind	Lyra
風飄	風逆	風北西	風南西	風北	風西	風	星女織
	켸 kēy 기 kī 후 hoō 우 oō	셰 sēy 이 ī 혹 hŏk' 후 hoō 우 oō	셰 sey 이 ī 난 nān 후 hoō 우 oō	혹 hŏk' 후 hoō 우 oō	셰 sēy 이 ī 후 hoō 우 oō	후 hoō 우 oō	
표 phyŏ 풍 phōong	역 gnyŏk 풍 phōong	셔 syō 북 pook 풍 phoōng	셔 syō 남 nām 풍 phoōng	북 pōok 풍 phoōng	셔 syō 풍 phoōng	ᄇᆞ pā ᄅᆞᆷ răm 풍 phoōng	직 tsik 녀 nyō 셩 syōng
효 hyŏ 우 oō 후 hoō 우 oō	무 moō 고 kŏ 우 oō 가 kā 셰 zēy	니 nī 시 sī 아 ā 나 nă 지 zī	하 hā 예 ēy 니 nī 시 sī	기 kī 다 tā 가 kā 셰 zēy	니 nī 시 sī 가 kā 셰 zēy	가 kā 셰 zēy	쇼 syŏk' 구 쇼 zyŏ 셰 sēy 이 ī

A genial shower	A constant rain	A shower of rain	Rain	Lightning	Clouds	A wasting wind	A fierce wind
雨祈	雨霖	雨驟	雨	電	雲	風殘	風暴
기우 kī oō	림우 lĭn oō	시우우 si oō oō	우 oō	뎐 tēn	운 oōn	산후우 zān hoō oō	호우후우 hŏ oō hōe oō
긔우 koōi oō	림우 lim oō	취우 tshyōoi oo	비우 pī oō	번개뎐 pōn kāi tyēn	구룸운 koō room ōon	잔풍 tsān phōong	포풍 phŏ phōong
아마고이 ā mā gŏ ī	나가아메 nā gā ā mēy	유우다지 yoō oō dā tsī	아메 ā mey	이나스마 ī nā zoŏ mā	구모 koō mŏ	나기가세 nā gī kā zēy	하야세 hā yā zēy

A cloudy day	A drought	A drizzly rain	A sudden rain	A clap of thunder	Thunder	A cessation of wind	A sudden wind
曀	旱	雨細	雨急	靂霹	雷	止風	風急
에이 ēy ī	간 kān	사이우 sā ī oō	규우우 kyōo oō oō	베기레기 pēy kī lēy kī	라이 lā ī	후우시 hōo ōo sī	규우후우 kyoō oō hōo oō
흐릴에 hōo rīr ē	ᄀᆞ믈한 kŭ mŏor hān	세우 sēy oō	급우 kōop oō	벽력 pyōk lyōk	우레뢰 oō lē lōi	풍지 phōong tsī	급풍 kōop phōong
구모루 koo mŏ roo	히데리 hī tē rī	고마아메 kŏ mā ā mēy	무라사메 moō rā sā mēy	가미나리 kā mī nā rī	이가스지 ī kā zoŏ tsī	가세야안다 kā zēy gā yān tā	규우나가세 kyoo oō nā kā zēy

Spring		A cloudy appearance	Mist	Dew	Hail	Snow	Fair weather
春		靄	霞	露	雹	雪	晴
슌 syēon	時候	아 ā 이 ī	가 kā	로 lō	학구 hāk	셰쯔 sēytsi	셰 sēy 이 ī
봄 pŏm 츈 tshyōon	Times and Seasons	아 ā 즈 tsoŏ 랑 rāng 이 ī 애 āī	노 nŏ 을 ŏŏr 하 hā	이 ī 슬 soŏr 로 rŏ	무 moō 릐 rŏoī 박 pāk	눈 noōn 셜 syēr	갤 kāir 쳥 tshyēng
하 hā 루 roō		모 mŏ 야 yā	가 kā 스 soŏ 미 mī	즈 tsoŏ 유 yoē	히 hī 노 nŏ 아 ā 메 mēy	유 yōe 기 kī	하 hā 루 roō 루 roō

Summer		A lucky influence	Fog	Hoarfrost	Sleet	A rainbow
夏		氣瑞	霧	霜	霰	虹
가 kā			뮈 boō	소 sŏ 우 oō	션 tēyn	고 kŏ 우 oō
녀 nyō 름 roŏm 하 hā		셔 syē 긔 kĕeī	안 ān 개 kāī 무 mōo	서 sō 리 rī 상 sāng	싸 ssā 눈 nōon 션 syōn	무 moō 지 tāī 게 kā 홍 hŏng
나 nā 즈 tsoŏ		ᅀᅳ soŏ 이 ī 기 kī	기 kī 리 rī	시 sī 모 mŏ	아 ā 라 rā 례 rēy	니 nī ᅀᅵ zī

倭語類解

Japanese words … explained Vol. I

二

A month	A fertile year	A complete year	Last year	Following year	This year	A year of age / A twelvemonth	Autumn
月	年豊	年朞	年去	年翌	年今	歲	秋
겨쯔 këyts'					곤넨 kŏn nēn	세이 sëy ī	시우 sī oō
돌월 tăr wŏr	풍년 phoong nyŏn	긔년 kŏoī nyŏn	거년 kŏ nyŏn	익년 ĭk nyŏn	금년 kŏom nyŏn	힛ㅅ셰 hăis sëy	ᄀᆞ올츄 kă ăr tshyōo
과지 kwă tsī 괏쯔 kwăts'	호우넨 hŏ oō nēn	기넨 kī nēn	교넨 kyŏ nēn	요쿠넨 yŏk nēn	곤넨 kŏn nēn	사이 sā ī	아기 ā kī

The First month	A barren year	A whole year	The coming year	Next year	That year	A year	Winter
月正	年凶	年周	年來	年明	年當	年	冬
쇼우겨쯔 syŏ oō këyts'		시우넨 sī oō nēn		메이넨 mēy ī nēn		넨 nēn	도우 tŏ oō
졍월 tsyŏng wŏr	흉년 hyŏong nyŏn	쥬년 tsyoō nyŏn	ᄅᆡ년 lăi nyŏn	명년 myŏng nyŏn	당년 tăng nyŏn	ᄒᆡ년 hăi nyŏn	겨으동 kyŏ oŏ tŏr
쇼우괏쯔 syŏ oō gwăts'	교우넨 kyŏ oō nēn	슈우넨 syoō oō nēn	라이넨 lā ī nēn	묘우넨 myŏ oō nēn	도우넨 tŏ oō nēn	도시 tŏ sī	후유 hoō yoō

Lastmonth	This month	The 12 th month	The tenth month	The eighth month	The sixth month	The fourth month	The second month
月去	月今	月二十	月十	月八	月六	月四	月二
	고계쯔 kīn kēyts'	시우니계쯔 si oo nī kēyts'	시유계쯔 sī oo kēyts	히쪼계쯔 hāts' kēyts	로구계쯔 lŏk' kēyts'	시계쯔 sī kēyts	니계쯔 nī kēyts'
거월 kō wōr	금월 koom wōr	십이월 sip i wōr	십월 sip wōr	팔월 phār wōr	륙월 lyook wōr	ᄉᆞ월 sā wōr	이월 ī wōr
교예쯔 kyŏ gēyts'	곤예쯔 kŏn gēyts'	ᅀᅵ우니꽈쯔 zī oo nī gwāts'	ᅀᅵ우꽈쯔 sī oo gwāts'	하찌꽈쯔 hā tsī gwāts'	로구꽈쯔 lŏk' gwāts'	시꽈쯔 sī gwāts	니꽈쯔 nī gwāts'

Next month	That month	Intercalary month	The 11th month	The ninth month	The seventh month	The fifth month	The third month
月來	月當	月閏	月一十	月九	月七	月五	月三
		쥰계쯔 zyoon kēyts'	시우이지계쯔 sī oo ī tsī kēyts	규유계쯔 kyoo oo kēyts'	시쯔계쯔 sits' kēyts'	고계쯔 gŏ kēyts	산계쯔 sān kēyts'
리월 lāi wōr	당월 tāng wōr	윤월 yoon wōr	십일월 sip ir wōr	구월 koo wōr	칠월 tshir wōr	오월 ŏ wōr	삼월 sām wōr
라이예쯔 lā ī gēyts'	도우예쯔 tŏ oo gēyts'	우로우즈기 oo rŏ oo tsoŏ kī	ᅀᅵ우이지꽈쯔 zī oo ī tsī gwāts'	구꽈쯔 koo gwāts'	시찌꽈쯔 si tsī gwāts'	고꽈쯔 gŏ gwāts	산과쯔 sān kwāts'

倭語類解

Japanese words assorted and explained Vol.

三

Steady heat Aug. 23	Middle of the dog days July 27.	Dragon boat festival 5th moon 5th day	Spring festival Feb. 4	A time	The wane of the moon	A decade	First quarter
處暑	中伏	端午	立春	時節	晦	旬	上弦
			리 rī 우 oō 슌 syoōn		과 kwā 이 ī	슌 syoōn	
쳐 ts'hyŏ 셔 syŏ	즁 tsyŏong 복 pŏk	단 tăn 오 ŏ	립 rip 츈 ts'hyoōn	시 sī 절 tsyŏr	그 koŏm 믐 oŏm 회 hŏi	열 yŏr 흘 hoŏr 슌 syoōn	샹 syāng 현 hyŏn
쇼 syŏ 쇼 syŏ	쥬 tsyoō 우 oō 후구 hōok'	단 tăn 고 gŏ	릳 rit 슌 syoōn 셰쯔 sěyts' 분 poōn	시 zī 셰쯔 sēyts'	즈 tsoŏ 모 mŏ 고 gŏ 리 rī	도 tŏ 우 oō 까 kkā 쇼 syŏ 슌 zyoōn	쇼 zyŏ 우 oō 겐 gēyn
The 7th day of the 7th moon	Close of the dog days Aug. 6.	First of the dog days July 17.	Feast of the tombs April 6.	A holiday	New moon	Full moon	Last quarter
七夕	末伏	初伏	寒食	名日	朔	望	下弦
시쯔 sīts' 셰 sēy 기 kī	마쯔 māts' 후구 hoōk'			메 mēy 이 ī 시쯔 zīts'	사구 săk'	보 bŏ 우 oō	
칠 ts'hīr 셕 syŏk	말 mār' 복 pŏk	초 ts'hŏ 복 pŏk	한 hān 식 sīk	명 myōng 일 īr	초 ts'hŏ 하 hă 르 ră 삭 săk	보 pŏ 롬 rŏm 망 māng	하 hā 현 hyŏn
나 tā 나 nā 바 bā 다 tā	빧 bāt 부구 poōk'	쇼 syŏ 후구 hoōk'	간 kān 쇼구 syŏk'	셋 sēyt 구 koō	즈 tsoŏ 이 ī 다 tā 지 tsī	즈 tsoŏ 기 kī 나 nā 가 kā	게 gēy 견 kēyn

In a short time	The day before yesterday	Tomorrow	Yesterday	A day	Close of the year	Excursion season The 9th day of 9th moon	Seedtime Sept. 8.
日頃	日昨再	日明	日昨	日	日臘	陽重	種百
게 këy 이 ï 시쯔 zïts'	사 sä 이 ï 삭 säk' 시쯔 zïts'	메 mëy 이 ï 시쯔 zïts'	사구 säk' 시쯔 zïts'	시쯔 zïts'			
경 kyŏng 일 ïr	재 tsäi 작 tsäk 일 ïr	명 myŏng 일 ïr	작 tsäk 일 ïr	날 när 일 ïr	랍 läp 일 ïr	즁 tsyŏng 양 yäng	빅 päik 죵 tsyŏng
교 kyŏ 우 oō 시쯔 zïts'	잇 ït 사구 säk' 시쯔 zïts'	묘 myŏ 우 oō 니 nï 지 tsï / 아 ä 스 soŏ	기 kï 노 nŏ 우 oō	니 nï 지 tsï	로 lŏ 우 oō 시쯔 zïts'	죠 tsyoŏ 우 oō 요 yŏ 우 oō	햐구 hyäk' 슈 syoŏ 우 oō

What day	Future day	This very day	Following day	To day	New year's eve	Winter Solstice Dec. 21.	Mid Autumn 8th moon 15th day
日何	日後明	日即	日翌	日今	夕除	至冬	夕秋
가 kä 시쯔 zïts'	메 mëy 이 ï 고 kŏ 우 oŏ 시쯔 zïts'			긴 kïn 시쯔 zïts'	쇼 zyŏ 셰 sëy 기 kï		시 sï 우 oō 셰 sëy 기 kï
하 hä 일 ïr	명 myŏng 후 hoŏ 일 ïr	즉 tsoŏk 일 ïr	익 ïk 일 ïr	금 koŏm 일 ïr	졔 työi 셕 syŏk	동 tŏng 지 tsï	츄 ts'hyoŏ 셕 syŏk
잇 ït 가 kä	아 ä 삳 sät 뎨 të	소구 sŏk' 시쯔 zïts'	요구 yŏk' 시쯔 zïts'	곤 kŏn 니 nï 지 tsï / 교 kyŏ 우 oō	오 ŏ 우 oō 조 tsoŏ 모 mŏ 묘 gŏ 리 lï	도 tŏ 우 oō 시 zï	슈 syoŏ 우 oŏ 셰 sëy 기 kï

倭語類解 上

These words translated and explained I.

時候 Times and Season

Moonlight night	Early	Daylight	Morning	Clearday	All day long	Day time	Howmany days
夜月	早	曉	朝	明平	日終	晝	日幾
계 kēyts' 쯔 야 yā	소 sŏ 우 oō	교 kyŏ 우 oō	됴 tyŏ 우 oō			쥬 tsyoō 우 oō	기 kī ᅀ zīts' 쯔
월 wŏr 야 yā	일 ir 올 oŏr 조 tsŏ	사 sā 베 pēy 효 hyŏ	아 ā 참 tshăm 죠 tsyŏ	평 phyēng 명 myōng	죵 tsyŏng 일 ir	낫 nāt 쥬 tsyoō	긔 kŏoi 일 ir
즈 tsoŏ 기 kī 요 yŏ	하 hā 야 yā 시 sī 스 tsoŏ 도 tŏ	아 ā 가 kā 즈 tsoŏ 기 ki	계 kēy 사 sā 아 ā 사 sā	혜 hēy 이 ī 메 mēy 이 ī	시 sī 우 oō ᅀ zīts' 쯔	히 hī 루 roō	이 ik 구 ᅀ zīts' 쯔

Candle light	Late	Dusk	Evening	Twilight	All night long	Night time	A short day
點更	晩	暮	夕	陽夕	夜達	夜	晷短
	빤 bān	뽀 bŏ	셰 sēy 기 kī	셰 sēy 기 kī 요 yŏ 우 oō	다 tāts' 쯔 야 yā	야 yā	단 tā 기 kī
경 kyōng 뎜 tyōm	느 noŏ 즐 tsoŏr 만 mān	져 tsyō 믈 mŭn 모 mŏ	나 nā 조 tsŏ 셕 syŏk	셕 syŏk 양 yāng	달 tār 야 yā	밤 pām 야 yā	단 tān 구 koō
고 kŏ 우 oō 뎬 ttēn	구 koō 레 rēy 가 kā 다 tā	히 hī 우 goō 레 rēy 구 koō 레 rēy	유 yoō 우 oō 베 pēy	유 yoō 우 oō 히 hī	요 yŏ 모 mŏ 스 soŏ 아 gā 라 rā	요 yŏ 루 roo	미 mī 니 nī 카 kā 이 ī 히 hī 가 kā 에 gēy

5

From 11a.m. to 1 p.m.	From 7 to 9 a.m.	From 3 to 5 a.m.	From 11p.m. to 1 a.m.	This hour	An hour	Yesterday evening	Bedtime
時午	時辰	時寅	時子	時此	時	夕昨	定人
오 gŏ 시 sī	신 sin 시 sī	인 in 시 sī	시 sī 시 sī	시 sī 시 sī	시 sī	시구 sak' 세 sēy 기 kī	신 sin 데 te 이 ī
오 ŏ 시 sī	진 tsin 시 sī	인 in 시 sī	ᄌᆞ tsă 시 sī	ᄎᆞ tshă 시 sī	ᄯᆡ stăi 시 sī	작 tsak 셕 syŏk	인 in 뎡 tyŏng
The 9th hour	The 5th hour	The 7th hour	The 9th hour				
고 kŏ 고 kŏ 노쪼 nŏts' 도 tŏ 기 kī	이 i 즈쯔 tsoots' 도 tŏ 기 kī	나 nā 나쯔 nāts' 도 tŏ 기 kī	고 kŏ 고 kŏ 노쪼 nŏts' 도 tŏ 기 kī	고 kŏ 노 nŏ 도 tŏ 기 kī	도 tŏ 기 kī	사구 sak' 유 yoo 우 oo	간 kān 요 yŏ 메 mēy

From 1 to 3p.m.	From 9 to 11a.m.	From 5 to 7 a.m.	From 1 to 3 a.m.	What hour	That hour	This evening	Hourglass done
時未	時巳	時卯	時丑	時何	時其	夕今	漏罷
미 mī 시 sī	시 sī 시 sī	보 bŏ 우 ōō 시 sī	지구 tsik' 시 sī	가 kā 시 sī	기 kī 시 sī	긴 kin 세 sēy 기 kī	하 hā 이 ī 로 lŏ 우 ōō
미 mī 시 sī	ᄉᆞ să 시 sī	묘 myŏ 시 sī	츅 tshyook 시 sī	하 hā 시 sī	기 kī 시 sī	금 koŏm 셕 syŏk	파 phā 루 loō
The 8th hour	The 4th hour	The 6th hour	The 8th hour				
야쯔 yāts' 도 tŏ 기 kī	요쯔 yŏts' 도 tŏ 기 kī	무쯔 mōots' 도 tĕ 기 kī	야쯔 yāts' 도 tĕ 기 kī	이 ī 즈 tsoŏ 오 gŏ 로 rŏ	소 sŏ 노 nŏ 도 tŏ 기 kī	곤 kŏn 세 sēy 기 kī	곤 kŏn 요 yŏ 메 mēy

Cold	Heat	Warmth	Dusky	Clear	Shade	From 7 to 9 p.m.	From 3 to 5 p.m.
冷	暑	温	昏	明	陰	時戌	時申
례 lĕy 이 ī	쇼 syŏ	온 ŏn	곤 kŏn	메 mĕy 이 ī	인 in	슈쯔 zyŏots' 시 sī	신 sin 시 sī
찰 tshăr 랭 lăng	더 tŏ 울 oŏr 셔 syŏ	드 tă 솔 săr 온 ŏn	어 ŏ 으 oŏ 롬 roŏm 혼 hŏn	볼 păr 글 koŏr 명 myŏng	그 koŏ 롬 roŏr 음 cŏm	술 syoor 시 sī	신 sin 시 sī
						The 5th hour	The 7th hour
히 hī 야 yā 비 pī 야 yā 시 sī	아 ā 즈 tsoŏ 이 ī	아 ā 다 tā 다 tā 가 kā	구 koŏ 레 rĕy	아 ā 기 kī 라 rā 가 kā	가 kā 게 gĕy	이 ī 즈쯔 tsoŏts' 도 tŏ 기 kī	나 nā 나쯔 nāts' 도 tŏ 기 kī
Frigid	Great Heat	Genial warmth	Dark	Bright	Light Sunshine	From 9 to 11 p.m.	From 5 to 7 p.m.
凉	熱熅	和暄	暗	朗	陽	時亥	時酉
료 lyŏ 우 oŏ	구 koŏ 세쯔 zĕyts'	견 kĕyn 과 kwā	안 ān	로 lŏ 우 oŏ	요 yŏ 우 oŏ	가 gā 이 ī 시 sī	이 ī 우 oŏ 시 sī
서 sŏ 놀 noŏr 량 lyāng	구 koŏ 열 yŏr	훤 hwŏn 화 hwā	아 ā 득 toŏk 홀 hăr 암 âm	볼 păr 글 koŏr 량 lāng	볃 pyŏt 양 yāng	히 hāi 시 sī	유 yoŏ 시 sī
						The 4th hour	The 6th hour
스 soŏ 즈 zoŏ 시 sī 이 ī	무 mōo 스 soŏ	노 nŏ 노 nnŏ 가 kā	구 koŏ 라 rā 시 sī	호 hŏ 기 gī 라 rā 까 kkā	히 hī 나 nā 다 tā	요쯔 yŏts' 도 tŏ 기 kī	무쯔 mŏots 도 tŏ 기 kī

Kăng	Woo	Ping	Keă
庚	戊	丙	甲
고 kŏ 우 oō	보 bŏ 우 oō	헤 hēy 이 ī	고 kŏ 우 oō
경 kyōng	무 moō	병 pyōng	갑 kāp
Metal senior 가 kā 노 nŏ 예 ēy	Earth senior 즈 tsoŏ 지 tsī 노 nŏ 예 ēy	Fire senior 히 hī 노 nŏ 예 ēy	Wood senior 기 kī 노 nŏ 예 ēy

Sin	Ke	Ting	Yih
辛	己	丁	乙
신 sīn	기 kī	데 tē 이 ī	이 쯔 īts'
신 sĭn	긔 koŏī	뎡 tyōng	을 ŏŏr
Metal junior 가 kā 노 nŏ 또 ttŏ	Earth junior 즈 tsoŏ 지 tsī 노 nŏ 또 ttŏ	Fire junior 히 hī 노 nŏ 또 ttŏ	Wood junior 기 kī 노 nŏ 또 ttŏ

干支

Horary characters

Todryiu the sun	Toshineon Reflection	Severe cold
曝	照	寒
호 hŏ 우 oō	쇼 syŏ 우 oō	간 hān
몰 măr 뢰 rŏī 일 ĭr 포 phŏ	비 pī 쵤 ts'hoir 죠 tsyŏ	춀 ts'hăr 한 hān
후 hŏ 스 soŏ	데 tē 루 roō	사 sā 무 moō 이 ī

	Shining	Shade of the sun
	暎	影日
	예 ēy 이 ī	시 쯔 zits' 예 ēy 이 ī
	부 pă 일 ăir 영 yōng	일 ĭr 영 yōng
	사 sā 사 sā 이 ī	히 hī 가 kā 게 gēy

倭語類解

Japanese words ... and explanation Vol.

六

地理 Terrestrial objects	Sëuh	Shin	Woo	Shin	Yin	Tsze	Jin
	戌	申	午	辰	寅	子	壬
	슈쯔 syoots'	신 sin	오 gŏ	신 sin	인 in	시 si	ᅀᅵ zin
	슐 syoor	신 sin	오 ŏ	진 tsin	인 in	ᄌᆞ tsă	임 im
	Dog	Ape	Horse	Dragon	Tyger	Rat	Water senior
	이 ī 누 noō	사루 sar'	우 oō 마 mā	다즈 tāts	도 tŏ 라 rā	네 nē	미 mī ᄉᆞ zoŏ 노 nŏ 에 ēy
	Hae	Yew	We	Sze	Maou	Chow	Kwei
	亥	酉	未	巳	卯	丑	癸
	가 gā 이 ī	이 ī 우 oū	미 mī	시 sī	보 bŏ	지구 tsik'	기 kī
	해 hăi	유 yoō	미 mī	ᄉᆞ să	묘 myŏ	츅 tshyook	계 kēy
	Pig	Fowl	Sheep	Snake	Rabbit	Ox	Water junior
	이 ī	도 tò 리 rī	히즈 hīts' ᅀᅵ zi	미 mī	우 oō	우 oō 시 sī	미 mī ᄉᆞ zoŏ 노 nŏ 또 ttŏ

地理 Ter- obj-

A bank	A mound	A rocky precipice	A rugged hill	A peak	The brow of a hill	Earthquake	The earth
岸	丘	壁石	峴	峯	山禿	震地	地
간 kān	규우 kyoō oō	세기혜기 sēy kī hēy kī	견 keyn	후우 hō oō	도구산 tŏk' sān		지 tsī
물언덕안 mōor ōn tŏk' ān	두던구 toō tŏn koō	석벽 syŏk pyŏk	고개현 kŏ kāi hyen	뫼ㅅ봉오리보 mŏis pōng o ri pōng	독산 tŏk sān	디진 tī tsīn	따디 ttā tī
기시 kī sī	오가 ō kā	뵤우뿌이와 pyŏ oō boō ī wā	사가 sā kā	미네 mī nē	하애야마 hā gēy yā mā	지신 tsī sin	즈지 tsoō tsī

A ravine	Tableland open country	A lofty precipice	A precipitous hill	A mountain top	The foot of a hill	A hill	A plain country
壑	原	壁絶	巖	嶺	麓山	山	地平
각구 gāk'	옌 gēyn	세쯔혜기 zēyts' hēy kī	간 gān	레이 lēy ī	산로구 sān lŏk'	산 sān	
굴헝학 koōr hōng hāk	언덕원 ōn tŏk wōn	절벽 tsyŏr pyŏk	바회암 pā hŏī ām	재령 sāi lyŏng	산록 sān lŏk'	뫼ㅅ산 mŏis sān	평디 phyŏng tī
구보다 koō pŏ tā	하라 hā rā	다가이와 tā kā ī wā	이와 ī wā	이다다기 ī tā tā kī	야마노후모도 yā mā nŏ hoō mŏ tŏ	야마 yā mā	혜이지 hēy ī tsī

Japa[nese] wo[rds] assoc[iated] [and] expla[ined] Vol.

七

The stones of a brook	A fairy stone	Water travelling	A footpath	A crooked road	A road	A cave	A desert plain
磧	石怪	路水	路徑	路彎	路	洞	野
셰기 sēy kī	과이셰기 kwā ī sēy ki		계이로 kēy ī lŏ	완로 wān lŏ	로 lŏ	도우 tŏ oŏ	야 yē
쟉벌젹 tsyāk pyŏr tsyŏk	과셕 kŏī syŏk	슈로 syoō lŏ	경로 kyōng lŏ	만로 mān lŏ	길로 kīr lŏ	골통 kŏr tŏng	들야 toŏr yā
미스아사노이시 mī zoŏ ā sā nŏ ī sī	맨셰기 bŏn sēy kī	스이로 soŏ ī lŏ	고미지 kŏ mī tsī	미와리미지 mā wā rī mī tsī	미지 mī tsī	호라 hŏ rā	노바라 nŏ pā rā

Earth Mould	Pebbles	A stone	Land travelling	A slanting road	A street	A valley	Wasteland
土	礫	石	路陸	路斜	街	谷	郊
도 tŏ	려기 lēy kī	셰기 sēy kī	리구로 lĭk' lŏ	샤로 syā lŏ	아이 gā ī	곡구 gŏk'	고우 kyŏ oŏ
흙토 hărk thŏ	몽오리돌륵 moŏng ŏ rī tŏr roŏk	돌셕 tŏr syŏk	륙로 lyŏok lŏ	샤로 syā lŏ	거리가 kō rī kā	골곡 kŏr kŏk	들교 toŏr kyŏ
즈지 tsoŏ tsī	즈뿌데 tsoŏ boŏ tē	이시 ī sī	리구지 lĭk' tsī	나나메미지 nā nā mēy mī tsī	지마다 tsī mā tā	다니 tā nī	하루노 hā roo nŏ

地理 8

A hillock	A cave	A cavern	A pitfall	Mire	Ashes	Dust	Sand
凸	穴	窟	陥	渟泥	灰	塵	沙
뎓쯔 tēts'	겨쯔 kēyts'	고쯔 kŏts'	간 kān	데이네이 dē ī nō ī	파이 kwā ī	신 zīn	샤 syā
ᄲᅩ죡텰 spŏ tsyŏk thyŏr	구무혈 koō moō hyŏr	구무굴 koō moō koŏr	새질함 skō tsīr hām	니녕 nī nyŏng	ᄌᆡ회 tsăī hŏī	틔ᄭᅳᆯ진 thŏōis koŏr tsīn	모래사 mŏ rē sā
나가다가 nā kā tā kā	아나 ā nā	이와야 ī wā yā	오도시아나 ŏ tŏ sī ā nā	누다 noō tā	하이 hā ī	지리 tsī rī	스나 soŏ nā

A hollow	A steep place	A den	A hole	A pit	Mud	Small dust	Fine sand
凹	崎嶇	窖	塡	坎	泥	埃	沙細
오우 ŏ oō	기구 kī koō	고우 kŏ oō	뎐 tēn	간 kān	데이 dē ī	아이 ā ī	사이샤 sā ī syā
오목오 ŏ mŏk ŏ	긔구 koŏī koō	굴교 koŏr kyŏ	메올뎐 mēy ŏr tyŏn	굴헝감 koŏr hŏng kām	즌흙니 tsoŏn hărk nī	몬지의 mŏn tsăī ăī	셰사 sēy sā
나가구보 nā kā koō pŏ	계와시이 kēy wā sī ī	아나홀데 ā nā hŏt tē	하미이례 hā mī ī rēy	다마리미ㅅ tā mā rī mī zoŏ	도로 dŏ rŏ	호고리 hŏ kŏ rī	고마스나 kŏ mā zoŏ nā

倭語類解

Japa… wo… assor… an… expla…

A waterfall	A fountain	A stream	An island	A lake	A large river		Mountain vapour
布瀑	泉	川	島	湖	江		嵐
보 pŏk' 구 호 hŏ	션 sēyn	쳔 sēyn	도 tŏ 우 oō	고 kŏ	고 kŏ 우 oō	江湖	란 lān
폭 p'hŏk 포 p'hŏ	심 săīm 쳔 táhyōn	내 nāī 쳔 táhyōn	셤 syōm 도 tŏ	가 kă 람 răm 호 hŏ	물 mōor 강 kāng	Rivers and Lakes	람 lām 긔 kŏŏī 람 lām
다 tā 기 kī 다 tā 기 kī 노 nŏ 미 mī ᅀ zoŏ	이 ī ᅀ zoŏ 미 mī	가 kā 와 wā	시 sī 마 mā	미 mī ᅀ zoŏ 우 oō 미 mī	미 mī ᅀ zoŏ 우 oō 미 mī 예 ēy		이 ī 라 rā 시 sī

A whirlpool	A spring	A marsh	A high island	A river	The sea		
潭	源	澤	島絶	河	海		
담 tān	원 gēyn	닥 tāk'	졀 zēyts' 도 tŏ 우 oō	가 kā	가 kā 이 ī		
소 sŏ 담 tām	근 koŏn 원 wōn 원 wōn	못 mŏt 퇵 t'hăik	졀 tsyōr 도 tŏ	하 hā 슈 syoō 하 hā	바 pā 다 tā 희 haī		
요 yŏ 도 dŏ 미 mī 미 mī ᅀ zoŏ	미 mī 나 nā 모 mŏ 도 tŏ	사 sā 와 wā	오 ŏ 기 kī 노 nŏ 시 sī 마 mā	미 mī ᅀ zoŏ 가 kā 와 wā	우 oō 미 mī		

A well	A ferry	A rivulet	A bay	A shore A strand	A flat bank	A deep abyss	A small Creek
井	津	溪	灣	濱	汀	淵	浦
셰이 sēy ī	신 sin	계이 kēy ī	완 wān	힌 hīn	뎨이 tē ī	연 eyn	호 hŏ
우물졍 oō moōr tsyōng	나루진 nă ră tsīn	시내계 sī nāi kēy	물구뷔만 mōor koō pooi mān	물ᄀᆞ빈 moōr kă pīn	물ᄀᆞ뎡 moōr kă tyōng	못연 mŏt yŏn	개포 kāi phŏ
이 ī	즈 tsoō	호소아와 hŏ sŏ gā wā	마와리미스 mā wā rī mī zoŏ	하마 hā mā	미애와 mī gī wā	후치 hoō tsī	우라 oō rā

A hot well	Collection of water	A stream in valley	A stream	An islet A coast	An isle	A pool	A rapid
井温	渠	澗	派	渚	洲	池	灘
온셰이 ōn sēy ī	교 kyŏ	간 kān	하이 hā ī	쇼 syŏ	시우 sī oō	지 tsī	단 dān
온졍 ŏn tsyōng	개천거 kăi tshyŏn kō	시내간 sī nāi kān	물가리파 moōr kā rāi phā	물ᄀᆞ져 moōr kă tsyō	물ᄀᆞ쥬 moōr kă tsyoō	못지 mŏt tsī	여흘탄 yō hoŏr thān
유이 yoō ī	미스 mī zoŏ	다니미스 tā nī mī zoŏ	미스미다 mī zoŏ mī tā	나애사 nā gī sā	미스빠다 mī zoŏ bā tā	이계 ī kēy	나다셰 nā dā sēy

倭語類解

Japa... w... assor... ar... expla... Vol.

Deep	Pure Clear	To ebb	To flow as a stream	Against the stream	High water	Water Pearl An icicle	Water
深	清	潰	流	水逆	水潮	鈴水	水
신 sīn	세이 sēy ī	과이 kwā ī	라우 lī oō	게기스이 kēy kī soō ī	됴우스이 tyō oō soō ī	스이래이 soō ī lēy ī	스이 soō ī
깁흘심 kip hŏr sīm	몱글쳥 măr koōr tshyēng	혀여질계 hō yō tsīr koōē	흘읔류 hoōr oōr ryoō	역슈 yŏk syoō	죠슈 tsyō syoō	슈령 syoō lyōng	물슈 moōr syoō
후가시 hoō kā sī	기요시 kī yō sī	히루 hīr'	나가루루 nā gā roōrī	무고우시오 moō kō oō sī ō	미시시오 mī zī sī ō	미스다마 mī zoō tā mā	미스 mī zoō

Shallow	Muddy	To rise as the tide	A wave	With the stream	Low water	The ocean	Rain water
淺	濁	溢	波	流順	水汐	宗水	潦
선 sēyn	다구 tāk'	이쯔 its'	하 hā	쥰리우 zyoōn lī oō	세기스이 sēy kī soō ī	스이소우 soō ī sō oō	로우 lō oō
엳틀쳔 yōt t'hŏor tshyŏn	흐릴탁 hoŏ rīr t'hāk	너물일 nŏ moōr īr	믈ㅅ결파 moōrs kyōr p'hā	슌류 syoōn lyoō	셕슈 syŏk syoō	슈종 syoō tsŏng	비ㅅ물료 pīs moōr ryō
아사시 ā sā sī	니꼬루 nī gō roō	아후루루 ā hoō roōr'	나미 nā mī	오이시오 ō ī sī ō	히시오 hī sī ō	노나가 nō nā kā	아마미스 ā mā mī zoō

To thaw	To flow off	To soak	To sprinkle	To leak	To steep in water	To bubble	To float
澌	注	滋	灑	漏	涵	湧	浮
시 sī	슈 syoō	ᅀᅵ zī	사 sā 이 ī	로 lŏ 우 oō	간 kān	요 yŏ 우 oō	후 hoō 우 oō
성 sŏng 에 āī 싀 sŏŏī	부 poō 을 oŏr 주 tsoō	부 poō ᄅᆞᆯ răr ᄌᆞ tsă	ᄲᅮ spoō 릴 rīr 쇄 swāī	ᄉᆡᆯ săĭr 루 loō	ᄌᆞᆷ tsăm 길 kīr 함 hām	소 sŏ ᄉᆞᆯ săr 용 yŏng	ᄯᅳᆯ ttoŏr 부 poō
시 sī 미 mī 도 tŏ 게 gēy	모 mŏ 리 rī	후 hoō 예 ēy 루 roō	소 sŏ 소 sŏ 구 goō	모 mŏ 루 roō	가 kā 조 tsoŏ 구 goō	미 mī 스 zoō 와 구 wāk'	우 oō 가 kā 무 moō / 우 oō 구 koō

To congeal	To draw water	To moisten	To wash	To drip To trickle	To drown	Foam	To sink
凝	汲	濕	洵	滴	溺	泡	沉
ᅌᅭ ŏyō 우 oō	규 kyoō 우 oō	이 ī 우 oō	도 tŏ 우 oō	테 tē 기 kī	데 dē 기 kī	호 hŏ 우 oō	진 tsīn
물 moŏr 엉 ŏng 긜 kŏŏir 응 ŏŏng	기 kī 를 roŏr 급 koŏp	저 tsŏ 즐 tsoŏr 습 soŏp	일 ĭr 도 tŏ	믈 tŏŏr ᄯᅥᆯ oŏr 뎍 tyŏk	ᄲᅡ spā 질 tsĭr 닉 nik	거 kŏp 품 phoōm 포 phŏ	ᄌᆞᆷ tsăm 길 kīr 침 ts'hīm
가 kā 다 tā 마 mā 루 roō	구 koō 무 moō	누 noō 루루 roŏr'	유 yoō 루 roō	시 sī 다 tā 다 dā 루 roō	오 ŏ 보 pŏ 루 roŏr	미 mī 스 zoŏ 노 nŏ 아 ā 와 wā	시 sī 조 tsoŏ 무 moō

倭語類解

Japanese words associated and explained Vol.

十

Before	The left	The south	The East		A marsh Fever	To melt	Ice
前	左	南	東	方位	瘴	消	氷
션 sēyn	사 sā	난 nān	도 to 우 oō		쇼 syŏ 우 oō	쇼 syŏ 우 oō	효 hyŏ 우 oō
앏 ārp 젼 tsyŏn	욀 ŏīr 좌 tswā	남 nām 녁 nyŏk 남 nām	동 tŏng 녁 nyŏk 동 tŏng	Places and Positions	쟝 tsyāng 긔 kooī 쟝 tsyāng	ᄉᆞ sā 르 rā 질 tsīr 쇼 syŏ	어 ŏ 룸 room 빙 pīng
마 mā 예 ēy	히 hī 다 tā 리 ri	미 mī 나 nā 미 mi	히 hi 가 gā 시 sī		쇼 syŏ 우 oō 기 ki	기 kī 유 yoō 루 roō	고 kŏ 오 ŏ 리 rī

Behind	The right	The north	The West			Slippery	To freeze
後	右	北	西			滑	凍
고 kŏ 우 oō	이 ī 우 oō	혹 hŏk'	세 sēy 이 ī			괏 kwāts	도 tŏ 우 oō
뒤 toōī 후 hoō	올 ŏr 흘 hoŏr 우 oō	북 poōk 녁 nyŏk 북 pŏk	셔 人 syos 녁 nyok 셔 syŏ			믯 mīt 그 koō 러 rŏ 올 ŏr 활 hwār	얼 ŏr 동 tŏng
우 oō 시 sī 로 ro / 노 nŏ 지 tsī	미 mī 기 gī	기 kī 다 tā	니 nī 시 sī			나 nā 메 mēy 라 rā 가 kkā	고 kŏ 오 ŏ 루 roō

...語類解上

...nese words ...ted ...d ...ined I.

方位 Plac... and Pos...

11 上

倭語類解

Jap wo asso a expl Vol.

On all sides Everywhere	A corner	A side A position	Lateral	Outside In front	Within	In the middle	Above
面四	隅	方	傍	表	内	中	上
	구 goō	호 hŏ 우 oō	호 hŏ 우 oō	효 hyŏ 우 oō	따 dā 이 ī	쥬 syoō 우 oō	쇼 syŏ 우 oō
ᄉᆞ sā 면 myōn	모 soŏ 롱 cōng 이 ī 오 oŏ	모 mŏ 방 pāng	곁 kyŏt 방 pāng	밧 pāt 표 p'hyŏ	안 ān 닋 nāi	가 ka 온 ōn 딕 kān 즁 tsyoong	우 ōōs ㅅ 샹 syāng
시 sī 면 myōn	스 soō 미 mi	가 kā 다 tā	가 kā 다 tā 와 wā 라 rā / 소 sŏ 바 pā	오 ŏ 모 mŏ 대 tē	우 oō 지 tsī	나 nā 가 kā	가 kā 미 mi / 우 oō 예 ēy

The eight points	The four quarters	The bottom	On one side	Inside	Without	Between	Below
方八	方四	底	邊	裡	外	間	下
하 hāts' 쯔 호 hŏ 우 oō		데 tē 이 ī	헨 hēyn	리 lī	과 kwā 이 ī	간 kān	가 kā
팔 p'hār 방 pāng	ᄉᆞ sa 방 pāng	밑 mit 뎌 tyō	ᄀᆞ kăs ㅅ 변 pyōn	속 sŏk 리 lī	밧 pāt 긔 ōi	ᄉᆞ sā 이 ī 간 kān	아 ā 래 rāi 히 hā
바 pāts' 쯔 가 kā 다 tā	시 sī 호 hŏ 우 oō	소 sŏ 고 kŏ	호 hŏ 토 tŏ 리 rī	우 oō 라 rā	호 hŏ 가 kā	아 ā 이 ī 다 dā	시 sī 모 mŏ / 지 tsī 다 tā

一

Husbands' Father	Uncle	Foster father	Mother	A near Relative	Grandfather	Great Grandfather	
舅	父叔	父養	母	親	父祖	父祖曾	
규 kyoō 우 oō	시 sik' 구 후 hoō		뫼 bŏ 우 oō	신 sīn	소 sŏ 후 hoō	조 zŏ 우 oō 소 sŏ 후 hoō	人倫
싀 soŏī 아 a 비 pī 구 koō	슉 syoōk 부 poō	양 yāng 부 poō	어 ŏ 미 mī 모 mŏ	어 ŏ 버 pō 이 ī 친 ts'hīn	조 tsŏ 부 poō	증 tsoōng 조 tsó 부 poō	Human Relations
슈 syoō 우 oō 도 tŏ 오 ŏ	오 ŏ 지 tsī	요 yŏ 우 oō 후 hoō	하 hā 하 hā	오 ŏ 야 yā	찌 dsī 시 zī	히 hi 오 ŏ 오 ŏ 지 tsī	
Husbands' mother	Aunt	Foster mother	Father & Mother	Father	Grand mother	Great Grandmother	
姑	母叔	母養	妣考	父	母祖	母祖曾	
고 kŭ	시 sīk' 구 뫼 bŏ 우 oō		고 kŏ 우 oo 히 hī	후 hoō	소 sŏ 뫼 bŏ 우 oō	조 zŏ 우 oō 소 sŏ 뫼 bŏ 우 oō	
12 싀 sŏoī 어 ō 미 mi 고 kŏ	슉 syoōk 모 mŏ	양 yāng 모 mŏ	고 kŏ 비 pi	아 ā 비 pi 부 poō	조 tsŏ 모 bŏ	증 tsŏong 조 tsŏ 모 bŏ	
슈 syoō 우 oō 도 tŏ 메 mēy	오 ŏ 바 pā	요 yŏ 우 oō 뫼 bŏ 우 oo	지 tsī 지 tsī 하 hā 하 hā	지 tsi 지 tsi	빠 bā 바 pa	히 hī 빠 bā 바 pā	

Son	Younger sister	Younger brother's wife	Twins	Younger Brother	Husband and wife	Wife	Wife's Father
子	妹	嫂弟	生同	弟	婦夫	妻	舅外
시 sĭ	ᄜᅢ이 bā ĭ	데이소우 tē ĭ sŏ oō	도우쇼우 tŏ oō syŏ oō	데이 tē ĭ		셰이 sēy ĭ	과이규우 kwā ĭ kyoō oō
아들ᄌᆞ ā toŏr sā	아ᄋᆞ누시미 ā ă noō sĭ măĭ	뎨수 tēy soō	동싱 tŏng săing	아ᄋᆞ뎨 ā ă tēy	부부 poō poō	안해쳐 ān hāi ts'hyŏ	외구 ŏĭ koō
무스고 moō soŏ kŏ	이모오도 ĭ mŏ ŏ tŏ	오도도요메 ŏ tŏ tŏ yŏ mēy	오나시하라 ŏ nā sĭ hā rā	오도도 ŏ tŏ tŏ	후후우 hŏo hoō oō	즈마 tsoŏ mā	하하까다노오지 ha ha kka tā nŏ ŏ tsĭ

Foster child	Sister's husband	Elder sister	Elder brother's wife	Brethren	Elder Brother	Second wife	Husband
子養	夫妹	姉	嫂兄	弟兄	兄	室後	夫
	ᄜᅢ이후 bā ĭ hoō	시 sĭ	계이소우 kēy ĭ sŏ oō	계이데이 kēy ĭ tē ĭ	계이 kēy ĭ		후 hoō
양ᄌᆞ yāng tsă	미부 măĭ poō	몯누의ᄌᆞ măt noō ŏoĭ tsă	형수 hyŏng soō	형뎨 hyŏng tēy	몯형 măt byŏng	후실 hoō sĭx	지아비부 tsĭ ā pĭ poō
요우시 yŏ oō sĭ	이모우도옫도 ĭ mŏ oō tŏ ŏt tŏ	아네 ā nē	아니요메 ā nĭ yŏ mēy	교우다이 kyŏ oō tā ĭ	아니 ā nĭ	고우시쯔 kŏ oō sĭts'	옫도 ot tŏ

倭語類解

Japanese words assorted and explained Vol

A second wife	Sisters-in-law	Wife's sister's child	Cousins	Grandson	Niece	Son-in-law	Son's Wife
孽庶	娌妯	娣妻	弟兄從	孫	女姪	婿	婦
쇼 syŏ 예쯔 gĕyts	지구 tsik' 리 lī	세 sēy 이 ī 난 nān	쇼 syoō 우 oō 게 kēy 이 ī 데 tē 이 ī	손 sŏn	지쯔 tsits' 쇼 zyŏ	세 sēy 이 ī	후 hoō 우 oō
셔 syō 얼 ōr	츅 ts'hyŏok 리 lī	쳐 ts'hyō 남 nām	죵 tsyōng 형 hyōng 뎨 tēy	손 sŏn 즈 tsă 손 sŏn	질 tsīr 녀 nyō	사 sā 회 hōī 셔 syō	며 myō 느 nă 리 rī 부 poō
게 kĕy 샤 syā 구 koō 하 hā 라 rā	아 ā 이 ī 요 yŏ 메 mēy	고 kŏ 슈 zyoō 우 oō 도 tŏ	이 ī 도 tŏ 고 kŏ	마 mā 꼬 gŏ	메 mēy 이 ī	무 moō 고 kŏ	요 yŏ 메 mēy

A wet nurse	Principal wife	Brothers-in-law	Distant cousins	Great grandson	Sister's child	Nephew	Daughter
母乳	室嫡	婿同	從再	孫曾	甥	姪	息女
슈 zyoō 뽀 bŏ 우 oō	데 tē 기 kī 시쯔 sīts'	도 tŏ 우 oō 세 sēy 이 ī	사 sā 이 ī 쇼 syŏ 우 oō	소 zŏ 우 oō 손 sŏn	세 sēy 이 ī	지쯔 tsits'	쇼 zyŏ 소구 sŏk'
유 yoō 모 mŏ	뎍 tyŏk 실 sīr	동 tŏng 셔 syō	지 tsăī 죵 tsyōng	증 tsăng 손 sŏn	싱 săing 질 tsīr 싱 săing	족 tsŏk 하 hā 질 tsīr	녀 nyŏ 식 sik
메 mēy 노 nŏ 도 tŏ	혼 hŏn 사 sā 이 ī	아 ā 이 ī 무 moō 고 kŏ	시 sī 이 ī 쥬 syoō 우 oō 데 tē 이 ī	히 hī 마 mā 꼬 gŏ	고 kŏ 시 zī 우 oō 도 tŏ	오 ŏ 이 ī	무스 moōs 메 mey

Name	A youth	An old friend	A friend	A clan	Relations by marriage	Relations by blood	A concubine
名	兒幼	舊親	友朋	族一	戚	親	妾
메 mēy 이 i	이 i 우 oō ᅀᅵ zi	신 sin 규 kyoō 우 oō	호 hŏ 우 oō 이 ī 우 oō	이 its' 쯔 소 zŏk' 구	세 sēy 기 kī	신 sin	쇼 syō 우 oō
일 ir 홈 hŏm 명 myŏng	유 yoō ᄋᆞ ă	친 tshin 구 koō	붕 poong 우 oō	일 ir 족 tsŏk	겨 kyō 레 rǎi 척 ts'hyŏk	친 tshin 홀 hăr 친 ts'hin	쳡 tshyŏp 쳡 ts'hyŏp
나 nā	따 dā 기 kī 꼬 gŏ	ᅀᅡ zī 간 kān 즈 tsoŏ 기 kī	도 tŏ 모 mŏ 다 tā 지 tsī	이 ī 지 tsī 소 zŏk' 구	하 hā 하 hā 노 nŏ 시 sī 다 tā 시 sī 이 ī	사 sī 다 tā 시 sī 이 ī	떼 tē 가 kā 께 kēy

Designation	Surname	A little child	A colleague in office	A family connected by marriage	A household	Kindred	The son of a concubine
字	姓	兒孩	官同	家婚	家一	族	子孽
ᅀᅵ zi	셰 sēy 이 ī	가 kā 이 ī ᅀᅵ zī		곤 kŏn 가 kā	이 its' 쯔 가 kā	소 zŏk' 구	게 gēytă 쯔 시 sī
ᄌᆞ tsă ᄌᆞ tsă	셩 syōng 셩 syōng	ᄒᆡ hăi ᄋᆞ ă	동 tŏng 관 kwān	혼 hŏn 가 kā	일 ir 가 kā	겨 kyō 레 rǎi 족 tsŏk	얼 ŏr ᄌᆞ tsă
아 ā ᅀᅡ zā 나 nā	묘 myŏ 우 oō ᅀᅵ zī	야 yā 야 yā	또 dŏ 우 oō 관 kwān	연 ēyn 샤 zyā 아 ā 야 yā 기 kī 또 dŏ 노 nŏ	잇 it 가 kā 잇 it 게 kēy	이 ī 지 tsī 루 rŏ 이 ī	소 sŏ 시 sī

倭語類解

Japanese words assorted and explained Vol.

十三

倭語類解上

A hero	A retired Scholar	Famous women	A filial child	A worthy man	A man	人品	Distinctive Mark
豪傑	隱士	烈女	孝子	君子	人		别號
					신 zīn		
호 hŏ 걸 kōr	은 oōn ᄉᆞ sǎ	렬 lyōr 녀 nyō	효 hyŏ ᄌᆞ tsǎ	군 koōn ᄌᆞ tsǎ	사 sā ᄅᆞᆷ rām 인 īn	Sorts of Men	별 pyōr 호 hŏ
교 gŏ 우 oō 계 즈 kēyts	인 in 시 sī	례 즈 lēyts' 죠 zyŏ	교 kŏ 우 oō 시 sī	군 koōn 시 sī	히 hī 도 tŏ		베 쯔 bēyts' 교 gŏ 우 oō

人品 Sorts of Men

A superior	A brave man	A scholar	Excellent Scholars	A faithful minister	A sage	Family name
長者	英雄	士	烈士	忠臣	聖人	氏
죠 tsyŏ 우 oō 샤 syā		시 sī	례 쯔 lēyts' 시 sī			시 sī
장 tsyāng 쟈 tsyā	영 yōng 웅 oōng	션 syōn 비 păī ᄉᆞ sǎ	렬 lyōr ᄉᆞ sǎ	츙 tshyōong 신 sīn	셩 syōng 인 īn	각 kāk 시 sī 시 sī
오 ŏ 도 tŏ 나 nā 슈 syoō	예 ēy 이 ī 유 yoō 우 oō	사 sā 무 moō 라 rā 이 ī	렌 lēyt 시 sī	쥬 tsyoō 우 oō 신 sīn	세 sēy 이 ī 신 zīn	우 oō 시 zī 소 sō 옌 ēyn 도 tŏ 노 nŏ

14 一

倭語類解

A clown A peasant	A little boy	An adult	Vulgar people	A squire A gentleman	A priest of the sect Taou	A teacher	A worthless man
夫田	童小	丁	人下	班两	士道	師	人小
뎬 tēn 후 hoō	쇼 syŏ 우 oō 도 tŏ 우 oō	뎨 tē 이 ī	가 kā 산 zīn	료 lyŏ 우 oō 한 hān	도 tŏ 우 oō 시 sī	시 sī	쇼 syŏ 우 oō 신 zīn
텬 tyōn 부 poō	쇼 syŏ 동 tŏng	장 tsăng 뎡 tyōng 뎡 tyōng	하 hā 인 in	량 lyāng 반 pān	도 tŏ 亽 să	스 soō 승 sŏong 亽 să	쇼 syŏ 인 īn
뎐 dēn 뿌 boō 노 nŏ 우 oō 닌 nin	고 kŏ 도 tŏ 모 mŏ	댠 tāt 샤 syā 모 mŏ 노 nŏ	시 sī 모 mŏ 시 zī 모 mŏ	례 lēy 기 kī 례 lēy 기 kī	야 yā 마 mā 부 poō 시 sī	시 sī 쇼 syŏ 우 oō	고 kŏ 비 pī 도 tŏ

A shop-keeper	A errand boy	A young person	The people	A common man	A genius of the hills	A disciple	A learned man
人市	令使	童	民	人常	人仙	子弟	生儒
시 sī 신 zīn	시 sī 레 lēy 이 ī	도 tŏ 우 oō	민 mīn	죠 zyŏ 우 oō 신 zīn	션 sēyn 신 zīn	뎨 tē 이 ī 시 sī	쥬 zyoō 쇼 syŏ 우 oō
시 sī 인 īn	亽 să 령 lyŏng	아 ā 희 hāi 동 tŏng	빅 păik 셩 syōng 민 mīn	샹 syāng 인 īn	션 syōn 인 īn	뎨 tēy 즈 tsă	유 yoō 싱 săing
마 mā 지 tsī 닌 nin	즈 tsoŏ 예 ēy 모 mŏ 지 tsī	와 wā 라 rā 베 pēy	다 tā 미 mī	시 sī 다 tā 시 zī 다 tā	야 yā 마 mā 히 hī 도 tŏ	데 dē 시 sī	쥬 zyoō 샤 syā 징 tsīng 고 kŏ 다 tā 지 tsī

十四

倭語類解 上

Chinese words ... I.

人品 Sorts of Men

A puppet	A courier	A woodman	A waterman	A falconer	A founder	A mechanic	A conjurer
傀(儡)	飛脚	樵夫	浦漢	鷹師	鑄匠	匠人	術者
과이 kwā ī		쇼우후 syŏ oō hoō	호간 hŏ kān	요우시 yŏ oō sī	슈쇼우 syoō syŏ oō	쇼우신 syŏ oō zīn	
광대괴 kwāng tāi kŏi	비각 pī kāk	쵸부 tshyŏ poŏ	포한 phŏ hān	응ᄉᆞ oōng sā	쥬장 tsyoō tsyāng	장인 tsyāng īn	술자 syoōr tsyā
가루와사시 kā roō wā zā sī	히갸구 hī kyāk'	기고리 kĭ kŏ rĭ	아마 ā mā	다가쇼우 tā kā syŏ oō	이모노시 ī mŏ nŏ sī	쇼구닌 syŏk' nīn 사이구닌 sā īk' nīn	쥬즈샤 zyoōts' zyā

15

A comedian	A player / One of weak abilities	A runner	A fisherman	A huntsman	A ostler	A caster / A smith	A fortune teller
戯子	輕才人	歩行	漁翁	獵戶	理馬	冶匠	卜者
기시 kī sī	게이사이신 kēy ī sā ī zīn	호고우 hŏ kŏ oō		료우고 lyŏ oō kŏ	리빠 lī bā	야쇼우 yā syŏ oō	보구샤 pŏk' syā
희ᄌᆞ hŏoī tsă	경지인 kyŏng tsăī īn	보항 pŏ hāng	어옹 ŏ ŏng	렵호 lyŏp hŏ	리마 lī mā	야장 yā tsyāng	복자 pŏk tsyā
교우겐사루가구 kyŏ oō gēyn sār gāk'	가루와사 kā roō wā zā	가지요리유구 kā tsī yŏ rī yŏok'	교오우 gyŏ ŏ oō	가리우도 kā rī oō dŏ	빠이 bā ī	가시 kā zī	우라나이샤 oō rā nā ī zyā

Abeggar	Anorphan	Awidower	A maid-servant	Aservant	Afemale dentist	Asorcerer	Ajuggler
人乞	孤	鰥	婢	僕	婆牙	巫	術幻
기쯔신 kīts' zīn	고 kŏ	관 kwān	히 hī	보구 pŏk'	갸하 gā hā	뮤 boō	겐쥬쯔 geyn zyōots'
걸인 kŏr in	외로올고 ŏi rŏ ŏr kŏ	홀아비환 kŏr ā pī hwān	죵비 tsyŏng pī	죵복 tsyŏng pŏk	아파 ā phā	무당무 moō tāng moō	환술 hwān syoŏr
고즈지기 kŏ tsoŏ tsī kī	히도리미 hī tŏ rī mī	야모뗴 yā mŏ mēy	게쇼 kēy zyŏ	계라이 kēy rā ī	스와이로우쇼 soŏ wā ī rŏ oō zyŏ	미고 mī kŏ	마호우 mā hŏ oō

Arobber	Achildless person	Awidow	A hired servant	Aslave	Aprostitute	Awizard	Anequestrian
盗强	獨	寡	工雇	奴	妓女	覡	才上馬
고우도우 kŏ oō tŏ oō	도구 tŏk'	과 kwā	고고우 kŏ kŏ oō	도 dŏ	죠기 zyŏ kī	게기 kēy kī	바쇼우사이 bā syŏ oō sā ī
강도 kāng tŏ	호올독 hŏ ŏr tŏk	홀어미과 hŏr ŏ mī kwā	고공 kŏ kŏng	죵노 tsyŏng nŏ	녀기 nyŏ kī	화랑이격 hwā rāng ī kyŏk	마상지 mā tsyāng tsāī
즈요기누스히도 tsoŏ yŏ kī noōs' hī tŏ	히도리 hī tŏ rī	꼬게 gŏ kēy	야도아우또 yā tŏ ī oō ttŏ	야즈꼬 yā tsoŏ gŏ	계이세이 kēy ī sēy ī	호사 hŏ sā 간나에 kān nā gī	교구 kyŏk' 빠노리 bā nŏ rī

倭語類解

Japanese words assembled and explained Vol.

十五

倭語類解上

Japanese words sorted and explained I. I.

身體 Human Body

身體 Body and Its parts

The pupil of the eye	The eye	The temples	The cheeks	The fore-head	The crown	The body
瞳	目	鬢	腮	額	頂	身
도우 tŏ oō	모구 mŏk'	빈 pin	사이 sā ī	가구 kāk	데이 tē ī	신 sin
눈부쳐동 noōn poō tshyā tŏng	눈목 noōn mŏk	귀밋빈 kooī mit pin	뺨싀 spyām sooī	니마ᄋᆡᆨ nī mā ăik	뎡바기뎡 tyōng pā kī tyōng	몸신 mŏm sīn
히도미 hī tŏ mī	메 mēy	비애 pī gēy	오도아이 ŏ tŏ gā ī	히다이 hī tā ī	이다다기 ī tā dā kī	미 mī

The eye ball	The white of the eye	The eye brows	The cheek bones	The countenance	The skull	The head
眸	睛白	眉	頰	顏	髗	頭
뽀우 bŏ oō	하구세이 hāk sēy ī	메 bī	교우 kyŏ oō	안 gān	로 lŏ	도우 tŏ oō
눈망올모 noōn māng ŏr mŏ	백정 păik tsyŏng	눈섭미 noōn sŏp mī	보죠개협 pŏ tsyŏ kăi hyŏp	낫안 năt ān	대골로 tăi kŏr lŏ	마리두 mā rī too
마나고 mā nā gŏ	시로다마 sī rŏ tā mā	마유 mā yoō	호우사기 hŏ oō sā kī	가오 kā ŏ	죠우즈지 tsyŏ oō tsoŏ tsī	가미 kā mī; 고우베 kŏ oō pēy

16 十六

Shedding of the teeth 齔齠	The front teeth 齒門	The teeth 齒	The tongue 舌	The mouth 口	The nostril 孔鼻	The nose 鼻	The eyelash 瞼	
됴 tyŏ 우 oō 신 sīn	몬 mŏn 시 sī	시 sī	셰 zēyts 쯔	고 kŏ 우 oō	ᄞᅵ bī 고 kŏ 우 oō	ᄞᅵ bī	켄 kēyn	
됴 thyŏ 츤 ts'hŏon	문 moōn 치 ts'hī	니 nī 치 ts'hī	혀 byō 셜 syōr	입 īp 구 koō	비 pī 공 kōng	코 k'hŏ 비 pī	눈 noōn 두 toō 에 āī 검 kōm	Ja v ass exp Vo
하 hā ᅌᅡ gā 미 mī	무 moō 고 kŏ 우 oō ᄞᅡ bā	하 hā	시 sī 다 tā	구 koō 지 tsī	하 hā 나 nā 노 nŏ 스 soŏ	하 hā 나 nā	마 mā 부 poō 다 tā 메 mēy 후 hoō 다 tā	

The throat 喉咽	The dog teeth 齒臭	The grinders 牙	The gums 齦	The lip 脣	The dimple under the nose 中人	The bridge of the nose 梁鼻	The ear 耳
인 īn 고 kŏ 우 oō	오 ŏ 우 oō 시 sī	ᅌᅡ gá	ᅌᅵᆫ gīn	신 gīn	신 zīn 쥬 tsyoō 우 oō	ᄞᅵ bī 료 lyŏ 우 oŏ	ᅀᅵ zī
인 īn 후 hoō	오 ŏ 치 ts'hī	엄 ōm 니 nī 아 ā	닛 kis 무 mooē 음 oŏm 훈 hooŏn	입 īp 시 sī 울 oōr 슌 syōor	인 in 즁 tsyōng	비 pī 량 lyāng	귀 koŏī 이 ī
논 nŏn 도 tŏ	오 ŏk' 구 ᄞᅡ bā	기 kī ᄞᅡ bā	하 hā ᅌᅮ goō 기 kī	구 koō 지 tsī ᄞᅵ bir 루	닌 nin 쥬 tsyoō 우 oō	고 kŏ 바 pā 나 nā	미 mī 미 mī

Thewrist	The back of the hand	The arm-pit	The arm	The neck	White mustachios	Whiskers	Mustachios
腕手	背手	腋	臂	項	鬚白	鬚勒	鬚
시 sī 우 oō 완 wān	사 sī 우 cō 하 hā 이 ī	예 ēy 다 kī	히 hi	교 kŏ 우 oō	하구 hāk' 바쪼 pāts'	로구 lŏk' 슈 syoō	슈 syoō
슈 syoō 완 wān	슈 syoō 비 păī	겨 kyō 드 toŏ 랑 rāng 이 ī 외 ăīk	풀 phăr 비 pī	목 mŏk 항 hāng	빅 păk 발 pār	록 loŏk 슈 syoō	나 nā 룻 rŏt 슈 syoō
데 tē 구 koō 비 pī	데 tē 노 nŏ 고 kŏ 우 oō	와 wā 기 kī 노 nŏ 시 sī 다 tā	히 hī 시 zī	구 koō 비 pī	시 sī 라 rā 게 gēy	호 hŏ 우 oō 히 hī 게 gēy	우 oō 와 wā 히 hī 게 gēy

A finger	The palm of the hand	The hand	The elbow	The shoulder	The chin	Hair	Beard
指	掌	手	肘	肩	頤	髮	髯
시 sī	쇼 syŏ 우 oō	시 sī 우 oō	쥬 tsyoō 우 oō	견 kēyn	이 ī	바쪼 pāts'	션 zēyn
손 sŏn 가 kā 락 rāk 지 tsī	손 sŏn 바 pā 당 tāng 장 tsyāng	손 sŏn 슈 syoō	풀 phăr 구 koō 미 mī 쥬 tsyoō	엇 ōt 게 kē 견 kyŏn	톡 t'hăr 이 i	터 t'ho 럭 rōk 발 pār	나 nā 룻 rŏt 염 yŏm
유 yoō 비 pi	다 tā 나 nā 고 gŏ 고 kŏ 로 rŏ	데 tē	힌 hīn 시 zī 노 nŏ 후 hoō 시 sī	가 kā 다 tā	아 ā 기 gī	가 kā 미 mī 게 gēy	시 sī 다 tā 히 hī 게 gēy

The buttocks	The navel	The spine	The nipples	The fist	The little finger	The middle finger	The thumb
臀	臍	脊	乳	拳	指小	指長	指拇
둔 tŏn	셰 sēy 이 ī	셰 sēy 기 kī	유 zyoō	켠 kēyn	쇼 syŏ 우 oō 시 sī	죠 tsyŏ 우 oō 시 sī	보 bŏ 우 oō 시 sī
볼 pŏr 기 kī 둔 toōn	빗 pāi 삽 skŏp 졔 tsēy	등 toōng 므 mă 르 ră 쳑 ts'hyŏk	졋 tsyŏt 유 yoō	주 tsoō 머 mō 귀 kwī 권 kwŏn	쇼 syŏ 지 tsī	쟝 tsyāng 지 tsī	모 mŏ 지 tsī
시 sī 리 rī	호 hŏ 소 zŏ	셰 sēy 보 pŏ 네 nē	지 tsī	고 kŏ 부 poō 시 sī	고 kŏ 유 yoō 비 pī	다 tā 가 kā 다 tā 가 kā 유 yoō 비 pī	오 ŏ 야 yā 유 yoō 비 pī

The anus	The loins	The belly	The back	The breast	The nails	The third finger	The fore finger
尻	腰	腹	背	胷	爪	指名無	指人指
고 kŏ 우 oō	요 yŏ 우 oō	후 hoōk 구	하 hā 이 ī	교 kyŏ 우 oō	소 sŏ 우 oō	보 boō 메 mēy 이 ī 시 sī	시 sī 진 zīn 시 sī
옹 ŏng 미 mī 니 nī 고 kŏ	허 hō 리 rī 요 yŏ	빈 pāi 복 pŏk	등 toōng 비 pāi	가 kā 슴 sām 흉 hyoōng	손 sŏn 톱 t'hŏp 조 tsŏ	무 moō 명 myŏng 지 tsī	지 tsī 인 īn 지 tsī
시 sī 리 rī 사 sā 기 kī	고 kŏ 시 sī	하 hā 라 rā	셰 sēy 나 nā 가 kā	무 mōō 네 nē	즈 tsoō 메 mēy	베 bēy 니 nī 사 sā 시 sī 유 yoō 비 pī	히 hī 도 tŏ 사 sā 시 sī 유 yoō 비 pī

倭語類解

Japan... wo... assor... an... expla... Vol.

十七

倭語類解上

Chinese words sorted and explained. I.

身體 Human Body

18

Muscles	Marrow	The heel	The instep	The shin	The leg		
肌	髓骨	跟	背足	脛	脚	陰門	陽物
기 kĭ		근 kŏn	소구 sŏk' 하이 hāi	계이 kēy ī	갸구 kyāk'	인 īn 몬 mŏn	요 yŏ 우 oō 모쯔 mŏts'
솔 săr 과 kŏoī	골 kŏr' 슈 syoō	발 pār 뒤 tooī 측 ts'hŏok 근 kon	족 tsyŏk 비 pāi	종 tsyōng 아 ā 리 rī 뼝 kyāng	다 tā 리 rī 과 kāk	음 oŏm 문 moŏn	양 yāng 물 moŏr
하 hā 다 tā 예 yē	고쯔 kŏts' 스이 zoŏi	기 kī 비 pī 스 soŏ	아 ā 시 sī 노 nŏ 고 kŏ 우 oō	고 kŏ 바 boō 로 rŏ	하 hā 기 gī	모 mŏ 보 pŏ	마 mā 라 rā

Sinews	Skin	A bone	The sole of the foot	The foot	The knee	The thigh	
筋	皮	骨	足掌	足	膝	腿	陰囊
근 kĭn	히 hī	고쯔 kŏts'	소구 sŏk' 슈 syŏ 우 oō	소구 sŏk'	시쯔 sĭts'	다 tā 이 ī	인 īn 노 nŏ 우 oō
힘 hĭm 쏠 stsŏot 근 koŏn	가 kā 족 tsŏk 피 p'hī	쌔 spyō 골 kŏr	족 tsyŏk 장 tsyāng	발 pār 족 tsyŏk	무 moō 룹 roŏp 슬 soŏr	신 sŏoĭn 다 tā 리 rī 퇴 t'hŏī	음 oŏm 낭 nāng
스 soŏ 시 zī	가 kā 와 wā	호 hŏ 네 nē	아 ā 시 sī 노 nŏ 우 oō 라 rā	아 ā 시 sī	히 hī 사 zā	모 mŏ 모 mŏ	긴 kīn 다 tā 마 mā

Urine	The blood	The bladder	The stomach	The six entrails	The lungs	The liver	The five viscera
尿	血	膀胱	胃	六腑	肺	肝	五臟
뇨 nyŏ 우 oō	계쯔 kēyts	호 hŏ 우 oō 고 kŏ 우 oō	이 ī	로 lŏk' 구 후 hoō	하 hā 이 ī	간 kān	
오 ŏ 좀 tsŏm 뇨 nyŏ	피 phī 혈 hyŏl	방 pāng 광 kwāng	양 yāng 위 oōī	륙 lyoŏk 부 poō	부 poō 화 hwā 폐 p'hēy	간 kān 간 kān	오 ŏ 장 tsāng
이 ī 바 bā 리 rī	지 tsī	보 bŏ 우 oō 고 kŏ 우 oō	구 koō 소 sŏ 후 hoō 구 koō 루 roō	롯 rŏt 보 boō	지 tsī 와 wā 다 tā	기 kī 모 mŏ	오 gŏ 소 sŏ 우 oō

Excrement	The pulse	The 3 parts of the body	The gall bladder	Intestines	The kidnies	The coats of the stomach	The heart
屎	脉	三膲	膽	腸	腎	脾	心
기 kī			단 tān	죠 tsyŏ 우 oō	신 zīn	히 hī	신 sīn
똥 stŏng 시 sī	뫽 măik 뫽 măik	삼 sām 쵸 ts'hyŏ	쓸 ssŏor 개 kăi 담 tām	애 āi 장 tsyāng	콩 k'hŏng 팟 phăt 신 sīn	만 mān 하 hā 비 pī	념 nyŏm 통 t'hŏng 심 sīm
구 koō 소 sŏ	먀구 myăk	산 sān 쇼 zyŏ 우 oō	기 kī 모 mŏ 도 tŏ	하 hā 라 rā 와 wā 다 tā	호 hŏ 소 ssŏ 베 mēy 구 goō 루 roō	와 wā 기 kī 모 mŏ 노 nŏ	고 kŏ 고 kŏ 로 rŏ

倭語類解 Japanese words used and explained Vol

十八

倭語類解 上

ese / ds / ted / d / ined / I.

容貌

oun- / and / ppe

Delicate	Good	Beautiful	Firm & strong	The manner	The face		Foul wind
妙	好	美	莊	樣	面	容貌	積
묘우 myŏ oŏ	교우 kŏ oŏ	뼤 bī	쇼우 sŏ oŏ		면 mēyn		히 hī
묘홀묘 myŏ hăr myŏ	죠홀호 tsyŏ hoŏr hŏ	아름다올미 ā răm tā ŏr mī	싁싁홀장 soŏik soŏik hăr tsāng	모양양 mŏ yāng yāng	낟면 năt myŏn	Countenance and appearance	방귀비 pāng koŏī pī
묘우나 myŏ oŏ nā	고노무요시 kŏ nŏ moŏ yŏ sī	메데도우 mēy tē tŏ oŏ	사가리 sa kā rī	요우 yŏ oŏ	오모데 ŏ mŏ tē		헤히루 hēy hī roŏ
Handsome	Clean & tidy	Pretty	Elegant	The appearance	The form		
姿	淨	姸	秀	儀	形		
시 sī	세이 sēy ī	견 kēyn	시우 sī oŏ	기 gī	계이 kēy ī		
즈틔즈 tsă thăi tsă	조홀졍 tsŏ hŏr tsyŏng	고올연 kŏ ŏr yŏn	빼혀날슈 spā hyŏ năr syoŏ	거동의 kŏ tŏng ŏoī	얼굴형 ŏr koŏr hyŏng		
스가다 soŏ gā tā	기례이 kī rey ī	가오요시 kā ŏ yŏ sī	히이네루 hī ī nnē roo	도리나리 tŏ rī nā rī	가다지 kā tā tsī		

19 一上

倭語類解

Japanese words assorted and explained Vol.

Small	Fullgrown	Scurfy	Pockmarked	Ugly	Disgusting	Fat Lusty	Fine
少	成長	垢	麻面	醜	媸	肥	嬌
쇼우 syŏ oō	죠우세이 tsyŏ oō sey i	고우 kŏ oō	면마 mēyn mā	시우 si oō	시 si	히 hī	교우 kyŏ oō
져믈쇼 tsyō moŏr syŏ	잡싱 tsyăng syŏng	싀구 stăi koō	면마 myŏn mā	더러울츄 tō rō oŏr ts'hyooi	무울치 mooi oŏr ts'hī	슬질비 săr tsir pī	교틔교 kyŏ t'hăi kyŏ
와가이 wā kā i	오유루 ŏ yoō roō	아가 ā kā	션규 sēyn kyoō	미니구시 mī nī koō sī	미구루시 mī goō roō sī	고예루 kŏ ēy roō	고비 kŏ pī

Young	Old Aged	Meagre Wasted	Scarred	Wrinkled	Vulgar Filthy	Lean Thin	Figure
稚	老	悴憔	痕	皺	陋	瘦	態
지 tsī	로우 lŏ oō		콘 kŏn	시우 sī oō	로우 lŏ oō	시우 sī oō	다이 tā i
어릴치 o rīr ts'hī	늘글로 noōr koōr lŏ	쵸쉐 ts'hyŏ ts'hyōoēy	허물흔 hō moōr hoōn	찡걸추 tsing koōir ts'hoō	더러울루 tō rō oōr roō	여윌수 yō ōir soō	틔도틔 t'hăi tŏ t'hăi
오사나이 ŏ sā nā ī	도시요리 tŏ sī yŏ rī / 오이 ŏ ī	쇼우스이 syŏ oō soŏ ī	기스아도 kī zoŏ ā tŏ	시와 sī wā	기다나이 kī tā nā ī	야스루 yā soŏ roo	와사 wā zā

十九

Perspiration sweat	Respiration	The animal spirits	Life	Spirit	氣息 Spirit and Breath	A shadow	Longlived
汗	吸呼	神精	命	氣		影	壽
간 kān	고 kŏ 규 kyoo 우 oō		며 mēy 이 ī	기 kī		예 ēy 이 ī	시 sī 우 oō
삼 stăm 한 hăn	호 hŏ 흡 hoŏp	졍 tsyōng 신 sīn	목 mŏk 숨 soōm 명 myōng	긔 koōī 운 oōn 긔 koōī		그 kŏ 림 rīm 자 tsă 영 yōng	목 mŏk 숨 soōn 슈 syoō
아 ā 셰 sey	이 ī 기 kī 즈 tsoŏ 가 kā 이 ī	셰 sēy 이 ī 신 sın	이 ī 노 nŏ 지 tsī	기 kī 예 gēy		가 ka 예 gēy	이 ī 노 nŏ 지 tsī

Tears	Yawning	Moisture	The breath	Strength		A trace A footstep	Short lived
淚	欠呵	液津	息	力		跡	夭
루 loō 이 ī	가 kā 간 kān		숙 sŏk'	륙 lyŏk'		셰 sēy 기 kī	요 yŏ 우 oō
눈 noōn 물 moōn 루 roō	가 kā 흠 hoŏm	진 tsīn 익 ăīk	쉼 sōoīm 식 sīk	힘 hīm 력 lyŏk		자 tsā 최 ts'hŏī 젹 tsyŏk	일 īr 즉 tsoŏk 을 oŏr 요 yŏ
나 nā 미 mī 다 dā	아 ā 구 koō 비 pī	신 sīn 예 ēy 기 kī	야 yā 스 soŏ 무 moō	지 tsī 가 kā 라 rā		아 ā 도 tŏ	하 hā 야 yā 구 koō 시 sā 스 soŏ 루 roō

To sound	A sound	To ridicule	To smile	To blow the nose	To snore	To spit	Spittle
響	音	咄	嚬	涕鼻捧	鼾	唾	涎
교우 kyŏ oō	인 in	도쯔 tŏts'	힌 hĭn	고우삐데이 kŏ oō bī tē ī	간 kān	다 tā	연 ēyn
울이일향 oōr ī ir hyāng	소리옴 sŏ răi oŏm	혀차돌 hyŏ ts'hăr tŏr	싱길빈 sing kōoir pin	힝비톄 hăing pī t'hēy	코고올한 k'hŏ kŏ oŏr hān	춤밧틀라 ts'hoŏm pāt t'hoor t'hā	춤연 ts'hōom yon
히비구 hī pī koō	오도 ŏ tŏ	시다우쯔 sī tā oots'	히소무 hī sŏ moō	하나후구 hā nā hoo koō	이비기 ī pī kī	즈바기하구 tsoŏ pā kī hāk'	즈바기 tsoŏ pā kī

To call	A voice	To sigh	To laugh	Wind in the stomach	Snot Snivel	To sneeze	To slabber
呼	聲	歎	笑	鳴腹	涕鼻	嚏	涎流
고 kŏ	세이 sēy ī	단 tān	쇼우 syŏ oo	후구메이 hoŏk' mēy ī	삐데이 bī tē ī	데이 tē ī	리우엔 lī oō ēyn
부롤호 poō roŏr hŏ	소리셩 sŏ răi syōng	탄식탄 t'hān sīk t'hān	우옴쇼 oō oōm syŏ	복명 pŏk myōng	비톄 pī t'hēy	자최옴톄 tsă ts'hoĭ oŏm t'hēy	류연 lyoō yōn
요뿌 yŏ boō	고예 kŏ yē	나게기 nā gēy kī	와라우 wā rā oō	하라나리 hā rā nā rī	하나시루 hā nā sī roō	굳샤미 koōt syā mi	즈바기요다레 tsoŏ pā kī yŏ dā rēy

Fear	Hilarity	To be pleased	To injure	Anger	To abhor	Grief	Clamour
驚	暢	悅	寃	忿	怨	憂	喧
계 kēy 이 ī	쟈 tsyŏ 우 oō	예 ēyts' 쯔	연 ēyn	훈 hoōn	연 ēyn	이 ī 우 oō	견 kēyn
놀 nŏr 날 nār 경 kyŏng	싀 sooī 훤 hwōn 홀 hăr 쟝 ts'hyăng	깃 kĭt 글 koŏr 열 yŏr	셜 syŏr 올 oŏr 원 wōn	분 poōn 홀 hăr 분 poōn	원 wōn 망 māng 원 wōn	근 koōn 심 sīm 우 oō	솓 sōot 두 toō 어 ŏ 릴 rīr 훤 hwōn
오 ŏ 도 dŏ 로구 rŏk'	하 hā 레 rēy 야 yā 가 kā	우 oō 레 rēy 시 sī 이 ī	가 kā 나 nā 시 sī 무 moō	이 ī 기 kī 도 tŏ 우 oō 루 roō	우 oō 라 rā 무 moō	우 oō 레 rēy 이 ī	야 yā 가 kā 마 mā 시 sī

Cheerful	Dread	To fret	To pity	Indignation	To hate	Sorrow	Concern
快	畏	鬱	憐	恚	恨	悶	愁
과 kwā 이 ī	이 ī	우 oōts' 쯔	련 lēyn	이 ī	곤 kŏn	빈 bīn	시 sī 우 oō
쾌 k'hwai 홀 hăr 쾌 k'hwai	두 toō 릴 rīr 외 ŏī	답 tăp 답 tăp 홀 hăr 울 oŏr	어 ŏ 엿 yŏt 블 poŏr 련 lyŏn	애 ăī 도 tŏ 롤 rŏr 에 ē	혼 hăn 홀 hăr 혼 hăn	민 mīn 망 māng 민 mīn	근 koōn 심 sīm 수 soō
고 kŏ 고 kŏ 로 rŏ 요 yŏ 시 śī	오 ŏ 소 sŏ 레 rēy	후 hoō 사 sā 갈 kā 루 roō 우 oō 또 ttŏ 시 sī	아 ā 와 wā 레 rēy 무 moō	무 moō 넨 nēn 구 koō 지 tsī 오 ŏ 시 sī	우 oō 라 rā 무 moō 루 roō	메 mēy 이 ī 와 wa 구 koō	기 kī 즈 tsoō 까 kkā 이 ī

倭語類解

Japanese words assorted and explained Vol.

To labour	To be ashamed	To forbear	To perceive	To harbour in the mind	To consider	A sigh Long breath	Elevated
勞	恥	忍	悟	懷	念	息大	興
로 lŏ 우 oō	지 tsī	신 zĭn	오 gŏ	과 kwā 이 ī	녠 nēn	다 tā 이 ī 속 sŏk'	
슈 syōo 고 kŏ 로 rŏ 올 oŏr 로 rŏ	붓 poōt 그 kŏo 릴 rīr 치 ts'hī	참 ts'hăm 올 oŏr 인 īn	세 skăī 칠 ts'hīr 오 ŏ	품 p'hōom 올 oŏr 회 hŏī	념 nyōm 려 ryŏ 념 nyōm	대 t'hāī 식 sĭk	흥 hoŏng 미 mī 흥 hoŏng
신 sīn 로 lŏ 우 oō	하 hā 즈 tsoŏ 까 kkā 시 sī	시 sī 노 nŏ 부 poō / 고 kŏ 라 rā 에 ēy	사 sā 메 mēy 사 sā 도 tŏ 루 roo	후 hoō 도 tŏ 고 kŏ 로 rŏ	넨 nēn 오 ŏ 이 ī 레 rēy	다 tā 메 mēy 이 ī 기 kī	교 kyō 우 oō

	To be exhausted	To repent	To bear patiently	To forget	To hanker after	To think	Affected
	困	悔	耐	忘	戀	思	感
	곤 kŏn	과 kwā 이 ī	다 tā 이 ī	모 mŏ 우 oō	렌 lēyn	시 sī	간 kān
	잇 ĭt 불 poŏr 곤 kŏn	뉘 noōī 웃 oōt 츨 ts'hoŏr 회 hŏī	견 kyŏn 딜 tĭr 내 nāī	니 nī 즐 tsoŏr 망 măng	그 koŏ 릴 rīr 련 lyōn	싱 săĭng 각 kăk 亽 să	늣 noŏt 길 kīr 감 kăm
	구 koō 다 tā 비 bī 레 rēy	구 koō 야 yā 무 moō	간 kān 닌 nĭn	와 wā 수 soŏ 루 roō	유 yoō 가 kā 시 sī 우 oō	오 ŏ 모 mŏ 우 oō	가 kā 다 tā 시 zī 게 kēy 나 nā 이 ī

二一

倭語類解上

ese
ds
ed
d
ned
I.

性情

性情

Nature and affections

Fidelity	Virtue	Propriety	Benevolence	Holy sagelike	The will	Nature
忠	德	禮	仁	聖	志	性
쥬 tsyoō 우 oō		레 lēy 이 ī	신 zin	셰 sēy 이 ī	시 sī	셰 sēy 이 ī
츙 tshyoōng 셩 syōng 츙 tshyoōng	큰 k'hoōn 덕 tŏk	례 lēy 도 tŏ 리 lēy	어 ā. 질 tsir 인 in	셩 syōng 인 in 셩 syōng	뜯 stoōt 지 tsī	텬 t'hyōn 셩 syōng 셩 syōng
쥬 tsyoō 우 oō 세쯔 sēyts'	도구 tŏk'	레 lēy 이 ī 애 gī	요 yŏ 시 sī	헌 hīn 지 tsī 리 rī	고 kŏ 고 kŏ 로 rŏ 사 zā 시 sī	우 oō 미 mī 즈 tsoŏ 기 kī

Nat- and aff-

Filial piety	Practice	Wisdom	Righteousness	Clever	Intention	Affections
孝	行	智	義	賢	意	情
고 kŏ 우 oō	고 kŏ 우 oō	지 tsī		견 kēyn	이 ī	셰 sēy 이 ī
효 hyŏ 도 tŏ 효 hyŏ	힝 hăing 실 sīr 힝 hăing	지 tsī 혜 hēy 지 tsī	올 ŏr 홀 hoŏr 의 oŏī	어 ŏ 질 tsir 현 hyōn	뜯 stoŏt 의 oŏī	뜯 stoŏt 졍 tsyong
고 kŏ 오 ŏ 고 kŏ 오 ŏ	고 ko 우 oō 셰 sēy 기 kī	지 tsī 예 ēy	기 gī	가 kā 시 sī 고 kŏ 시 sī	고 kŏ 고 kŏ 로 rŏ 기 gī	나 nā 사 sā 게 kēy

22

In telli-gent	To plan Scheming	Bravery	Talent	Respectful To respect	Pure	Humility	Sincerity
明聰	謀	勇	才	敬	廉	謙	誠
	맛 bŏ 우 oō	요 yŏ 우 oō		겨 kēy 이 ī	련 lēyn	켜 kēyn	셰 sēy 이 ī
총 tshŏng 명 myong	쇠 skŏī 모 mŏ	놀 năr 뵐 nāīr 용 yŏng	지 tsăī 조 tsŏ 지 tsăī	공 kŏng 경 kyōm 경 kyōm	청 tshŏng 렴 lyōm 렴 lyōm	겸 kyūm 손 sŏn 겸 kyūm	정 tsyūng 셩 syūng 셩 syōng
소 sŏ 우 oō 메 mēy 이 ī	하 hā 가 kā 루 roō	이 ī 시 sī 무 moō	사 sā 이 ī	우 oō 야 yā 마 mā 우 oō	셰 sēy 이 ī 렌 lēyn	헤 hēy 리 rī 구 koō 따 dā 루 roō	셰 sēy 이 ī 신 sīn

Penetra-tion	Ingenious	Boldness Ferocious Fierceness	Ability To be able	Careful	Chaste	Yielding	Faithful-ness
悟穎	慧	猛	能	愼	貞	讓	信
여 ēy 이 ī ㅇ고 gŏ	계 kēy 이 ī	모 mŏ 우 oō	노 nŏ 우 oō	신 sīn	뎨 tē 이 ī	쇼 zyŏ 우 oō	신 sīn
여 yō 오 ŏ	슬 soŏr 긔 koŏī 혜 hēy	밍 măīng 녈 nyōr 밍 măīng	느 noŏng 올 hăr 능 noŏng	삼 sām 갈 kār 신 sīn	고 kŏ 들 toŏr 졍 tsyōng	스 să 양 yāng 양 yāng	미 mī 들 toor 신 sīn
하 hā 즈 tsoŏ 메 mēy 이 ī	리 rī 고 kŏ 우 oō	다 tā 계 kēy 시 sī	요 yŏ 구 koō	즈 tsoŏ 즈 tsoŏ 시 sī 무 moō	맏 māt 스 soŏ ㅇ구 goō	신 sīn 샤 syāk' 구	다 tā 노 nŏ 미 mī

倭語類解

Japanese words assorted and explained Vol..

二三

Sorrow	Joy	To enquire into minutely	Hard Stiff	Liberal	Amicable Harmonious	Correct	Honest
哀	喜	詳	剛	寬	和	端正	純朴
아 ā 이 ī	기 kī	쇼 syŏ 우 oō	고 kŏ 우 oō	관 kwān	과 kwā	단 tān 쇼 syŏ 우 oō	쥰 zyoōn 하구 hāk'
슬 soŏr 플 p'hŏor 이 ăī	긷 kīt 글 koŏr 희 koŏī	즈 tsă 세 sēy 샹 syāng	근 koŏt 셜 sēr 강 kāng	너 nŏ 를 roŏr 관 kwān	고 kŏ 롤 rŏr 화 hwā	단 tān 졍 tsyōng	슌 syoōn 박 pāk
나 nā 끠 gŏ 리 rī	요 yŏ 로 rŏ 고 kŏ 비 pī	구 koō 와 wā 시 sī 우 oō	즈 tsoŏ 요 yŏ 시 sī	오 ŏ 우 oō 이 ī 나 nā	야 yā 와 wā 라 rā 구 goō	다 tā 다 dā 시 sī 이 ī	쇼 syoōn 보구 bŏk'' / 스 soō 나 nā 오 ŏ

Delight	Anger	To examine	Diligent	Pliant Soft	Obedient Complying	Cautious	Upright
樂	怒	察	敏	柔	順	小心	純直
라구 lāk'	도 dŏ	사쯔 sāts'	빈 bīn	시 zī 우 oō	쥰 zyoōn	쇼 syŏ 우 oō 신 sīn	쥰 zyoōn 죠구 tsyŏk'
즐 tsoŏr 길 kīr 락 rāk	노 nŏ 홀 hăr 노 nŏ	술 săr 필 p'hīr 찰 tshār	민 mīn 쳡 ts'hyŏp 민 mīn	부 poō 드 toŏ 러 rŏ 올 ŏr 유 yoō	슌 syoōn 홀 hăr 슌 syoon	쇼 syŏ 심 sīm	슌 syoōn 직 tsik
오 ŏ 모 mŏ 시 sī 로 rŏ 구 kkoō	하 hā 라 rā 다 tā 데 tē	삳 sāt 스 soŏ 루 roō	사 sā 도 tŏ 시 sī	야 yā 와 wā 라 rā 가 kā	고 kŏ 우 oō 쥰 zyoōn	즈 tsoŏ 즈 tsoŏ 시 sī 무 moo	쇼 syŏ 우 oō 도 tŏ 우 oō

Sincere	Economical	Strong	Firm	Good	Niggardly	Lust	Love
款誠	儉	强	壯	善	吝	慾	愛
세 sēy 이 ī 관 kwan	켠 kēyn	교 kyŏ 우 oŏ	소 sŏ 우 oŏ	셴 seyn	린 lin	요구 yŏk'	아 ā 이 ī
셩 syŏng 관 kwān	검 kōm 소 sŏ 검 kōm	강 kāng 홀 hăr 강 kāng	장 tsāng 홀 hăr 장 tsāng	잘 tsăr 홀 hăr 션 syŏn	린 lin 홀 hăr 린 lin	욕 yŏk 심 sĭn 욕 yŏk	스 să 랑 rāng 이 ăi
도 tŏ 리 rĭ 모 mŏ 즈 tsoŏ	켠 kēyn 야구 yāk'	고 kŏ 와 wā 시 sĭ	사 sā 관 kān 나 nā 루 roŏ	요 yŏ 이 ī / 요 yŏ 시 sĭ	시 sĭ 마쯔 māts'	요구 yŏk' 신 sĭn	이 ī 도 tŏ 오 ŏ 시 sĭ

Stubborn	Extravagant	Weak	Robust	Bad	Sparing	Covetousness	Hatred
執固	奢	弱	健	惡	惜	貪	憎
고 kŏ 시 sĭ 우 oŏ	샤 syā	샤구 zyāk'	켠 kēyn	아구 āk'	셰 sēy 기 kĭ	단 tān	소 sŏ 우 oŏ
고 kŏ 집 tsip	샤 syā 치 ts'hī 샤 syā	약 yāk 홀 hăr 약 yāk	건 kŏn 장 tsāng 건 kŏn	모 mŏ 질 tsĭr 악 āk	앗 āt 길 kĭr 셕 syŏk	탐 t'hām 홀 hăr 탐 t'hām	뮈 mŏoi 올 ŏr 즁 tsoŏng
이 ī 즈 tsoŏ 즈 zoŏ 나 nā	요 yŏ 오 gŏ 루 roŏ	요 yŏ 와 wā 시 sĭ	스 soŏ 고 kŏ 야 yā 가 kā	아 a 시 sĭ 시 sĭ / 니 nĭ 구 koo 시 sĭ	오 ŏ 시 sĭ 무 moŏ	무 moŏ 사 sā 보 bŏ 루 roŏ	니 nĭ 구 koo 무 moo

倭語類解

Japanese words assorted and explained Vol. I

二三

To err	Stupid	Diligent	Just Up right	Cruel	Abrupt	Haughty	Real Certain
迷	愚	勤	正公	忍殘	突唐	慢倨	實確
뻬 bēy 이 ī	구 goō	긴 kīn	고 kǒ 우 oō 쇼 syǒ 우 oō	ᅀᅡᆫ zān ᅀᅵᆫ zīn	도 tō 우 oō 도쯔 tǒts'	교 kyǒ 만 mān	가구 kāk' 시쯔 zits'
아 ā 득 toǒk 홀 hǎr 미 mī	어 ō 릴 rīr 우 oō	부 poō 즈 tsoǒ 런 rōn 홀 hǎr 근 koǒn	공 kōng 정 tsyōng	잔 tsān 인 īn	당 tāng 돌 tǒr	거 kō 만 mān	확 hwāk 실 sīr
마 mā 요 yǒ 우 oō	오 ǒ 로 rǒ 까 kkā	즈 tsoǒ 도 tǒ 무 moō 루 roō	스 soǒ 나 nā 오 ǒ	아 ā 사 sā 마 mā 시 sī	다 tā 이 ī 기 kī 나 nā	오 ǒ 오 ǒ 헤 hēy 이 ī 나 nā	다 tā 시 sī 까 kkā 나 nā

To mislead	Unskilful	Idle	Partial Depraved	Lecherous Wanton	Floating Unsettled	Vague	Stiff
惑	拙	懶	僻偏	惡姦	濫汎	濶迂	強木
고구 kǒk'	세쯔 sěyts'	란 lān	헨 hēyn 헤 hēy 기 kī	간 kān 아구 āk'	한 hwān 란 lān	우 oō 과쯔 kwāts'	보구 bǒk' 교 kyǒ 우 oō
혹 hǒk' 홀 hǎr 홀 nǒk'	조로 tsǒr 올 hǎr 졸 tsǒr	게 kē 어 ǒ 를 roǒr 란 lān	편 phyōn 벽 pyōk	간 kān 악 āk	범 pōm 람 lām	오 ǒ 활 hwār	목 mǒk 강 kāng
마 mā 요 yǒ 우 oō 호 hǒ 레 rēy	즈 tsoǒ 다 tā 나 nā 시 sī	오 ǒ 고 kǒ 다 tā 루 roō	예 ēy 고 kǒ 히 hī 기 kī	가 kā 다 tā 마 mā 시 sī 이 ī	오 ǒ 우 oō 베 pēy 나 nā	스 soǒ 이 ī 산 sān	긷 kit 시 sī 구 koō

語類解上 性情 24

A word	言語 words and Expressions	Lewd Debauched	Empty vacant	Perverse Selfwilled	Profligate	Ingenious clever	Hasty
言		亂淫	虛	愎	恣	巧	躁
연 geyn			교 kyŏ	혹 hŏk	시 sī	고우 kŏ oŏ	소우 sŏ oŏ
말 mār 숨 sām 언 ŏn		음 ŏŏm 란 lān	허 hŏ ㅅ stŏir 될 허 hŏ	퍅 p'hyāk 홀 hăr 퍅 p'hyāk	방 pāng ᄌᆞ tsă ᄌᆞ tsă	공 kŏng 교 kyŏ 교 kyŏ	조 tsŏ 홀 hăr 조 tsŏ
고 kŏ 도 tŏ 바 pā		인 in 란 lān	무 moŏ 나 nā 시 sī 이 ī	단 tān 개 kkī 나 nā	고 kŏ 고 kŏ 로 rŏ 마 mā 마 mā	다 tā 구 koŏ 미 mī	고 kŏ 고 kŏ 로 rŏ 미 mī 시 zī 가 kkā 이 ī

Expressions			Disobedient	Foolish	Libidinous Lewd	Artful	Dull
辭			惡悖	癡	姦	術	鈍
시 zi			하 hā 이 ī 아구 āk	지 tsi	간 kān		돈 dŏn
말 mār 솜 săm 스 să			패 p'hāi 악 āk	어 ŏ 릴 rir 치 ts'hī	간 kān 사 sā 간 kān	지 tsāi 조 tsŏ 술 syuŏr	둔 toŏn 홀 hăr 둔 toŏn
모 mŏ 노 nŏ 가 gā 다 tā 리 ri			오 ŏ 우 oŏ 도 dŏ 우 oŏ 나 nā	구 goŏ 지 tsī / 오 ŏ 로 rŏ 소 sŏ 가 kkā	와 wā 루 roŏ 가 gā 시 sī 고 kŏ 이 ī	슈즈 zyoŏts	돈 dŏn 나 nā

倭語類解

Japanese words assorted and explained Vol. I

二四

To pledge in drinking	To open one's mouth	To deliberate To consult	To inform To proclaim	To hear	To announce	To reprove	To question To ask
酢酬	口開	論議	告	聞	稟	諫	問
시 sī 우 oō 사구 sāk'	가 kā 이 ī 고 kŏ 우 oō	긔 gī 론 lŏn	교 kŏ 우 oō	븐 boōn	힌 hīn	간 kān	븐 boōn
슈 syoō 자 tsāk'	기 kăi 구 koō	의 ŏŏī 론 lŏn	고 kŏ 홀 hăr 고 kŏ	들 toŏr 닐 nīr 문 moōn	픔 p'hoōm 홀 hăr 픔 p'hoōm	간 kān 홀 hăr 간 kān	무 moō 름 roŏr 문 moōn
유 yoō 이 ī 고 kŏ 다 tā 에 ēy	구 koō 지 tsī 오 ŏ 히 hī 라구 rāk'	소 sŏ 우 oō 딴 dān 다 dā 잇 gŏ 우 oō	시 sī 라 rā 세 sĕy 즈 tsoō 에 gey	기 kī 가 kā 세 sēy	무 măŏō 시 sī 아 ā 애 gēy	이 ī 사 sā 무 moō	도 tŏ 우 oō

Will it do, or not?	To commence a discourse	To debate	To accuse To defend one's self	To tell To publish	To intreat To beg	To admonish To enjoin	To answer To reply
否可	論開	論公	訴	白	請	誡	答
가 kā 후 hoō	가 kā 이 ī 유 yoō		소 sŏ	하구 hāk'	세 sēy 이 ī	가 kā 이 ī	도 tŏ 우 oō
가 kā 부 poō	기 kăi 유 yoō	공 kŏng 론 lŏn	할 hăr 소 sŏ	숣 sŏr 올 ŏr 뵉 păik	청 tshyŏng 홀 hăr 청 tshyŏng	경 kyŏng 계 kēy 계 kēy	디 tăi 답 tāp 답 tāp
요 yŏ 시 sī 아 ā 시 sī	사 sā 도 tŏ 스 soŏ	고 kŏ 우 oō 론 lŏn	소 sŏ 시 sī 루 roō	유 yoō 이 ī 와 wā 게 kēy	마 mā 네 nē 구 koō 구 koō 세 sēy 이 gī	이 ī 마 mā 시 sī 메 mēy	고 kŏ 다 tā 예 ēy

25

Playful talk	Chit chat Leisure talk	An oath Agreement	To praise	A constant attendant	To direct	To transmit a message	To take up To lift up
談弄	談閑	盟	譽	介紹	揮指	喝傳	起提
로우단 lŏ oō tān	간단 kān tān	메이 mēy ī	요 yŏ	쇼우가이 syŏ oō kā ī	시기 sī kī	텐가쯔 tēn kāts'	데이기 tē ī kī
롱담 lŏng tām	한담 hān tām	밍셰밍 māing sēy māing	기릐예 kī rīr ēy	쇼개 syŏ kāi	지휘 tsī hooī	젼갈 tsyōn kār	뎨긔 tēy kooī
조우단 zŏ oō tān	시즈가니가달루 sī tsoŏ kkā nī kā tār'	지게리 tsī gī rī	호메루 hŏ mēyr'	나가사빠구 nā kā sā bāk'	사시스 sā sī zoŏ	도리즈게 tŏ rī tsoŏ gī	오고스 ŏ kŏs'

To jest To joke	Empty words	A covenant To engage	To exhort	To assent to	To know one's duty	To order To command	To receive an order
弄嘲	言空	約	勸	諾許	委知	付分	付當
도우로우 tŏ oō lŏ oō	고우엔 kŏ oō gēyn	야구 yāk'	관 kwān	교다구 kyŏ dāk'	지이 tsī ī	분후 poōn hoō	도우후 tŏ oō hoō
죠롱 tsyŏ lŏng	공언 kŏng on	언약약 ŏn yāk yāk	권홀권 kwōn hăr kwōn	허낙 hŏ näk	지위 tsī oōī	분부 poōn poō	당부 tang poō
아사계루 ā zā kēyr'	소라고도 sŏ rā gŏ tŏ	야구소구 yāk' sōk	시유루 sī yoō roo / 스스무 soŏ soŏ moō	우게고우 oō kēy kŏ oō	후레 hoō rēy / 시라세 sī rā sēy	이이즈게 ī ī tsoŏ kēy	이이즈계 ī ī tsoŏ kēy

倭語類解 上

Japanese Words Collected and Explained Vol. I.

言語 Words and Expressions

To meditate / To be silent	To boast / To be proud	To vilify	To slander / To calumniate	To chide	To strive	To go to law / To plead	A whisper
默	矜	毁	讒	叱	爭	訟	附耳語
모구 mŏk'	교우 kyŏ oō	기 ki	산 zān	시쯔 sits'	소우 sŏ oō	쇼우 syŏ oō	후시교 hoō zī gyŏ
줌줌묵 tsăm tsăm mōok	쟈랑궁 tsyā rāng kōong	헐훼 hŏr hwōi	춤소참 tshām sŏ tshām	꾸지즐즐 skoō tsī tsoŏr tsoŏr	드톨징 tă thŏr săing	숑亽숑 syŏng sā syŏng	부이어 poō ī ŏ
야하리 yā hā rī	호고루 hŏ kŏr'	구스례 koō zoŏ rēy	산소우 sān sŏ oō	시가루 sī kā roō	아라소우 ā rā sŏ oō	구시 kóō zī	소소나구 sŏ sŏ nāk'

To stammer	To distinguish	To ridicule / To jeer	To flatter	To seduce / To mislead	To interrogate	To incite a quarrel	Verbose / Loquacious
訥	辯	譏	諛	誘	詰	嗾	譫語
도쯔 dŏts'	변 pēyn	기 ki	유 yoō	이우 ī oō	기쯔 kits'	소우 sŏ oŏ	션교 sēyn gyŏ
말구듈눌 mār koō toŏr noŏr	말잘홀변 mār tsār hăr pyōn	비우솔긔 pī oō soŏr koŏī	아당홀유 ā tāng hăr yoō	달낼우 tār nāir oō	힐난홀힐 hīr nān hăr hīr	쵸길주 tshyŏ kir tsoō	셤어 syōm ō
구지도모루 koō tsī dŏ mŏr'	벤졔쯔 pēyn zēyts'	나부루 nā poō roō	헤쯔로우 hēyts' rŏ oō	다라스 tā rā soŏ	나시루 nā zī roō	히소까니유우 hī sŏ kkā nī yoō oō	우쯔쯔고도바 oō tsoŏts' kŏ tŏ bā

26 二十六

A little / Rather much	To return / Back again	And	All		To speak disorderly	To speak roughly	To borrow expressions / To pretend
頗	返	而	凡	語辭	發妄	澁語	托假
하 hāā	헨 hēyn	ᅀᅵ zī	한 hān		모 mŏ 우 oō 바쯔 pāts'	교 gyŏ 시 sī 우 oō	가 kā 다구 tāk'
자 tsă 못 mŏt 파 phā	도 tŏ 로 rŏ 혈 hyŏr 반 pan	말 mār 니 nī 올 oŏr 이 ī	무 mŏō 릇 rŏot 범 pom	Particles	망 māng 발 pār	어 ŏ 삽 sāp	가 kā 탁 t'hāk
고 kŏ 도 tŏ 니 nī	가 kā 예 ēy 데 tē	시 sī 고 kŏ 우 oō 시 sī 데 tē	오 ŏ 요 yŏ 소 sŏ		뫼 bŏ 우 oō 하 hā	구 koō 지 tsī 시 sī 부루 poōr'	다구 tāk' 스 soŏ 루 roō

Shall, Will / About to be	Necessary	In, at	By, with, In order to		To reveal a secret	To praise ones-self	To compliment
将	須	扵	以		泄漏	稱自	頉稱
쇼 syŏ 우 pŏ	슈 syoō	요 yŏ	이 ī		로 lŏ 우 oō 세쯔 sēyts'	ᅀᅵ zī 쇼 syŏ 우 oō	쇼 syŏ 우 oō 다쯔 tāts'
장 tsyāng 찻 tshăt 장 tsyāng	모 mŏ 로 rŏ 미 mī 슈 syoo	늘 noŏr 어 ŏ	ᄡᅥ psŏ 이 ī		루 loō 설 syŏr	자 tsā 칭 tshing	칭 tshing 탈 t'hār
하 hā 다 tā 조 tsoŏ 애 gī	가 kā 마 mā 예 ēy 데 tē	오 ŏ 이 ī 데 tē	몯 mŏt 데 tē		모 mŏ 라 rā 스 soŏ	ᅀᅵ zī 만 mān	가 kā 고 kŏ 즈 tsoō 게 kēy

倭語類解

Japanese words associated and explained Vol

倭語類解 上

...nese ...rds ...cted ...nd ...uned ...I.

語辭

Part-

How	Just Merely	Rather Better	Still	But	Also Again	Yet Still	Which
幾	姑	寧	猶	但	又	尤	所
기 kĭ	고 kŏ	녕 nē 이 ĭ	이 ĭ 우 oō	단 tān	이 ĭ 우 oō	이 ĭ 우 oō	쇼 syŏ
거 kŏ 의 oŏĭ 긔 koŏĭ	아 ā 직 tsĭk 고 kŏ	출 tshăr 아 ā 리 rĭ 녕 nyōng	오 ŏ 히 hĭ 려 ryō 유 yoō	다 tā 만 mān 단 tān	또 ttŏ 우 oō	더 tō 욱 ōok 우 oō	바 pā 소 sŏ
다 tā 분 poŏn	마 즈 māts'	세 sēy 메 mēy 데 tē	나 nä 오 ŏ 시 sĭ	다 tā 다 tā 시 sĭ	마 mā 다 tā	나 nā 오 ŏ	오 ŏ 루 roō

27

二七

What	To obtain To get	Vainly only	Very	Only	More	Self One's-self	That
何	得	徒	最	惟	更	自	其
가 kā	도 구 tŏk	도 tŏ	사 sā 이 ĭ	이 ĭ	고 kĕ 우 oō	시 zĭ	기 kĭ
엇 ōt 지 tsĭ 하 hā	시 sĭ 러 rō 곰 kŏm 득 took	흔 hăn 갓 kāt 도 tŏ	[illegible] kă 상 tsăng 최 tshŏĭ	오 ŏ 직 tsik 유 yoō	다 tā 시 sĭ 킹 kăing	스 soŏ 스 soŏ 로 rŏ 즈 tsă	그 koŏ 기 kĭ
도 dŏ 우 oō 시 sĭ 떼 ttē 나 nā 셰 zēy 니 nĭ	예 ēy 루 roō	히 hĭ 도 tŏ 예 ēy 니 nĭ	이 ĭ 고 kŏ 우 oō	다 tā 다 dā	가 kā 사 sā 비 nē 데 tē	미 mĭ 즈 tsoŏ 가 kā 라 rā	소 sŏ 노 nŏ

Therefore	Because	Especial	Ought Suitable	To do To make	Then, after that	If	Then consequently
故	因	特	宜	爲	卽	若	方
고 kŏ	인 in	도구 tŏk'	긔 gī	이 ī	소구 sŏk'	샤구 zyāk'	호우 hŏ ōō
짐 tsīm 즛 tsoŏt 고 kŏ	인 in 홀 hăr 인 in	특 thŏŏk 별 pyŏr 특 t'hŏŏk	맛 māt 당 tāng 의 oŏī	홀 hăr 위 ooī	즉 tsoŏk 재 tsăī 즉 tsoŏk	만 mān 일 ir 약 yāk	바 pā 야 ya 흐 hoŏ 로 rŏ 방 pāng
고 kŏ 도 to 사 sā 라 ra	욧 yŏt 데 tē	도구 tŏk' 벳 bēyt 즈 tsoŏ	몯 mŏt 도 tŏ 모 mŏ	나 nā 루 roō	스 soŏ 나 nā 와 wā 지 tsī	모 mŏ 시 sī / 만 mān 니 nī 지 tsī	사 sā 이 ī 쥬 tsyoō 우 ōō

But However	Finally	To dare May be	Every	All together	Luckily In case that	Past Done	Whether, or, any, some
然	竟	敢	每	皆	幸	曾	或
연 zeyn	게 kēy 이 ī	간 kān	빠 bā 이 ī	가 kā 이 ī	고 kŏ 우 ōō	소 sŏ 우 ōō	고구 kŏk'
그 koŏ 럴 rŏr 연 yŏn	마 mā 참 tshăm 내 năī 경 kyŏng	감 kăm 히 hi 감 kăm	매 măī 양 yāng 매 măī	다 tā 개 kăi	힝 hăing 혀 hyŏng 힝 hăing	일 ir 즉 tsoŏk 증 tsoŏng	혹 hŏk 혹 hŏk
시 sī 가 ka 레 rēy 바 pā	오 ŏ 와 wā 루 roō 마 mā 데 tē	아 ā 예 ēy 데 tē	마 mā 이 ī	미 mā 나 nā	모 mŏ 시 sī	가 kā 즈 tsoŏ 데 ttē	아 ā 루 roō 이 ī 와 wā

nese rds ted d ained 1.

語辭

Extreme	Must To compel	To cause To make	To speak	It is, Yes	Correspond-ing	Since	Finally Forthwith
極	必	使	曰	是	應	旣	遂
격 kyŏk'	히ᄶ hits'	시 sī	예ᄶ ēyts'	시 sī	요 yŏ 우 ŏŏ	기 kī	스 soŏ 이 ī
극 kŏŏk ᄒᆞᆯ hăr 극 kŏŏk	반 pan 듯 tŏŏt 필 p'hĭr	ᄒᆞ hă 어 yŏ 곰 kŏm ᄉᆞ să	ᄆᆞᆯ măr 왈 wār	이 ī 시 si	벅 pŏk 벅 pok 응 ŏŏng	임 īm 의 ŏŏī 긔 kŏŏī	드 toŏ 듧 tooĭr 슈 syoō
싱 sī 고구 gŏk'	가 kā 나 nā 라스 raz'	셰 sey 시 sī 메 mēy	노 nŏ 나 tā 모 mŏ 우 ŏŏ	고 kŏ 레 rēy	신 sīt ᄭᅡ kkā 도 tŏ	스 soŏ 데 tē 니 nī	즈 tsoŏ 이 ī 니 ni

Part

28

二

May, Can Ought	Although	To give to	To say	This	Truly	Moreover	To happen Now & then
可	雖	與	云	此	誠	況	適
가 kā	스 soŏ 이 ī	요 yŏ	운 ŏŏn	시 sī	셰 sey 이 ī	교 kyŏ 우 ŏŏ	데 tē 기 kī
ᄋᆞᆯ ŏr ᄒᆞᆯ hăr 가 kā	비 pī 록 rŏk 슈 syoō	다 tā 몯 mŏr 여 yŏ	니 nī ᄅᆞᆯ răr 운 ŏŏn	이 ī ᄎᆞ ts'hă	진 tsīn 실 sīr 노 nŏ 셩 syŏng	ᄒᆞ hă ᄆᆞᆯ moŏr 며 myŏ 황 hwāng	마 mā 즘 tsăm 뎍 tyŏk
베 pēy 구 koō	다 tā 도 tŏ	아 ā 다 tā	유 yoŏ 우 ŏō	고 kŏ 노 nŏ	마 mā 고 kŏ	이 ī 완 wān	오 ŏ 리 rī
베 pey 기 kī	예 ey	유 yoo 루 roo			도 tŏ	야 yā	후 hoō 시 si

To sit down		Want, need Requisite	Other Different	General Universal	Carelessly Any how	Empty In vain	From out of
坐		要	别	都	聊	空	自
사 zā	動静	요 yŏ 우 oō	베쯔 pēyts'	도 tŏ	료 lyŏ 우 oō	고 kŏ 우 oō	시 zi
안 ān 졸 tsoŏr 좌 tswā	Motion and Rest	종 tsŏng 요 yŏ 요 yŏ	다 tā 름 roŏr 별 pyor	모 mŏ 둘 tŏr 도 tŏ	에 āi 오 ŏ 라 rā 지 tsi 로 rŏ	쇽 syŏk 졀 tsyŏr 업 ŏp 살 sār 공 kŏng	부 poō 들 t'hoŏr 자 tsā
이 ī 도 tŏ 루 roō		간 kān 요 yŏ 우 oō / 가 kā 나 nā 메 mey	가구 kāk' 베쯔 pēyts'	스 soŏ 베 pēy 데 tē	이 ī 사 sā 사 sā 가 kā	이 ī 다 tā 즈 tsoŏ 라 rā	요 yŏ 리 rī

To rise up		Every, all	Together with	Every one	Addicted to Devotedly Entirely	Suddenly	To wish To desire
起		諸	并	各	專	忽	願
기 kī		죠 zyŏ	헤 hēy 이 ī	가구 kāk'	센 sēyn	고쯔 kŏts'	완 gwān
닐 nir 긔 kooi		모 mŏ 들 toŏr 제 tsēy	아 hā 올 ŏr 병 pyŏng	각 kāk 각 kāk	오 ŏ 로 rŏ 젼 tsyŏn	문 moōn 득 toŏk 홀 hŏr	원 wŏn 홀 hăr 원 wŏn
오 ŏ 기 kī		모 mŏ 로 rŏ 모 mŏ 로 rŏ	소 sŏ 예 ēy 데 te	오 ŏ 노 nŏ 오 ŏ 노 nŏ	몯 mŏt 바 pā 기 [illegible] 더 ri	다 tā 지 tsī 마 mā 지 tsi	넹 nē 고 gŏ 우 oo

倭語類解

Japanese words associated and explained Vol.

二八

倭語類解上

These words dotted and joined I.

動靜 Motion and Rest.

To look down	To go out	To advance	To return	To go To depart	To move To stir	To walk	To stand
俯	出	進	還	去	動	行	立
후 hoō	슈ㅈ syoōts'	신 sīn	관 kwān	고 kǒ	도 tǒ 우 oō	고 ko 우 oǒ	리 lī 우 oō
구 koō 볼 poǒr 부 poō	날 nār 출 ts'hyoōr	나 nā 올 ǒr 진 tsīn	도 tǒ 라 rā 올 ǒr 환 hwān	갈 kār 거 kǒ	움 oōm 즉 tsǒok 일 īr 동 tǒng	녈 nēyr 힝 hāing	셜 syǒr 립 līp
구 koō 로 rǒ 뿌구 bǒok'	이 ī 스루 zoǒr'	스 soǒ 스무 soǒm'	가 kā 예루 ēyr'	유구 yōok'	우 oō 꼬고 gǒk'	아 ā 루구 roōk'	다 tā 지 tsī

29

To look up	To go in To enter	To retire To retreat	To revert	To come	To walk up and down	To run	To step
仰	入	退	歸	來	徊徘	走	步
교 kyǒ 우 oō	뉴 nyoō 우 oō	다 tā 이 ī	기 kī	라 lā 이 ī	하 hā 이 ī 과 kwā 이 ī	소 sǒ 우 oǒ	호 hǒ
우 oō 럴 rōr 앙 āng	들 toǒr 입 ip	무 moō 를 roǒr 퇴 t'hōi	도 tǒ 라 rā 갈 kār 귀 kwī	올 ǒr 릭 lāi	빅 pāi 회 hōi	돌 tǎr 올 oǒr 주 tsoō	거 kō 름 roōm 보 pǒ
아 ā 오 ǒ 구 goō	이루 īr'	시 sī 리 rī 소구 zǒk'	모 mǒ 도루 dǒr'	기 kī 다루 tār'	다 tā 지 tsī 마 mā 와루 wār'	하 hā 시루 sīr	아 ā 유 yoō 미 mī

To squint	To gaze, to contemplate	To be still To be quiet	To bend To crook	To follow To comply	To worship To bow down	To ascend To mount	To upset To fall down
眄	顧	靜	屈	隨	拜	登	顚
면 meyn	고 kŏ	셰 sey 이 ī	구ᇧ kōots'	스 zoō 이 ī		도 tŏ 우 oō	뎐 tēn
훌 hoŏr 궐 kwir 면 myōn	도 tŏ 라 rā 볼 pŏr 고 kŏ	고 kŏ 요 yŏ 졍 tsyŏng	구 koō 불 poŏr 굴 koon	ᄯᆞᆯ stă 올 roŏr 슈 syoo	졀 tsŏr 비 păi	오 ŏ 를 roŏr 등 tŏong	업 ōp 더 tŏ 질 tsīr 뎐 tyōn
후 hoō 리 rī 가 kā 에 ēy 리 rī 미 루 nīr'	가 kā 에 ēy 리 rī 미 루 nīr'	시 sī 즈 tsoŏ 가 kā 니 nī	가 kā 까 gā 마 루 mār'	시 sī 다 tā 꼬 gŏ 우 oō	하 hā 이 ī	아 ā 까 루 gār'; 노 nŏ 보 루 pŏr'	다 tā 오 ŏ 레 rēy 후 hoō 시 sī

To peep To pry	To look to To hope for	To detain To remain	To straiten To stretch out	To drive out To expel	To bow, to make a bow	To descend To go down	To lay prostrate
窺	望	留	伸	逐	揖	降	沛
기 kī	뽀 bŏ 우 oō	리 rī 우 oō	신 sīn	지 구 tsīk'	이 ī 우 oo	고 kŏ 우 oō	하 hā 이 ī
엿 yōt 볼 pŏr 규 kyoō	ᄇᆞ pā 랄 răr 망 māng	머 mŏ 믈 mŏŏr 류 ryoō	펼 p'hyŏr 신 sīn	ᄶᅩᆺ stsŏ 출 ts'hăr 츅 ts'hyook	읍 oŏp 홀 hăr 읍 oŏp	ᄂᆞ nā 릴 rīr 강 kāng	졋 tsyōt 바 pā 질 tsīr 패 p'hāī
우 oō 가 kā 꼬 gŏ 우 oō	노 nŏ 좀 무 zŏm'	도 tŏ 또 dŏ 마 루 mār'	노 nŏ 베 pēy	옫 ŏt 가 kā 계 kēy	이 ī 조 tsoŏ	사 sā 까 gā 리 rī; 구 koō 따 루 dār'	아 ā 오 ŏ 노 nŏ 구 koō

倭語類解

Japa[nese] wo[rds] assor[ted] ar[e] expla[ined] Vol.

二十九

倭語類解 上

Chinese words noted and romanised I.

動靜 Motion and Rest

To carry To bear	To bring in the hand	To hold under the arm	To hold with both hands	To hold fast	To point	The twinkling of an eye	To see
擔	擕	擁	掬	持	指	瞬	見
담 tān	계 kēy 이 ī	요 yŏ 우 oō	긱 kik' 구	지 tsī	시 sī	슌 syoōn	견 kēyn
멜 mēr 담 tām	잇 it 글 koŏr 휴 hyoō	씰 skīr 옹 ŏng	우 oō 휠 hwīr 국 koŏk	가 kā 질 tsīr 지 tsī	가 kă 륻 răt 칠 ts'hīr 지 tsī	눈 noōn 삼 skăm 쟈 tsya 길 kīr 슌 syoōn	볼 pŏr 견 kyōn
니 nī 나 nā 우 oō	다 tā 즈 tsoŏ 사 sā 예루 ēyr'	와 wā 기 kī 하 hā 사무 sām'	스 soŏ 구 koō 우 oō	모 mŏ 즈 tsoō	사 sā 시 sī	메 mēy 다 tā 다 tā 기 kī	미루 mīr'

30

To strike To knock	To uphold To assist	To embrace	To scratch	To grasp	To beckon	To close the eyes	To look repeatedly
扣	扶	抱	搔	操	揮	瞑	瞥
고 kŏ 우 oō	후 hoō	호 hŏ 우 oō	소 sŏ 우 oō	소 sŏ 우 oō	기 ki	메 mēy 이 ī	베쯔 pēyts'
두 toō 드 tă 릴 rīr 고 kŏ	붇 poōt 들 toŏr 부 poō	안 ān 올 oŏr 포 p'hŏ	글 koŏr 글 koŏr 소 sŏ	잡 tsāp 올 oŏr 조 tsŏ	두 toō 를 toŏr 휘 hoōī	눈 noōn 가 kă 믈 moŏr 명 myōng	눈 noōn 금 kŏom 져 tsyō 길 kīr 별 pyōr
다 tā 다구 tāk	도 tŏ 릳 rīt 즈구 tsoŏr'	이 ī 다구 dāk'	가구 kāk'	도루 tŏr	데 tē 마 mā 네구 nēk'	메 mēy 우 oō 후 hoō 사가 sāg'	시 sī 바 pā 라구 rāk' 미루 mīr'

To deliver To rescue	To roll up	To pick up To gather	To beat To knock	To lift To heave	To pull To row	To push To shove along	To rub in the hand
拯	捲	拾	打	擡	控	推	捏
쇼 zyŏ 우 oŏ	권 kēyn	시 sī 우 oŏ	다 tä	다 tä 이 ī	고 kŏ 우 oŏ	스 soŏ 이 ī	네 쯔 nēts'
건 kŏn 질 tsĭr 증 tsŏng	거 kŏ 들 toŏr 권 kwŏn	주 tsoŏ 울 oŏr 습 soŏp	칠 ts'hīr 다 t'hä	들 toŏr 대 täī	당 tăr 길 wīr 공 kŏng	밀 mīr 츄 ts'hyoŏ	바 pyä 빌 pwīr 녈 nyŏr
스 soŏ 구 koŏ 우 oŏ	마 구 mäk'	히 hī 로 rŏ 우 oŏ	우 즈 oōts'	아 ä 구 루 goŏr'	고 구 kŏg'	오 ŏ 스 soŏ	모 mŏ 무 moŏ

To clasp the hands	To sweep	To rouse To shake	To wipe	To prop To support	To touch To feel	To shake	To dust To wipe away dust
拱	掃	抖	拭	撐	捫	搖	拂
교 kyŏ 우 oŏ	소 sŏ 우 oŏ	도 tŏ 우 oŏ	쇼 구 syŏk'	도 tŏ 우 oŏ	몬 mŏn	요 yŏ 우 oŏ	후 쯔 hōots'
스고 skŏ 줄 tsoŏr 공 kŏng	쓸 ssoŏr 소 sŏ	뻘 ptŏr 두 toŏ	쓰 ssoŏ 슬 soŏr 식 sĭk	괴 kŏī 올 ŏr 탱 t'häng	문 män 질 tsĭr 문 moŏn	흔 hoŏn 들 toŏr 요 yŏ	뻘 ptŏr 칠 ts'hīr 불 poŏr
고 kŏ 마 mā 누 구 noŏk'	하 hā 와 구 wäk'	후 hoŏ 리 rī 스 soŏ 즈 루 tsoŏr'	누 noŏ 구 goŏ 우 oŏ	사 sā 사 sā 에 루 ēyr'	나 nā 즈 루 tsoŏr'	유 yoŏ 사 sā 주 구 tsoŏk'	후 hoŏ 리 rā 스 soŏ 데 tē / 하 hā 라 rā 우 oŏ

倭語類解

Japanese words assorted and explained Vol.

三十

倭語類解上 Chinese words sorted and explained I. 宮室 Buildings

To dream	To sleep / To doze	To lie down to sleep	To step over	To kick	To kneel	To couch	To climb
夢	眠	臥	踰	蹴	跪	蹲	攀
보 bŏ 우 oō	멘 mēyn	과 gwā	유 yoō	시구 sīk'	기 kī	손 sŏn	한 hān
꿈 skoŏm 몽 mŏng	조 tsŏ 올 ăr 면 myŏn	누 noŏ 올 oŏr 와 wā	넘 nŏm 올 oŏr 유 yoō	찰 ts'hăr 축 ts'hyŏok	꿀 skoŏr 개 kŏoē	쭛 tsoŏt 구 koŏ 릴 rīr 준 tsoōn	밟 pāt 들 toŏr 반 pān
유 yoō 메 mēy	네 nē 무 moō 리 rī	후 hoō 세 sēy	고 kŏ 시 sī	계루 kēyr'	히 hī 사 zā 마 mā 즈구 tsoŏk'	즈구 tsoŏk' 바 pā 우 oŏ	나 nā 스루 zoŏr'
31 三一	To go to rest / To lodge	To lie prostrate	To upset / Upside down	To trample	To stumble	To squat	To dance / To jump
	宿	伏	倒	蹈	蹶	踞	躍
	시구 sīk'	후구 hoōk'	도 tŏ 우 oō	도 tŏ 우 oō	계쯔 kēyts'	교 kyŏ	야구 yāk'
	잘 tsār 숙 syoŏk	업 ŏp 될 twīr 복 pŏk	걷 kŏt 구 koŏ 러 rŏ 질 tsīr 도 tŏ	밟 părp 올 oŏr 도 tŏ	거 kŏ 칠 ts'hīr 궐 kwŏr	거 kŏ 러 rŏ 안 ān 줄 tsoŏr 거 kŏ	뛸 stoōīr 약 yāk
	네루 nēr'	후 hoō 시 sī	사 sā 가 kā 사 sā 마 mā	후 hoō 무 moō	조 tsoŏ 마 mā 즈구 tsoŏk'	고 kŏ 시 sī 가 kā 게루 kēyr'	오 ŏ 도 dŏ 리 rī

倭語類解

Japanese words associated and explained

Vol.

宮室

Buildings

A side room	A front room	A bed room	A house	An upper chamber	The great Interior	A palace
廊	廳	閨	家	樓	内大	宮
로 lŏ 우 oō		계 kēy 이 ī	가 kā	로 lŏ 우 oō	다 tā 이 ī 따 dā 이 ī	규 kyoō 우 oō
행 hăng 랑 răng 랑 răng	집 tsīp 텽 t'hō	도 tŏ 장 tsāng 규 kyoō	집 tsīp 가 kā	다 tā 릭 rīk 루 roō	대 tăi 내 năi	집 tsīp 궁 koōng
나 nā 가 gā 야 yā	데 tē 이 ī	네 nē 야 yā 구 koō 즈 tsoō 로 rŏ	이 ī 예 ēy	니 nī 가 kā 이 ī	오 ŏ 오 ŏ 우 oō 지 tsī	미 mī 야 yā

A cottage A straw shed	A kitchen	A sitting room A parlour	A room A chamber	A pavilion	A hall	The precincts of the palace
屋茅	厨	廊舍	房	亭	殿	闕
보 bŏ 우 oō 오 ŏk' 구	쥬 tsyoō 우 oō	샤 syā 로 lŏ 우 oō	호 hŏ 우 oō	데 tē 이 ī	뎐 tēn	계쯔 kēyts'
모 mŏ 옥 ŏk	부 poō 억 ŏk 쥬 tsyoō	샤 syā 랑 lāng	구 koō 들 toŏr 방 pāng	뎡 tyōng 자 tsă 뎡 tyōng	집 tsīp 뎐 tyōn	집 tsīp 궐 kwōr
와 wā 라 rā 야 yā	구 koō 리 rī 야 yā	자 zā 시 sī 기 kī	헤 hēy 야 yā 후 hoō 사 sā	데 tē 이 ī 시 sī	도 tŏ 노 nŏ	긴 kīn 리 rī

三一

倭語類解 上

Chinese words ... and ... I.

宮室 Buildings

A Tile	Eaves	A rafter	A pillar	A stanchion	A beam	A privy	A lodge A stage
瓦	簷	椽	柱	梲	樑	厠	棚
와 gwā	연 eyn	뎬 tēn	죠 tsyŏ	세쯔 seyts'	료 lyŏ 우 oō	속 sŏk	호 hō 우 oō
지 tsi 새 sāi 와 wā	쳠 ts'hyŏm 하 hā 쳠 tshyŏm	셔 syŏ 연 yŏn	기 kī 동 tŏng 쥬 tsyoō	디 tāi 공 kong 졀 tsyŏr	들 toŏr ᄉ보 spŏ 량 lyāng	뒤 toōi ᄉ간 skān 측 ts'hook	가 kā 가 kā 붕 poōng
가 kā 와 wā 라 rā	노 nŏ 기 kī	다 tā 루 roō 기 kī	하 hā 시 sī 라 rā	고 kŏ 우 oō 료 lyŏ 우 oō	우 oō 즈 tsoŏ 빠 bā 리 rī	가 kā 와 wā 야 yā	가 kā 리 rī 야 yā

A door	A roof	A penthouse	The base of a pillar	A post	A cross beam	A coal hole	A stable
門	甍	箔葺	礎	棟	桁	幕炭	廐
몬 mŏn	모 mŏ 우 oō	이 ī 하구 hāk'	소 sŏ	도 tŏ 우 oō	고 kŏ 우 oō	단 tān 마구 māk'	규 kyoō 우 oō
문 moōn 문 moōn	기 kī 싀 soŏ rī 밍 māing	위 wī 박 pāk	쥬 tsyoō 츄 tshyoō 초 ts'hŏ	므 mă 르 rā 동 tŏng	도 tŏ 리 rī 힝 hāing	탄 t'hān 막 māk	외 ŏī 양 yāng 구 koō
가 kā 도 dŏ	하 hā 후 hoō	고 kŏ 마 mā 이 ī	이 ī 시 sī 즈 tsoŏ 예 ēy	무 moō 나 nā 기 gī	계 key 다 tā	스 soŏ 미 mī 고 gŏ 야 yā	무 boō 마 mā 야 yā

32

三二

A wainscoat	A board	A railing	A lock	An inner door	A window	To open	A bar
壁	子板	杆欄	鈸	户	窓	開	扉柴
헤 hey 기 ki	한 hān 시 sī		쥬쯔 zyoots	고 kŏ	소 sŏ 우 oō	가 kā 이 ī	사 sā 이 ī 히 hī
바 pă 람 rām 벽 pyŏk	판 p'hān 자 tsă	란 lān 간 kān	비 păi 목 mŏk 쇠 syŏor	지 tsī 게 kē 호 hŏ	창 ts'hāng 창 ts'hāng	열 yŏr 기 kăi	싀 swī 비 pī
가 kā 베 pey	아 ā 마 mā 도 dŏ	란 lān 간 kān	즈 tsoŏ 보 pŏ 아 gā 네 nē	도 tŏ	마 mā 도 dŏ	아 ā 계루 keyr	시 sī 바 pā 아 gā 기 kī

A grating	A gallery	A screen	A fastening	A pivot A hinge	Window Grating	To shut	A bolt
櫨	樓林	子障	釕	樞	櫺窓	閉	櫞
레 lēy 이 ī	마쯔 māts' 로 lŏ 우 oō		료 lyŏ 우 oō	스 soŏ 우 oō	조 sŏ 우 oō 레 dēy 이 ī	헤 hēy 이 ī	산 sān
둉 tyoōng 긷 kīt 령 lyōng	말 mār 루 roō	장 tsyāng 자 tsă	걸 kŏr 새 săi 료 lyŏ	지 tsī 도 tŏ 리 rī 츄 ts'hyoō	창 ts'hāng 령 lyōng	닫 tā 틀 toŏr 폐 p'hēy	빋 pīt 장 tsyāng 산 swān
누 noō 기 kī	엔 ēyn 다 tā 가 kā 도 tŏ 노 nŏ	쇼 syŏ 우 oō 시 zī	가 kā 계 kēy 아 gā 네 nē	구 koō 루루 roōr	나 nā 가 kā 기 kī	다 tā 계루 tēr 도 tŏ 즈루 zoōr	관 kwān 누 noō 기 kī

Chinese words ... ted ... nd ... ined I.

宮室

A terrace	A garden	Wooden steps A ladder	A door blind	A frame A stand	A hanging board	A screen for the sun	A chimney
臺	園	梯	簾	架	板懸	陽遮	堗
다 tā 이 ī	연 ēyn	데 tē 이 ī	렌 lēyn	가 kā	겐 kēyn 한 hān	샤 syā 요 yŏ 우 oō	도 tŏts' 쯔
되 tāi 대 tāi	동 tŏng 산 sān 원 wōn	사 sā 다 tă 리 rī 데 tēy	발 pār 렴 lyŏm	시 sī 렁 rŏng 가 kā	현 hyŏn 판 p'hān	챠 tshyā 양 yang	굴 koŏr 독 tŏk 돌 tŏr
우 oō 데 tē 나 nā	소 sŏ 노 nŏ	가 kā 게 kēy 하 hā 시 sī	스 soŏ 다 dā 레 rēy	다 tā 나 nā	가 kā 게 kēy 이 ī 다 tā	긷 kīt 가 kā 게 kēy	게 kēy 무 moō 리 rī 다 dā 사 sī

City and Sub-

Stairs	A court	Foundation	Do. made of beads	A table	A clothes stand	A screen for the face	A fireplace
陛	庭	基	簾珠	子卓	椸	靣遮	口竈
헤 hēy 이 ī	데 tē 이 ī	기 kī	슈 syoō 렌 lēyn	다 tāk 구 시 sī	이 ī	샤 syā 멘 mēyn	소 sŏ 우 oō 고 kŏ 우 oō
섬 sŏm 폐 p'hēy	뜰 stoŏr 뎡 tyŏng	터 t'hŏ 긔 kŏoī	쥬 tsyoō 렴 lyŏm	탁 t'hāk 자 tsă	홰 hwāi 이 ī	챠 tshyā 면 myŏn	조 tsŏ 구 koō
기 kī 사 zā 하 hā 시 sī	니 nī 와 wā	야 yā 시 sī 기 kī	다 tā 마 mā 스 soŏ 다 da 레 rēy	즈 tsoŏ 구 koō 에 ēy	이 ī 고 kŏ 우 oō	가 kā 오 ŏ 가 kā 구 koō 시 sī	헤 hēy 즈 tsoŏ 이 ī 구 koō 지 tsī

33 三三

城郭

Cities and Suburbs

A city	A mandarin's court	Ancestral Temple	A kingdom A nation
城	宮	廟宗	國
셰 sēy 이 ī	관 kwān		국 kŏk
셩 syŏng 셩 syăng	구 koō 와 wī 관 kwān	종 tsŏng 묘 myŏ	나 nā 라 rā 국 koŏk
시 sī 로 rŏ	구 koō 보 pŏ 우 oō	소 sŏ 우 oō 뵤 byŏ 우 oō	구 koō 니 nī

A fence	A wall	Flower steps
籬	墻	階花
리 lī	쇼 syŏ 우 oō	과 kwā 가 kā 이 ī
울 oŏr 셥 sŏp 리 lī	담 tām 쟘 tsyŏm	화 hwā 계 kēy
마 mā 가 gā 기 kī	가 kā 기 kī	과 kwā 단 dān

Suburbs	Government office	National altars	A capital city
郭	府	稷社	京
곽 kwāk	후 hoō		교 kyŏ 우 oō
밧 pāt 셩 syŏng 곽 kwāk	마 mā 을 ăr 부 poō	샤 syā 직 tsik	셔 syŏ 울 oŏr 경 kyŏng
호 hŏ 가 kā 시 sī 로 rŏ	즈 tsoŏ 가 kā 사 sā	샤 syā 쇽 syŏk'	미 mi 야 yā 고 kŏ

To repair	A stone wall	Flagstones
理修	築	石薄
시 sī 우 oō 리 lī	직 tsik'	학 hāk' 셰 sēy 기 kī
슈 syoō 리 lī	쌓 psăr 츅 tshyŏok	박 pāk 셕 syŏk
슈 syoō 리 lī	이 ī 시 sī 가 gā 기 kī	우 oō 스 soō 이 ī 시 sī

倭語類解

Japanese words associated and explained Vol.

三三

倭語類解上

...ese ...ds ...ted ...nd ...ined ...I.

城郭

Foreign parts	A post	A territory	A district	A stone bridge	A fire signal	A pass	A parapet
方外	驛	鎮	郡	矼	燧烽	關	堞
과 kwā 이 ī 호 hŏ 우 oō		진 tsin	군 goōn	고 kŏ 우 oō	호 hŏ 우 oō 스 soŏ 이 ī	관 kwān	됴 typ 우 oō
외 ŏī 방 pāng	억 ōk 역 yōk	진 tsīn 졍 tsyōng 진 tsīn	고 kŏ 올 ŏr 군 koōn	돌 tŏr ᄃᆞ tă 리 rī 강 kāng	봉 pŏng 슈 syoō	모 mŏ 개 kāī 관 kwān	셩 syōng 각 kāk 회 hŏī 텹 t'hyōp
이 ī 나 nā 가 kā	예 ēy 기 kī	시 sī 즈 tsoŏ 무 moōr' 루	고 kŏ 오 ŏ 리 rī	이 ī 시 sī 바 pā 시 sī	도 tŏ 우 oō 메 mēy 호 hŏ 우 oō 과 kwā	세 sēy 기 kī 몬 mōn	시 sī 로 rŏ 노 nŏ 가 kā 베 pēy

Cit- and Sub-

34

A by-place	A stand A stopping place	A lodging place	A town	A border	A bridge	A signal mound	A ditch
方邊	站	館	邑	境	橋	臺墩	濠
헨 hēyn 호 hŏ 우 oō	산 sān	관 kwān	이 ī 우 oō	게 kēy 이 ī	교 kyŏ 우 oō		고 kŏ 우 oō
변 pyōn 방 pāng	참 ts'hām 참 ts'hām	집 tsīp 관 kwān	고 kŏ 올 ŏr 읍 oŏp	지 tsī 경 kyōng 겅 kyōng	ᄃᆞ tă 리 rī 교 kyŏ	돈 tŏn ᄃᆡ tăī	히 hăī ᄌᆞ tsă 호 hŏ
벤 pēyn 뽀 bŏ 우 oō	도 tŏ 마 mā 리 rī	다 tā 데 tē	사 sā 도 tŏ	사 sā 가 kā 이 ī	하 hā 시 sī	돈 tŏn 다 ta 이 ī	호 hŏ 리 rī

A mound A cemetery	An arena An open space	A treasury A storehouse	A belfry	A parish	Neighbourhood	A hamlet	A village
[illegible]	場	庫	樓鐘	社	隣	村	鄕
고 kŏ 우 oō	죠 tsyoō 우 oō	고 kŏ	쇼 syŏ 우 oō 로 lŏ 우 oō	샤 syā	린 līn	손 sŏn	교 kyŏ 우 oō
장 tsyāng 승 soōng 후 hoō	터 t'hō 장 tsyāng	고 kŏs ㅅ 집 tsip 고 kŏ	죵 tsyŏng 루 loō	샤 syā 단 tān 샤 syā	이 ī 욷 ōot 린 līn	ㅁ mă 올 ăr 촌 ts'hŏn	싀 swī 골 kŏr 향 hyāng
드 tsoŏ 카 kā	빠 bā	고 kŏ 구 koō 라 rā	슈 syoō 로 lŏ 우 oō	야 yā 시 sī 로 tŏ	도 tŏ 나 nā 리 rī	무 moō 라 rā	후 hoō 루 roō 사 sā 도 tŏ

Pasturage	A shop An inn	A market	A granary A magazine	The gate of a village	A small village	A dwelling	A native village
場牧	店	市	倉	閭閻	里	居	鄕故
뽀 bŏk' 구 죠 tsyŏ 우 oō	덴 tēn	시 sī	소 sŏ 우 oō		리 lī	교 kyŏ	
목 mŏk 장 tsyāng	숟 soōt 막 māk 뎜 tyŏm	저 tsyō 제 tsē 시 sī	고 kŏs ㅅ 집 tsīp 창 ts'hāng	려 lyō 염 yōm	ㅁ mă 올 ăr 리 lī	살 sār 거 kō	고 kŏ 향 hyāng
마 mā 기 kī	하 hā 다 tā 왜 gō 야 yā 다 tā 나 nā	이 ī 치 tsī	구 koō 라 rā	료 lyŏ 엔 ēyn	사 sā 도 tŏ 리 lī	오 ŏ 루 roō	고 kŏ 교 kyŏ 우 oō

倭語類解
Japanese words associated and explained Vol

三四

官職 Office and Rank

Emperor	Heir apparent	A king	A prince of the empire	A great sovereign	A princess	The court
皇帝	太子	王	諸侯	大君	公主	朝廷
				다 tā 이 ī 군 koōn		
황 hwāng 뎨 tēy	태 thāi 즈 tsă	님 nīm 금 koŏm 왕 wāng	졔 tsēy 후 hoō	대 tāi 군 koōn	공 kŏng 쥬 tsyŏo	됴 tyŏ 뎡 tyŏng
고 kŏ 우 oō 테 tē 이 ī	다 ta 이 ī 시 sī	오 ŏ 우 oō	쇼 syŏ 고 kŏ 우 oō	오 ŏ 오 ŏ 기 kī 미 mī	교 kŏ 우 oō 슈 syoō	됴 tyŏ 우 oō 테 tē 이 ī

Empress	Wife of do. Eastern harem	Sons of the Nobility	A sovereign	The Imperial family	Princess's Husband	A minister
皇后	東宮	世子	君	宗室	駙馬	臣
			군 koōn			신 sīn
황 hwāng 후 hoō	동 tŏng 궁 koōng	셰 sēy 즈 tsă	님 nīm 금 koŏm 군 koōn	종 tsŏng 실 sir	부 poō 마 mā	신 sīn 하 hā 신 sīn
고 kŏ 우 oō 고 gŏ 우 oō	도 tŏ 우 oō 고 gōō 우 ōō	셰 sēy 이 ī 시 sī	기 kī 미 mī	소 sŏ 우 oō 시 sits' 쯔	후 hoō 바 bā	신 sīn 카 kkā

Instructor	An officer	An officer for receiving congratulation	A special messenger	Examiner	Keeper of the palace	General	A prime minister
導訓	負官	官慰接	使勅	使御	使府	將大	相丞
		쇼 syŏ 우 oō 이 ī 관 kwān		교 gyŏ 시 sī			
훈 hoōn 도 tŏ	관 kwān 원 wōn	접 tsyap 위 oōī 관 kwān	칙 ts'hik 亽 să	어 ō 亽 să	부 poō 亽 să	대 tāī 쟝 tsyāng	승 sōong 샹 syāng
훈 hoōn 도 dŏ 우 oō	관 kwān 인 īn	세 sēy 즈 tsoō 이 ī 관 kwān	죠 tsyŏ 구 koō 시 sī	가 구 kāk' 시 sī 메 mēy 즈 tsoō 키 kēy	후 hoō 시 sī	다 tā 이 ī 쇼 syŏ 우 oō	쇼 syŏ 우 oō 쇼 syŏ 우 oō

A runner (special)	An officer of the court	An officer for making congratulation	A faithful messenger	A messenger	Great Keeper	Overseer Director	Chief Minister
差別	官上堂	官慰問	使信	臣使	令守	司監	相宰
베 쪼 pēyts' 사 sā 이 ī		뽄 boōn 이 ī 관 kwān		사 sī 신 sīn			
별 pyōr 차 ts'hāī	당 tōng 샹 syāng 관 kwān	문 moōn 위 oōī 관 kwān	신 sīn 亽 sā	亽 sā 신 sīn	슈 syoō 령 lyōng	감 kām 亽 să	지 ts'āī 샹 syāng
벳 pēyt 사 sā 이 ī	도 dŏ 우 oō 쇼 syŏ 우 oō 관 kwān	에 ēy 기 kī 시 sī 도 tŏ 가 kā 이 ī 관 kwān	신 sīn 시 sī	쇼 zyŏ 우 oō 시 sī	슈 syoō 레 lēy 이 ī	관 kān 시 sī	사 sā 이 ī 쇼 syŏ 우 oō

倭語類解

Japanese words assorted and explained Vol.

三五

倭語類解 上

Japanese words explained and defined I.

官職

Offices and rank

Government	To direct To manage	A station	An office Employment	Interpreter	A military officer	A doctor A physician	A ready messenger
政	掌	位	職	通事	軍官	醫員	差備官
세 sěy 이 ī	쇼 syŏ 우 oō	이 ī				이 ī 인 in	
졍 tsyōng 亽 sā 졍 tsyōng	ᄀᆞ kă 음 oōm 알 ăr 쟝 tsyāng	벼 pyō 슬 săr 위 ŏōī	벼 pyŏ 슬 săr 직 tsik	통 thŏng 亽 sā	군 koon 관 kwān	의 wī 원 wŏn	차 tshāi 비 pī 관 kwān
마 mā 즈 tsoŏ 리 rī 고 gŏ 도 tŏ	즈 tsoŏ 가 kā 사 sā 도루 dŏr'	구 koō 라 rā 이 ī	쇼구 syŏk'	즈 tsoŏ 우 oō 시 zī	군 goōn 관 kwān	이 ī 샤 syā	사 sā 비 pī 관 kwan

An order	To sustain an office	Rank	To serve in an office	A scribe A secretary	A recorder	A painter	A beadle
令	任	品	仕	書吏	錄事	畫員	籌員
레 lĕy 이 ī	닌 zīn	힌 hīn	시 sī	쇼 syŏ 리 lī		과 kwā 인 in	쥬 tsyoō 유 yoō 인 in
령 lyōng 흘 hăr 령 lyŏng	맏 măt 들 toŏr 임 im	차 tshă 례 rĕy 픔 p'hoōm	벼 pyŏ 슬 săr 亽 să	셔 syā 리 lī	록 lŏk 亽 să	화 hwa 원 wŏn	쥬 tsyoō 원 wŏn
레 lĕy 이 ī 메 mĕy 이 ī	마 mā 가 kā 스 soŏ	시 sī 나 nā	슈 syoŏt 시 sī 즈 tsoŏ 가 kā 유루 yoor'	가 kā 기 kī 야구 yăk'	로구 lŏk 시 zī	에 ēy 가 kā 기 kī 에 ēy 시 sī	산 săn 쟈 zyā

36

An autograph	Friendly enquiry	Ceremonial presents	A card of ceremony	A written agreement	公式 General forms	Merit	To praise and blame	倭語類解 Japanese words assorted and explained Vol.
本手	情問	物禮	單禮	契書		名功	貶襃	
시우혼 sī oō hŏn	뽄세이 boōn sēy ī	레이모쯔 lēy ī mŏts					호우혠 hŏ oō hēyn	
슈본 syoō pŏn	문졍 moōn tsyāng	례물 lēy moor	례단 lēy tān	셔계 syŏ kēy		공명 kŏng myŏng	포폄 phŏ phyŏm	
슈뽄 syoō bŏn	몬쇼우 mŏn zyŏ oō	인모쯔 ĭn mŏts	레이단 lēy ī tān	쇼계이 syŏ kēy ī		고우메이 kŏ oō mēy ī	노오리히기빠시 nŏ ŏ rī hī kī bā sī	
Letter of information	Communication of orders	An engagement	A present of Local productions	A separate document		Emolument	To recommend & exalt	
聞啓	令傳	条約	物方	幅別		祿	擧薦	
			후우모쯔 hoō oō mŏts	베쯔후구 pēyts hōok		로구 lŏk	센교 sēyn kyŏ	
계문 kēy moōn	젼령 tsyŏn lyāng	약됴 yāk tyŏ	방물 pāng moōr	별복 pyŏr pŏk		녹록 nŏk lŏk	쳔거 tshyŏn kŏ	
게이뿐 kēy ī boōn	덴레이 tēn lēy ī	야구죠우 yāk zyŏ oō	도산 tŏ sān	벧뿌구 pēyt pook		지꾜우 tsī gyŏ oō	스스메아가루 soō soō mēy ā koor	三六

倭語類解 上

Chinese words sorted and explained I.

文學

Literature

37

三七

文學

Literature

Literature	A private seal	An answer	A transcript	A document	A table of contents	A sealed document
文	書圖	狀答	謄	籍文	錄目	子關
맨 boōn	도 tŏ 쇼 syŏ	도 tŏ 우 oō 죠 tsyŏ 우 oō	도 tŏ 우 oō	뿐 boōn 세 sēy 기 kī		관 kwān 시 sī
글 koōr 월 wōr 문 moōn	도 tŏ 셔 syŏ	답 tăp 장 tsāng	벋 pŏt 길 kĭr 등 toōng	문 moōn 젹 tsyŏk	목 mŏk 록 lŏk	관 kwān 존 tsā
후 hoō 미 mī	인 in 빤 bān	혜 hēyn 도 tŏ 우 oō	우 oō 즈 tsoōs' 스	뿐 boōn 자 tsyăk' 구	모 mŏk' 구 로 lŏk' 구	관 kwān 뿐 boōn

Learning To learn	A public seal	A seal	An epistle A letter	A record	A memorandum	A receipt A note
學	周交	印	簡書	錄記	記件	子單
가 kăk 구	교 kŏ 우 oō 시 sī 우 oō	인 in	쇼 syŏ 간 kān	기 kī 로 lŏk 구	견 kēyn 기 kī	단 tān 시 sī
비 pāi 홀 hor 혹 hăk	효 hyŏ 쥬 tsyoō	인 in 인 in	셔 syŏ 간 kān	긔 kwī 록 lŏk	건 kōn 긔 kwī	단 tān 존 tsā
마 mā 나 nā 뿌 boō	계 kēy 스 soō	인 in 즈 tsoō 이 ī	데 tē 가 gā 미 mī	시 sī 루 roō 스 soō	가 kā 기 kīts' 쯔 게 kēy	단 tān 간 kkān

倭語類解

Japanese words associated and explained Vol.

A stroke	The seal character	To compose love songs	To discuss	To read	To study	Work	To teach
畫	篆	月風	題	讀	習	夫工	教
	뎐 tēn		뎨 tē 이 ī	도구 dŏk	시 sī 우 oō	교 kŏ 우 oō 후 hoō	교 kŏ 우 oō
그 koŏ 을 oŏr 획 hŏik	젼 tsyōn 자 tsă 젼 tsyōn	풍 p'hoōng 월 wōr	글 koŏr 뎨 tēy 뎨 tēy	닐 nīr 글 koŏr 독 tŏk	니 nī 길 kīr 습 soŏp	공 kŏng 부 poō	가 kă 르 ră 칠 tshīr 교 kyŏ
과구 kwăk'	고 kŏ 몬 mŏn 시 zī	후 hoō 우 oō 예쯔 gēyts'	다 dā 이 ī	욤무 yŏm'	나 nā 로 rŏ 우 oō	구 koō 후 hoō 우 oō 계 kēy 이 ī 고 kŏ	오 ŏ 시 sī 유루 yoōr

A Jot	To write A writing	To rhyme	To comment	To chant	To discourse	To recite	To instruct
點	寫	韻次	註	吟	講	誦	訓
	샤 syā	시 sī 인 in		긴 gin	고 kŏ 우 oō	쇼 syŏ 우 oŏ	군 koōn
뎜 tyōm- 뎜 tyōm	쓸 ssoŏr 샤 syā	차 ts'hă 운 oōn	주 tsoō 낼 nāir 주 tsoō	을 oŏr 플 phoŏr 음 oŏm	강 kāng 할 hăr 강 kāng	외 ŏī 올 ŏr 숑 syŏng	가 kă 르 ră 칠 tshīr 훈 hoōn
뎬 tēn	가 kā 기 kī	와 wā 인 in	쥬 tsyoō 우 oō	긴 gin 주루 zoŏr'	고 kŏ 우 oō 샤구 syăk	쥬 tsyoō 우 oō 요 yŏ 미 mī	오 ŏ 시 sī 예 ēy

三十

倭語類解上 These words ... ted ... d ... ined I.

文學 Literature

38 三八

Variegated paper	A volume A roll	Liquid ink	A proverb	A diary	A copy	A half line	Correct Writing
紙紋	卷	墨水	文諺	記日	帖法	行半	書正
몬 mŏn 시 sī	켄 kēyn	스 soŏ 이 ī ᄫᅩ구 bŏk'	갠 gēyn 뿐 boōn	시쯔 zīts' 기 kī	호 hŏ 우 oō 됴 tyŏ 우 oō	한 hān 교 kŏ 우 oō	쇼 syŏ 우 oō 쇼 syŏ
문 moōn 지 tsī	권 kwōn 권 kwōn	슈 syoō 묵 moōk	언 ōn 문 moōn	일 ir 긔 kwī	법 pŏt 텹 t'hyōp	반 pān 힝 hăng	졍 tsyōng 셔 syō
가 kā 라 rā 가 kā 미 mī	마 mā 기 kī	스 soŏ 미 mī 에 ēy	온 ōn 몬 mŏn	닛 nīt 기 kī 히 hī 죠 tsyŏ 우 oō	데 tē 혼 hŏn	구 koō 즈 tsoŏ 시 sī	신 sīn

Coloured paper	Paper	A book	A picture	An almanack	A rough sketch	A penman	Running hand
紙色	紙	冊	畫	書曆	草記	筆能	書草
시 sī 기 kī 시 sī	시 sī	사구 sāk'	과 kwā	레 lēy 기 kī 쇼 syŏ	기 kī 소 sŏ 우 oō		소 sŏ 우 oō 쇼 syŏ
식 săik 지 tsī	죠 tsyŏ 회 hwī 지 tsī	칙 ts'hăik 칙 ts'hăik	그 koŏ 림 rīm 화 hwā	력 lyŏk 셔 syŏ	긔 kwī 초 ts'hŏ	능 noŏng 필 p'hir	초 ts'hŏ 셔 syō
이 ī 로 rŏ 가 gā 미 mī	가 kā 미 mī	쇼 syŏ 모쯔 mŏts'	에 ēy	고 kŏ 요 yŏ 미 mī	시 sī 다 tā 가 gā 기 kī	노 nŏ 우 oō 히즈 hīts'	소 sŏ 우 oō 시 sī

武備 Martial affairs

To draw up To arrange	To raise troops	Military affairs
陣	兵起	武
	기 kī 헤 hēy 이 ī	뿌 boō
진 tsīn 칠 tshīr 진 tsīn	긔 kwī 병 pyōng	호 hŏ 반 pān 무 moō
진 tsīn	헤 hēy 이 ī 오 ŏ 오 ŏ 고 kŏs' 스	뿌 boō 시 sī / 뿌 boō 관 kwān

To set in order	To lay in ambush	A soldier
齊整	兵伏	兵
세 sēy 이 ī 세 sēy 이 ī	후 hook' 구 헤 hēy 이 ī	헤 hēy 이 ī
졍 tsyōng 제 tsēy	복 pŏk 병 pyōng	군 koōn 亽 să 병 pyōng
다 tā 다 tā 시 sī 우 oō	후 hoō 새 sēy 세 zēy 이 ī	쯔 tsoō 와 wā 모 mŏ 노 nŏ

A book press	An ink stone dripper	An ink stone	A pencil
鎮書	滴硯	硯	筆
쇼 syō 진 tsīn	켄 kēyn 데 tē 기 kī	켄 kēyn	히 hits' 쯔
셔 syō 진 tsīn	연 yōn 뎍 tyōk	벼 pyō 로 lō 연 yōn	붓 poot 필 phīr
사 sā 산 sān	미 mī 스 zoō 이 ī 레 rēy	스 soō 스 zoō 리 rī	후 hoō 데 dē

	A writing table A desk	An inkstone box	Ink
	案書	箱硯	墨
	쇼 syō 안 ān	켄 kēyn 쇼 syō 우 oō	보 bŏk' 구
	셔 syō 안 ān	연 yōn 샹 syāng	먹 mŏk 묵 mook
	쯔 tsoō 구 koō 에 ēy	스 soō 스 zoō 리 rī 바 pā 고 kŏ	스 soō 미 mī

倭語類解

Japanese words assorted and explained Vol.

三八

倭語類解 上

These words … explained

I.

武備

Mar Aff.

To assail To surprise	To surround To besiege	To invade	To scuffle To wrangle	To fight To contend	An enemy An opponent	Dignity Might	The word of command
襲	圍	侵	鬪	戰	敵對	威	號令
시 sī 우 oō	이 ī	신 zīn	도 tŏ 우 oō	센 sēyn		이 ī	고 gŏ 우 oō 레 lēy 이 ī
엄 ōm 습 soŏp 홀 hăr 습 soŏp	에 ē 올 oōr 위 oōī	침 ts'hīm 노 nŏ 침 ts'hīm	싸 ssā 홀 hŏr 투 t'hoō	싸 ssa 홀 hŏr 젼 tsyōn	디 tăī 뎍 tyŏk	위 oōī 엄 ōm 위 oōī	호 hŏ 령 lyōng
오 ŏ 소 sŏ 우 oō	도 tŏ 리 rī 가 kā 곰 kŏm	오 ŏ 가스 kās'	켄 kēyn 과 kwā — 이 ī 시 sā 가 kā 이 ī.	익구 ik' 사 sā — 다 tā 다 tā 고 kŏ 우 oō	다 tā 이 ī 데 tē 기 kī	이 ī 기 kī 오 ŏ 이 ī	이 ī 이 ī 즈 tsoŏ 게 kēy

To straiten To distress	To go round To revolve	To pillage To plunder	To attack To punish	To challenge to battle	A robber	The field of battle	Severity Strictness
逼迫	匝	掠	伐	挑戰	賊	戰場	嚴
보 po 우 oō 하구 hāk'	소 sŏ 우 oō	랴구 lyāk'	바쯔 pāts'	됴 tyŏ 우 oō 센 sēyn	조구 zŏk'		엔 gēyn
핍 p'hīp 박 pāk	두 toō 룰 roŏr 잡 tsāp	노 nŏ 략 lyāk 략 lyāk	칠 ts'hīr 벌 pōr	도 tŏ 젼 tsyōn	도 tŏ 젹 tsōk 적 tsāk	젼 tsyōn 쟝 tsyāng	엄 ōm 홀 hăr 엄 ōm
세 sēy 마루 mār'	마 mā 와루 wār'	가 kā 스무 soŏm'	우즈 oōts'	이 ī 도 dŏ 미 mī 다 tā 다 tā 고 kŏ 우 oō	누스 noŏs' 메 bī 도 tŏ	센 sēyn 죠 tsyŏ 우 oō	기 kī 비 pī 시 sī 이 ī

39

三九

To take in a pit	To exterminate	A defeat	To pull out To draw out	To plunder	To lose sight of	To defend To guard	To rescue To deliver
坑	滅	敗	拔	刧	瞭失	防	援救
고 kŏ 우 oō	메쯔 meyts'	하 hā 이 ī	하쯔 hāts'	교 kyŏ 우 oō	시쯔 sits' 료 lyŏ 우 oō	호 hŏ 우 oō	규 kyoō 우 oō 엔 ēyn
묻 mōot 지 tsī 룰 roōr 깅 kăing	멸 myŏr 홀 hăr 멸 myŏr	패 p'hăi 홀 hăr 패 p'hăi	쌔 spā 힐 hĭr 발 pān	겁 kŏp 홀 hăr 겁 kŏp	실 sĭr 료 lyŏ	방 pāng 비 pī 방 pāng	구 koō 원 wōn
무 boo 메루 meyr	멘 mēyt 스 soō 호 hŏ 로 rŏ 부루 poōr'	야 yā 부 poō 레 rēy	누 nook'	오 ŏ 비 pī 야 yā 가스 kās'	미 mī 오 ŏ 도 tŏ 시 sī	후 hoō 세 sēy 구 goō	가 kā 세 sēy 이 ī

To rebel	To perish	To defeat To break	To surrender To yield	To take prisoner To capture	To fall into confusion	To defend the borders	To keep To maintain
叛	亡	破	降	擒	亂	戍	守
한 hān	모 mŏ 우 oō	하 hā	고 kŏ 우 oō	긴 kĭn	란 lān	슈 zyoō	슈 syoō
반 pān 홀 hăr 반 pān	망 mang 홀 hăr 망 māng	파 p'hā 홀 hăr 파 p'hā	항 hāng 복 pŏk 항 hāng	사 sā 로 rŏ 잡 tsăp 을 oŏr 금 koōm	어 ŏ 즈 tsoŏ 러 rŏ 올 ŏr 란 rān	슈 syoō 사 sā 리 rī 슈 syoō	직 tsĭk 힐 hwĭr 슈 syoō
소 sŏ 무 moō 기 kī	호 hŏ 로 rŏ 부 poō	야 yā 부 poō 레루 rēyr'	고 kŏ 우 oō 산 sān	이 ī 게 kēy 도루 dŏr'	미 mī 다 dā 루루 roōr'	볜 pēyn 뽀 bŏ 우 oō 니 nī 마 mā 모루 mŏr'	마 mā 모루 mŏr'

倭語類解

Japanese words assorted and explained Vol:

The hilt of a sword	A blade	A knife A small sword	A sword A sabre	Armour		To be reconciled	To desert
鐔	刃	刀	劒	甲	軍器	親和	叛背
도우 tŏ oō	인 zĭn	도우 tŏ oō	켄 kēyn	고우 kŏ oō		콰신 kwā sĭn	하이한 hā ī hān
바기답 pă kī tāp	놀인 năr ĭn	칼도 k'hār tŏ	환도검 hwān tŏ kŏm	갑옷갑 kăp ŏt kap	Military weapons	화친 hwā tshĭn	비반 păi pān
즈바 tsoŏ pā	야이빠 yā ī bā	고가다나 kŏ gā tā nā	즈루기 tsoŏ roō gī / 가다나 kā tā nā	요로이 y r ī		와단 wā dān	무혼 moō hŏn
A sheath A scabbard	The back of a sword	A sharp sword	A precious sword	A helmet			To revenge a quarrel
鞘	本刀	刀利	劒寶	冑			讎報
쇼우 syŏ oō	도우혼 tŏ oō hŏn	리도우 lĭ tŏ oō		쥬우 tsyoō oō			호우시우 hŏ oō sī oō
감풀쵸 kām p'hoōr ts'hyŏ	도본 tŏ pŏn	리도 lĭ tŏ	보검 pŏ kŏm	투구쥬 t'hoō koō tsyoō			보슈 pŏ syoō
사야 sā yā	고가다나노시데 kŏ gā tā nā nō sĭ dē	리켄 lĭ kēyn	호우켄 hŏ oō kēyn	가뿌도 kā boō tŏ			아다오호우수 ā dā ŏ hŏ oō zoŏr

Blunt weapons	To hit the centre	A target	The head of an arrow	An arrow	To bend a bow	A strong bow	Blunt
干	中	革貫	鏃	矢	彎	弓强	鈍
간 kān	쥬 tsyoō 우 oō	관 kwān 각 kāk' 구	소 sŏk' 구	시 sī	완 wān	고 kŏ 우 oō 규 kyoō 우 oō	돈 tŏn
방 kāng 패 p'hāi 간 kān	맏 māt 칠 ts'hīr 즁 tsyōong	관 kwān 혁 hyŏk	살 sār 믿 mīt 족 tsŏk	살 sār 시 sī	활 hwār 혈 hyōr 만 mān	강 kāng 궁 koōng	무 moō 될 twir 둔 toōn
다 tā 데 tē	아 ā 다 tār' 루	다 tā 데 tē 이 ī 다 tā	야 yā 노 nŏ 네 nē	야 yā	유 yoō 미 mī 오 ŏ 히 hik' 구	즈 tsoō 요 yŏ 유 yoō 미 mī	니 nī 부 poō 이 ī / 기 kī 레 rēy 누 noō

A spear A lance	A battle-ax	A mark, to shoot at	The shaft of an arrow	The but-end of an arrow	To shoot an arrow	A bowstring	A bow
戈	鉞斧	帿	[illegible]	筈	射	弦	弓
과 kwā	후 hoō 예 ēyts' 쯔	고 kŏ 우 oō	하 hāk' 구	과 kwāts' 쯔	샤 syā	갠 gēyn	규 kyoō 우 oō
창 ts'hāng 과 kwā	부 poō 월 wŏr	솔 sŏr 후 hoō	고 kŏ 도 tŏ 리 rī 박 pāk	오 ŏ 늬 nāi 괄 kwar	쏠 ssŏr 샤 syā	시 sī 위 ŏoī 현 hyŏn	활 hwār 궁 koōng
호 hŏ 고 kŏ	새 sēyts' 쯔 예 ēyts' 쯔	호 hŏ 마 mā 도 tŏ	히 hī 기 kī 메 mēy	야 yā 하 hāz' 스	유 yoō 미 mī 이 īr 루	유 yoō 미 mī 즈 tsoŏr' 루	유 yoō 미 mī

倭語類解

Japanese words assorted and explained

Vol.

軍器 (Mil: Wea...)

A gauntlet	A warrant A passport	A signal board	A standard A banner	A flag	Powder Gunpowder	A fowling piece	A bullet A pellet
甲掌	信標	牌	纛	旗	藥火	銃鳥	子彈
쇼 syŏ 우 oō 죠 tsyŏ 우 oō	효 hyŏ 우 oō 신 sīn	하 hā 이 ī	독구 dŏk'	기 kī	과 kwā 야 yāk' 구	됴 tyŏ 우 oō 죠 tsyŏ 우 oō	단 tān 시 sī
장 tsyang 갑 kāp	표 p'hyŏ 신 sīn	패 p'hāi 패 p'hāi	독 tŏok 독 tŏk	긔 kwī 긔 kwī	화 hwā 약 yāk	됴 tyŏ 춍 tshyōng	탄 t'hān ᄌᆞ tsă
고 kŏ 데 tē 가 kā 계 kēy	와 wā 리 rī 후 hoō	사 sā 애 gēy 후 hoō 따 dā	하 hā 우 goō 마 mā	하 hā 다 tā	구 koō 지 tsī 우스 goōs' 리 rī	텝 tēt 보 pŏ 우 oō	다 tā 마 mā

A thimble for archers	An armlet for archers	A soldier's billet	A canopy	A gong	A fire-rope A match	An iron ball	To let off a gun
指角	韝	符兵	盖	鉦	縄火	丸鐵	砲放
가 kāk' 구 시 sī	고 kŏ 우 oō		가 kā 이 ī	세 sēy 이 ī	과 kwā 쇼 zyŏ 우 oō	대 tēts' 쪼 왼 gwān	호 hŏ 우 oō 호 hŏ 우 oō
각 kāk 지 tsī	풀 p'hăr 지 tsī 구 koō	병 pyōng 부 poō	개 kăī 개 kăī	징 tsāing 졍 tsyong	화 hwā 승 soōng	텰 t'hyŏr 환 hwān	방 pāng 포 p'hŏ
유 yoō 비 pī 쪼 tsoō 노 nŏ	이 ī 아 gā 계 kēy	헤 hēy 이 ī 후 hoō	기 kī 누 noō 아 gā 사 sā	도 dŏ 라 rā	히 hī 나 nā 와 wā	텝 tēt 보 pŏ 노 nŏ 다 tā 마 mā	히 hī 즈 tsoō 즈 zoō 미 mī

To beget To bear young	To conceive To be pregnant	To marry a wife	To match To couple	A young lady A spinster	A mediator match-maker		Manacles Handcuffs
生	孕	娶	配	女處	媒中	婚娶	械
쇼 syŏ 우 oō	요 yŏ 우 oō	슈 syoō	하 hā 이 ī	쇼 syŏ 죠 zyŏ	츄 tsyoō 우 oō 빠 ba 이 ī	Marriage	가 kā 이 ī
날 nār 싱 săing	빌 păīr 잉 īng	쟝 tsyāng 가 kā 드 toŏ 릴 rīr 취 ts'hōoī	짝 stsāk 비 pāī	처 tshyŏ 녀 nyŏ	중 tsyoōng 매 māī		긔 kwī 계 kēy 계 kēy
무 moō 마루 mār'	하 hā 라무 rām'	메 mēy 도루 tŏr'	묘 myŏ 우 oō 도 tŏ	고 kŏ 무스 moōs' 메 mēy	나 nā 가 kā 다 tā 지 tsī		도 dŏ 우 oō 구 goō

To bring forth	The womb	The menses	To marry out a daughter	The 8 natal characters	Marriage
産	胎	水經	嫁	字八	姻婚
산 sān	다 tā 이 ī	계 kēy 이 ī 스 soō 이 ī	가 kā	하쯔 hāts' 지 zī	곤 kŏn 인 in
나 nā 흘 hŏr 산 sān	틔 t'hăī 틔 t'hăī	경 kyūng 슈 syoō	셔 syŏ 방 pāng 마 mā 칠 ts'hīr 가 kā	팔 p'hār 즈 tsă	혼 hŏn 인 in
우무 oōm'	하 hā 라 rā 고 gŏ 모루 moōr'	즈 tsoŏ 기 kī 야구 yāk'	요 yŏ 메 mēy 이 ī 리 rī	시 sī 아 ā 와 wā 세 sēy	곤 kŏn 레 lēy 이 ī

倭語類解

Japa... wo... assort... an... expla...

Vol.

四十一

倭語類解 上

These words noted and explained I.

宴享

A going to meet one	A host	A feast by the way	To bring up the feast	A feast A banquet		Swaddling clothes	A boy A male child
迎	人主	宴次路	宴上進	宴	宴享 Feasting and Entertainments	褓襁	男
게 gēy 이 ī	쥬 syoo 신 zin	로 lō 시 sī 연 ēyn	신 sīn 쇼 syŏ 우 oō 연 ēyn	연 ēyn		교 kyŏ 우 oō 호 hŏ 우 oō	난 nan
마 mā 즁 tsoōr 영 yōng	쥬 tsyoŏ 인 in	로 lŏ 차 tshā 연 yōn	진 tsin 샹 syāng 연 yōn	잔 tsan 치 tshāi 연 yōn		강 kang 보 pŏ	ᄉᆞ sā 나 nā 희 hāi 남 nām
무 moō 가 kā 이 ī	데 tē 이 ī 슈 syoō	노 nŏ 보 pŏ 리 ri 유 yoo 하 hā 지 tsī	후 hoō 우 oō 신 sīn 예 ēy	유 yoō 하 hā 지 tsī / 사 sī 가 kā 모 mŏ 리 ri		무 moŏ 즈 tsoŭ 기 kī / 시 sī 메 mēy 시 sī	오 ŏ 도 tŏ 고 kŏ

Feas. & Entert.

42

To receive & entertain	A guest	A feast on disembarking	The middle of a feast	A feast on embarking	Separation	A girl A female
待接	客	宴船上	宴中	宴船下	異離	女
쇼 syŏ 우 oō 다 tā 이 ī			쥬 tsyoō 우 oō 연 ēyn	게 kēy 션 sēyn 연 ēyn	리 lī 이 ī	죠 zyŏ
졉 tsyōp 디 tāi	손 sŏn 직 kāik	샹 syāng 션 syōn 연 yōn	즁 tsyoōng 연 yōn	하 hā 션 syōn 연 yōn	리 lī 이 ī	계 kēy 집 tsip 녀 nyō
셋 sēyt 다 tā 이 ī 지 tsī 소 sŏ 우 oō	갸구 kyāk'	쇼 zyŏ 우 oō 센 sēyn 연 ēyn	나 nā 가 kā 유 yoō 하 hā 지 tsī	사 sā 례 rēy 이 ī	사 sā 마 mā 다 tā 게 gēy	온 ōn 나 nā

To take leave	To constrain to eat rice	To gambol To frisk	A song A ballad	To be drunk Intoxicated	To pour out wine	Tea	To prepare To make ready
辭	食勸	舞	歌	醉	酒酌	茶	辦
시 zi	관 kwān 쇼쿠 syŏk'	부 boō	가 kā	스 soō 이 ī	사구 sāk' 슈 syoō	다 tā	변 pēyn
하 hā 직 tsik ᄉᆞ sā	권 kwŏn 식 sĭk	츔 tshoōm 츌 tshoōr 무 moō	노 nŏ 릐 răi 가 kā	츄 tshyoōi 홀 hăr 츄 tshyoōi	쟉 tsyăk 쥬 tsyoō	차 tshā 다 tā	쟝 tsyāng 만 mān 홀 hăr 판 phān
이 ī 도 tŏ 마 mā 오 gŏ 이 ī	메 mēy 시 sĭ 오 ŏ 시 sĭ 이루 ir'	마 mā 우 oō / 오 ŏ 도 dŏ 리 rĭ	우 oō 다 tā	요 yŏ 이 ī / 요 yŏ 우 oō	사 sā 계 kēy 즈가 tsoōg'	쟈 tsyā	교 kŏ 시 sĭ 라 ra 이 ī / 요 yŏ 우 oō 이 ī

A present at parting	To decline eating	To ramble To stroll	To sing	To awake from wine	To urge to take wine	To drink	To supply To offer up
餞	退膳	遊	唱	醒	酒使	飮	供
션 sēyn	센 sēyn 다 tā 이 ī	이 ī 우 oō	쇼 syŏ 우 oō	셰 sēy 이 ī	시 sĭ 슈 syoō	인 ĭn	교 kyŏ 우 oō
젼 tsyŏn 송 sŏng 젼 tsyŏn	션 syŏn 퇴 thŏi	놀 nŏr 유 yoō	부 poō 를 roŏr 챵 tshyang	셩 skăir 셩 syŏng	ᄉᆞ sā 쥬 tsyoō	마 mā 실 sĭr 음 oŏm	이 ī 바 pā 지 tsī 공 kŏng
하 hā 나 nā 무 moō 계 kēy	스 soō 뻬루 bēyr'	아 ā 소브 sŏb'	우 oō 도 tŏ 우 oō	사 sā 메루 mēyr'	스 soō 이 ī 교 kkyŏ 우 oō	노무 nŏm'	마 mā 가 ka 나 nā 이 ī 소 sŏ 노 nŏ 우 oō

A bell	To play / To strike	Psaltery	A guitar	A harp	Music	樂器 Musical Instruments	To present / To accompany
鐘	彈	箏	琵琶	琴	樂		送
쇼우 syŏ oō	단 tān	쇼우 syŏ oō	비하 bī hā	긴 kin	가구 gāk'		소우 sŏ oō
쇠북죵 sōī pook tsyŏng	톨탄 thăr t'hān	징징 tsăing tsăing	비파 pī p'hā	거문고금 kŏ moōn kŏ koŏm	풍류악 phoōng lyoō āk		보낼송 pŏ năi sŏng
즈리가네 tsoō rī gā nē	단스루 tān zŏor; 히구 hik'	히근 hī kŏn	비와 npī wā	고도 kŏ tŏ	하야시 hā yā sī		오구루 ŏ koō roō

A drum	A pan pipe / A sackbut	A fiddle-string	A kind of harp	A dulcimer	A tune
鼓	笙	絃	奚琴	瑟	調曲
고 kŏ	쇼우 syŏ oō	견 kēyn	가이긴 kā ī kin	시쯔 sits'	교구됴우 kyŏk' tyŏ oō
북고 pōok kŏ	싱황싱 săing hwăng săing	줄현 tsoōr hyōn	히금 hăi koōm	기약고슬 kăi yăk kŏ soŏr	곡됴 kŏk tyŏ
즈쯔미 tsoōds mī	히지리기 hī tsī rī kī	즈루 tsoōr'	고규우 kŏ kyoō oō	미와 mī wā	후시 hoō sī

倭語類解上 … these words … used … 樂器 Mus. Inst. 43 上三

梳洗 Combing and Washing	Cymbals	A small flute	A flute	To play on a pipe	To pipe To blow	A horn A long pipe	A long drum
	拍	笛口	笛	簫洞	嘯	角	鼓長
	하 구 hak'	고 kŏ 우 oō 데 tē 기 kī	네 tē 기 kī	노 tŏ 우 oō 쇼 syŏ 우 oō	쇼 syŏ 우 oō	가 구 kāk'	쇼 syŏ 우 oō 고 kŏ
	박 păik 판 păik	구 koo 뎍 tyŏk	뎌 tyŏ 뎍 tyŏk	동 tŏng 쇼 syŏ	슈 syoō 픙 p'hă 됨 răm 쇼 syŏ	쥬 tsyoō 라 rā 각 kāk	장 tsyāng 고 kŏ
	호 hŏ 도 dŏ 키 [illegible]	구 koo 지 [illegible] 호 hoō 에 ey	호 hoō 에 ēy	샤 syāk' 구 하 hā 지 tsī	우 oō 소 sō 후 구 hoōk'	다 tā 게 kēy 스 zoŏ 스 zoŏ	갓 kāt 고 kŏ

	To blow	A pipe	A fife	To blow a shell	To play gently	A trumpet	A musical stone
	吹	笳	篥	螺吹	嘯平大	叭喇	磬石
	스 soŏ 이 ī	가 kā	리 쯔 lits'	스 soŏ 이 ī 라 rā	다 tā 이 ī 혜 hēy 이 ī 쇼 syŏ 우 oō	라 lā 하 쯔 hāts'	세 sēy 기 kī 계 kēy 이 ī
	불 poōr 쥐 tshyooi	초 tshŏ 김 kīm 가 kā	피 p'hī 리 rī 률 ryuōn	쥐 tshŏoi 라 rā	대 t'hāī 평 p'hyŏng 쇼 syŏ	라 lā 발 pār	셕 syŏk 경 kyŏng
	후 구 hoōk'	시 sī 바 pā 호 hoō 에 ēy	후 hoō 기 kī 모 mŏ 노 nŏ	가 kā 이 ī	고 kŏ 유 zyoō 라 rā 이 ī	슈 syoō 라 rā 이 ī	린 rīn

倭語類解

Japa[nese] wo[rds] assort[ed] an[d] explai[ned] Vol.

A washing tub	To bathe	Combing apparatus	A comb brush	A comb	A tuft of hair	A knot of hair	To comb the head
盥	浴沐	貼梳	箚梳	梳	髻	鬟	頭梳
관 kwān	뽁구 bŏk' 요구 yŏk'	쇼 syŏ 됴 tyŏ 우 ōō	쇼 syŏ 셰 sēy 이 ī	쇼 syŏ	계 kēy 이 ī	관 kwān	쇼 syŏ 도 tŏ 우 ōō
낟 năt 씨 ssī 숟 sōŏr 관 kwān	목 mŏk 욕 yŏk	소 sŏ 텹 t'hyŏp	소 sŏ 셩 syōng	빗 pīt 소 sŏ	샹 syāng 토 thŏ 계 kēy	마 mā 리 rī 환 hwān	소 sŏ 두 tōō
다 tā 라 rā 이 ī	교 gyŏ 우 ōō 스 zōŭ 이 ī	빈 bīn 교 gŏ 리 rī	구 kōō 시 sī 하 hā 라 rā 이 ī	구 kōō 시 sī	다 tā 부 pōō 사 sā	가 kā 미 mī 노 nŏ 와 wā 애 gēy	가 kā 미 mī 유 yōō 우 ōō

梳洗

Comb. & Wash

To rinse the mouth	To wash	A cleaning of the head	A comb cleaner	A wooden comb	A double knot of hair	False hair	To shave the head
漱	洗	屑頭	角梳	櫛	髻丫	髢	頭剃
소 sŏ 우 ōō	셰 sēy 이 ī	도 tŏ 우 ōō 셰쯔 sēyts'	쇼 syŏ 각구 kăk'	시쯔 sīts'	아 ā 계 kēy 이 ī	데 tē 이 ī	데 te 이 ī 도 tŏ 우 ōō
양 yāng 치 ts'hī 질 tsīr 홀 hăr 수 sōō	씨 ssī 숟 sōŏr 셰 sēy	두 tōō 셜 syŏr	소 sŏ 각 kāk	어 ō 레 rē 빗 pīt 줄 tsōŏr	아 ā 계 kēy	돌 tăr 외 ăī 텨 t'hyōū	톄 t'hēy 두 tōō
구 kōō 지 tsī 스 sōŏ 스억 sōōg'	아 ā 로 rŏ 우 ōō	후 hōō 계 kēy	구 kōō 시 sī 노 nŏ 아 ā 가 kā 도 tŏ 리 rī	구 kōō 시 sī 히 hī 기 kī	가 kā 라 rā 고 kŏ 와 wā 애 gēy	네 nē 조 zŏ 예 ēy	가 kā 미 mī 소루 sŏr'

倭語類解

Japan[ese] wo[rds] assor[ted] an[d] expla[ined] Vol.

Tweezers	A finger ring	An armlet	A hairpin	A toilette	To anoint To besmear	Rouge	A tooth stick
子鑷	環指	釧	簪	·粧	塗	脂臙	水漱
됴 tyŏ 우 oo 시 si	시 si 관 kwan	션 seyn	신 sin	소 sŏ 우 oo	도 tŏ	연 ēyn 시 sī	소 sŏ 우 oo 뫽구 bŏk·
셥 syŏp 즈 tsă	지 tsī 환 hwăn	풀 phăr 쇠 sŏi 쳔 tshyon	빈 pui 혀 hyŏ 좀 tsăm	단 tān 장 tsāng 홀 hăr 장 tsāng	바 pā 를 roor 도 tŏ	연 yŏn 지 tsī	수 soŏ 목 mŏk
케 kēy 누 noŏ 기 kī	유 yoŏ 비 pi 아 gā 네 nē	우 oo 데 dē 아 gā 네 nē	간 kān 자 zā 시 sī	요 yŏ 소 sŏ 오 ŏ 이 i 시 si 닥구 tāk'	누루 noŏr'	뻬 bēy 니 ni	요 yŏ 우 oo 지 zi

	A looking glass	Girdle gems	An earring	To adorn To deck	False ornaments	Pomatum	Wash balls
	鏡	佩	珥	飾	糝	油蠟	子膩
	계 key 이 i	하 ha 이 i	시 zi	쇽구 syŏk'	산 sān	로 lŏ 우 oo 이 i 우 oo	시 si 시 si
	거 kŏ 울 oor 경 kyong	출 ts'hăr 패 phai	귀 kooi 엿 yot 골 kŏr 이 i	꾸 skoŏ 밀 mir 식 sik	뿌 spoŏ 릴 rir 숨 săm	랍 lăp 유 yoŏ	이 i 즈 tsă
	가 kā 아 gā 미 mi	사 sā 구루 goor'	미 mi 미 mi 아 gā 네 nē	가 kā 자루 zār'	고 kŏ 나 nā 가 ka 기 ki 계 kēy 쇼 syŏŏ	빈 bīn 즈 tsoŏ 케 key	아 ā 라 rā 이 i 고 kŏ

服飾 Clothes and Ornaments

Hairy clothes	A mantle	A batoon	A round collar	A head kerchief	A cap	A hat A bonnet
衣氅	衣表	笏	領團	巾頭	子帽	冠
쇼우이 syŏ oō ī	효우이 hyŏ oō ī	고쯔 kŏts'	단레이 dān lēy ī	도우긴 tŏ oō kīn	뽀우시 bŏ oō sī	관 kwān
챵의 tshyăng wi	표의 phyŏ wi	홀홀 hŏr hŏr	단령 tān lyŏng	두건 toō kān	모즈 mŏ tsă	관관 kwān kwān
게고로모 kēy kŏ rŏ mŏ	우와기 oō wā gī	샤구 syăk	단료우 dān lyŏ oō	즈긴 zoŏ kīn	게즈긴 kēy zoŏ kūn 게보시 kēy pŏ sī	관무리 kān moō rī

Wadded clothes	A coat	Clothes Apparel	A bib	A warm cap	A broad brimmed hat	A crape cap
襖	袍	衣	褙胷	帽煖	笠	帽紗
오우 ŏ oō	호우 hŏ oō	이 ī		단뽀우 dān bŏ oō	리우 lī oō	샤뽀우 syā bŏ oō
핫옷오 hăt ŏt ŏ	도포포 tŏ phŏ phŏ	옷의 ŏt wī	흉배 hyŏng păi	난모 nān mŏ	갓립 kăt lip	사모 sā mŏ
와다이레 wā tā ī rēy	하오리 hā ŏ rī	기루모노 kīr' mŏ nŏ	교우하이 kyŏ oō hā ī	미미오오이 mī mī ŏ ŏ ī	가사 kā sā	샤호우 syā hŏ oō

45

倭語類解

To cut out clothes	Trowsers Breeches Pantaloons	A belt	A rain dress	A rain mantle	A shirt	A folded garment	Fur dress
裁	袴	帶腰	衣簑	裝雨	衫汗	衣疊	裘
사 sā 이 ī	고 kō	요 yŏ 우 oō 다 tā 이 ī	사 sā 이 ī	우 oō 쇼 syŏ 우 oō	간 kān 산 sān	됴 tyŏ 우 oō 이 ī	규 kyoō 우 oō
무 mă 롤 răr 지 tshī	바 pā 지 tsī 과 kwā	요 yŏ 듸 tăī	사 sā 의 wī	우 oō 장 tsăng	한 hān 삼 sām	텹 thyŏp 의 wī	갇 kāt 옫 ŏt 구 koō
다즈 tāts'	하 hā 가 kā 마 mā / 바 pāt 지 tsī	고 kŏ 시 sī 오 ŏ 비 pī	미 mī 노 nŏ	아 ā 마 mā 구 goō	하 hā 다 dā 기 gī	다다무 tām'	가 kā 와 wā 기루 gīr' 모 mŏ 노 nŏ

A collar	A petticoat	An apron A garment	A girdle	A rain hat	An oilskin dress	A jacket	A single garment
領	褌	裳	帶	笠簑	衫油	衫	衣單
레 lēy 이 ī	곤 kŏn	쇼 syŏ 우 oō	다 tā 이 ī	사 sā 리 lī 우 oō	이 ī 우 oō 산 sān	산 sān	단 tān 이 ī
깃 kit 령 lyĕng	고 kŏ 의 wī 곤 kŏn	치 tshī 마 mā 샹 syāng	듸 twī 듸 tăī	사 sā 립 lip	유 yoō 삼 sām	젹 tsyŏk 삼 sām 삼 sām	단 tān 의 wī
에 ēy 리 rī	시 sī 다 tā 오 ŏ 비 pī	마 mā 에 ēy 가 kā 게 kēy / 모 mŏs' 스 소 sŏ	오 ŏ 비 pī	미 mī 노 nŏ 가 kā 사 sā	갇 kāt 바 pā	가 kā 다 tā 비 pī 라 rā	히 hī 도 tŏ 예 ēy 모 mŏ 노 nŏ

Japanese words assorted and explained Vol.

四五

Stockings socks	A pillow A bolster	A sleeping gown A coverlet	A kerchief	Button	A surplice	A fold A plait	A sleeve
襪	枕	衾	巾	紐	衲	襞	袖
베쯔 pēyts'	신 sīn	긴 kīn	긴 kīn	쥬우 tsyoō oō	도우 dŏ oō	헤기 hēy kī	시우 sī oō
보션 말 pŏ syōn māř	벼개 침 pyō kāī tshŏm	니블 금 nī poěr koŏm	슈건 건 syoō kōn kōn	돌막이 뉴 tăr māk ī nyoō	누덕이 납 noō tō kī nāp	주롬 벽 tsoō roōm pyŏk	소매 슈 să māī syoō
다비 tā pī	마구라 mā koō rā	후스마 오요기 hoō soō mā yŏ gī	데누구이 tē noō goō ī	뽀다 bŏ tā	사시계로모누 sā sī gīr' mŏ nŏ	히다 hī dā	소데 sŏ tē

Boots	Leggings Gaiters	A mattrass	Bare shouldered	Ribband A band	A tassel	A seam	A cloak
子靴	纏行	褥	袒	襻	纓	縫	幅
과시 kwā sī	고우텐 kŏ oō tēn	죡구 zyŏk'	단 tān	한 hān	에이 ēy ī	후우 hō oō	후구 hŏŏk
휘조 hwō tsā	힝젼 hāing tsyōn	요욕 yŏ yŏk	멜단 mēr tān	고롬반 kŏ rŏm pān	신영 skīn yŏng	홀봉 hŏr pŏng	폭복 phŏk pŏk
후가구즈 hoō kā goō tsoō	한뎐 hān dēn	후돈 hoō tăn	가다하다 kā tā hā dā	히모 hī mŏ	간무리노오 kān moō rī nŏ ŏ	누우 noō oō	하바 hā pā

Food Victuals Aliment	Boiled water Hot water	Noon rice Dinner	Rice Boiled rice		To put on To dress	Clogs Wooden Shoes	Shoes
饌	水熱	飯午	飯	飮食	着	屐	鞋
션 syōn	슈 zyoŏk' 구 스 soŏ 이 ī	오 gŏ 한 hān	한 hān	Eating and Drinking	쟈 zyak' 구	게 kēy 기 kī	아 ā 이 ī
반 pān 찬 tshān 찬 tshān	슉 syŏk 슈 syoō	오 ŏ 반 pān	밥 pāp 반 pān		닙 nīp 을 oŏr 챡 tshyak	격 kyŏk 지 tsī 극 koŏk	신 sīn 혜 hēy
메 mēy 시 sī 노 nŏ 사 sā 이 ī	유 yoō	히 hī 루 roō 이 ī 이 ī	메 mēy 시 sī		기 kir' 루	게 gēy 다 dā	구 koōts' 즈

Rice water Congee	Broth	Evening rice, supper	Early rice Breakfast			To strip off To undress	Straw shoes
粥	羹	飯夕	飯早			脫	鞋草
시 sik' 구	고 kŏ 우 oō	셰 sēy 기 kī 한 hān	소 sŏ 우 oō 한 hān			따 ttāts' 쯔	소 sŏ 우 oō 아 ā 이 ī
죽 tsyŏok 죽 tsyŏok	국 koōk 깅 kāing	셕 syŏk 반 pān	조 tsŏ 반 pān			벗 pŏ 슬 sŏor 탈 thār	초 tshŏ 혜 hēy
가 kā 유 yoō	슈 syoŏr' 루 / 아 āts' 즈 모 mŏ 노 nŏ	이 ī 우 oō 메 mēy 시 sī	아 ā 사 sā 메 mēy 시 sī			누 noŏk' 구	소 zŏ 우 oō 리 rī

倭語類解 上

Japanese words assorted and explained

Vol.

倭語類解 上

…ese …rds …ted …d …ned I.

飲食

Eat. &c Drink

Bread	Flour Paste	Minced meat	Sediment Lees	To ferment liquor	Savory food Fish. &c.	Thick wine Muddy wine	Wine Liquor
饅	麵	膾	滓	釀	肴	酒濁	酒
만 mān	면 mēyn	과 kwā 이 ī	시 sī	쇼 zyō 우 oō	고 kō 우 oō	다 tāk' 구 슈 syoō	슈 syoō
만 mān 두 toō 만 mān	국 koŏk 슈 syoō 면 myōn	회 hŏī 회 hŏī	조 tsoŏ 의 wī 지 tsāī	비 pī 즐 tsoŏr 양 yāng	안 ān 쥬 tsyoō 효 hyō	탁 thāk 쥬 tsyoō	술 soŏr 쥬 tsyoō
만 mān 쥬 zyōo 우 oō	소 sō 우 oō 멘 mēyn	나 nā 마 mās' 스	간 kān 스 soŏ	사 sā 계 kēy 즈 tsoō 구 koōr 루	사 sā 가 kā 나 nā	니 nī 고 gō 리 rī 사 sā 계 kēy	사 sā 계 kēy

Pulse Jelly	Sliced paste vermacelli	A. cake	Flesh Meat	Dregs Grains	Leaven Ferment	Hot wine	Clear wine
腐豆	麵刀	餅	肉	漉	麴	酒燒	酒淸
	도 tō 우 oō 멘 mēyn	헤 hēy 이 ī	니 nīk' 구	로 lōk' 구	기 kīk' 구	쇼 syō 우 oō 슈 syoō	
두 toō 부 poō	도 tō 면 myōn	셕 stōk 병 pyōng	고 kō 기 kī 육 yoōk	거 kō 를 roōr 록 rōk	누 noō 룩 roōk 국 koōk	쇼 syō 쥬 syoō	청 tshyōng 쥬 tsyoō
도 tō 우 oō 후 hoō	기 kī 리 rī 조 zō 우 oō 멘 mēyn	모 mō 지 tsī	시 sī 시 sī	고 kōs' 스	고 kō 우 oō 시 zī	쇼 syō 우 oō 쥬 tsyoō 우 oō	세 sēy 이 ī 슈 syoō

47

Sugar candy	Brown sugar	Confection Honey fruits Conserves	Crumbs Morsels	Vinegar	Pickled, or minced meat	Sweet pickle	Cow's milk Milk
糖冰	糖砂	果蜜	屑	醋	醢	醬甘	酪酡
효우도우 yŏ oō tŏ oō		미쯔과 mits' kwā	셰쯔 sēyts'	조 sŏ	가이 kā i	간쇼우 kān syŏ oō	다라구 tā lāk'
빙당 ping tāng	사당 sā tāng	밀과 mīr kwā	ᄀᆞ르셜 kă rā syōr	쵸조 tshŏ tsŏ	젓해 tsŏt hăī	감쟝 kām tsyāng	타락 t'hā lāk
고오리사도우 kŏ ŏ rī zā tŏ oō	샤도우 syā tŏ oō	미즈스계 mits' zoŏ kēy	고 kŏ	스 soŏ	시오가라 sī ŏ kā rā	미소 mī sŏ	우시노지 oō sī nŏ tsī

Comfits	White sugar	Sirup Treacle	Honey	Oil	Salt	A kind of Waterplant	Clear pickle Pure brine
糖花五	糖雪	糖飴	蜜	油	塩	菹	醬清
	셰쯔도우 sēyts' tŏ oō	이도우 ī tŏ oō		이우 ī oō	이연 ĭyn	쇼 syŏ	셰이쇼우 sēy ī syŏ oō
오화당 ŏ hwā tāng	셜당 syōr tāng	이당 ī tāng	ᄭᅮᆯ밀 skoŏr mir	기름유 kī roōm yoō	소곰염 sŏ kŏm yōm	딤ᄎᆡ조 thīm tshăī tsŏ	쳥쟝 tshyŏng tsyāng
고과도우 gŏ kwā tŏ oō	시로사도우 sī rŏ zā tŏ oō	아메 ā mēy	미쯔 mits'	아부라 ā poō rā	시오 sī ŏ	기미스이 kī mī soŏ ī	쇼우유우 syŏ oō yoō oō

倭語類解

Japanese words assorted and explained Vol.

倭語類解上

Chinese Words used and explained I.

飮食 Eating & Drinking

Cooked Dressed	To cool	To boil to rags overdone	To decoct	To broil To roast	To stew	Meal of the Dolichus Hirsutus	Candied orange peel
熟	清	爛	煎	炙	蒸	葛粉	丁橙
슈구 zyoŏk	세이 sēy ī	란 lān	션 sēyn	세기 sēy kī	죠우 zyŏ oō	가쯔훈 kāts' hoōn	도우데이 tŏ oō tē ī
니글쇽 nī koŏr syoŏk	식을졍 sik oŏr tsyōng	무로녹올란 moō rŏ nŏk ŏr rān	달힐젼 tār hīr tsyōn	구올젹 koō oŏr tsyŭk	씰증 stīr tsoŏng	갈분 kār poōn	동뎡 toŏng tyŏng
우무 oōm'	히유루 hī yoōr'	다다루루 tā dā roōr'	션스루 sēyn zoŏr' / 아우루 ā hoōr'	압부루 ā poōr'	무스 moōs'	구스 koō zoŏ	뿌슈관 boō syoō kān

48

To serve up	Raw	To congeal	To scald Hot water	To seeth	To fry in a pan	To boil To cook	Candied orange
盛	生	凝	湯	煮	炒	烹	餠橘
셰이 sēy ī	쇼우 syŏ oō	교우 gyŏ oō	도우 tŏ oō	쇼 syŏ	소우 sŏ oō	호우 hŏ oō	기쯔헤이 kīts' hēy ī
담을셩 tām oŏr syōng	날겁싱 năr kŏp săing	엉긜응 ŏng kwīr oŏng	끌을탕 skoŏr oŏr thāng	지질쟈 tsī tsīr tsyā	복글쵸 pŏk koŏr tshyŏ	삶물핑 săr moōr phăing	귤병 kyoōr pyŏng
모루 mŏr'	나마 nā mā	고무루 kŏ moōr'	와구 wāk'	니예루 nī ēyr'	이루 īr'	니루 nīr'	뿌시관 boō sī kān

Rank Rancid	A raw Smell	Fragrant	Salt Briny	Acrid Pungent	Sweet	To entertain To feast	To taste
羶	腥	焄	醎	辛	甘	餉	嘗
션 sëyn	셩이 sëy ī	군 koōn	간 kān	신 sīn	간 kān	쇼우 syŏ oō	쇼우 syŏ oō
노린젼 nŏ rīr tsyŏn	비린생 pī rīr syŏng	향긔훈 hyāng kwī hoōn	졸함 stsăr hām	미올신 măī ŏr sīn	돌감 tăr kām	먹일향 mŏk īr hyāng	맛볼샹 măt pŏr syāng
도로구사이 dŏ rŏk' sā ī	나마가사이 na mā goō sā ī	고우노니오이 kŏ oō nŏ nī ŏ ī	시오하유시 sī ŏ hā yoō sī	가라시 kā rā sī	아마시 ā mā sī	구와스 koō wās'	나무루 nā moōr'

Rotten	Aromatic	Stinking	Tasteless Insipid	Sour Acid	Bitter	A taste	To eat
腐	葷	臭	淡	酸	苦	味	食
후 hoō	군 koōn	시우 sī oō	담 tān	산 sān	구 koō	비 bī	쇼구 syŏk'
석굴부 sŏk koŏr poō	누릴훈 noō rīr hoōn	내츄 nai tshyoō	승거올담 soŏng kŏ oŏr tām	싈산 swīr sān	씁고 ssoŏr kŏ	맛미 măt mī	먹올식 mŏk oŏr sīk
구사루 koo sār'	가구사이 kā goō sā ī	가구 kā goō	마쯔구사이 mits' koō sā ī	스이이 soō ī ī	니가시 nī gā sī	아시와이 ā zī wī ī	구우 koō oō

倭語類解

Japanese words assorted and explained Vol.

四八

倭語類解 上

...ose ...rds ...ed ...d ...ned I.

飲食

Eat. & Drin...

To relish Agreeable	A stoppage in the throat	To spew out To spurt out	To hold in the mouth To contain	To bite	To suck	To smell To stink	Fetid putrid
嗜	塞咽	噴	含	齕	吮	嗅	臭腐
기 kī	인 īn 속 sŏk'	훈 hoōn	간 gān	고 kōts' 쯔	션 sēyn	규 kyoō 우 oō	후 hoō 시 sī 우 oō
즐 tsoēr 길 kīr 기 kī	인 īn 식 săik	뿜 spoōm 을 oōr 분 poōn	머 mŏk 음 oŏm 을 oōr 함 hām	너 nō 홀 hoŏr 홀 hoŏr	샐 spăr 연 yōn	맏 māt 틀 thŏor 후 hoō	부 poō 취 tshyoō
다 tā 시무 sīm'	논 nŏn 도 dŏ 후 hoō 사 sā 까루 găr'	하구 hāk'	후 hoō 구무 kōom'	가 kā 미 mī 기루 kīr'	스 soŏ 우 oō	니 nī 오 ŏ 이 ī 가 kā 구 goō	구 koō 소 sō 구 koō 사 sā 이 ī

Satisfied To be full	A dryness in the throat	To vomit	To taste in the mouth	To catch in the mouth	To lick	To swallow To gulp	Urinous smell
飽	乾喉	吐	口咂	噙	舐	呑	臭尿
호 hŏ 우 oō	고 kŏ 우 oō 간 kān	도 tŏ	소 sŏ 우 oō 고 kŏ 우 oō	긴 kīn	데 tē 이 ī	돈 tŏn	뇨 nyŏ 우 oō 시 sī 우 oō
배 pāi 브 poŏ 를 roŏr 포 p'hŏ	후 hoō 간 kān	토 t'hŏ 할 hăr 토 t'hŏ	잡 tsăp 구 koō	새 ssī 블 poŏr 금 koŏm	할 hăr 틀 thoŏr 뎌 tyŏ	숨 săm 킬 k'hīr 톤 t'hăn	뇨 nyŏ 취 tshyoō
하 hā 라 rā 가 gā 후 hōō 도 tŏ 이 ī	논 nŏn 도 dŏ 가 kā 와구 wāk'	도 tŏ 갸구 kyāk'	구 koō 지 tsī 나 nā 메 mēy 부 boō	구 koō 와 wā 예루 ēyr'	내 nē 부루 poōr'	노무 nŏm'	쇼 syŏ 우 oō 벤 peyn 구 koō 사 sā 이 ī

49

疾病

Sickness and Disease

To quench To extinguish	Smoke To smoke	To roast To bake	To burn	Fire	To be hungry To hunger	Starving Famished
熄	烟	燒	焚	火	飢	餒
쇽 sŏk	연 ēyn	쇼우 syŏ oŏ	훈 hŏon	화 kwā	긔 kī	요 yŏ
불새질식 poōr skō tsir sĭk	닉연 năī yōn	술올쇼 săr oŏr syŏ	불붇들분 poōr pōot thŏor poōn	불화 poōr hwā	주릴긔 tsoō rir kwī	술홀에 soŏr hoŏr ēy
히기유루 hī kī yoōr'	께무루 kēy moōr'	야구 yāk'	다구 tāk'	히 hī	가조렐루 kā tsoŏ rēyr' 우예루 oō ēyr'	이연 ī ēyn 구이니구이 koō ī nī koo ī

	A smoke jack	To boil rice To steam	To light a fire To dress food	Charcoal Coal	To thirst To be thirsty	To dislike To loathe
	鎖烟	炊	爨	炭	渴	厭
	연사 ēyn sā	스이 soŏ ī	산 sān	단 tān	갈 kāts	염 ēyn
	연쇄 yōn swāī	밥지올취 pāp tsī ŏŏr tshōōey	불지둘찬 poōr tsī toŏr tshān	숫탄 sōor t'hān	갈홀갈 kār hăr kār	술홀염 soŏr hoŏr yōm
	께무리마구 kēy moō rī māk'	메시다구 mēy sī tāk'	히다구 hī tāk'	스미 soŏ mī	가와구 kā wāk'	이도우 ī tŏ oō 스가누 soŏ kān'

倭語類解

Japanese words assorted and explained Vol.

Disziness	To take cold Inflammation	Diarrhoea	Vomiting	A phlegmatic disease	A catarrh	Loss of the voice	A sickness Disease
暈眩	風中	疾痢	噎嘔	病痰	寒傷	音失	病
	쥬 tsyoō 우 oō 우 hoō 우 oō	리 li 시 쯔 sits'		단 tān 헤 hēy 이 ī		시 쯔 sĭts' 인 īn	헤 hēy 이 ī
현 hyŏn 운 oōn	즁 tsyoōng 풍 phoōng	리 li 질 tsīr	구 koō 역 ngyŏk	담 tām 병 pyōng	상 syāng 한 hān	실 sīr 음 oōm	병 pyōng 병 pyōng
켠 kēyn 운 oōn	쥬 tsyoō 우 oō 부 poō	리 li 뵤 pyŏ 우 oŏ	오 ŏ 우 oō 케 kēy 기 kī	단 tān 뵤 pyŏ 우 oō	쇼 syŏ 우 oō 관 kān	고 kŏ 에 ēy 가 kā 레 rēy	야 yā 마 mā 이 ī

Headache	Inflammation in the head	Fever & Ague	Purging Looseness Dysentery	Colick Cholera	A periodical sickness	A slight cold	Pain Ache Agony
痛頭	風頭	疾瘧	瀉泄	亂霍	病時	感外	痛
도 tŏ 우 oō 도 tŏ 우 oō	도 tŏ 우 oō 후 hoō 우 oō	갸 꾸 gyāk' 시 쯔 sīts'	세 쯔 sēyts' 샤 syā		시 sī 헤 hēy 이 ī	과 kwā 이 ī 관 kān	도 tŏ 우 oō
두 toō 통 thŏng	두 toō 풍 phoōng	학 hāk 질 tsīr	설 syōr 샤 syā	곽 kwāk 란 lān	시 sī 병 pyōng	외 ŏi 감 kām	알 ār 홀 hoŏr 통 thŏng
스 zoŏ 즈 tsoŏ 우 oō	스 zoŏ 후 hoō 우 oō	오 ŏ 고 kŏ 리 rī	하 hā 라 rā 아 gā 군 koān 다 tā 리 rī	과 구 kwāk' 란 lān	하 hā 야 yā 리 rī 야 yā 마 mā 이 ī	가 kā 이 ī 게 kēy 가 kā 세 zēy	이 ī 다 tā 미 mī

Numbness of the feet	Numbness Palsy	To swell	Phlegm	Epilepsy	Prolapsus ani	Quinsy	Pain in the breast
麻足	木麻	腫	痰	疾癎	下帯	痹喉	痛胷
소 구 sŏk' 마 mā	마 mā 보 구 bŏk'	쇼 syŏ 우 oō	단 tān	간 kān 시 쯔 sits'			
족 tsyŏk 마 mā	마 mā 목 mŏk	부 poō 을 ŏr 종 tsyŏng	담 tām 담 tām	간 kān 질 tsir	대 tăi 하 hā	후 hoō 비 pi	흉 hyoōng 통 thŏng
시 sī 비 pī 리 rī 애 gā	시 sī 베 bī 레 rēy	하 hā 루 루 roŏr'	가 kā 스 soŏ 하 hā 기 kī	덴 tēn 간 kān	다 tā 이 ī 애 gēy	고 kō 우 oō 히 hī	교 kyō 우 oō 즈 tsoō 우 oō

Emission of semen	Numbness of the legs	Dropsical swelling	Dyspnoea To pant	Madness Delirium	Jaundice	Removal of thirst	Pain in the belly
泄夢	麻脚	脹	喘	狂	疸黄	渴消	痛腹
보 bō 우 oō 세 쯔 sēyts	갸 구 kyāk' 마 mā	죠 tsyŏ 우 oō	젠 zēyn	교 kyō 우 oō	고 kō 우 oō 다 쯔 tāts'		
몽 bŏng 셜 syŏr	각 kāk 마 mā	창 tshyāng 만 mān 창 tshyāng	천 tshyōn 만 mān 천 tshyōn	미 mī 칠 tshir 광 kwāng	황 hwāng 달 tār	쇼 syŏ 갈 kār	복 pŏk 통 thŏng
모 mŏ 우 oō 즈 zŏ 우 oō	스 soō 네 nē 시 sī 부 poō 리 rī	죠 tsyŏ 우 oō 만 mān	세 sēy 기 kī	기 kī 찌 tsī 애 gā 이 ī	오 ŏ 우 oō 단 dān	쇼 syŏ 우 oō 가 쯔 kāts'	후 구 hoŏk' 즈 tsoō 우 oō

倭語類解 上 疾病

A scab A cicatrice	The itch	A bile	A gathering	Eruption Kings evil	Scurf	Ulcer	Small pox
痂	癢	癰瘭	疣	瘢	癬	瘡	疹痘
가 kā	요 yō 우 oō	라 lā 례 lēy 기 kī	이 ī 우 oō	텐 tēn	션 sēyn	소 sŏ 우 oō	토 tŏ 우 oō 진 tsīn
더 tŏ 데 tē 가 kā	가 kă 려 ryō 올 ŏr 양 yāng	라 lā 력 lyōk	혹 hŏk 우 oō	어 ŏ 루 roō 러 rō 기 kī 뎐 tyōn	버 pŏ 즘 tsoŏm 션 syōn	창 tshāng 질 tsīr 창 tshāng	두 toō 진 tsīn
가 kā 사 sā 부 poō 다 tā	가 kā 유 yoō 이 ī	루 roō 이 ī 례 rēy 기 kī	이 ī 누 noō 노 nŏ 메 mēy 마 mā 메 mēy	나 nā 마 mā 스 zoŏ	가 kā 례 rēy 야 yā 마 mā 이 ī	가 kā 사 sā	호 hŏ 우 oō 소 sŏ 우 oō

To heal To restore	Pus Matter	Leprosy	A black speck A blotch	A spot A wart	A freckle	A sore	Measles
痊	汁膿	癩	黶	痣	疿	疥	疹麻
션 sēyn	노 nŏ 우 oō 시 sī 우 oō	라 lā 이 ī	연 ēyn	시 sī	후쯔 hoōts'	가 kā 이 ī	마 mā 진 tsīn
암 ām 굴 koōr 젼 tsyōn	농 nŏng 즙 tsoŏp	룡 lyŏng 병 pyŏng 래 lăi	샤 syā 마 mā 귀 koōi 염 yōm	기 kī 뮈 moōi 지 tsī	ᄯᅡᆷ stām ᄯᅱ stwī 불 poōr	옴 ŏm 개 kāi	마 mā 진 tsīn
이 ī 유루 yoōr'	우 oō 미 mī 시루 sīr'	가즈 kat 다 tā 이 ī	호구 hŏk' 로 rŏ	이 ī 보 pŏ	아 ā 셰 sēy 보 pŏ	히 hī 졘 zēyn 아 gā 시 ī	하 hā 시 sī 가 kā

51

To expire	A cripple A crumpled leg	A dwarf	Harelip	Blind	A squinting eye	A cataract	Baldness
絶氣	脚縮	子矮	唇缺	瞽	眼斜	瞙眼	頭禿
	슉 syŏok 구 갹 kyăk 구	와 wa 이 ĭ 시 sĭ	계 kēyts 쯔 신 sĭn	고 kŏ	샤 syā 간 găn	안 găn 마 māk' 구	도 tŏk' 구 도 bŏ 우 oō
긔 kwĭ 졀 tsyŏr	츅 tsĭnyŏok 각 kăk	왜 wăi 즈 tsă	결 kyŏr 슌 syoon	쇼 syŏ 경 kyŏng 고 kŏ	샤 syā 안 ăn	안 ăn 막 măk	독 tŏk 두 toō
기 kī 졔 쯔 zēyts	이 ī 시 sī 리 rī	잇 īt 슨 soŏn 뽀 bŏ	이 ī 구 koō 지 tsī	메 mēy 구 koō 라 rā	숑 sŏong 고 kŏ 우 oō	메 mēy 노 nŏ 호 hŏ 시 sī	하 hā 게 gēy 아 ā 다 tā 마 mā

To revive	Lame	An eunuch	Humpbacked	Dumb	One eyed	A speck on the eye	Deafness
甦	蹇	閹	背龜	啞	目一	肉瘤	聾
소 sŏ	견 keyn	언 ēyn	개 kĭ 하 hā 이 ĭ	아 ā	이 īts' 쯔 모 mŏk' 구	노 nŏ 우 oō 니 nĭk' 구	로 lŏ 우 oō
시 skăi 여 yŏ 날 năr 소 sŏ	절 tsŏr 건 kŏn	고 kŏ 쟈 tsyā 엄 ŏm	귀 koŏi 븨 păi	벙 pŏng 어 ŏ 리 rī 아 ā	일 ĭr 목 mŏk	노 nŏ 육 yŏok	귀 koŏi 먹 mŏk 을 ŏŏr 롱 lŏng
기 kī 즉 zoŏk' / 소 sŏ 세 sēy 이 ĭ	진 tsĭn 때 bā	후 hoŏ 우 goō 리 rĭ 나 nă 시 sĭ	세 sēy 무 moō 시 sĭ	오 ŏ 시 sĭ	가 kā 다 tā 메 mēy	도 dŏ 니 nĭk' 구	쥼 tsoŏm 보 pŏ 우 oō

倭語類解上

ese rds ed d ned I.

A coffin	A corpse A carcase	A funeral		To regulate To set to right	To cauterize To brand	Medicine Physick	To cure a sickness
棺	尸	喪	喪祭 Funerals and Sacrifices	理調	炙	藥	病救
관 kwān	시 sī	소 sŏ 우 oō		됴 tyŏ 우 oō 리 li	규 kyoō 우 oō	야 yāk' 구	규 kyoō 우 oō 혜 hēy 이 ī
관 kwān 지 tsăi 관 kwān	죽 tsoōk 엄 ōm 시 sī	싱 sīng ᄉᆞ să 상 sāng		됴 tyŏ 리 li	뜸 stoŏm 질 tsīr 구 koō	약 yāk 약 yāk	구 koō 병 pyōng
히 hī 즈 tsoō 기 kī	가 kā 바 pā 네 nē	후 hoō 고 kŏ 우 oō 모 mŏ		요 yŏ 우 oō 죠 tsyŏ 우 oō	야 yā 이 ī 도 tŏ	구 스 koōs' 리 rī	간 kān 뵤 byŏ 우 oō

喪祭 Fun: & Sacr.

Mourning	The soul A spirit	To die Death			To restore to health	To puncture	A vital remedy
服	魄魂	死			瘳	鍼	藥命
부 boōk' 구	곤 kŏn 하 hăk' 구	시 sī			쥬 tsyōo 우 oō	신 sīn	
닙 nīp 을 oŏr 복 pŏk	혼 hŏn 빅 pāăk	죽 tsoōk' 을 oŏr ᄉᆞ să			ᄒᆞ hă 릴 rīr 츄 tshyōo	침 tshīm 침 tshīm	명 myōng 약 yāk.
쇼 syŏ 우 oō 신 zīn	다 tā 마 mā 시 sī 이 ī	시 sī 누 루 noōr' 시 sī 스 soŏ			야 yā 마 mā 이 ī 이 ī 유 루 yoōr'	하 hā 리 rī 다 tā 데 tē	메 mēy 이 ī 야 구 yāk'

52

A temple	Temples and Pagodas	Fasting	Anniversary of a death	A sacrificial temple	A grave A tomb	To bury	To cry To lament
寺	寺刹	齋	日忌	堂祠	墓	埋	哭
시 zī		사 sā 이 ī	기 kī 싀 쯔 zīts'	시 sī 도 tŏ 우 oō	뽀 bŏ	빠 bā 이 ī	고 구 kŏk'
졀 tsyŏr 亽 sǎ		지 tsāi 계 kěy 지 tsāi	긔 kwī 일 ĭr	亽 sǎ 당 tāng	무 moŏ 덤 tŏm 묘 myŏ	무 moŏ 들 toŏr 믜 māi	울 oōr 곡 kŏk
데 tē 라 rā		모 mŏ 노 nŏ 이 ī 미 mī	이 ī 미 mī 비 pī / 쇼 syŏ 우 oō 신 zīn 비 pī	마 mā 즈 루 tsoŏr' 이 ī 예 ēy	즈 tsoŏ 가 kā / 하 hā 가 kā	우 oō 스 무 zoŏm'	나 구 nāk'

A pagoda		A sacrifice	A parental tablet	A tomb stone Monument	To inter	To condole
刹		祭	主神	碑	葬	弔
사 쯔 sāts'		셰 sēy 이 ī	신 sīn 슈 syoō	히 hī	소 sŏ 우 oō	됴 tyŏ 우 oō
졀 tsyŏr 찰 ts'hār		졔 tsēy 亽 sǎ 졔 tsēy	신 sīn 쥬 tsyoō	비 pī 셕 syāk 비 pī	무 moŏ 들 toŏr 장 tsāng	됴 tyŏ 문 moŏn 됴 tyŏ
고 kŏ 데 tē 리 rā		마 즈 māts' 리 rī	간 kān 누 noŏ 시 sī	셰 sēy 기 kī 히 hī / 다 tā 데 tē 이 ī 시 sī	소 sŏ 우 oō 레 rēy 이 ī	도 tŏ 무 moŏ 라 rā 이 ī

倭語類解上

寺刹

Temples and Pagodas

A ghost A devil	A cassock	A friar (Chinese)	A priest	A prayer To invoke	A divinity A demigod	An altar	A monastery A convent
鬼	袈裟	沙彌	僧	祈	菩薩	壇	菴
기 kī	갸 kā 샤 syā	샤 syā 비 bī	소 sŏ 우 oō	기 kī			안 ān
귀 kooī 신 sīn 귀 kooī	가 kā 사 sā	사 sā 미 mī	즁 tsyoāng 승 soōng	빌 pīr 괴 kwī	보 pŏ 살 sār	단 tān 단 tān	암 ām 즈 tsă 암 ām
가 kā 미 mī 오 ŏ 니 nī	게 kēy 사 sā	고 kŏ 소 zŏ 오 ŏ	보 bŏ 우 oō ᅀ zoŏ 슛 syoōt 게 kēy	이 ī 노 nŏ 리 rī	호 hŏ 사쯔 sāts'	단 dān	이 ī 오 ŏ 리 rī

53

A demon	A long gown	A priest's cap	A nun	An abbot A prior	An invisible being	Buddha	A tower A minaret
夜义	長衫	僧帽	尼	長老	靈	佛	塔
야 yā 사 sā	죠 tsyŏ 우 oō 산 sān	소 sŏ 우 oō 보 bŏ 우 oō	ᅀ| zī		레 lēy 이 ī	보쯔 pŏts'	
야 yā 차 tshā	쟝 tsyāng 삼 sām	승 soōng 모 mŏ	승 soōng 니 nī	쟝 tsyāng 로 lŏ	신 sīn 령 lyōng 령 lyŏng	부 poō 쳐 tsiyō 불 poōr	탑 thāp 탑 thāp
우 oō 무 moō 메 mēy 무구 moōk' 메 mēy	나 nā 가 gā 이 ī 기 kī 루 roō 모 mŏ 노 nŏ	모 mŏ 우 oō 스 soŏ	아 ā 마 mā 미 mī 고 kŏ 니 nī	죠 tsyŏ 우 oō 로 lŏ 우 oō	레 lēy 이 ī 켄 keyn	호 hŏ 도 tŏ 케 kēy	도 tŏ 우 oō

倭語類解 Japanese vo[cabulary] assort[ed] an[d] explai[ned] Vol.

刑獄 Punishments and Imprisonments

To lay hold of	To imprison / To confine	To take / To apprehend	To punish / To fine	To disobey / To transgress	To put in order / To govern / To control	Punishment
拘	囚	拿	罰	犯	治	刑
구 koō	시우 sī oō	다 tā	바쯔 pāts'	한 hān	지 tsī	케이 kēy ī
걸릴구 kōr rīr koō	가돌슈 kā tōr syoō	자바드릴나 tsā pā toō rīr nā	죄줄벌 tsōi tsoōr pōr	범ᄒᆞᆯ범 pōm hār pōm	다ᄉᆞ릴치 tā sā rīr tshī	형벌형 hyōng pōr hyōng
가가루 kā kār'	도라와레 tō rā wā rēy	도라히구 tō rā hīk'	즈미 tsoō mī	오가스 ō kās'	오사마루 ō sā mār'	케이빠즈 kēy ī bāts'

A prison / A gaol	To arrest / To restrain	To bind / To tie up	To steal	A fault / offence	A crime / A sin, Blame	A law / A rule
獄	禁	縛結	偷	過	罪	法
교구 gyŏk'	긴 kīn	계쯔 kēyts' 하구 hăk'	도우 tŏ oō	과 kwā	사이 sā ī	호우 hŏ oō
옥옥 ŏk ŏk	금ᄒᆞᆯ금 koŏm hăr koŏm	결박 kyōr pāk	도적질ᄒᆞᆯ투 tŏ tsŏk rīr hăr thoō	허물과 hō moōr kwā	허물죄 hō moōr tsŏī	법법 pōp pōp
로우 rŏ oō / 교구 gyŏk 야 yā	긴ᅀᅳ루 kīn zoōr'	시바루 sī pār'	누스무 noo soōm'	아야마지 ā yā mā tsī / 기ᅀᅮ kī zoŏ	도가 tŏ gā	노리 nŏ rī

倭語類解 上

Chinese words noted and explained I.

刑獄

Punishment and Imprisonment

To tattoo in the face	To degrade from office To discard	To let go To discharge	To decide To determine	To make public	To investigate To examine	To interrogate To scrutinize	To bamboo To beat
黥	黜	放	斷决	公屬	覈查	訊	笞
계 kēy 이 ī	슈 쯔 tsyōots'	호 hŏ 우 oŏ	계 쯔 kēyts' 단 dān	조 구 zŏk' 고 kŏ 우 oŏ	사 sā 가 구 kāk'	신 zīn	다 tā 이 ī
조 tsă 지 tsăi 경 kyōng	내 nāi 칠 tshŭr 츌 tshyoŏr	노 nŏ 흘 hoŏr 방 pāng	결 kyŏr 단 tān	쇽 syŏk 공 kōng	사 sā 힉 hăik	쳐 tsyŏ 쥴 tsoŏr 신 sīn	티 thăi 쟝 tsyāng 티 thăi
이 ī 레 rēy 스 zoo 미 mī	다 dā 스 soŏ 지 sī 리 rī 조 zŏ 구 루 koŏr'	하 hā 나 즈 năts'	나 nā 지 tsī 아 ā 기 kī	도 tŏ 리 rī 아 ā 게 gēy 결 kēyt 쇼 syŏ	긴 gīn 미 mī	세 sēy 메 mēy	고 kŏ 즈 tsoŏ 에 ēy

54

五四

To prick	To reprimand To condemn	To forgive To pardon	To excuse	To clear up a matter	To search to the bottom	To send up a statement	To cudgel To bastinado
刺	讁	赦	恕	明發	刷推	招捧	杖
시 sī	다 구 tāk'	샤 syā	쇼 zyŏ		스 soŏ 이 ī 사 sā 이 ī	호 hŏ 우 oŏ 쇼 syŏ 우 oŏ	쵸 tsyŏ 우 oŏ
지 tsăi 를 roŏr 조 tsă	죄 tsŏi 쥴 tsoŏr 젹 tsyŏk	샤 syā 흘 hăr 샤 syā	졉 tsyŏp 을 oŏr 셔 syŏ	발 pār 명 myōng	츄 tshyoŏ 쇄 swāi	봉 pŏng 쵸 tshyŏ	막 māk 대 tāi 쟝 tsyāng
사 sā 스 soŏ	나 nā 가 스 găs	유 yoŏ 루 스 roŏs'	하 hā 가 루 kār'	하 hā 즈 tsoŏ 메 mēy 이 ī	오 ŏ 시 sī 즈 tsoŏ 메 mēy	구 koŏ 지 tsī 가 gā 기 kī	즈 tsoŏ 에 ēy

倭語類解

Japa
w
asso
a
expl
Vol.

籌數

Calculation and Reckoning

To behead To decapitate	To kill To slay
斬	殺
산 săn	사쯔 săts'
베 pē 힐 hīr 참 ts'hām	죽 tsoŏk 일 ir 살 săr
기ᄅ kīr'	고로스 kŏ rŏs'

To stick the head on a pole	To strangle
示梟	絞
교 gyŏ 우 oō 시 zī	고 kŏ 오 oō
효 hyŏ 시 sī	교 kyŏ 홀 hăr 교 kyŏ
교 kyŏ 우 oō 슈 syoō	시 sī 메 mĕy 고로스 kŏ rŏs'

Seven	Five	Three	One	To count To calculate To compute
七	五	三	一	筭
시쯔 sĭts'	괴 gŏ	산 săn	이쯔 ĭts'	쥬 tsyoō 우 oō
닐 nīr 곱 kŏp 칠 ts'hīr	다 tâ 숫 săt 오 ŏ	셕 sŏk 삼 sām	호 hăn 일 ir	혬 hĕym 쥬 tsyoō
나 nā 나쯔 nāts'	이 ī 즈쯔 tsoōts'	믿쯔 mĭts'	히 hī 도쯔 tŏts'	산 sān 료 ryŏ 우 oō

Eight	Six	Four	Two	To reckon A number
八	六	四	二	數
하쯔 hăts'	로구 lŏk'	시 sī	니 nī	스 soŏ
여 yŏ 듧 tărp 팔 p'hăr	여 yŏ 슷 soŏt 륙 lyoŏk	넉 nŏk 亽 să	두 toŏ 이 ĭ	혬 hĕym 수 soŏ
야쯔 yats'	무쯔 moōts'	요ᄃ쯔 yŏts'	후 hoŏ 다쯔 tăts'	가 kā 스 zoŏ

A gurbit A Chin foot	A pint 1½ catty	A pecul 120 catties	A dram 1/10 of an oz.	A catty 1⅓ pound	A myriad	A hundred	Nine
尺	升	石	錢	斤	萬	百	九
셰 sēy 기 kī		셔 syō 가 kī	센 sēyn				큐 kyoō 우 oō
자 tsā 챡 tshyăk	되 tōï 승 soōng	셤 syōm 셕 syŏk	돈 tŏn 젼 tsyōn	근 koōn 근 koōn	일 ir 만 mān 만 mān	일 ir 빅 păik 빅 păik	아 ā 홉 hŏp 구 koō
샤 쿠 syāk'	쇼 syŏ 우 oō	잇 īt 뵤 pyŏ 우 oō	몸 mŏm 메 mēy	긴 kīn	만 mān	햐 구 hyāk'	고 kŏ 고 kŏ 노 쯔 nŏts'

Calc and Reck

An inch	A piece of cloth	A gantang 12 catties A peck	5 grains 1/100 of an oz.	An ounce	A lac	A thousand	Ten
寸	疋	斗	分	両	億	千	十
	히 쯔 hīts'	도 tŏ 우 oō	분 poōn				시 sī 우 oō
치 tshī 촌 tshŏn	필 phīr 필 phīr	말 mār 두 toō	푼 phoōn 분 poōn	량 lyăng 량 lyăng	억 ŏk 억 ŏk	일 ir 쳔 tshyŏn 쳔 tshyŏn	열 yŏr 십 sip
순 soōn	히 hī 기 kī	도 tŏ	훈 hoōn	료 lyŏ 우 oō	오 구 ŏk'	센 sēyn	도 tŏ 우 oō

55

To trade / To deal	To set a price	True price / Real value	Goods / Commodities	To buy		One thing	A handful
販	價講	直	貨物	買	買賣	一隻	一握
한 hān	고 kō 우 oō 가 kā	죠구 tsyŏk'	모쯔 mŏts' 과 kwā	빠 bā 이 ī		이쯔 īts' 세 sēy 기 kī	이쯔 īts' 아구 āk'
흥 hŏong 판 phān 판 phān	강 kāng 가 kā	갑 kāp 직 tsik	물 moōr 화 hwā	살 sār 매 māi	Buying and Selling	일 ir 쳑 ts'hyŏk	일 ir 악 āk
아 ā 기 kī 나 nā 이 ī	네 nē 구 goō 미 mī	아 ā 다 tā 이 ī / 네 nē 단 dān	시 sī 로 rŏ 모 mŏ 노 nŏ	고 kŏ 우 oō		히 hī 도 tŏ 고 kŏ 오 ŏ 리 rī	히 hī 도 tŏ 니 nī 기 gī 리 rī

A Capital / The main thing	To barter	Market price	A price / Cost	To sell	One head of cattle	A fingerfull / A pinch
本	易	直市	價	賣	一駄	一撮
혼 hŏn	예 ēy 기 kī	시 sī 죠구 tsyŏk'	가 kā	빠 bā 이 ī	이쯔 īts' 다 tā 이 ī	이쯔 īts' 사쯔 sāts'
밑 mit 본 pŏn	밧 pāi 골 kŏr 역 yāk	시 sī 직 tsik	갑 kāp 가 kā	풀 p'hār 매 māi	일 ir 태 thāi	일 ir 촬 ts'hwar
모 mŏ 도 tŏ	가 kā 예루 ēyr'	소 sŏ 우 oō 빠 bā	아 ā 다 tā 이 ī	우루 oōr'	이 ī 지 tsī 다 dā	히 hī 도 tŏ 쯔 tsoŏ 마 mā 미 mī

Japanese words associated and explained Vol.

	House Rent, To give on trust	To repay To pay down	The side	A witness	A pledge	A debt	To borrow	Gain Profit
	貰家	償	邊	人證	質	債	借	利
	가 kā 셰 sēy 이 ī	쇼 syō 우 oō	현 hēyn	쇼 syō 우 oō 신 zīn	시 sī	사 sā 이 ī	샤 syā	
	가 kā 셰 sēy	가 kā 플 p'hŏor 샹 syāng	변 pyōn 리 rī 변 pyōn	증 tsŏong 인 in	볼 pŏr 모 mŏ 지 tsī	빋 pīt 채 ts'hāi	빌 pīr 챠 tsbyā	리 lī 홀 hăr 리 lī
買賣	야 yā 진 tsīn	스 soŏ 마 mā 스 soŏ 즈 tsoŏ 구 goō 노 nŏ 우 oō	뿌 boō 연 gīn	우 oō 게 kēy 닌 nīn	시 sī 지 tsī	가 kā 게 kēy	가 kā 루 roō	리 lī

Buy and Sell	To set aside evidence	To take as a loan	Double	To secure To hold fast	A bond A security	To pawn To pledge	To lend A loan	To get gain
	徵推	賃	倍	保	文明	當典	貸	利與
	스 soō 이 ī 죠 tsyō 우 oō	닌 nīn	하 hā 이 ī	호 hŏ 우 oō	메 mēy 이 ī 뽄 boōn	텐 tēn 도 tŏ 우 oō	다 tā 이 ī	
56	츄 tšhyoŏ 징 tsīng	셰 sēy 낼 nāir 님 nīm	갑 kāp 졀 tsyōr 비 pāi	보 pŏ 둘 tŏor 보 pŏ	명 myōng 문 mōon	뎐 tyōn 당 tāng	술 sōr 디 tāi	홍 hoōng 리 lī
	와 wā 기 kī 마 mā 예 ēy 이 ī 다 dā 스 soō	진 tsīn	배 bā 이 ī	다 tā 모 mŏ 즈 tsoŏ	데 tē 가 gā 다 tā	시 sī 지 tsī 모 mŏ 쏘 ts'	가 kā 시 sī	교 kyŏ 우 oō 리 lī

倭語類解

上終

Poor. Indigent	A midsman A party concerned	To hold mutual pledge	To put off
貧	謀同	執分	移推
힌 hīn	도 tŏ 우 oō 뽀 bŏ 우 oō	분 poōn 시 sī 우 oō	스 soŏ 이 ī 이 ī
가 kā 난 nān 홀 hăr 빈 pīn	동 tŏng 모 bŏ	분 poōn 집 tsīp	츄 tshyoŏ 이 ī
빈 pan 나 nā 루 roŏ	나 nā 가 kā 마 mā	와 wā 계 kēy 데 tē 도 tōr' 루	후 hoō 리 rī 가 kā 에 gī

The borders of life	Rich	A merchant A trader A dealer	Wealth Possessions
涯生	富	賈商	產財
	후 hoō 우 oō	쇼 syŏ 우 oō 고 kŏ	
싱 săing 아 ăī	가 kā 음 ăm 열 yōr 부 poō	샹 syāng 고 kŏ	지 tsăī 산 sān
쇼 syŏ 우 oō 야 gā 이 ī	도 tŏ 무 moō	아 ā 기 kī 비 pī 도 tŏ	사 zā 이 ī 산 sān

倭語類解 下

Japanese expressions assorted and explained Vol. II.

國號 Names of Countries

The Sung Dynasty	The Suy Dynasty	The Shŭh Dynasty	The Tsin Dynasty	The Yin Dynasty	The Yu Emperor
宋	隋	蜀	秦	殷	虞
소 sŏ 우 oō	스 soō 이 i	쇼구 syŏk'	신 sīn	인 in	구 goō
송 sŏng 나 nā 라 rā 송 sŏng	슈 syoō 나 nā 라 rā 슈 syoō	촉 tshyŏk 나 nā 라 rā 촉 tshyŏk	진 tsīn 나 nā 라 rā 진 tsīn	은 oŏn 나 nā 라 rā 은 oŏn	우 oō 나 nā 라 rā 우 oō
소 sŏ 우 oō 고구 kŏk'	스 soŏ 이 i 고구 kŏk'	쇼구 syŏk' 고구 kŏk'	신 sīn 고구 kŏk'	인 in 고구 kŏk'	구 goō 고구 kŏk'

The Yüen Dynasty	The Tong Dynasty	The Tsin Dynasty	The Han Dynasty	The Chow Dynasty	The Hëa Dynasty
元	唐	晉	漢	周	夏
겐 gēyn	도 tŏ 우 oō	신 sin	간 kān	시 sī 우 oō	가 kā
원 wŏn 나 nā 라 rā 원 wŏn	당 tāng 나 nā 라 rā 당 tāng	진 tsīn 나 nā 라 rā 진 tsīn	한 hān 나 nā 라 rā 한 hān	쥬 tsyoō 나 nā 라 rā 쥬 tsyoō	하 hā 나 nā 라 rā 하 hā
겐 gēyn 고구 kŏk'	가 kā 라 rā	신 sīn 고구 kŏk'	간 kān 고구 kŏk'	슈 syoō 고구 kŏk'	가 [illegible] 고구 kŏk'

倭語類解

Japanese words assorted and explained Vol.

The Wuy Country	The Yen Country	The Tsoo Country	The Woo Country	The Chin Country	The Chin Country	The Loo Country	The Ming Dynasty
魏	燕	楚	吳	陳	鄭	魯	明
기 gī	연 ēyn	소 sŏ	고 gŏ	진 tsīn	데 tē 이 ī	로 lŏ	메 mē 이 ī
위 ōoī 나 nā 라 rā 위 ōoī	연 yōn 나 nā 라 rā 연 yōn	초 ts'hŏ 나 nā 라 rā 초 ts'hŏ	오 ŏ 나 nā 라 rā 오 ŏ	진 tsīn 나 nā 라 rā 진 tsīn	졍 tsyōng 라 rā 졍 tsyōng	로 lŏ 나 nā 라 rā 로 lŏ	명 myōng 나 nā 라 rā 명 myōng
기 gī 고구 kŏk'	연 ēyn 고구 kŏk'	소 sŏ 고구 kŏk'	고 gŏ 고구 kŏk'	진 tsīn 고구 kŏk'	데 tē 이 ī 고구 kŏk'	로 lŏ 고구 kŏk'	메 mē 이 ī 고구 kŏk'

The Tsaou Country	The Hān Country	The Tse Country	The Yuēh Country	The Tsae Country	The Tsaou Country	The Wuy Country	The Tsing Dynasty
趙	韓	齊	越	蔡	曹	衛	清
스 soŏ 우 oō	간 kān	셰 sēy 이 ī	에쯔 ēyts'	사 sā 이 ī	소 sŏ 우 oō	에 ēy 이 ī	셰 sēy 이 ī
죠 tsyŏ 나 nā 라 rā 죠 tsyŏ	한 hān 나 nā 라 rā 한 hān	졔 tsēy 나 nā 라 rā 졔 tsēy	월 wŏr 나 nā 라 rā 월 wŏr	채 ts'hāī 나 nā 라 rā 채 ts'hāī	조 tsŏ 나 nā 라 rā 조 tsŏ	위 oōī 나 nā 라 rā 위 oōī	쳥 ts'hyōng 나 nā 라 rā 쳥 ts'hyōng
쇼 syŏ 우 oō 고구 kŏk'	간 kān 고구 kŏk'	셰 sēy 이 ī 고구 kŏk'	엣 ēyt 고구 kŏk'	사 sā 이 ī 고구 kŏk'	소 sŏ 우 oō 고구 kŏk'	에 ēy 이 ī 고구 kŏk'	셰 sēy 이 ī 고구 kŏk'

倭語類解下

	Lew-kew	Japan	The state Leaou	The 100 Tse states	The three Han states	The Keih country	The Ting country	The Ke country
	球琉	本日	遼	濟百	韓三	虢	滕	杞
		시 zits' 쯔 혼 hŏn	료 lyŏ 우 oō	햐 구 hyăk' 셰 sēy 이 ī		곽 구 kwăk'	도 tŏ 우 oō	기 kī
…ese …rds …ted …d …ned II.	류 lyoō 구 koō	일 ĭr 본 pŏn	료 lyŏ 나 nā 라 rā 료 lyŏ	박 păik 졔 tsēy	삼 săm 한 hān	괵 kŏik 나 nā 라 rā 괵 kŏik	등 tŏăng 나 nā 라 rā 등 toŏng	긔 kwī 나 nā 라 rā 긔 kwī
國號	리 li 우 oō 기 kī 우 oō	니 nī 혼 hŏn	료 lyŏ 우 oō 고 구 kŏk'	햐 구 hyăk' 사 이 sāi	산 săn 간 kān	곽 구 kwăk' 고 구 kŏk'	도 tŏ 우 oō 고 구 kŏk'	기 kī 고 구 kŏk'

Nam of Coun	Mongolia	Cochin China	The state Kim	Corea	The Sin Lo state	Corea	The Seih country	The Heu country
	古蒙	南安	金	麗高	羅新	鮮朝	薛	許
			긴 kīn		신 sīn 라 lā		셰 쯔 sēyts'	교 kyŏ
58 五八	몽 mŏng 고 kŏ	안 ān 남 nām	금 koŏm 나 nā 라 rā 금 koŏm	고 kŏ 려 lyŏ	신 sīn 라 lā	죠 tsyŏ 션 syŏn	셜 syŏr 나 nā 라 rā 셜 syŏr	허 hŏ 나 nā 라 rā 허 hŏ
	모 mŏ 우 oō 고 kŏ	안 ān 난 nān	긴 kīn 고 구 kŏk'	고 kŏ 우 oō 라 이 lai	신 sīn 로 lŏ 우 oō	됴 tyŏ 우 oō 션 sēyn	셰 쯔 sēyts' 고 구 kŏk'	교 kyŏ 고 구 kŏk'

A plough share	To till the ground	A bank or mound	An acre	A field Arable land	田農 Agricul-ture	The northern barbarians	Tartary
耒	耕	堰堤	畝	田		狄北	子㺚
라이 lāi	교 kŏ 우 oō	테 tē 이 ī 엔 ēyn	호 hŏ 우 oŏ	텐 tēn			다 tāts 쯔 시 sī
싀다 stā 뷔 pwī 뢰 rŏi	밧 pāt 갈 kār 경 kyōng	텨 tē 언 ōn	이 ī 랑 rāng 묘 myŏ	밧 pāt 뎐 tyōn		븍 poŏk 뎍 tyŏk	달 tār 즈 tsă
스 soŏ 기 kī	다 tā 아 gā 에 스 ēys	쓰 tsŏots' 즈 미 mī	우 oō 네 nēy	다 tā		호 구 hŏk' 대 tē 기 kī	달 tāt 단 tān

A hoe	A plough	Husband man Farmer	A field path	Plantation Rice field		The wild Tartars	The southern Barbarians
鉏	犂	農	町	沓		胡	蠻南
쇼 syŏ	리 rī	노 nŏ 우 oǭ	데 tē 이 ī	도 tŏ 우 oō		고 kŏ	
호 hŏ 믜 măī 서 sŏ	보 pŏ 십 sĭp 리 rī	녀 nyŏ 름 roŏm 지 tsī 을 oŏr 농 nŏng	밧 pāt 거 kŏ 리 rī 뎡 tyōng	논 nŏn 답 tāp		오 ŏ 랑 rāng 캐 kāī 호 hŏ	남 nām 만 mān
구 koō 사 sā 도 tŏ 리 rī	가 kā 라 스 rās' 기 kī	노 nŏ 우 oō 사 구 sāk'	마 mā 지 tsī	하 hā 다 tā 케 kēy		에 ēy 비 bī 스 soŭ	난 nān 반 bān

倭語類解

Japan... wo... assor... an... explai... Vol.1

A flail	Straw	A reap hook	Old corn	To bring forth fruit	To throw up earth	The blade of corn	To plant
枷	藁	鎌	陳	實結	培	苗	植栽
가 kā	고 kŏ 우 oö	렌 lēyn	진 tsīn	께 kēyts' 쯔 시 zīts 쯔	빠 bāi' 이	뱌 byŏ 우 oō	사 sā 이 ī 쇼 syōk' 구
도 tŏ 리 rī 깨 tshāi 가 kā	딥 tīp 고 kŏ	낟 nāt 렴 ryōm	묵 mōok 을 oŏr 진 tsīn	결 kyōr 실 sīr	붇 poōt 도 tŏ 둘 toŏr 배 pāī	이 ī 삭 sāk 묘 myŏ	재 tsāī 식 sik
이 ī 너 nŏ 우 oōts' 즈	와 wā 라 rā	가 kā 마 ma	후 hoō 루 roō 이 ī	니 nā 리 rī 낟 nāt 다 tā	즈 tsoŏ 지 tsī 고 kŏ 우 oō	나 nā 에 ēy	우 oō 에 ēy 즈 tsoŏ 게 kēy

To beat	A bundle	To mow To reap To crop	Waste ground	Fruitless	To hoe To weed	The ear of corn	To sow A seed
擣	束	刈	荒	實不	耘	穗	種
도 tŏ 우 oō	소 sŏk' 구	애 gā 이 ī	코 kŏ 우 oō	후 hoōts' 쯔 시 zīts' 쯔	운 oōn	스 soō 이 ī	쇼 syŏ 우 oō
무 moŏ 드 tă 릴 rĭr 도 tŏ	묵 moōk 글 koŏr 속 sŏk	불 pooīr 애 āī	거 kō 출 tshoŏr 황 hwāng	불 pōor 실 sīr	기 kī 음 oŏm 알 ăir 운 oōn	이 ī 삭 sāk 슈 syoō	씨 ssī 종 tsyŏng
다 tā 다 tāk' 구	즈 tsoŏ 가 kā 누 noōr' 루	가 kār' 루	아 ā 라 rā 시 sī	나 nā 리 rī 나 nā 이 ī	구 koö 사 sā 도 tŏr' 루	호 hŏ	다 tā 너 nō

59

倭語類解

Japan… wo… assor… and explan… Vol.I

To store up	To collect	To gather in fruits	Husk of grain	A sieve	A whet stone	A pestle	A stone pestle
藏	儲	收	稃	箕	礑	杵	碓
소 sŏ 우 oō	죠 tsyŏ	시 sā 우 oō	후 hoō	기 ki	가 kā 이 ī	죠 syŏ	다 이 tāi
감 kăm 출 tshoor 장 tsăng	저 tsyō 츄 tshyoō 저 tsyō	거 kŏ 둘 toor 슈 syoō	벼 pyŏ 겁 kŏp 풀 p'hoor 부 poō	키 k'hī 긔 kwī	매 māi 의 wī	공 kŏng 이 ī 저 tsyō	방 pāng 하 hā 디 tāī
다 tā 시 sī 나 무 nām'	모 mŏ 우 oō 뎨 kēy	오 ŏ 사 sā 무 루 moōr'	모 mŏ 미 mi 누 noō 가 kā	미 mī	히 hī 기 kī 우 스 ŏŏs'	기 kī 네 nēy	가 kā 라 rā 우 스 oŏs'

Country Cottage	To heap up	To receive	Bran	A close sieve	To grind	To bray To pound in a mortar	A mortar
墅	積	納	糠	籭	磨	舂	臼
쇼 syŏ	셰 sēy 기 kī	노 nŏ 우 oō	고 kŏ 우 oō	하 hā	마 mā	쇼 syŏ 우 oō	켜 kyŏ 우 oō
농 nŏng 소 sŏ 셔 syō	싸 ssā 흘 hoŏr 젹 tsyŏk	드 toŏ 릴 rīr 납 nāp	겨 kyŏ 강 kāng	깨 kkā 블 pōor 파 p'hā	골 kăr 마 mā	찌 tstsī 홀 hoŏr 숑 syŏng	확 hwāk 구 koō
노 nŏ 우 oō 사 구 săk' 외 gŏ 야 yā	즈 무 tsoŏm'	오 ŏ 사 무 sām'	누 noō 가 kā	히 루 hīr'	도 tŏ 예 gēy	즈 구 tsŏok'	즈 tsoŏ 기 kī 우 스 oŏs'

倭語類解 下

(Chinese Words … II.)

禾穀 Corn and Grain

Barley	Millet	Ricecorn	Early Paddy	Corn		Provisions Revenue	Tribute
麰	黍	米粳	稻	禾	禾穀	糧	貢
뽀 bŏ 우 oō	쇼 syŏ	고 kŏ 우 oō 뻬 bēy 이 ī	도 tŏ 우 oō	콰 kwā		료 lyŏ 우 oō	고 kŏ 우 oō
보 pŏ 리 rī 모 mŏ	기 kī 장 tsāng 셔 syŏ	경 kyŏng 미 mī	벼 pyŏ 도 tŏ	벼 pyŏ 화 hwā	Corn and Grain	량 lyāng 식 sik 량 lyāng	받 pāt 찰 ts'hīr 공 kŏng
무 moō 기 gī	기 kī 비 pī	우 oō 루 roō 시 si 꼬 gŏ 메 mēy	모 mŏ 이 ī / 이 ī 네 nē	아 ā 라 rā 이 ī 네 nē		한 hān 마 mā 이 ī	미 mī 즈 tsŏo 기 kī

60

Wild Barley	Barbadoes millet	Glutinous Rice	Rice	Grain			Toll, Tax, Rent
麰耳	稷	糯	米	穀			稅
시 zī 뽀 bŏ 우 oō	쇼구 syŏk'	따 dā	뻬 bēy 이 ī	고구 kŏk'			세 zēy 이 ī
이 ī 모 mŏ	피 p'hī 직 tsik	찹 tshāp 쌀 psār 나 nā	쌀 psār 미 mī	곡 kŏk 식 sik 곡 kŏk			공 kŏng 세 sēy 세 sēy
야 yā 마 mā 무 moō 기 gi	히 hī 예 ēy	모 mŏ 지 tsī 꼬 gŏ 메 mēy	고 kŏ 메 mēy	고구 kŏk' 모쯔 mŏts'			가 kā 다 tā 긴 gin

倭語類解 Japanese words assorted and explained Vol. 二

菜蔬 Vegetables

Wild vegetables	Coix, Job's tears	Real Sesame	Rye	Buckwheat	Peas	Wheat
菜	苡薏	荏真	薥薥	蕎	豆小	麥
사 sā 이 ī	이 ī 이 ī	신 sīn 싄 zīn	쇼구 syŏk' 쇼구 syŏk'	교우 kyŏ ōō	쇼우 syo ōō 도우 tŏ ōō	배구 bīk'
나 nă 믈 măr 채 tshăi	의 wī 이 ī	진 tsīn 임 īm	촉 tshyŏk 촉 tshyŏk	모 mŏ 밀 mīr 교 kyŏ	쇼 syŏ 두 toŏ	밀 mīr 믹 maĭk
야 yā 사 sā 이 ī	요 yŏ 구 koō 이 ī / 스 soŏ 스 soŏ 다 dā 마 mā	외 gŏ 마 mā	기 kī 삐 bī	소 sŏ 빠 bā	아 ā 스 zoŏ 기 kī	고 kŏ 무 mōo 기 gī

Herbs	Barley shoots	Water Sesame clary	Maize Turkish corn	Paddy	Kidney beans Green gram	Beans, pulse
蔬	芽麥	荏水	黍玉	粟	豆菉	豆大
쇼 syŏ	배구 bāk' 가 gā	스 soō 이 ī 싄 zīn	교구 gyŏk' 쇼 syŏ	조구 zŏk'	로구 lŏk' 도 tŏ 우 ōō	다 tā 이 ī 도 tŏ 우 ōō
나 nā 믈 măr 소 sŏ	믹 maĭk 아 ā	슈 syoō 임 īm	옥 ŏk 셔 syō	조 tsŏ 속 sŏk	록 lŏk 두 toō	대 tāī 두 toō
구 koō 사 sā 삐 bī 라 rā / 소 sŏ 사 sā 이 ī	무 moō 기 gī 메 mēy 예 ēy	예 ēy 고 kŏ	도 tŏ 우 ōō 기 kī 비 bī	아 ā 와 wā	마 mā 사 sā 라 rā	마 mā 메 mēy

Sallad	Chinese Collyflower	Calabash	Cucumber	Leeks Scallions	Onions	Ginger	Turnip Radish
萵	菘	瓠胡	苽黃	薤	葱	薑	蔔蘿
과 kwā	스 soō 우 oō	고 kŏ 고 kŏ	교 kŏ 우 oō 과 hwā	갸 kā 이 ī	소 sŏ 우 oō	교 kyŏ 우 oō	라 lā 후구 hook'
부 poō 루 roō 와 wā	빠 păi 치 tshăi 숑 syŏng	호 hŏ 호 hŏ	황 hwāng 과 kwā	부 poō 치 tshăi 히 hăi	파 phā 총 tshŏng	성 tsăing 강 kāng 강 kāng	라 lā 복 pŏk
지 tsī 사 sā	다 tā 간 kān	뱝 bŏ 우 oō 뱌 boō 라 rā 가 kā 뱝 bō 쟈 tsyā	기 kī 우 oō 라 rā	니 nī 라 rā	네 nē 기 gī	쇼 syŏ 우 oō 가 gā 하 hā 시 zi 가 kā 미 mī	따 dā 이 ī 곤 kŏn

Fern, Brake	Mallows	Brinjal Eggplant	Winter Melon	Melon	Garlick	Mustard plant	Rape, Turnip
蕨	葵	茄	苽冬	苽	蒜	芥	菁
계쪼 kēyts	기 kī	가 kā		과 kwā	산 sān	가 kā 이 ī	세 sēy 이 ī
고 kŏ 사 sā 리 rī 궐 kwŏr	아 ā 옥 ŏk 규 kyoō	가 kā 지 tsī 가 kā	동 tōng 과 kwā	외 ŏī 과 kwā	마 mā 놀 när 숸 swŏn	겨 kēy 조 tsā 개 kăi	쇠 sŏoīr 무 moō 우 oō 청 tshyong
와 wā 라 rā 삐 bī	아 ā 오 ŏ 이 ī	나스 nās' 삐 bī	도 tŏ 우 oō 과 gwā	우 oō 리 rī	닌 nin 니구 năk'	가 kā 라 rā 시 sī	호 hŏ 소 sŏ 네 nē

Wild onions	Taro Arum Aquaticum	A certain plant	Young reeds	The Fir Fungus	Fragrant Mushroon	A toadstool Wild Mushroon	Pursa pastoris
葱野	芋	茉	蔘	耳松	蕈香	菌	薺
야 yā 소 sǒ 우 oō	우 oō	쥬 zyoōts' 쯔	신 sīn	숑 syǒ 우 oō 시 zī	고 kǒ 우 oō 신 sīn	긴 kīn	셰 sēy 이 ī
야 yā 총 ts'hŏng	토 t'hǒ 란 rān 우 oō	삼 sām 쥬 tsyoō 출 tshyoōn	더 tŏ 덕 tŏk 삼 sām	숑 syŏng 이 ī	향 hyāng 심 sīm	버 pǒ 슷 soǒt 균 kyoōn	낭 nāng 이 ī 졔 tsēy
히 hīr' 루	사 sā 도 tǒ 이 ī 모 mǒ	오 ǒ 게 kēy 라 rā	도 tǒ 도 tǒ 기 kī	마 māts' 즈 다 tā 게 kēy	시 sī 이 ī 다 tā 게 kēy	나 nā 바 bā	나 nā 즈 zoǒ 나 nā

Red onions	Wild Basil	White Goosefoot	Lucky stalk	Wild yams Potatoes	Stone Fungus	Shoots of bamboo	Blite Amaranthus oleraceus
葱紫	蘇	藜	莄苦	薯	耳石	筍	莧
시 sī 소 sǒ 우 oō	소 sǒ	레 lēy 이 ī	기 kīts' 쯔 고 kǒ 우 oō	쇼 syǒ	셰 sēy 기 kī 시 zī	슌 syoōn	간 kān
쟈 tsă 총 ts'hŏng	차 ts'hă 조 tsǒ 기 kī 소 sǒ	도 tǒ 톨 t'hărs ㅅ 려 lyǒ	길 kīr 경 kyŏng	마 mā 셔 syō	셕 syŏk 이 ī	쥭 tsyŏok 슌 syoōn 슌 syoōn	비 pī 름 roǒm 현 hyŏn
네 nē 부 boō 가 kā	시 sī 소 sǒ	아 ā 가 kā 자 zā	기 kī 교 kyǒ 우 oō	야 yā 마 mā 이 ī 모 mǒ	이 ī 와 wā 다 tā 게 kēy	다 tā 게 kēy 노 nǒ 고 kǒ	히 hī 유 yoō

倭語類解 下

Japanese words assorted and explained Vol. I

Fruit	果實 Fruits	Yellow horns	Seamoss	Mint	Bearded knotgrass	Celery Parsley	Dock
果		角黃	衣海	藿甘	蓼	芹	蕩
과 kwā		고 kŏ 우 oō 가 kāk' 구	가 kā 이 ī 이 ī	간 kān 곽 kwāk 구	료 lyŏ 우 oō	긴 kin	테 tē 이 ī
과 kwā 실 sīr 과 kwā		황 hwāng 각 kāk	해 hāī 의 wī	감 kām 곽 kwāk	엳 yōt 귀 kwī 료 lyŏ	미 mī 나 nā 리 rī 근 kŏm	소 sŏ 로 rŏ 장 tsyāng 이 ī 뎨 tēy
고 kŏ 노 nŏ 미 mī		도 tŏ 고 kŏ 로 rŏ 뎬 tēn 구 goō 사 sā	노 nŏ 리 rī	와 wā 가 kā 메 mēy	다 tā 데 dē	셰 sēy 리 rī	시 sī 노 nŏ 네 nē

Product	Shoots	Sweet moss	Eringo	Waternut	A kind of grass	Sorrel
實	茅	苔甘	帶海	菱	蓿苜	醬酸
시 zīts' 쯔	야 iā	간 kān 다 tā 이 ī	가 kā 이 ī 다 tā 이 ī	료 lyŏ 우 oō		산 sān 쇼 syŏ 우 oō
62 열 yŏr 미 mǎī 실 sīr	엄 ōm 아 ā	감 kām 태 t'hāī	해 hāī 대 tāī	말 mār 암 ām 룽 roŏng	목 mŏk 슉 syoŏk	산 sān 장 tsyāng
미 mī	메 mēy 야 ā 시 sī	아 ā 마 mā 노 nŏ 리 rī	곤 kŏn 뿌 bŏo	히 hī 시 sī	모 mŏk' 구 슈 syōok' 구	이 ī 다 tā 도 tŏ 리 rī; 스 zoč 이 ī 쇼 skŏ

White apricot	Pomegranate	Chinese Fig	Fruit of the Fir tree	Pumelo	Small orange	Sweet orange	Dragon's eyes
杏銀	榴石	柿	子栢	子柚	柑橘	橘	眼龍
긘 gīn 교 kyŏ 우 ōō	셔 sōy 기 kī 리 lī 우 ōō	시 sī	학 hāk' 시 sī	이 ī 우 ōō 시 sī	기쯔 kits' 간 kān	기쯔 kits'	
은 ōŏn 힝 hăing	석 syŏk 류 lyoō	감 kām 시 sī	빅 păik 즈 tsă	유 yoō 즈 tsă	귤 kyoor 감 kām	귤 kyoor 귤 kyoor	룡 lyong 안 ān
긘 gīn 안 ān	ᅀᅡ구 zāk' 로 lŏ	가 kā 기 kī	마즈 māts' 노 nŏ 미 mī	유 yoō ᅀ zoŏ	긷 kīt 간 kān	다 tā 지 tsī 바 bā 나 nā	료 lyŏ 우 oō 간 gān

Peach	Apricot	Dried do.	Pear	Pistachenut	Honey orange	Common orange	Li-tchi
桃	杏	柿乾	梨	子榧	柑蜜	子柑	芰茘
도 tŏ 우 ōō	교 kyŏ 우 ōō	간 kān 시 sī	리 lī	히 hī 시 sī	미쯔 mits' 간 kān	간 kān 시 sī	
복 pŏk 숑 syōng 화 hwā 도 tŏ	살 săr 고 kŏ 향 hăing	간 kān 시 sī	빈 păī 리 lī	비 pī 즈 tsă	밀 mīr 감 kām	감 kām 즈 tsă	러 lō 지 tsī
모 mŏ 모 mŏ	안 ān ᅀ zoŏ	구 koō 지 tsī 가 gā 기 kī	나 nā 시 sī	가 kā 야 yā 노 nŏ 미 mī	미 mī 간 kān	구 koō 넌 nen 보 bŏ	레 lēy 이 ī 시 sī

倭語類解

Japa… wo… assor… ar… expla… Vol. I

一二

倭語類解下

Chinese words collected and explained II.

果實

Fruit

63

Wild Grapes	Anacorn	Asweetpear Agreengage	Chesnut	Jujube Date	A sour plum	Damson	Walnut
葡山	實橡	棠	栗	棗	柰	李	桃胡
산 sān 도 tǒ 우 oō	쇼 syǒ 우 oō 시쯔 zīts'	도 tǒ 우 oō	[illegible]쯔 its'	조 sǒ 우 oō	따 Jā 이 ī	리 lı	고 kǒ 도 tǒ 우 oō
산 sān 도 tǒ	샹 syāng 실 sīr	아 ǎ 가 kā 외 ǒi 당 tāng	밤 pām 률 ryoōr	대 tāī 쵸 ts'hyǒ 죠 tsǒ	엇 ōt 내 nāī	외 ǒi 올 ǎt 리 lī	호 hǒ 도 tǒ
야 yā 마 mā 뿌 boō 도 dǒ 우 oō	가 kā 시 sī 노 nǒ 미 mī	이 ī 마 mā 나 nā 시 sī	구 koǒ 리 rī	나쪼 nāts' 메 mēy	가 kā 라 rā 나 nā 시 sī	스 soǒ 모 mǒ 모 mǒ	쿠 koō 루 roō 미 mī

Strawberry	Grapes	Plum	Yellow Chesnut	Haselnut	Papaya	An Apple	Cherry
莓	萄葡	實梅	栗黃	榛	瓜木	檎林	桃櫻
마 mā 이 ī	호 hǒ 도 tǒ 우 oō	마 mā 이 ī 시쯔 zīts'	교 kǒ 우 oō 리쯔 līts'	신 sin	뽁구 bǒk' 과 kwā	린 līn 긴 kīn	오 ǒ 우 oō 도 tǒ 우 oō
[illegible] stāng 올 āc 기 kī 믜 māī	포 p'hǒ 도 tǒ	믜 māī 실 sīr	황 hwāng 률 ryoōr	개 kāī 음 ǎm 신 sīn	목 mǒk 과 kwā	림 līm 금 koǒm	앙 āng 도 tǒ
이 ī 지 tsī 꼬 gǒ	뿌 boō 도 dǒ 우 oō	부 boō 메 mēy 노 nǒ 미 mī	가 kā 찌 tsī 구 goō 리 rī	하 hā 시 sī 빠 bā 미 mī	켄 kēyn 보 pǒ 가 gā 나 nā 시 sī 뽀 bǒ 기 kēy	린 līn 꼬 gǒ	유스 yoōs' 라 rā

Gold ore	A treasure Precious things		Kernel	Real Melon	Water pepper	Five taste seed	Winter cherry Red aunt
金泥	寶	珍寶	核	苽眞	椒川	子味五	娘姑紅
	호 hŏ 우 oo		각 kăk'	신 sin 과 kwā			고 kŏ 우 oŏ 고 kŏ 로 lŏ 우 oŏ
니 nī 금 koŏm	보 pŏ 비 păi 보 pŏ	Precious things	씨 ssī 핵 hăik	진 tsīn 과 kwā	쳔 tshyŏn 쵸 tshyŏ	오 oŏ 미 mī 즈 tsă	홍 hoŏng 고 kŏ 랑 lāng
데 dē 이 ī 긴 kān	다 tā 가 kā 라 rā		사 sā 네 nē	맛 măt 과 kwā	션 seyn 쇼 syŏ 우 oŏ	고 gŏ 미 ī 시 sī	호 hŏ 오 ŏ 즈 zoŏ 기 kī
Silver	Gold		A stalk	Gourd watermelon	Wild pepper	Pepper	A Kind of date
銀	金		蔕	苽西	椒山	椒胡	梗
긴 gīn	긴 kin		데 tē 이 ī	셰 sēy 이 ī 과 kwā			션 sēyn
은 oŏn 은 oŏn	쇠 sŏī 금 koŏm		꼭 skŏk 지 tsī 레 thēy	셔 syŏ 과 kwā	산 sān 쵸 tshyŏ	호 nŏ 쵸 tshyŏ	두 tă 리 răi 염 yŏn
시 sī 로 rŏ 가 kā 네 nē	고 kŏ 가 gā 네 nē		호 hŏ 소 ssŏ	스 soŏ 이 ī 과 kwā	산 sān 쇼 syŏ 우 oŏ	고 kŏ 쇼 syŏ 우 oŏ	시 sī 라 rā 구 goŏ 미 mī

倭語類解 Japa[nese] wo[rds] asse[mbled] a[nd] expla[ined] Vol.

下

...ese ...rds ...ed ...d ...ined

II.

珍寶

...keeping ...things

Ashell	Crystal	Tortoise shell	Cornelian	Amber	Aperfeet pearl	Apearl	Quick Silver
貝	晶水	瑁玳	瑙瑪	珀琥	珠孔無	珠	銀水
빠 bā 이 ī	스 sōo 아 ī 쎄 sēy 이 ī	다 tā 이 i 뽀 bŏ 우 oō	빠 bā 노 nŏ 우 oō		뿌 boō 고 kŏ 우 oō 슈 syōo	슈 syoō	스 soō 이 ī 긴 gīn
자 tsyā 기 kāi 패 phāi	슈 syōō 징 tsyŏng	디 tāi 모 mŏ	마 mā 노 nŏ	호 hŏ 박 pāk	무 mōo 공 kŏng 쥬 tsyoō	구 koō 솔 săr 쥬 tsyōo	슈 syōo 운 ŏon
가 kā 이 ī	스 soō 이 ī 쇼 syŏ 우 oō	볘 bēyt 고 kŏ 우 oō	메 mēy 도 lŏ 우 oō	코 kŏ 하구 hāk'	마 mā 고 kŏ 야 yā 노 nŏ 다 tā 마 mā	다 tā 마 mā	미 mī 즈 zŏo 가 kā 네 nē
Copper	Agreen shell	Glass	Bee's-Wax	Coral	Ajewel Agem	Arock pearl	Cash Money
銅	鈿螺	璃琉	蠟蜜	瑚珊	玉	珠珍	錢
도 tŏ 우 oō	라 lā 덴 tēn	리 lī 우 oō 리 lī			교구 gyŏk'	진 tsīn 슈 syōo	션 sēyn
구 koō 리 lī 동 tŏng	라 lā 뎐 tyōn	류 lyoō 리 lī	밀 mīr 랍 lāp	산 sān 호 hŏ	옥 ŏk 옥 ŏk	진 tsīn 쥬 tsyoō	돈 tŏn 젼 tsyōn
아 ā 가 kā 와 gā 네 nē	아 ā 오 ŏ 와 gā 이 ī	삐 bī 이 ī 도 dŏ 로 rŏ	미쓰 mīts' 로 lŏ 우 oō	산 sān 고 gŏ	다 tā 마 mā 이 ī 시 sī 다 tā 마 mā	아 ā 와 wā 삐 bī 노 nŏ 다 tā 마 mā	제 zēy 니 nī

64

倭語類解

Japan[ese] wo[rds] assort[ed] an[d] expla[ined] Vol.I

Ivory	To fuse	To cast metals To found	Copper bars	Native copper	Iron	Pewter	Tin Brass
牙象	鍊	鑄	銅尺	銅生	鐵	鑞	錫
죠 syŏ 우 oō 가 gā	련 reyn	쥬 syōo	샤구 syāk' 도 tŏ 우 oō	쇼 syŏ 우 oō 도 tŏ 우 oō	데쯔 tets'	로 rā 우 oō	샤구 syāk'
샹 syāng 아 ā	니 nī 길 kīr 련 ryŏn	지 tsī 울 oŏr 주 tsoō	척 tshyŏk 동 tŏng	싱 sāing 동 tŏng	쇠 sŏī 텰 thyŏr	납 nāp 랍 rāp	쥬 tsyoō 셕 syŏk 셕 syŏk
소 zŏ 우 oō 게 gēy	비루 pīr' 가 kī 도 tŏ 우 oō	이루 īr'	죠 tsyŏ 우 oō 도 dŏ 우 oō	아 ā 라 rā 아 ā 가 kā 가 gā 네 nē	구 koō 로 rŏ 가 gā 네 nē	스 soŏ 스 zoŏ	신 sīn 쥬 tsyoō 우 oō

Cinnabar	Rhinoceros horn	To melt	Queen's metal	Smelted copper	Black copper	Lead Black lead	Gong metal Bet metal
砂朱	角犀	鎔	錫含	銅熟	銅烏	鉛	鍮
	세 sēy 이 ī 가구 kāk'	요 yŏ 우 oō	간 gān 샤구 syāk'		우 oō 도 tŏ 우 oō	엔 ēyn	쥬 tsyoō 우 oō
쥬 tsyōo 사 sā	셔 syŏ 각 kāk	노 nŏ 길 kīr 용 yŏng	함 hām 셕 syŏk	슉 syōok 동 tŏng	오 ŏ 동 tŏng	면 myŏn 연 yŏn	놋 nŏt 유 yōo
슈 syoō 샤 syā	사 sā 이 ī 가구 kāk'	도 tŏ 라 rā 가스 kās' 가 kā 네 nē 와구 wāk'	도 tŏ 단 tān	쥬구 zyoōk 도 dŏ 우 oō	샤구 syāk' 도 dŏ 우 oō	나 nā 마 mā 리 rī	사 sā 하 hā 리 rī

倭語類解下

Chinese words Noted and Explained II.

布帛

Cloth and Silk

Satin	Brocade Variegated silk		Glue	Wax	Brimstone Sulphur	Alum	Borax
緞	錦	布帛	阿膠	蠟	硫黃	白礬	硼砂
단 dān	긘 kin		아 ā 고 kŏ 우 oō	로 lŏ 우 oō	리 lī 우 oō 고 kŏ 우 oō	햑구 hāk' 한 hān	
비 pī 단 tān 단 tān	바 pā 단 tān 금 koŏm	Cloth and Silk	아 ā 교 kyŏ	밀 mīr 랍 lāp	류 lyoō 황 hwāng	빅 pāīk 반 pān	붕 pōong 사 sā
단 tān 모 mŏ 노 nŏ 돈 tŏn 스 soŏ	기 kī 누 noō		니 nī 가 kā 와 wā	미쯔 mīts' 가스 kās'	유 yoō 오 oŏ 우 oō	묘 myŏ 우 oō 반 pān	호 hŏ 우 oō 샤 syä

65

Damask Ornamented silk	Silk Tissue			White wax vegetable wax	Saltpetre Nitre	Arsenic	Magnet Loadstone
粧緞	帛			白蠟	焰硝	砒礵	磁石
소 sŏ 우 oō 단 dān	햑구 hāk'			햑구 hāk' 로 lŏ 우 oō			지 zī 셰 sēy 기 kī
장 tsāng 단 tān	깁 kip 빅 pāik			빅 pāik 랍 lāp	염 yōm 쵸 ts'hyŏ	비 pī 상 sāng	쟈 tsă 셕 syŏk
니 nī 시 sī 기 kī	오 ŏ 리 rī 모 mŏ 노 nŏ			기 kī 노 nŏ 야 yā 니 nī	엔 ēyn 쇼 syŏ 우 oō	히 hī 소 sŏ 우 oō	시 zī 샤구 syāk'

Bombasin Cottonsilk	Gauze	Thin silk of Hangchow	Flowered silk	Wide silk	Fine silk sarcenet	Close silk	Twilled silk
紬綿	紗	羅杭	紬花	織廣	紋	段閃	段縇
메 mēyn 유 yoō 우 oō		고 kŏ 우 oō 라 lā	과 kwā 유 yoō 우 oō	고 kŏ 우 oō 쇼구 syŏk'	몬 mŏn	센 sēyn 단 dān	센 sēyn 단 dān
면 myŏn 쥬 tsyoō	김 kīm 사 sā	항 hāng 라 lā	화 hwā 쥬 tsyoo	광 kwāng 직 tsik	어 ō 르 roŏ 누 noō 쿨 koŏr 무 moōn	셤 syŏm 단 tān	션 syōn 단 tān
즈 tsŏo 무 mōo 기 gī	샤 syā	로 lŏ 샤 syā 로 lŏ	사 sā 야 yā	히 hi 로 rŏ 슈 syoō 스 soŏ	아 ā 야 yā	슈 syoō 스 soŏ	란 lān 견 kēyn

Camlet	Thin silk	Taffeta	Puckered Crape	Square-wove silk	Embroidery	Gold thread	Rolled silk
織交	羅	綾	紗走	紬方	綉	線金	段冒
고 kŏ 우 oō 쇼구 syŏk'	라 lā	료 yŏ 우 oō	소 sŏ 우 oō 샤 syā	호 hŏ 우 oō 유 yoō 우 oō	시 sī 우 oō	긴 kin 센 sēyn	뵤 bŏ 우 oō 단 dān
교 kyŏ 직 tsik	깁 kīp 라 lā	깁 kīp 릉 rŏong	주 tsoō 사 sā	방 pāng 쥬 tsyōo	슈 syoō 질 tsīr 슈 syoō	금 koŏm 션 syŏn	모 mŏ 단 tān
손 sŏn 나 nā 이 ī	우스 oōs' 모 mŏ 노 nŏ	린 lin 즈 zoŏ	지 tsī 리 rī 면 mēyn	몬 mŏn 나 nā 시 sī	누 noō 이 ī	긴 kīn 란 lān	마 mā 기 kī 니 nī 시 sī 기 kī

倭語類解

Japanese words assorted and explained Vol.

Loose words sorted and defined II.

布帛

Cloth and Silk

66

A loom	Raw silk	Spinning wheel	Cotton screw	Yellow cloth for priests	Oil cloth	Silky Cotton	Calico Soft cloth
機	繅	車紡	車壓	布[illegible]	布麻黑	綿木	布潤
기 kī	소 sŏ 우 oō	호 hŏ 우 oō 교 kyŏ	오 ó 우 oō 교 kyŏ	쇼 syo 우 oo 호 hŏ	고 kŏk' 구 마 mā 호 hŏ	모 mŏk' 구 면 mēyn	슌 zyoōn 호 hŏ
틀 thoŏr 괴 kwī	실 sīr 혈 hyŏr 소 sŏ	방 pāng 거 kŏ	압 āp 거 kŏ	싱 sāing 포 p'hŏ	흑 hŏk 마 mā 포 p'hŏ	목 mŏk 면 myŏn	윤 yŏon 포 p'hŏ
하 hā 다 tā	마 mā 와 wā 다 tā	이 ī 도 tŏ 히 hī 기 kī 구 koŏ 루 roŏ 마 mā	와 wā 다 tā 자 zā 비 pī 도 tŏ 리 rī	기 kī 히 hī 라 rā	아 ā 부 boŏ 라 rā 누 nōo 노 nŏ	모 mŏ 멘 mēyn	윤 yōon 부 boŏ
A comb A shuttle	Silky thread	A cocoon A Bombyx	Cotton	Dimity Soft cotton cloth	Cloth	Grass cloth	Three measures
梭	絲	繭	綿	子許	布	布苧	升三
사 sā	시 sī	켄 kēyn	면 mēyn	교 kyŏ 시 sī	호 hŏ	죠 tsyŏ 호 hŏ	산 sān 쇼 syŏ 우 oō
북 poŏk 사 sā	실 sīr 사 sā	고 kŏ 티 t'hī 견 kyŏn	소 sŏ 옴 ŏm 면 myŏn	허 hŏ 자 tsā	뵈 pŏī 포 p'hŏ	저 tsyŏ 포 p'hŏ	삼 sām 승 soŏng
오 ŏ 사 sā	이 ī 도 tŏ	이 ī 도 tŏ 마 mā 기 kī	와 wā 다 tā —	도 tŏ 로 rŏ 멘 mēyn	누 noō 노 nŏ	사 sā 라 rā 시 sī	삼 sām 소 sŏ 에 gī

[illegible] color	Dark green	An indigo color Blue	Oil green	Crimson	The woof	To weave	A shuttle
色香沉	青鴉	藍	綠油	紅大	緯	織	筬
쇼 [illegible] 고 kō 우 oō 쇼구 syŏk'	아 à 세 sēy 이 ī	란 lān	이 ī 우 oō 료구 lyŏk'	다 tā 이 ī 고 kŏ 우 oō	이 ī	쇼구 syŏk'	세 sēy 이 ī
침 shĭm 향 hyang 색 săik	아 ā 청 tshyŏng	족 tsŏk 람 lām	유 yōo 록 lŏk	대 tāi 홍 hŏng	ᄡᅵ psī 위 oōī	ᄶᅡᆯ stsăr 직 tsik	ᄇᆞ pă ᄃᆡ tāi 셩 syŏng
고 kŏ 우 oō 이 ī 로 rŏ	루 roō 리 rī 곤 kŏn	아 ā 이 ī 이 ī 로 rŏ	미루 mīr' 쟈 tsyā	모 mŏ 미 mī 이 ī 로 rŏ 히 hī	요 yŏ 고 kŏ	오루 hŏr'	히 hī

Tea color	Purple	Grass green	Pea green	Peach colour	Scarlet	The warp	To spin
色茶	芝紫	綠草	綠豆	紅桃	紅真	經	紡
다 tā 쇼구 syŏk'	시 sī 시 sī	소 sŏ 우 oō 료구 lyŏk'	도 tŏ 우 oō 로구 lyŏk'	도 to 우 oō 고 kŏ 우 oō	신 sīn 고 kŏ 우 oŏ	게 kēy 이 ī	호 hŏ 우 oō
다 tā ᄉᆡᆨ săik	ᄌᆞ tsă 지 tsī	초 tshŏ 록 lŏk	두 toō 록 lŏk	도 tŏ 홍 hŏng	진 tsīn 홍 hŏng	놀 năr 경 kyŏng	질 tsīr 삼 sām 방 pāng
쟈 tsyā 이 ī 로 rŏ	무 moō 라 ra 사 sā 기 kī 이 ī 로 rŏ	모 mŏ 요 yŏ 에 gī	도 tŏ 리 rī 노 nŏ 고 kŏ 이 ī 로 rŏ	모 mŏ 모 mŏ 이 ī 로 rŏ	혼 hŏn 모 mŏ 미 mī	다 tā 데 tē	하 hā 다 tā 오 nŏ 리 rī

Yellow powder	Gamboge	Yellow	Red Carmine	Ornament	To dye	Color of firblossom
黃丹	石雄黃	黃	紅	彩	染	松花色
고 kŏ 우 oō 단 tān	세 sēy 기 kī 유 yoō 우 oō 고 kŏ 우 oō	고 kŏ 우 oō	고 kŏ 우 oō	사 sā 이 ī	션 zēyn	쇼 syŏ 우 oō 과 kwā 쇼구 syŏk'
황 hwāng 단 tān	셕 syŏk 웅 ŏong 황 hwāng	누 noō 르 roŏr 황 hwāng	블 poŏr 글 koŏr 홍 hŏng	채 tshāi 석 sāik 채 tshāi	믈 moŏr 드 toŏ 릴 rīr 염 yŏm	숑 syŏng 화 hwā 석 sāik
오 ŏ 우 oō 단 dān	오 ŏ 오 ŏ 우 oō	기 kī 나 nā	아 ā 가 kā	이 ī 로 rŏ 도 dŏ 루 roō	소 sŏ 메루 mēyr'	우 oō 구 goō 이 ī 스 soŏ 쟈 tsyā
彩色 Ornaments and Colours						
Yellow Varnish	Yellow ochre	Peach yellow	Vermilion	A colour	To soak	Color of tender grass
黃漆	石雌黃	桃黃	朱紅	色	潤	軟草色
고 kŏ 우 oō 시쯔 sits'	세 sēy 기 kī 시 sī 고 kŏ 우 oō	도 tŏ 우 oō 고 kŏ 우 oō	슈 syoō 고 kŏ 우 oō	쇼구 syŏk'	쥰 zyoōn	센 sēyn 소 sŏ 우 oō 쇼구 syŏk'
황 hwāng 칠 tshir	셕 syŏk ᄌᆞ tsă 황 hwāng	도 tŏ 황 hwāng	쥬 tsyoō 홍 hŏng	빗 pit 석 sāik	져 tsŏ 츌 tsoŏr 윤 yoōn	연 yŏn 초 ts'hŏ 석 sāik
슌 syoōn 게 kēy 이 ī	기 kī 이 ī 로 rŏ	니 nī 즈 tsoŏ 지 tsī 이 ī 로 rŏ	슈 syoō	이 ī 로 rŏ	후 hoō 에루 ēyr'	도 tŏ 구 kōo 사 sā 이 ī 로 rŏ

A rusty color	A yellowish green	Green	Black	Azure Flower colour	Purple	Cerulean Azure	White
鉎垢	三綠	綠	黑	青花	三青	青	白
쇼 syŏ 우 oō 고 kŏ 우 oō	산 sān 료구 lyŏk'	료구 lyŏk'	고구 kŏk'	셰 sēy 이 ī 과 kwā	산 sān 셰 sēy 이 ī	셰 sēy 이 ī	하구 hāk
싱 sǎing 구 koō	삼 sām 록 lŏk	프 p'hǎ 를 roǒr 록 lŏk	거 kŏ 믈 moǒr 흑 hŏk	청 ts'hyŏng 화 hwā	삼 sām 청 tshyŏng	프 p'hoǒ 를 roǒr 청 tshyŏng	흰 hoǐn 빅 pǎik
사 sā 비 pī	이 ī 와 wā 료구 lŏk' 쇼 syŏ 우 oō	미 mī 도 dŏ 리 rī	구 koō 로 rŏ	아 ā 오 ŏ 하 hā 나 nā 이 ī 로 rŏ	곤 kŏn 쇼 zyŏ 우 oō	아 ā 오 ŏ	시 sī 로 rŏ

To smear To daub	A dusky color	Verdigrease	Varnish Lacker	Lotus leaf color	Berlin blue	Flower purple	White lead Ceruse
塗漆	霾花	銅綠	漆	荷葉	回回青	二青	粉
도 tŏ 시쯔 sits	빠 bā 이 ī 과 kwā	도 tŏ 우 oō 료구 lyŏk'	시쯔 sits'	가 kā 요 yŏ 우 oō	과 kwā 이 ī 과 kwā 이 ī 셰 sēy 이 ī	니 nī 셰 sēy 이 ī	훈 hoōn
도 tŏ 칠 ts'hir	믹 mǎi 화 hwā	동 tŏng 록 lŏk	옷 ŏt 칠 ts'hir	하 hā 엽 yĕp	회 hŏi 회 hŏi 청 tshyŏng	이 ī 청 tshyŏng	분 poōn 분 poōn
누루 noōr'	가 kā 뻬 bī	로구 lŏk' 쇼 syŏ 우 oō	우루 oōr' 시 sī	구 koō 사 sā 소 zŏ 메 mēy	소 sŏ 메 mēy 즈 tsoō 케 kēy 구스 goōs' 리 rī	하 hā 나 nā 곤 kŏn 쇼 zyŏ 우 oō	시 sī 로 rŏ 이 ī 고 gŏ 훈 hoōn

倭語類解

Japan… wo… assor… an… explan… Vol.

倭語類解 下

…nese words …rted and …ined II.

器具

Tools and Implements

A safe	A drawer	A trunk A basket	A shop A stall	A tool Instrument		A light color	A landscape
廚眼仟	極	籠	欌	器	器具 Tools and Implements	淡	繪蒔
센 sēyn 간 gān 쥬 tsyoō 우 oō	간 kān	로 lŏ 우 oō	소 sŏ 우 oō	기 kī		단 tān	시 zī 과 kwā 이 ī
쳔 tshyōn 안 ān 쥬 tsyoō	함 hām 함 hām	롱 lŏng 롱 lŏng	장 tsāng 장 tsāng	그 koŏ 릇 roŏt 긔 kwi		믈 moŏr 근 koŏr 담 tām	시 sī 회 hŏi
단 tān 스 soŏ	함 hām 빼 bīts' 쯔	즈 tsoŏ 스 zoŏ 라 rā	도 tŏ 따 dā 나 nā	우 oōts' 즈 와 wā 모 mŏ 노 nŏ		우 oō 스 soŏ 이 ī	마 mā 기 kī 에 ēy

A double handled ink stone	A cabinet	Portmanteau A leather trunk	A chest	Utensil A vessel		Party-color Piebald	To shine Light
硯掛雙	極層	籠皮	樻	皿		斑	光
소 sŏ 우 oō 가 kā 이 ī 켄 kēyn	오 zŏ 우 oō 간 kān	히 hī 로 lŏ 우 oō	기 kī	메 mēy 이 ī		한 hān	고 kŏ 우 oo
쌍 ssang 괘 kwāi 연 ēyn	층 tshoŏng 함 hām	피 phī 롱 lŏng	궤 koōēy 궤 koōēy	그 koŏ 릇 roŏt 명 myŏng		어 ŏ 록 rŏk 반 pān	빗 pīt 광 kwāng
숭 soŏng 기 kī 유 zyoō 우 oō	쥬 zyoō 우 oō 빠 bā 고 kŏ	가 kā 와 wā 고 gŏ	히 hī 즈 tsoŏ	사 sā 라 rā		마 mā 다 dā 라 rā	히 hī 가 kār' 루

68

六十八

A mattrass	A mat	A screen	A chair	A couch A bedstead	A lock	A box	A portable ink stone
席方	席	風屛	椅交	床	鑰	子箱	硯掛
호 hŏ 우 oō 세 sēy 기 kī	세 sēy 기 kī	헤 hēy 이 ī 후 hoō 우 oō	교 kŏ 우 oō 이 ī	쇼 syŏ 우 oō	야구 yāk'	쇼 syŏ 우 oō 시 sī	가 kā 이 ī 겐 kēyn
방 pāng 셕 syŏk	돗 tŏt 셕 syŏk	병 pyŏng 풍 p'hoōng	교 kyŏ 의 wī	상 sāng 상 sāng	열 yōr 쇠 sŏī 약 yāk	상 syāng ᄌᆞ tsă	괘 kwāī 연 yōn
시 sī 도 tŏ 네 nē	무 moō 시 sī 로 rŏ 고 gŏ 자 zā	뵤 byŏ 우 oō 부 poō	교구 kyŏk' 로구 rŏk'	유 yoō 가 kā 젠 zēyn	가 kā 기 gī	하 hā 고 kŏ	가 kā 계 kēy 스 soōz' 스 리 rī

A thin mat	A floor mat	A shade	A table	A bench	To lock	A key	An escritoir
衣地	席疊	子簇	几	床繩	之鎖	子鎖	硯掛皮
지 tsī 이 ī	됴 tyŏ 우 oō 세 sēy 기 kī	소구 sŏk' 시 sī	기 kī	죠 zyŏ 우 oō 쇼 syŏ 우 oō	사 sā 시 sī	사 sā 시 sī	히 hī 가 kā 이 ī 겐 kēyn
디 tī 의 wī	텹 t'hyōp 셕 syōk	족 tsŏk ᄌᆞ tsă	착 t'shāik 상 sāng 궤 koōē	승 sōong 상 sāng	쇄 swāī 지 tsī	쇄 swāī ᄌᆞ tsă	피 phī 괘 kwāī 연 yōn
우 oōs' 스 베 pēy 리 rī	다 tā 다 tā 미 mī	가 kā 계 kēy 모 mŏ 노 nŏ	오 ŏ 시 sī 마 mā 스 zoŏ 기 kī	쇼 syŏ 우 oō 기 gī	오 ŏ 로스 xŏs'	됴 dyŏ 우 oō	가 kā 와 wā 스 soōz' 스 리 rī 바 bā 고 kŏ

倭語類解

Japa… w… asso… a… expl… Vol.

三十五頁 下 These words selected and explained II. 器具

A clock	Fire irons	A fan	A canopy	A curtain	A screen for the sun	A parasol	A bamboo mat
自鳴鐘	火鐵	扇	鋪	帳	遮日	日傘	簟
싀 zī 메 mēy 이 ī 쇼 syŏ 우 oō	과 kwā 데쯔 tēts'	센 sēyn	호 hŏ	죠 tsyŏ 우 oō	쟈 tsyā 싀쪼 zīts'	싀쯔 zīts' 산 sān	덴 tēn
자 tsă 명 ngyōng 종 tsyŏng	화 hwā 렬 t'hyōr	부 poō 체 tshē 션 syōn	폘 p'hyōr 포 p'hŏ	장 tsyāng 장 tsyāng	챠 tshyā 일 ir	일 īr 산 sān	삳 sāt 뎜 tsyōm
도 tŏ 계 kēy 이 ī	히 hī 우 oō 지 tsī	오 ŏ 오 ŏ 기 gī	시 sī 기 kī 모 mŏ 노 nŏ	노 nŏ 렌 rēyn	히 hī 오 ŏ 이 ī	히 hī 아 gā 사 sā	샤 syā 지 tsī

Tools and Impl. 69 六十九

A spy glass	Candle screen	A chimney A pipe	To spread To expand	Musquito curtains	A tent	An umbrella	A rug A carpet
千里鏡	輪畵	煙竹	陳	蚊帳	幕	雨傘	氊
션 sēyn 리 lī 계 kēy 이 ī	린 līn 도 tŏ	연 ēyn 지구 tsīk'	진 tsin	훈 hoōn 죠 tsyŏ 우 oō	마구 māk'	우 oō 산 sān	션 sēyn
쳔 ts'hyōn 리 lī 경 kyōng	륜 lyoōn 도 tŏ	연 yōn 쥭 tsyoōk	베 pē 플 p'hoōn 진 tsIn	문 moōn 장 tsyāng	장 tsyāng 막 māk 막 māk	우 oō 산 sān	담 tām 젼 tsyōn
모 mŏ 우 oō 메 mēy 아 gā 네 nē	시 sī 아바 bā 리 rī	기 kī 세루 sēyr'	히 hī 로 rŏ 애루 gēyr'	가 kā 죠 tsyŏ 우 oō	죠 tsyŏ 우 oō 마구 māk' 덴 tēn 마구 māk'	카 kā 라 rā 가 kā 사 sā	모 mŏ 우 oō 센 sēyn

A metal tray	A round tray, a dish	A wine cup	A wine press	A coffer A casket	A pitcher A pan	A weight	Spectacles
鉦盤	盤	杯	酒榨	盒	瓶	錘	眼鏡
소 sō 우 oō 한 hān	한 hān	바 pā 이 ī	슈 syoō 사 sā	고 kō 우 oō	혜 hēy 이 ī	즈 tsoō 이 ī	안 gān 계 kēy 이 ī
징 tsāing 반 pān	반 pān 반 pān	잔 tsān 빅 pāī	쥬 tsyoō 자 tsā	합 hāp 합 hāp	병 pyōng 병 pyōng	드 tā 림 rīm 츄 tshyöö	안 ān 경 kyōng
가 kā 나 nā ᄠᅩᆫ bǒn.	마 mā 루 roō ᄠᅩᆫ bǒn	사 sā 가 kā ᄌᆞ zoǒ 기 kī	사 sā 가 kā ᄠᅮ boō 네 nē	쥬 zyoō 우 oō	도 tǒk' 구 리 rī	오 ǒ 모 mǒ 리 rī	메 mēy 가 gā 네 nē

A cup	A square tray	A ladle	A wine boiler	A bottle A chalice	A flowered pitcher	A basket for weighing	Scales, steelyards
椀	四角盤	勺	酒煎子	鐏	畵瓶	簽	稱
	시 sī 가 kāk' 구 한 hān	샤 syāk' 구	슈 syoō 션 sēyn 시 sī	손 sǒn	과 kwā 혜 hēy 이 ī	션 sēyn	쇼 syǒ 우 oō
지 tsī 완 wān 완 wān	ᄉᆞ sǎ 각 kāk 반 pān	구 koō 기 kī 작 tsyāk	쥬 tsyoō 젼 tsyōn ᄌᆞ tsǎ	술 sōor 준 tsoōn 준 tsoōn	화 hwā 병 pyōng	사 sā 슬 soǒr 쳠 tshyōm	저 tsǒ 울 oūr 칭 tshīng
완 wān	오 ǒ 시 sī 기 kī	샤 syā	사 sā 게 kēy 약 yāk 관 kwān	사 sā 게 kēy 다 tār' 루	과 kwā 힌 hīn	가 kā 고 gǒ	하 hā 가 kā 리 rī

倭語類解

Japan[ese] wo[rds] asso[ciated] a[nd] expl[ained] Vol.

	Bellows	To cover	A kettle	A small pan	A pan	A spoon.	A platter	A pot
	爐風	之盖	鑵	鏊	鍋	匙	楪	鉢
	후 hoō 우 oō 로 lŏ	가 kā 이 ī 사 sā	관 kwān	교 kŏ 우 oō	[illegible] tē 이 ī	시 sī	됴 tyŏ 우 oō	하쯔 hāts'
III.	풍 phoōng 로 lŏ	개 kāī 지 tsī	단 tān 지 tsī 관 kwān	노 nŏ 고 kŏ 오 ŏ	솟 sŏt 둉 tyōng	술 soŏr 시 sī	뎝 tyōp 시 sī 뎝 tyōp	바 pā 리 ri 발 pār
器具	후 hoō 이 ī 이고 gŏ	후 hoō 다 tā 오 ŏ 기 kī 셰루 sēyr'	약 yāk 관 kwān	교 kŏ 나 nā 뻬 bēy	나 nā 베 pēy	사 sā 시 zī	사 sā 라 rā	하 hā 지 tsī

Tools and Impl-	Water bellows	A furnace	A lid A cover	A frying pan	A caldron	Chop sticks	A glass	A earthen pot
	爐風水	爐	盖	鐵煎	釜	箸	子鐘	鉢砂
	스 soŏ 이 ī 후 hōo 우 oō 로 lŏ	로 lŏ	가 kā 이 ī	셴 sēyn 데쪼 tēts'	후 hoō	죠 tsyŏ	쇼 syŏ 우 oō 시 sī	샤 syā 하쯔 hāts'
70	슈 syoō 풍 phoōng 로 lŏ	화 hwā 로 lŏ 로 lŏ	두 toō 에 ē 개 kāī	젼 tsyōn 렬 thyār	가 kā 마 mā 부 poō	져 tsyō 져 tsyō	죵 tsyŏng 차 tsă	사 sā 발 pār
	스 soŏ 이 ī 후 hoō 로 lŏ	히 hī 빠 bā 지 tsī	후 hoō 다 tā	교 kŏ 으부 boō 나 nā 뻬 bēy	가 kā 마 mā	하 hā 시 sī	죠구 tsyŏk'	사 sā 하 hā 지 tsī

A dried gourd	A bucket	A pail	A jug	A boiler	Porcelain Earthenware	An incense pot	A portable stove
蘆葫	斗水	桶水	缸	甑	陶	盒香	爐仙神
고 kŏ 로 lŏ	스 soō 이 ī 도 tŏ 우 oō	스 soō 이 ī 도 tŏ 우 oō	고 kŏ 우 oō	소 sŏ 우 oō	도 tŏ 우 oō	고 kŏ 우 oō 고 kŏ 우 oō	신 sīn 션 syōn 로 lŏ
호 hŏ 로 lŏ	슈 syoō 두 toō	슈 syoō 통 thŏng	항 hāng 항 hāng	시 sī 로 rŏ 증 tsoŏng	질 tsīr 긋 kōt 도 tŏ	향 hyāng 합 hāp	신 sīn 션 syōn 로 lŏ
효 hyŏ 우 oō 단 tān	즈 tsoŏ ᄆ부 boō 레 rēy	미 miz' 스 하 hāz' 스	즈 tsoŏ ᄆ보 bŏ	고 kŏ 시 sī 기 kī	야 yā 기 kī 모 mŏ 노 nŏ	고 kŏ 우 oō ᄆ바 bā 고 kŏ	노 nŏ ᄆ부 boō 로 rŏ

A sacrificial vessel	A dried calabash	A hoop	A tub A butt A barrel	A bowl	A jar	A brass basin	A censer
俎	瓢	箍	桶	盆	瓮	鐥	爐香
쇼 syŏ	효 hyŏ 우 oō	고 kŏ	도 tŏ 우 oō	혼 hŏn	오 ŏ 우 oō	션 sēyn	
도 tŏ 마 mā 조 tsŏ	박 pāk 표 phyŏ	테 thē 고 kŏ	통 thŏng 통 thŏng	동 tŏng 힋 hāi 분 poōn	독 tŏk 옹 ŏng	다 tā 야 yā 션 syōn	향 hyāng 로 lŏ
마 mā 나 nā 이 ī 다 tā	하 hā 계 kēy 히 hī 사 sā ᄀ고 gŏ	다 tā 계 kēy 노 nŏ 와 wā	오 ŏ 계 kēy	가 kā 나 nā 오 ŏ 기 kī	가 kā 메 mēy	가 kā 나 nā 다 dā 라 rā 이 ī	고 kŏ 우 oō 로 lŏ

倭語類解

Japanese words assorted and explained Vol.I

七

倭語類解 下

器具 Tools and Implements

A sack	A thatch	A flower basket	To carry a lantern	A candle stick	A lantern	A strainer	A sieve
囊	苞	筐	挑燈	燭臺	燈	笊	篩
노 nŏ 우 oō	돈 tŏn	교 kyŏ 우 oō	됴 tyŏ 우 oō 도 tŏ 우 oō	쇼 syŏk' 구 다 tā 이 ī	도 tŏ 우 oō	소 sŏ 우 oō	시 sī
주 tsoō 머 mŏ 니 nī 낭 nāng	슴 stoōm 둔 toōn	광 kwāng 조 tsŏ 리 rī 광 kwāng	도 tŏ 등 toŏng	쵸 tshyŏ 듸 tăī	등 toŏng 잔 tsān 등 toŏng	죠 tsyŏ 릐 răī 조 tsŏ	사 shē 스 să
긴 kīn 쟈 tsyāk' 구	도 tŏ 마 mā	하 hā 나 nā 가 ka 오 gŏ	히 hī 가 kā 기 kī 다 tā 즈 tsoŏr' 루	도 tŏ 우 oō 다 dā 이 ī	안 ān 도 dŏ 우 oō	고 kŏ 메 mēy 유 yoō 리 rī 이 ī 가 kā 기 kī	후 hoō 루 rōo 이 ī

71

A bag	A straw screen	A hamper	To extinguish a lamp	A lamp	A taper A candle	A fish basket	A bamboo sieve
帒	草簾	笥	滅燈	燈火	燭	筲	竹篩
다 tā 이 ī	소 sŏ 우 oō 렌 lēyn	시 sī	메 mēyts' 쯔 도 tŏ 우 oō	도 tŏ 우 oō 과 kwā	쇼 syŏk' 구	세 sēy 이 ī	지 tsīk' 구 시 sī
부 poō 대 tāī 듸 tăī	초 tshŏ 렴 lyōm	싁 soŏk 스 să	멸 myăr 등 toŏng	등 toŏng 화 kwā	쵸 tshyŏ 쵹 tshyŏk	솔 sŏr 셩 syōng	쥭 tsyoŏk 스 să
후 hoōk' 구 로 rŏ	아 ā 기 kī 다 tā 와 wā 라 rā	오 ŏ 오 ŏ 고 gŏ 리 rī	히 hī 게 kēy 스 soŏ	됴 tyŏ 우 oō 시 zī 아 gā 시 sī 라 rā	로 lŏ 우 oō 소 sŏk' 구	빠 bā 렌 rēyn	메 mēy 도 tŏ 오 ŏ 시 sī

A prop A post	A besom A broom	A mangle	A washing block	A line	A angle A fishhook	A castnet A net	A case
林	箒	硏	砧	緪	釣	網	槖
마쯔 māts'	시 sī 우 oō	견 kēyn	진 tsīn	고 ko 우 oō	됴 tyŏ 우 oō	모 mŏ 우 oō	다구 tāk'
말 mār ᄯᅩᆨ stŏk 말 mār	뷔 poōī 츄 ts'hyoō	연 yōn 연 yōn	다 tā 도 tŏ 미 mī 참 ts'hīm	줄 tsoōr 공 koōng	낙 nāk 시 sī 됴 tyŏ	고 kŏ 불 poŏr 망 māng	쟈 tsyā ᄅᆞ rā 락 rāk
다 dā 구 goō 이 ī	호 hŏ 우 oō 기 kī	야 yā 겐 gēyn	기 kī 누 noō 다 tā	스 zoō 나 nā	즈 tsoō 리 rī	아 ā 미 mī	후구 hoōk' 루 rō

A file A string	A straw basket	A torch	A fuller's club	A cord	An angling rod	A net-string	A bundle a pack
串	簣	炬	槌木	繩	竿	綱	袱
션 seyn	기 kī	교 kyŏ	뵉구 bŏk' 다 tā 이 ī	쇼 zyŏ 우 oō	간 kān	고 kŏ 우 oō	후구 hoōk'
곧 kŏt 치 ts'hī 쳔 ts'hyōn	삼 sām 래 rāī 궤 kwē	홰 hwāī 거 kō	목 mŏk 퇴 t'hŏī	노 nŏ 승 soŏng	낙 nāk 대 tāī 간 kān	벼 pyō 리 rī 강 kāng	보 pŏ 복 pŏk
호 hŏ 구 goō 시 sī	텐 tēn 몯 mŏt 고 kŏ	다 tā 이 ī 마즈 māts'	기 kī 누 noō 다 tā 다 tā 기 kī	나 na 와 wā	즈 tsŏō 리 rī 소 sŏ 오 ŏ 사 sā 오 ŏ	아 ā 미 mī 노 nŏ 오 ŏ 오 ŏ 스 zŏo 나 nā	후 hoō 로 rŏ 시 sī 기 kī

倭語類解

Japan[ese] wor[ds] assort[ed] an[d] expla[ined] Vol.

七十一

倭語類解下 Chinese words ... explained I.

器具 Tools and impl-

A nail	An awl	A hatchet An axe	An adze	A file	An iron hammer	A forge	A tube A pipe
釘	錐	斧	鐁	鑢	椎鐵	冶	筩
뎨 tē 이 ī	스 soō 이 ī	후 hoō	훈 koōn	료 lyŏ	뎨 tēts 쯔 다 ta 이 ī	야 yā	교 kŏ 우 oō
못 mŏt 뎡 tyōng	송 sŏng 곳 kŏt 츄 ts'hyoō	도 tŏ 치 tshăi 부 poō	자 tsā 괴 kŏi 분 poōn	줄 tsoōr 려 lyŏ	텰 thyōr 퇴 thŏi	풀 p'hoōr 무 moō 야 yā	홍 hŏng 옹 hŏng
구 koō 에 gī	기 kī 리 rī	요 yŏ 기 kī 오 ŏ 노 nŏ	됴 tyŏ 우 oō 노 nŏ 오 ŏ	야 yās' 스 리 rī	싈 zīt 데 tē 이 ī	후 hoō 이 ī 교 gŏ	도 tŏ 이 ī

72

A staple A cramp	A bore	A chizel	A plane	A saw	Pincers	A sledge-hammer	A trough
釘蛭	鑽	鑿	鉋	鋸	鉗	鎚	槽
시 sits' 쯔 데 tē 이 ī	산 sān	사 sāk' 구	호 hŏ 우 oō	교 kyŏ	견 kēyn	다 tā 이 ī	소 sŏ 우 oō
질 tsīr 뎡 tyōng	비 pī 비 poŏī 찬 ts'hān	살 skoŏr 착 ts'hāk	대 tăī 파 p'hā 포 p'hŏ	톱 lŏp 거 kō	집 tsīp 게 kē 겸 kyōm	쇠 sŏī 마 mā 치 tshī 퇴 t'hŏī	귀 koŏī 우 oō 조 tsŏ
가 kās' 스 까 gā 이 ī	마 mā 예 ēy 기 gī 리 rī	노 nŏ 미 mī	가 kā 나 nā	노 nŏ 교 kŏ	히 hī 빠 bā 사 sā 미 mī	가 kā 나 nā 즈 zŏō 지 tsī	하 hā 미 mī 이 ī 레 rēy

A smoothing iron	A needle	A chopping knife	A bell	A circle A ring	A trowel	A small hoe	A spade
斗熨	針	刀斫	鈴	環	鏝	枚	鐝
우쯔 oōts' 도 tŏ 우 oō	신 sīn	샤구 syăk' 도 tŏ 우 oō	례 lēyn 이 ī	관 kwān	만 mān	견 kēyn	계쯔 kēyts'
울 oŏr 두 toō	바 pā 놀 năr 침 tshīm	쟉 tsăk 도 tŏ	방 pāng 올 ŏr 령 lyōng	골 kŏr 회 hŏī 환 hwān	쇠 sŏī 손 sŏn 만 mān	가 kā 래 rāī 홈 hŏm	광 kwāng 이 ī 궐 kwŏr
히 hī 노 nŏ 시 sī	하 hā 리 rī	구 koō 사 sā 기 kī 리 rī	스스 soŏz'	와 wā	사 sā 비 pī	고스 kŏs' 기 kī	구 koō 와 wā

A thimble	An iron heater	Shears	A clasp-knife	A small bell	A hook	An iron rake	A hoe
銲	鐵烙	子剪	刀挟	鐃	鉤	把鐵	鉀
간 kān	라구 lāk' 데쯔 tēts'	션 sēyn 시 sī	교 kyŏ 우 oō 도 tŏ 우 oō	도 dŏ 우 oō	고 kŏ 우 oō	데쯔 tēts' 하 hā	소 sŏ 우 oō
셜 stăīr 한 hān	락 lāk 텰 t'hyōr	젼 tsyōn ᄌ tsă	협 hyōp 도 tŏ	뇨 nyŏ 령 lyōng 뇨 nyŏ	갈 kār 구 koō 리 rī 구 koō	텰 t'hyōr 파 p'hā	삽 sāp 삽 sāp
소 sŏ 소구 sŏk' 리 rī	고 kŏ 데 tē	하 hā 사 sā 미 mī	약 yăk 모 mŏ 우 oō	후 hoō 우 oō 례 lēy 이 ī	가 kā 기 gī	구 koō 사 sā 가 kā 이 ī	스 soŭ 기 kī

Japanese words assorted and explained Vol. I

七十二

...ese words ...ted d ...ined

II

鞍轡 Sadlery

A bit	A breast band	Saddle ornament	A covering for a saddle	A saddle		To chop	A handle
銜馬	帶胸	韂	甲鞍	鞍	鞍轡	斫	柄
바 bā 간 kān	교 kyŏ 우 oŏ 다 tā 이 ī	션 sēyn	안 ān 고 kŏ 우 oŏ	안 ān		샤구 syăk'	헤 hēy 이 ī
마 mā 함 hām	흉 hyŏng 듸 tăi	드 tă 래 răi 첨 tshyŏm	안 ān 갑 kăp	기 kī 르 roŏ 마 mā 안 ān	Sadlery	짝 skăk 쿨 koŏr 쟉 tsyăk	주 tsă 로 rŏ 병 pyōng
구즈 koŏtsŭ 와 wā	무 moŏ 나 nā 가 gā 이 ī	아 ā 오 ŏ 리 rī	구 koŏ 라 rā 오 ŏ 오 ŏ 이 ī	구 koŏ 라 rā		계 kēy 스루 zoŏr'	즈 tsoŏ 가 kā

A bridle	A curb	A stirrup	A girth	A pannier saddle		To pierce To bore	A grind stone
轡	勒	子鐙	帶肚	鞍馱		之鑽	礪
히 hī	로구 lŏk'	도 tŏ 우 oŏ 시 sī	도 tŏ 다 tā 이 ī	다 tā 이 ī 안 ān		산 săn 시 sī	레 lēy 이 ī
혁 hyŏk 비 pī	굴 koŏr 에 ē 륵 lŏŏk	등 toŏng 자 tsă	두 toŏ 듸 tăi	태 thăi 안 ān		찬 tshăn 저 tsŏ	숫 soŏt 돌 tŏr 려 lyŏ
다즈 tātsŭ 나 nā	가 kā 미 mī 가 kā 계 kēy	아 ā 뿌 boŏ 미 mī	하 hā 라 rā 오 ŏ 비 pī / 하 hā 루 roŏ 비 pī	니 nī 구 goŏ 라 rā		모 mŏ 모 mŏ	도 tŏ 이 ī 시 sī

73

A boat A canoe	A vessel A ship		To hire a horse	To load	A saddle band	Breech-leather	A rein
船小	船	舟車 Ships and Carriages	馬雇	擔荷	鞁	鞦	韁
쇼 syŏ 우 oō 션 seyn	션 sēyn		고 kŏ 빠 bā	가 ka 숀 sŏn	히 hī	시 sī 우 oō	교 kyŏ 우 oō
쇼 syŏ 션 syōn	비 păi 션 syūn		고 kŏ 마 mā	하 hā 죤 tsŏn	기 ki 르 roŏ 마 mā 지 tsī 올 oŏr 피 p'hī	고 kŏ 돌 tăr 개 kăi 츄 tshyoō	쥬 tsyoō 리 ri 올 oōr 강 kāng
고 kŏ 부 poē 네 ne	후 hoō 네 nē / 부 poō 네 nē		다 dā 진 tsin	니 ni 교 gŏ 시 sī 라 rā 예 ēy	구 koō 라 rā 시 si 기 kī	시 sī 리 ri 가 gā 이 ī	구 koō 지 tsī 스 zoŏ 나 nā
A fast sailing vessel	A ship A junk			To unload	A horse's load	A whip	A saddle cloth
船快	船大			卸	物卜	鞭	韉
과 kwā 이 i 션 sēyn				샤 syā	보구 pŏk' 모쯔 mots'	벼 pēyn	션 sēyn
쾌 Khwāi 션 syōn	대 tăi 션 syōn			부 poō 리 ri 올 oōr 사 sā	복 pŏk 믈 mōor	채 tshāi 편 p'hyōn	언 ōn 치 tshī 쳔 tshyōn
하 hā 야 yā 후 hoō 네 nē	다 tā 이 ī 션 sēyn			니 nī 오 ŏ 로스 rŏs'	니 nī 모즈 mŏts'	무 moō 지 tsī	빠 bā 션 sēyn / 다 tā 오 ŏ 이 ī

倭語類解下 … ese / rds / ted / d / ained … 舟車

Ships and Carri- 74 三[illegible]

A leadline	An anchor	A large oar A scull	A sail	A stern	A float	A fishing boat	A fly boat
繩龍	碇	櫓	帆	梢船	槎	船漁	船飛
료우쇼우 ryŏ ōō zyŏ ōō	데이 tē ī		한 hān	션소우 sēyn sŏ ōō	사 sā	쑈션 syŏ sēyn	
룡승 lyŏng scŏng	닫뎡 tat tyŏng	노로 nŏ rŏ	돋범 tŏt pōm	션쵸 syōn tshyŭ	승사사 suŏng sā sā	어션 ō syōn	비션 pī syōn
미나와 mī nā wā	이가리 ī kā rī	로 lŏ	호 hŏ	후네노도모 hoō nē nŏ tŏ mŏ	우기기 oō kī kī	우오즈리부네 oō ŏ tsŏr ri poō nē	히션 hī sēyn

A cabin	A cable	A pole A boat hook	A mast	A rudder	A prow A stem	A raft	A trading boat
房艙	纜碇	篙	檣	柁	頭船	筏	船商
소우호우 sŏ oō hŏ oō	데이란 tē ī lān	고우 kŏ oō	쇼우 syŏ oō	다 tā	션도우 sēyn tŏ oō	바쯔 pāts'	쇼우션 syŏ oō sēyn
창방 tshāng pāng	뎡람 tyōng lām	사홧대고 sā hwāt tāī kŏ	돋대쟝 tŏt tāī tsyāng	치타 tshī tshā	션두 syōn toō	셔벌 stē pōr	샹션 syāng syōn
야우라 yā goō rā	이가리ᅀᅳ나 ī kā rī zoŏ nā	미ᅀᅡ오 mī zā ŏ	호바시라 hŏ pā sī rā	가ᅀᅵ kā zī	후네노오모데 hoō nē nŏ ŏ mŏ tē	이가다 ī kā tā	아기나이부네 ā kī nā ī boō nē

To ford	To push along a boat	To cast anchor	To hoist sail	To register a vessel	A vessel's hold	A marine	Floor timber
渡	舟盪	碇抛	蓬掛	船點	倉船	[illegible]格	子板船
도 tŏ —	도 tŏ 우 oō 시 sī 우 oō	호 hŏ 우 oō 데 tē 이 ī	가 kā 이 ī 호 hŏ 우 oō	텬 tēn 셴 sēyn	셴 sēyn 소 sŏ 우 oō	가 kăk' 구 쑨 goōn	셴 sēyn 한 hăn 시 sī
건 kŏn 널 nŏr 도 tŏ	탕 thăng 쥬 tsyoō	포 p'hŏ 뎡 tyūng	괘 kwāi 봉 pŏng	뎜 tyŏm 션 syŏn	션 syŏn 창 tshăng	격 kyŏk 군 koōn	션 syŏn 판 phăn ᄌ tsă
와 wā 다 tăr' 루	후 hoō 네 nē 오 ŏ 스 soŏ	이 ī 가 kā 리 rī 오 ŏ 로스 rŏs' 이 ī 가 kā 리 rī 이 ī 례 rēy	호 hŏ 가 kā 계 kēy	후 hoō 나 nā 계 kēy 뿐 boōn	셴 sēyn 산 sān 야 yā 라 rā 이 ī	스 soŏ 이 ī 후 hoō	스 soŏ 이 ī 다 tā

To moor a vessel	To paddle	To get up the anchor	To take in sail	To tack	To clear out a vessel	A sailor A crew	A scoop
泊	撓	碇拔	篷卸	篷扯	船出	工沙	戽
하 hāk 구	도 dŏ 우 oō	하 hāts' 쓰 데 tē 이 ī	샤 syā 호 hŏ 우 oō	시 sī 호 hŏ 우 oō	슈 syoōts' 쯔 셴 sēyn	샤 syā 고 kŏ 우 oō	고 kŏ
부 poō 툴 thoŏr 박 pāk	저 tsŏ 울 oŏr 뇨 nyŏ	발 pār 뎡 tyōng	샤 syā 봉 pŏng	지 tsī 봉 pŏng	출 tshyoōr 션 syōn	사 sā 공 kŏng	푸 p'hă 래 rāī 호 hŏ
도 tŏ 마 mār' 루	오 ŏ 시 sī	이 ī 가 kā 리 rī 아 ā 게 루 gēyr'	호 hŏ 오 ŏ 오 ŏ 로스 rŏs'	호 hŏ 오 ŏ 히 hĭk' 구	슌 syŏot 셴 sēyn	센 sēyn 도 dŏ 우 oō	아 ā 가 kā 도 tŏ 리 rī

倭語類解 下 舟車

To turn round	A wheel	A sedan chair	A chariot	To repair a vessel	To swim	A vessel in a fog	An unsteady wind
轉	輪	子轎	輦	葺修	泅	船暈	風漂
뎐 tĕn	린 lĭn	쿄 kyŏ 우 oō 시 sĭ	렌 lĕyn	시 sī 우 oō 시 sī 우 oō	시 sī 우 oō	운 oōn 센 sēyn	효 hyŏ 우 oō 후 hoō 우 oō
구 koō 을 oōr 젼 tsyōn	박 pāk 회 hōī 륜 lyoōn	교 kyŏ ᄌ tsă	련 lyōn 련 lyōn	슈 syoō 즙 tsoōp	헤 hē 음 oŏm 슈 syoō	운 oōn 션 syōn	표 p'hyŏ 풍 p'hoōng
우 oō 다 tā 다 tā	구 koōr' 루 마 mā 노 nŏ 와 wā	고 kŏ 시 sĭ	데 tē 우 goōr' 루 마 mā	후 hoō 나 nā 슈 syōo 리 rī 후 hoō 나 nā 부 boō 신 sīn	오 ŏ 요 yŏg' 우	후 hoō 네 nē 니 nī 요 yŏ 우 oō	효 hyŏ 우 oō 리 rī 우 oō

To convey To transport	To ride An equipage	A small do	A car A carriage	To fumigate a vessel	To dive	A shipwreck To founder	Unsafe anchorage
輸	駕	轎小	車	燻煙	迷	船破	泊漂
유 yoō	가 kā	쇼 syŏ 우 oō 쿄 kyŏ 우 oō	쿄 kyŏ	연 ēyn 군 koōn	베 bī		
슈 syoō 운 ōōn ᄒᆞᆯ hăr 슈 syoō	멍 mĕng 에 ē 가 kā	쇼 syŏ 교 kyŏ	술 soōr 위 roōī 거 kŏ	연 yōn 훈 hoōn	무 moō ᄌ tsă 미 mī 미 mī	파 p'hā 션 syōn	표 p'hyŏ 박 pāk
하 hā 교 kŏb' 부	노 nŏ 리 rī 가 kā 고 gŏ	노 nŏ 리 rī 모 mŏ 노 nŏ	구 koōr' 루 마 mā	후 hoō 네 nē 다 tā 데 dē	가 kāts 즈 개 gī	하 hā 센 sēyn	효 hyŏ 우 oō 하 hāk' 구

75 二十

Dice	To play at chess	A box of chess-men	Chess	Amusements		To pull To hawl	To load To carry
六雙	碁着	桶碁	碁	技雜	技戲	曳	載
소 sŏ 우 oō 로구 lŏk'	ᅀᅣ구 zyăk 기 kī	기 kī 도 tŏ 우 oō	기 kī	ᅀᅭ zŏ 우 oō 게 gī		예 ēy 이 ī	사 sā 이 ī
쌍 ssăng 륙 lyōok	착 tshyăk 긔 kwī	긔 kwī 통 thŏng	바 pā 독 tŏk 긔 kwī	잡 tsăp 기 kī	Tricks and Plays	쓸 skoŏr 을 oŏr 예 ēy	시 sī 룰 roŏr 지 tsăī
스 soŏ ᅌᅭ gŏ 로구 lăk	ᅌᅭ gŏ 우 oō 즈 tsoŏ	ᅌᅭ gŏ ᅌᅨ gēy	ᅌᅭ gŏ	나 nā 구 goō 사 sā 미 mī 고 kŏ 도 tŏ		히구 hīk	노 nŏ 스루 soŏr'
Cards	The game of chess	Chess-men	A chess board	Plays The drama		To drag	To mount To ride
牌紙	奕	子碁	局	戲		牽	乘
시 sī 하 hā 이 ī	예 ēy 기 kī	기 kī 시 sī	교구 kyŏk	기 kī		켄 kēyn	쇼 syŏ 우 oō
지 tsī 패 phāi	장 tsyāng 긔 kwī 혁 hyăk	긔 kwī ᄌᆞ tsă	판 phān 국 koōk	노 nŏ 른 răt 회 hŏī		읻 it 글 koŏr 견 kyŏn	톨 thăr 승 soŏng
가 kăr' 루 다 tā	쇼 syŏ 우 oō 게 gī	ᅌᅭ gŏ 이 ī 시 sī	ᅌᅭ gŏ 빤 bān	교 kyŏ 우 oō ᅌᅦᆫ gēyn		고 kŏ 게 gī	노루 nŏr'

倭語類解

Japan[ese] wor[ds] assort[ed] an[d] explai[ned] Vol. I

A fabulous bird (male)	A bird		To lose	A swing	A hand ball	Gambling	To pin at chess
鳳	鳥		負	韆鞦	毬	賭	碁假
	됴 tyŏ	飛禽	후 hoō 우 oō	사 sā 우 oō 션 sēyn	규 kyoō 우 oō	도 tŏ	가 kā 기 kī
봉 păng 황 hwāng 봉 păng	새 sāi 됴 tyŏ	Flying Birds	질 tair 부 poō	츄 tshyoō 쳔 tshyōn	쥭 tsyōok 방 pāng 올 ŏr 구 koō	나 nā 기 kī 도 tŏ	가 kā 긔 kwī
호 hŏ 우 oō	도 tŏ 리 rī		마 māk' 구 루 roō	바 bā 사 sā 교 gŏ	데 tē 마 mā 리 rī	가 kā 계 kēy	하 hā 사 sā 미 mī 쇼 syŏ 우 oō 이 gī

A fabulous bird (female).	A phenix A divine bird			To win	A foot ball	A lot	To take a hand
凰	鸞			勝	毽	鬮	拏
				쇼 syŏ 우 oō	견 kēyn	규 kyoō 우 oō	호 hŏ 우 oō
봉 pŏng 황 hwāng 황 hwāng	란 lān 됴 tyŏ 란 lān			이 ī 긜 kwīr 승 soŏng	져 tsyŏ 기 kī 곤 kōn	졉 tsyōp 이 ī 구 koō	훈 hoōn 슈 syoō 방 pāng
오 ŏ 우 oō	란 lān			갓 kāts' 즈	마 mā 리 rī	구 koō ᅀᅵ zī	쇼 zyŏ 왼 gŏn

76

A wild goose	A diver	A heron / A large stork	A sort of wild goose / A swan	An eagle	A parrot	Mandarin duck	A stork
鴈	鷀	鸛	鵠	鷲	鵡鸚	鴦鴛	鶴
안 gān	시 zī	관 kwān	곡 kŏk'	시 sī 우 oō		엔 ēyn 오 ŏ 우 oō	각 kāk'
기 kī 러 rŏ 기 kī 안 ān	두 toō 루 roō 미 mī 자 tsă	한 hān 새 sāi 관 kwān	고 kŏ 해 hē 곡 kŏk	수 soō 리 rī 츄 tshyōo	잉 āing 무 moō	원 wōn 앙 āng	화 hwā 학 hāk
가 kā 리 rī	노 nŏ 즈루 tsoŏr'	오 ŏ 오 ŏ 도 tŏ 리 rī	고 kŏ 우 oō	와 wā 시 sī	오 ŏ 우 oō 무 moō	오 ŏ 시 sī 도 tŏ 리 rī	즈루 tsoŏr'

A falcon	A wild duck	A fishing cormorant	A sort of wild duck	A crane / A small heron	A large bird	A green duck	A peacock
鷹	鷗	鷀鸕	鳧	鷺白	鵬	翠翡	雀孔
요 yŏ 우 oō	오 ŏ 우 oō	로 lŏ 시 zī	복 bŏk'	학 hāk' 로 lŏ	호 hŏ 우 oō		고 kŏ 우 oo 샥 syāk'
매 māi 응 ŏng	갈 măr 며 myŏ 기 kī 구 koō	로 lŏ 자 tsă	다 tā 와 wā 기 kī 목 mŏk	백 pāik 로 lŏ	새 sāi 붕 poōng	비 pī 취 tshyōō	공 kŏng 쟉 tsyāk
다 tā 가 kā	가 kā 모 mŏ 메 mēy	우 oō 노 nŏ 도 tŏ 리 rī / 누 noō 레 rēy 사 sā 기 kī	노 nŏ 간 gān	시 sī 라 rā 사 sā 기 gī	다 tā 이 ī 호 hŏ 우 oō	히 hī 스 soŏ 이 ī	구 koō 쟉 zyāk'

倭語類解

Japanese words assorted and explained Vol.

七十六

倭語類解下

[...]ese [...]rds [...]ted [...]d [...]ined II

飛禽 Birds

77

A turtle dove	A king-fisher	A nightingale	A wren	A lark	A horned owl	A kite	A sparrow hawk
鳲	鸂	鸎	鷯鷦	鶊鶬	鶹鵂	鳶	鸇
시 sī	계 kēy 이 ī	오 ŏ 우 oō	쇼 syŏ 우 oō 료 lyŏ 우 oō	소 sō 우 oō 고 kŏ 우 oō	큐 kyoō 우 oō 리 lī 우 oō	엔 ēyn	센 sēyn
뻑 pŏk 국 kook 새 sāī 시 sī	비 pī 오 ŏ 리 rī 계 kēy	꾇 kŏīt 고 kŏ 리 rī 잉 ĭăng	츠 tshoō 료 lyŏ	창 tshāng 경 kyōng	휴 hyoō 류 lyoo	쇼 syŏ 로 lŏ 기 kī 연 yōn	새 sāī 매 māī 젼 tsyōn
갇 kāt 고 kŏ 도 tŏ 리 rī	가 kā 와 wā 셰 sēy 미 mī	우 oō ㅇ구 goō 아 ā 스 soŏ	미 mī 소 sŏ 사 sā ㅿㅏ zā 이 ī	히 hī 빠 bā 리 rī	요 yŏ 다 tā 가 kā	도 tŏ 배 bī	하 hā 이 ī 다 tā

An owl	A goose	A snipe	A wagtail	A cuckoo	A partridge	A water fowl	A buzzard A kind of hawk
梟	鵝	鷸	鴒鶺	鵑杜	鴣鷓	鷁	鶻
쑈 syŏ 우 oō	ㅇ가 gā		셰 sēy 기 kī 레 lēy 이 ī	도 tŏ 켄 kēyn		이 쯔 its'	고 쯔 kŏts'
옫 ŏt 바 pā 미 mī 효 hyŏ	게 kē 유 yoō 아 ā	도 tŏ 요 yŏ 새 sāī 휼 hyoŏr	쳑 tshyŏk 령 lyŏng	두 toō 견 kyōn	쟈 tsyā 고 kŏ	부 pă 룸 răm 가 kā 비 pi 일 ĭr	송 sŏng 골 kŏr 매 māī 골 kŏr
후 구 hoŏk 로 rŏ	도 tŏ 우 oō ㅇ간 gān	기 쯔 kīts	이 ī 시 sī 다 tā 라 rā 기 kī	호 hŏ 도 tŏ 도 tŏ ㅇ기 gī 스 soŏ	샤 syā 고 kŏ	후 hoō 나 nă 도 dŏ 리 rī	하 hā 야 yā ㅂ부 boō 사 sā

A feather	A hen	A bat	A duck	A crow A raven	A domestic fowl	A wood pecker	A swallow
羽	雛	蝙蝠	鴨	烏	鷄	鴷	鷰
우 oō	[illegible] soō 우 oō	헨 hēyn 후 hook' 구	오 ŏ 우 oō	우 oō	케 kēy 이 ī	레 lēyts' 쯔	연 ēyn
짓 tsīt 우 oō	삿 sāt 기 kī 추 tshoo	편 p'hyōn 복 pŏk	오 ŏ 리 rī 압 āp	가 kā 마 mā 괴 kŏi 오 ŏ	닭 tărk 계 kēy	닷 tāt 뎌 tyŏ 구 koō 리 rī 렬 ryŏr	져 tsyŏ 비 pī 연 yōn
하 hā 네 nê	히 hī 요 yŏ 고 kŏ	고 kŏ 우 oō 무 mōo 리 rī	가 kā 모 mo	가 kā 라 rās' 스	니 nī 와 wā 도 tŏ 리 rī	기 kī 다 tā 다 tā 기 kī	즈 tsoŏ 빠 bā 메 mēy

A wing	A chattering sparrow	A sparrow	A qoo[illegible]	A magpie	A pigeon A dove	Pheasant	A rock swallow
翼	噪雀	雀	鶉	鵲	鳩	雉	胡鷰
욕 yŏk' 구	샥 syāk' 구 소 sŏ 우 oo	샥 syāk' 구	슌 zyoon	샥 syāk' 구	규 kyoō 우 oō	지 tsī	고 kŏ 연 ēyn
놀 nār 개 kāī 익 ik	쟉 tsyāk 조 tsŏ	춤 tshăm 새 sāi 쟉 tsyāk	몯 [illegible] 초 [illegible] 라 rā 기 ki 슌 zyoon	가 kā 치 tshī 쟉 tsyāk	비 pī 들 toŏr 기 kī 구 koō	셩 skwōng 치 tshī	호 hŏ 연 yōn
즈 tsoŏ 비 pā 사 sā	스 sooz' 스 메 mēy 사 sā 와 wā 우 goō	스 sooz' 스 메 mēy	우 oŏz 스 라 rā	가 kā 사 sā 사 sā 기 gī	하 hā 도 tŏ	기 kī 시 zī	아 ā 나 nā 즈 tsoŏ 빠 bā 메 mēy

倭語類解

Japan[ese] wo[rds] asso[rted] an[d] expla[ined] Vol.

A beast A brute		A bait for birds	To nestle A nest	To peck	To fly	An egg	A beak A bill
獸		餌鳥	巢	啄	飛	卵	嘴
시우 sī oō	走獸	됴시 tyǒ zī	소우 sǒ oō	닥 tāk'	히 hī	란 lān	사 sī
즁싱슈 tsoǒng sīng syǒo	Running Beasts	됴이 tyǒ ī	깃드릴소 kit toǒ rīr sǒ	조올탁 tsǒ oǒr thāk	놀비 nā p	알란 ār rān	부리췌 poō rī tshyōoey
지구쇼우 tsīk' syǒ oō		도리노예 tǒ rī nǒ ēy	스즈구루 soǒ tsoǒ koǒr'	예히로우 ēy hī rǒ oō	도부 tǒ	다마고 tā mā gǒ	구지빠시 kōo tsī bā sī

A fabulous beast An unicorn			To roost To alight To perch	To grasp with the claw	To crow To sing	To plume the feathers	A talon A claw
麒麟			棲	攫	鳴	刷羽	距
			셰이 sēy ī	과구 kwāk	메이 mey ī	사이우 sā ī oō	교 kyǒ
긔린 kwī līn			깃드릴셔 kīt toǒ rīr syǒ	더위출확 tǒ ooī tshūr hwāk	울명 oor myǒng	쇄우 swāī oō	며느리톱거 myō nā rī t'hǒp kō
기린 kī līn			스무 soǒm'	즈가무 tsoǒ kām'	나구 nāk'	하우시도루 hā oō sī tǒr'	즈메 tsǒo mēy

A cow	A colt A nag	A piebald horse	A white horse	A dappled horse	A horse	A tyger	A lion
牛	駒	馬駁	馬白	馬驄	馬	虎	獅
규 gyoō 우 oō	구 koō	학 hăk 빠 bā	학 hăk' 빠 bā		빠 bā	고 kŏ	시 sĭ
쇼 syŏ 우 oō	미 măĭ 야 yā 지 tsĭ 구 koō	박 pak 마 nā	빅 păĭk 마 mā	총 tshŏng 마 mā	몰 măr 마 mā	범 pŏm 호 hŏ	스 să 지 tsăĭ 스 să
우 oō 시 sĭ	고 kŏ 마 mā	마 mā 다 dā 라 rā 무 moō 마 mā	시 sĭ 로 rŏ 무 mōo 마 mā	소 sŏ 우 oō 빠 bā	무 boō 마 mā	도 tŏ 라 rā	시 sĭ 시 sĭ

倭語類解

Japanese words assorted and explained Vol.I

A calf	A camel	A gelding	A spotted horse	A red horse	A charger A fine horse	A leopard	An elephant
犢	駝	馬騸	馬騅	馬赤	馬駿	豹	象
도 구 tŏk'	다 tā	셴 sēyn 빠 bā	즈 tsoŏ 이 ī 빠 bā	셰 sēy 기 kī 빠 bā	쥰 zyōon 빠 bā	후 hŏ 우 oō	쇼 syŏ 우 oō
쇠 syŏī 야 yā 지 tsĭ 독 tŏk	약 yāk 대 tăĭ 타 t'hā	션 syon 마 mā	츄 tshyoō 마 mā	젹 tsyŏk 마 mā	쥰 tsyŏn 마 mā	표 p'hyŏ 범 pŏm 표 p'hyŏ	고 k'hŏ 기 k'hī 리 rī 샹 syāng
우 oō 시 sĭ 노 nŏ 고 kŏ	라 lāk' 구 다 dā	긴 kīn 두 toō 기 kī 무 moō 마 mā	가 kā 스 soŏ 게 gēy	아 ā 가 kā 무 mōo 마 mā	슌 syoōn 메 mēy	효 hyŏ 우 oō	조 zŏ 우 oō

...ese
...rds
...ted
...d
...ined
II.

走獸

...um.
Beasts

A lamb	An arctic fox	A monkey An ape	A Musk deer	A wolf	A rhinoceros	A bear	An ass
羔	狸	猿	麝	狼	犀	熊	驢
고 kŏ	리 lī	엔 ēyn	샤 zyā	로 lŏ 우 oŏ	세 sēy 이 ī	유 yōo 우 oŏ	료 lyŏ
염 yŭm 쇼 syŏ 고 kŏ	솕 sărk 리 lī	잔 tsăin 납 năp 이 ī 원 wŏn	사 sā 향 hyāng 노 nŏ 로 rŏ 샤 syā	일 ir 히 hī 랑 rāng	무 mōo 쇼 syŏ 셔 syō	곰 kŏm 웅 oāng	나 nā 귀 kooī 려 lyŏ
히 hits' 즈 시 zī 노 nŏ 고 kŏ	스 soŏ 리 rī	사 săr' 루	샤 zyā 고 kŏ 우 oŏ	오 ŏ 오 ŏ 가 kā 메 mēy	사 sā 이 ī	구 koŏ 마 mā	우 oŏ 사 sā 기 gī 무 mōo 마 mā

79

A squirrel A woodrat	A goat A sheep	A fox	A mouse deer	A deer A stag	A wild dog	A great bear	A mule
貂	羊	狐	獐	鹿	豺	羆	騾
됴 tyŏ 우 oō	요 yŏ 우 oō	고 kŏ	쇼 syŏ 우 oō	로 lŏk' 구	사 sā 이 ī	히 hī	라 lā
돈 tōn 피 p'hī 료 lyŏ	양 yāng 양 yāng	여 yŏ 으 oŏ 호 hŏ	노 nŏ 로 lŏ 장 tsyāng	사 sā 숨 săm 록 lŏk	승 soŏng 랑 rāng 이 ī 싀 soŏī	곰 kŏm 비 pī	노 nŏ 새 sāī 라 ra
기 kī 네 nēz' 스 미 mī	히 hits' 즈 시 zī	기 kī 즈 tsŏo 네 nē	구 koō 시 zī 가 kā	시 sī 가 kā	야 yā 마 mā 이 ī 누 noō	시 sī 우 goō 마 mā	로 rŏ 무 moō 마 mā

A cat	A cur A dog	A pig	A hare A rabbit	A rat A mouse	A flying squirrel	Badger	Land otter Beaver
猫	狗	猪	兎	鼠	鼯	貒	獺山
요 byŏ 우 oō	고 kŏ 우 oō	죠 tsyŏ	도 tŏ	소 sŏ	고 gŏ	단 tān	산 sān 다쯔 tāts'
괴 kōī 묘 myŏ	개 kāī 구 koō	돝 tŏt 제 tsēy	톳 thŏt 기 kī 토 thŏ	쥐 tsoōī 셔 syŏ	드 tă 람 rām 이 ī 오 ŏ	오 ŏ 소 sŏ 리 rī 단 tān	산 sān 달 tār
네 nē 고 kŏ	이 ī 누 noō	부 boō 다 tā	우 oō 사 sā 기 gī	네즈 nēz' 미 mī	리 rī 스 sŏo	마 mā 미 mī	다 tā 누 noō 기 kī

Female Beast	A hound A shaggy dog	A wild hog	A hedgehog Porcupine	A weasel	A mole	Glutton	River otter
雌	狵	猪山	蝟	狖	鼢	貛	獺水
사 sā	호 hŏ 우 oō	산 sān 죠 tsyŏ	이 ī	고 kŏ 우 oō	훈 hoōn	관 kwān	스 soŏ 이 ī 다쯔 tāts
암 ām 자 tsă	더 tŏ 펄 phŏr 개 kāī 방 pāng	산 sān 제 tsēy	고 kŏ 솜 sŏm 돝 tŏt 위 oōī	쪽 tsyŏk 접 tsyŏp 이 ī 핑 phāng	두 toō 더 tŏ 쥐 tsoōī 분 poōn	담 tām 뷔 pōoī 환 hwān	슈 syŏo 달 tār
메 mēy 스 soo	게 kēy 부 bŏo 구 kŏo 이 ī 누 nŏo	이 ī 노 nŏ 시 sī 시 sī	기 kī 즈 tsoŏ	이 ī 다 tā 지 tsī	무 mŏo 구 goŏ 라 rā	덴 tēn	가 kā 와 wā 우 oō 소 sŏ

倭語類解

Japan... wo... asso... an... expla... Vol

七十九

To drive	To train a dog	To gore	To bark	A paw	Hair	A horn	Male Beast
驅	狃	觸	吠	踶	毛	角	雄
구 koō	쥬 tsyōo 우 oō	조구 zŏk'	하 hā 이 ī	데 tē 이 ī	뽀 bŏ 우 oō	가구 kāk'	유 yōo 우 oō
몰 mŏr 구 koō	버 pō 릇 roŏt 뉴 nyoō	찌 tstsi 를 roŏr 죡 tshyŏk	즈 tsoŏ 즐 tsŏor 폐 p'hēy	출 tshăr 톄 tēy	터 thŏ 럭 rŏk 모 mŏ	섈 spoōr 곽 kāk	수 sōo 웅 oŏng
오 ŏ 우 oō	구 koō 셰 sēy	호 hoō 흘 룰 roōr' 루	호 hŏ 유 률 yōor' 루	계 kēy 루 roō	계 gēy	즈 tsoŏ 노 nŏ	오 ŏ 수 sōo

	To gallop	To ride on horse back	To break in a horse	To gnaw	To neigh To roar	A hoof	A tail	A mane
	馳	騎	馴	噬	嘶	蹄	尾	鬣
	지 tsī	기 ki	슌 syoōn	세 zēy 이 ī	셰 sēy 이 ī	데 tē 이 ī	뻬 băi	료 yŏ 우 oō
80	돌 tăr 닐 nīr 치 tshī	톨 thār 긔 kwī	길 kīr 드 toŏ 릴 rīr 슌 syoōn	물 meōrs ㅅ 셔 syō	울 oōr 식 sik	굽 koōp 톄 tēy	쇠 skŏ 리 ri 미 mī	갈 kār 기 kī 립 rīp
	가 kā 게 루 kēyr	노 루 nŏr'	나 nā 레 rēy 나 nā 루 루 roōr'	가 무 kām'	이 ī 뽀 bŏ 우 oō	히 hī 조 tsoŏ 메 mēy	오 ŏ	다 tā 데 tē 가 gā 미 mī

倭語類解

Japanese words assorted and explained Vol.

水族

Aquatic animals

A sturgeon	Stock fish	Scissar fish	Salmon	Mullett	A fish	A dragon
民魚	大口魚	鱸魚	鰱魚	鯔魚	魚	龍
민 mīn 교 kyŏ	대 tāi 이 ī 교 kŏ 우 oō 교 kyŏ	로 lō 교 kyŏ	련 lēyn 교 kyŏ	시 sī 교 kyŏ	교 kyŏ	료 lyŏ 우 oō
민 mīn 어 ō	대 tāi 구 koō 어 ŏ	로 lō 어 ō	련 lyōn 어 ŏ	치 tshwī 어 ō	고 kŏ 기 kī 어 ō	미 mī 르 roŏ 룡 lyŭng
니 nī 베 pēy 우 oō 오 ŏ	다 tā 라 rā	스 soŏ 스 zoŏ 기 kī	사 sā 게 kēy	이 ī 셰 sēy 고 gŏ 이 ī	우 oō 오 ŏ	다 tāts' 즈

Stone bream	A silver mouthed fish	A sea spider	Plaise	A shark	A carp	A crocodile
家鷄魚	銀口魚	八梢魚	魴魚	鯊魚	鯉魚	蛟龍
가 kā 계 kēy 이 ī 교 kyŏ	은 gīn 고 kŏ 우 oō 교 kyŏ	하 hāts' [illegible] 소 sŏ 우 oō 교 kyŏ	호 hŏ 우 oō 교 kyŏ	사 sā 교 kyŏ	리 lī 교 kyŏ	고 kŏ 우 oō 료 lyŏ 우 oō
가 kā 계 kēy 어 ō	은 oōn 구 kōo 어 ŏ	팔 phār 쵸 tshyŏ 어 ō	방 pāng 어 ō	사 sā 어 ō	리 lī 어 ō	교 kyŏ 룡 lyŭng
다 tā 이 ī	아 ā 유 yoō	다 tā 고 kŏ	보 boō 리 rī	사 sā 메 mēy	고 kŏ 이 ī	아 ā 마 mā 료 lyŏ 우 oō

Stone fish	Catfish	Pomfret	Old school fish	An eel	A large white fish	A porpoise	A perch
魚石	魚鮎	魚鮩	道古	魚鱣	魚芒	魚鮪	魚鮒
셰 sēy 기 kī 교 kyŏ	뎬 dēyn 교 kyŏ	헤 hēy 이 ī 교 kyŏ	고 kŏ 도 tŏ 우 oō 교 kyŏ	션 sēyn 교 kyŏ	보 bŏ 우 oō 교 kyŏ	이 ī 교 kyŏ	후 hoō 교 kyŏ
셕 syŏk 어 ō	뎜 tyŏm 어 ō	병 pyŏng 어 ō	고 kŏ 도 tŏ 어 ō	젼 tsyŏn 어 ō	망 māng 어 ō	유 yoō 어 ō	부 pōo 어 ō
이 ī 시 sī 모 mŏ 지 tsī / 우 goō 지 tsī	나 nā 마 mā 즈 tsoŏ	마 mā 나 nā 가 gā 즈 tsoŏ 오 ŏ	사 sā 바 pā	우 oō 나 nā 기 gī	사 sā 와 wā 라 rā	시 sī 비 pī	후 hoō 나 nā

A mud eel	Sea blubber	A river porpoise	A salmon trout	Cuttle fish	A bream	A skate	A turbot A flounder
魚鰍	魚鏡	魨河	魚松	魚賊烏	魚鱖	魚洪	魚廣
시 sī 우 oō 교 kyŏ	계 kēy 이 ī 교 kyŏ	가 kā 돈 tŏn	쇼 syŏ 우 oō 교 kyŏ	우 oō 소 구 zŏk' 교 kyŏ	게 쯔 kēyts 교 kyŏ	고 kŏ 우 oō 교 kyŏ	고 kŏ 우 oō 교 kyŏ
츄 tshyoō 어 ō	경 kyōng 어 ō	하 hā 돈 tŏn	송 syōng 어 ō	오 ŏ 적 tsŏk 어 ō	궐 kwŏr 어 ō	홍 hŏng 어 ō	광 kwāng 어 ō
도 dŏ 죠 tsyŏ 우 oō	에 ēy 비 pī 가 kā 네 nē	후 hoō 우 goō	마 mā 스 soŏ	이 ī 가 kā	아 ā 사 sā 지 tsī / 다 tā 나 nā 고 gŏ	에 ēy 이 ī	가 sā 레 rēy 이 ī

Dressed limpit	Tripang	A cockle	A crab	A tortoise	Isinglass Fish glue	A small sea spider	Green-boned fish
鰒熟	蔘海	蛤	虫倒	龜	鰾	梢八小	魚鯖
슈 zyōok 구 우 hoōk' 구	가 kā 이 ī 신 sīn	고 kŏ 우 oō	도 tŏ 우 oō 쥬 tsyōo 우 oō	기 kī	효 hyŏ 우 oō	쇼 syŏ 우 oō 하 hāts' 쯔 소 sŏ 우 oō	셰 sēy 이 ī 교 kyŏ
슉 syoōk 복 pŏk	히 hăī 숨 săm	죠 tsyŏ 개 kāī 합 hap	도 tŏ 충 tshyōong	거 kō 복 pŏk 귀 koōī	부 poō 레 rē 표 p'hyŏ	쇼 syŏ 팔 p'hār 쵸 ts'hyŏ	청 tshyōng 어 ō
이 ī 데 tē 아 ā 와 wā 비 pi	나 nā 마 mā 고 kŏ 다 tā 와 wā 라 rā 외 gŏ	하 hā 마 mā 오구 goō 리 rī	이 ī 시 sī 아 gā 니 ni	가 kā 메 mēy	니 nī 베 pēy	마 mā 나 nā 다 tā 고 kŏ	셰 sēy 아 gā 이 ī
Dried limpits	A limpit A rocksucker	A mirscle	A spiral shell fish	Land tortoise	A whale	A scale	A seasnail
鰒全	鰒生	蛤紅	螺	鼈	鯨	鱗	魚古乾
션 sēyn 후 hoōk 구	쇼 syŏ 우 oō 후 hoōk' 구	고 kŏ 우 oō 고 kŏ 우 oō	라 lā	베 pēyts' 쯔	게 kēy 이 ī	린 līn	간 kān 고 kŏ 교 kyŏ
젼 tsyōn 복 pŏk	싱 sāīng 복 pŏk	홍 hŏng 합 hāp	쇼 syŏ 라 rā 라 rā	쟈 tsyā 라 rā 벌 pŏr	고 kŏ 릐 răī 경 kyōng	비 pī 놀 nār 린 rīn	간 kān 고 kŏ 어 ŏ
호 hŏ 시 sī 아 ā 와 wā 비 pī	아 ā 와 wā 비 pī	아 ā 아 gā 이 ī	사 sā ㅿ아 zā 에 ēy	스 soŏ 본 pŏn	구 koō ㅿ이 zī 라 rā	우 oō 로 rŏ 구 koōz' ㅿ 우 oō 로 rŏ 고 kŏ	갇 kāt 즈 tsoō 우 oō 부 poō 시 sī

倭語類解 一

Japanese words asserted and explained Vol.I

八十一

A firefly	A lisard	A snake	A reptile An insect		A fish bait	Sea weed	A crab
螢	蝘	蛇	蟲	昆蟲	餌魚	花石	蟹
계 kēy 이 ī	연 ēyn	샤 syā	쥬 tsyōō 우 oō		교 kyŏ 시 zī	셰 sēy 기 kī 과 kwā	가 kā 이 ī
반 pan 도 tŏ 형 hyŏng	도 tŏ 마 mā 비 pāi 얌 yām 연 yŏn	비 pāi 얌 yām 샤 syā	베 pēy 레 rēy 츙 tshyoōng	Insects and worms	어 ō 이 ī	셕 syŏk 화 hwā	게 kāi 히 hāi
호 hŏ 다 tā 루 roō	이 ī 모 mŏ 리 rī	헤 hēy 비 pī	무 moō 시 sī		우 oō 오 ŏ 노 nŏ 예 ēy	고 kŏ 하 gā 기 kī	가 kā 니 nī

	A silkworm	A butter fly	An adder A poisonous snake	A boa con strictor		A shrimp A prawn	An oval muscle
	蠶	蝶	蛇毒	蟒		鰕	膓蝗
	잔 zān		독 dŏk' 구 샤 syā	모 mō 우 oō		가 kā	셰 sēy 이 ī 죠 tsyŏ 우 oō
82	누 noō 에 ē 잠 tsăm	나 nā 뷔 pwī 뎝 tyŏp	독 tŏk 샤 syā	구 koō 렁 rōng 이 ī 망 māng		새 sāi 오 ŏ 하 hā	셩 syōng 쟝 tsyāng
	가 kā 이 ī 고 gŏ	됴 tyŏ 우 oō	히 hī 라 rā 구 koō 지 tsī 마 mā 무 moō 시 sī	우 oō 와 wā 바 bā 미 mī		예 ēy 비 pī	세 sēy 이 ī 쇼 syŏ 우 oō

倭語類解

A leech	A slug A snail	A gnat A musquito	An earwig	A cricket	A grasshopper A mantis	A dragon fly	A bee
蛭	蝸	蚊	蛄	蟀蟋	螂螳	蜓	蜂
시 sits' 쯔	과 kwā	훈 hoōn	고 kŏ	시 sīts' 쯔 소 sŏts' 쯔	도 tŏ 우 oō 로 lŏ 우 oō	데 tē 이 ī	호 hŏ 우 oō
거 kō 머 mō 리 rī 질 tsīr	돌 tăr 팡 phāng 이 ī 와 wā	모 mŏ 긔 kwī 문 moōn	도 tŏ 로 rŏ 래 rē 고 kŏ	실 sāir 솔 sŏr	당 tāng 랑 lāng	잔 tsān 자 tsā 리 rī 뎡 tyōng	벌 pōr 봉 pŏng
히 hī 루 roō	다 dā 이 ī 료 lyŏ 오 oō / 과 kwā 규 gyoō 우 oō	가 kā	계 kēy 라 rā	기 kī 리 rī 기 gī 리 rīs' 스	가 kā 마 mā 기 kī 리 rī	돈 tŏn 뽀 bŏ 우 oō	하 hā 지 tsī

Japanese words assorted and explained Vol. I

An ant	A locust	A beetle	A fly	A curling worm	An ephemera A flying ant	A locust	Cockchafer Tree beetle
蟻	虫蝗	虻	蠅	蛩	蝣蜉	蚱	蟬
기 gī	고 kŏ 우 oō 쥬 tsyoō 우 oō	모 mŏ 우 oō	요 yŏ 우 oō	교 kyŏ 우 oō	후 hoo 이 ī 우 oō	사 sāk' 구	션 sēyn
가 kā 얌 yām 이 ī 의 wī	황 hwāng 츙 tshyōong	등 toōng 의 ik 밍 māing	ᄑᆞ phă 리 rī 승 soōng	뵈 pŏī 짱 stsāng 이 ī 공 kŏng	부 poō 유 yoō	묏 mŏīt 도 tŏ 기 kī 작 tsāk	매 māī 얌 yām 이 ī 션 syōn
아 ā 리 rī	이 ī 나 nā 무 moō 시 sī	아 ā 부 poō	하 hā 이 ī	하 hā 다 tā 오 ŏ 리 rī 무 moō 시 sī	후 hoō 유 yoō 우 oō	이 ī 나 nā 고 gŏ	세 sēy 미 mī

八十二

倭語類解下

…nese …rds …pted …d …ined II.

昆虫 Insects and worms

A tick	A frog	A sort of toad	A cater-pillar	A louse	A flea	A centipede	An earth worm
蜆	蛙	蟾	蠹	蝨	蚤	蜈蚣	蚯蚓
히 hī	와 wā	섬 sēyn	도 tŏ	시 쯔 sīts'	소 sŏ 우 oō	야 gŏ 고 kŏ 우 oō	큐 kyōo 우 oō 인 īn
진 tsīn 듸 toōī 비 pī	개 kāī 구 koō 리 rī 와 wā	두 toō 텁 thōp 이 ī 셤 syōn	좀 tsŏm 두 toō	니 nī 슬 soŏr	벼 pyŏ 록 rŏk 조 tsŏ	오 ŏ 공 kŏng	구 koō 인 īn
다 dā 니 ni	가 kā 예 루 ēyr'	와 wā 구 koō 도 dŏ 우 oō	시 sī 미 mī	시 sī 라 rā 미 mī	노 nŏ 미 mī	무 moō 가 kā 데 dē	미 mī 미 mī ᅀ zōo

83

A mite	A tadpole	A large toad	A toad	A nit	A stinking insect	A spider	A maggot
蛆	蝌蚪	蟾蜍	蝦蟆	蟣	臭虫	蛛	蠼螋
소 sŏ	과 kwā 도 tŏ 우 oō	셤 sēyn 쇼 zyŏ	가 kā 마 mā	기 kī	시 sī 우 oō 쥬 tsyōo 우 oō	쥬 tsyoō	셰 sēy 기 kī 과 구 kwāk
귀 koōī 더 tŏ 기 kī 저 tsyō	과 kwā 두 toō	셤 syōm 여 yō	하 hā 마 mā	혀 hyŏ 긔 kwi	취 tshyoōī 충 tshyōong	거 kō 믜 mwī 쥬 tsyoō	쵸 tshyōk 화 hwā
우 oō ᅀ시 zī	가 kā 예 루 ēyr' 고 kŏ	히 hī 기 kī 가 kā 이 루 īr'	가 kā 와 ᅀ wāz'	시 sī 라 rā 미 mī 노 nŏ 고 kŏ	나 nā 구 koō 메 mēy	구 koō 모 mŏ	샤 구 syāk' 도 tŏ 리 rī 무 mōo 시 sī

A deflected fir	Trumpet flower Bignonia	Cedar Pine	A tree	樹木 Trees and woods	Injury done by insects	Small insects	A grub worm
栢側	桐梧	松	樹		損虫	蚑	蠐
	오 gŏ 도 tŏ 우 oō	쇼 syŏ 우 oō	슈 syoō		쥬 tsyoō 우 oō 손 sŏn	기 kī	세 sēy 이 ī
측 tshook 빅 pāik	오 ŏ 동 tŏng	솔 sŏr 숑 syŏng	나 nā 모 mŏ 슈 syoō		츙 tshyoong 손 sŏn	긜 kwīr 기 kī	굼 koōm 벙 pōng 이 ī 재 tsēy
소구 sŏk' 바구 pāk'	기 kī 리 rī 노 nŏ 기 kī	마즈 māts'	기 kī		무 moō 시 sī 구 koō 이 ī	하 hā 우 oō 무 moō 시 sī	스구 sook' 모 mŏ 무 moō 시 sī

Mulberry	Cypress	Bamboo	Cassia cinnamon		Insects at the bottom of vessels	To crawl as an insect
桑	栢	竹	桂		蟠	蠢
소 sŏ 우 oō	하구 hāk'	지구 tsik'	계 kēy 이 ī		한 hān	슌 zyoon
뽕 spŏng 나 nā 모 mŏ 상 sāng	잣 tsāt 빅 pāik	대 tāi 죡 tsyŏok	계 kēy 슈 syoō 계 kēy		서 sŏ 릐 rīr 반 pān	구 koō 무 moō 거 kŏ 릐 rīr 쥰 tsyoōn
구 koō 와 wā 노 nŏ 기 kī	마즈 māts' 노 nŏ 기 kī	다 tā 게 kēy	가즈 kāts' 라 rā 노 nŏ 기 kī		와 wā 다 dā 가 kā 마루 mār'	우 oō 오 gŏ 우 oō 오 gŏ 스루 soōr'

倭語類解 — Japa[nese] wo[rds] asso[ciated] an[d] expla[ined] Vol.

Sycamore tree Planetree	Sandal wood	Guaiacum Lignum vitæ	Paper tree	A large kind of oak	A large kind of fir	Spindle tree	Chinese Fir
楓	檀	槐	楮	楙	檜	冲杜	杉
후 hoō 우 oō	단 tān	괘 kwā 이 ī	죠 tsyŏ	사 sā 우 oō	과 kwā 이 ī		산 sān
신 siu 나 nā 모 mŏ 풍 p'koōng	박 pāk 달 tār 단 tān	회 hŏī 화 hwā 괴 kŏī	닥 tāk 저 tsyō	ㄱ kă 래 rāī 츄 tshyoō	젼 tsōt 나 nā 모 mŏ 회 hŏī	두 toō 충 tshyōong	익 ik 개 kāī 삼 sām
가 ka 이 ī 데 dē	뱌구 pyāk' 단 dān	연 ēyn 유 zyoō 노 nŏ 기 kī	가 kā 시 zī 노 nŏ 기 kī	하 hā 사 sā 기 gī	히 hī 노 nŏ 기 kī	도 tŏ 쥬 tsyōo 우 oō	스 soŏ 기 gī

倭語類解下

...ese words ...ted ...d ...ined II.

樹木

...rees and woods

84

Brazil wood	Birch	A wood used in making furniture	Varnish tree	An oak	The elm	A willow	Palm
蘇木	樺	椵	漆	橡	楡	柳	棕櫚
	과 kwā	가 kā	시쯔 sits'	쇼 syŏ 우 oō	유 yoō	리 lī 우 oō	소 sŏ 우 oŏ 료 lyŏ
소 sŏ 목 mŏk	봇 pŏt 화 hwā	과 kŏī 나 nā 모 mŏ 가 kā	옷 ŏt 나 nā 모 mŏ 칠 tshīr	도 tŏ 토 thŏ 리 rī 샹 syāng	느 noŏ 롬 roŏm 나 nā 모 mŏ 유 yoŏ	버 pŏ 들 toŏr 류 lyōo	종 tsōng 려 lyŏ
소 sŏ 모구 bŏk'	가 kā 바 pā 노 nŏ 기 kī	히 hī 노 nŏ 기 kī	우루 oōr' 시 sī 노 nŏ 기 kī 하 hā 제 zēy	도 tŏ 지 tsī 노 nŏ 기 kī	니 nī 레 rēy 노 nŏ 기 kī	야 yā 나 nā 기 gī	슈 syōo 로 lŏ

A plank	A bud	Branch	The trunk of a tree	A parasite	A bramble A thorny bush	Hovenia	A wood used for axle trees
板	蘖	枝	株	寄生	荊	枳	檢
한 hān	계쯔 keytsŭ	시 sī	쥬 tshyoō	기 kī 쇼 syŏ 우 oō	계 kēy 이 i	기 ki	켠 kēyn
널 nār 판 phān	초 tshŏ 리 ri 얼 ŏr	가 kā 지 tsi 지 tsi	낟 nāt 쥬 tsyoō	긔 kwi 싱 sāing	가 kā 싀 swi 형 hyōng	링 rāing 즈 tsă 기 ki	검 kōm 평 phāing 검 kōm
이 i 다 tā	예 ēy 다 dā 사 sā 기 ki	예 ey 다 dā	구 koō 이 i 졔 zēy	야 yā 도 dŏ 리 ri 기 ki	이 i 도 dŏ 라 rā	가 kā 라 rā 다 tā 지 tsi	무 moō 구 koō 노 nŏ 기 ki

倭語類解 Japanese words ... explained Vol.

Timber Materials	A leaf Foliage	A twig	Root	Red sycamore	The fruit of the pine	A tree used for making bows	Dolychips Polystachies
材	葉	梢	根	丹楓	松子	杻	藤
사 sā 이 ī	요 yō 우 oō	소 sŏ 우 oō	곤 kŏn	단 tān 후 hoō 우 oō	쇼 syŏ 우 oō 시 sī	쥬 tsyoō 우 oō	도 tŏ 우 oō
지 tsāi 목 mŏk 지 tsāi	닙 nip 엽 yŏp	나 nā 모 mŏ 슴 skoŏm 쵸 tshyŏ	불 puŏr 희 hwi 근 kŏn	단 tān 풍 phōong	송 syŏng 즈 tsă	싸 ssā 리 ri 뉴 nyoō	등 toŏng 등 toŏng
사 zā 이 ī 목 mŏk' / 주 tsoŏk' 리 kĭ	하 hā	고 kŏ 스 zŏo 예 ēy / 고 kŏ 예 ēy 다 dā	네 nē	모 mŏ 민 mīn 지 tsi	마 māts' 즈 즈 tsoŏ 우 gŏo 리 ri	하 hā 이 gī	후 hoō 시 zī

倭語類解 下

These words sorted and explained II.

花草 Flowers and Grass

Sun flower	Plum Blossom	Moutan	A flower	Flowers and Grass	Firewood	A forest A grove	Rotten wood
葵花	梅花	牡丹	花	花草	薪	林	朽
기 kī 과 kwā	마 mā 이 ī 과 kwā		과 kwā		신 sīn	린 līn	우 oō
규 kyōō 화 hwā	매 māī 화 hwā	목 mŏk 단 tān	곳 kŏt 화 hwā		섭 sōm 신 sīn	수 soō 풀 phoŏr 림 līm	서 sō 글 kŏŏr 후 hoō
아 ā 오 ŏ 이 ī 노 nŏ 하 hā 나 na	무 moō 메 mēy 노 nŏ 하 hā 나 nā	뽀 구 bŏk' 단 tān	하 hā 나 nā		다 tā 기 kī 기 gī	하 hā 야 yā 시 sī	구 kōo 지 tsī 기 kī 구 koō 지 루 tsĭr'

Pear Blossom	Chrysanthemum Marigold	Paeony	A waterlily A lotus		Cordwood A faggot	A thicket. Underwood	A float A raft
海棠花	菊花	芍藥	蓮花		柴木	藪	楂
가 kā 이 ī 도 dŏ 우 oō 과 kwā	기 구 kīk' 과 kwā		렌 lēyn 과 kwā		사 sā 이 ī 뽀 구 bŏk'	소 sŏ 우 oō	사 sā
히 hāī 당 tang 화 hwā	국 kōōk 화 hwā	쟉 tsyāk 약 yāk	련 lyŏn 화 hwā		싀 swī 목 mŏk	덤 tōm 불 pŏr 수 soō	등 toōng 걸 kŏr 사 sā
가 kā 이 ī 도 dŏ 우 oō 노 nŏ 하 hā 나 nā	기 구 kīk' 노 nŏ 하 hā 나 nā	샤 구 syāk' 야 구 yāk'	하 hā 스 soŏ 노 nŏ 하 hā 나 nā		시 sī 바 pā	구 koō 사 sā 무 mōo 라 ra 야 yā 부 boō	기 kī 리 rī 가 kā 부 poō

86 八五

Sumach	Hibiscus Syrian Mallow	Knotgrass flower	Cockscomb flower	Honey suckle	Hesitation flower	A lily	Rose
萸茱	花槿	花蓼	花冠鷄	花銭金	躅躑	丹山	薇薔
슈 syōo 유 yōo	긴 kīn 과 kwā	료 lyŏ 우 oō 과 kwā	계 kēy 이 ī 관 kwān 과 kwā		데 tē 기 kī 죠구 tsyŭk'	산 sān 단 tān	
슈 syōo 유 yōo	근 koŏn 화 hwā	료 lyŏ 화 hwā	계 kēy 관 kwān 화 hwā	금 koŏm 전 tsyōn 화 hwā	쳑 ts'hyŏk 쵹 ts'hyŏk	산 sān 단 tān	장 tsāng 미 mī
구 gōo 미 mī	무 mōo 구 kōo 게 gēy 노 nŏ 하 hā 나 nā	다 tā 계 kēy 노 nŏ 하 hā 나 nā	계 kēy 이 ī 도 tŏ 우 oō 노 nŏ 하 hā 나 nā	긴 kīn 센 sēyn 과 kwā	사 sāts' 츠 기 kī	유 yoō 리 rī	쇼 syŏ 우 oō 비 bī

Willow blossoms	Marsh Mallows	Carnation Pink	Bastard saffron	Garden balsam	Illumine hill red	American honey suckle	Tulip-tree
絮柳	蓉芙	花竹石	花紅	花仙鳳	紅山暎	花鵑杜	花夷辛
리 ī 우 oō 쇼 zyŏ			고 kŏ 우 oō 과 kwā		예 ēy 이 ī 산 sān 고 kŏ 우 oō	도 tŏ 견 kēyn 과 kwā	신 sīn 이 ī 과 kwā
류 lyoō 셔 syŏ	부 pōo 용 yŏng	셕 syŏk 쥭 ts'hyook 화 hwā	홍 hŏng 화 hwā	봉 pŏng 션 syŏn 화 hwā	영 yŏng 산 sān 홍 hŏng	두 toō 견 kyŏn 화 hwā	신 sīn 이 ī 화 hwā
야 yā 나 nā 기 gī 노 nŏ 하 hā 나 nā	후 hoō 요 yŏ 우 oō	셰 sēy 기 kī 지구 tsik' 과 hwā	베 pēy 니 nī	호 hŏ 우 oō 센 sēyn 과 kwā	기 kī 리 rī 시 sī 마 mā	즈즈 tsoōtsi 시 zī 노 nŏ 하 hā 나 nā	고 kŏ 부 boō 시 sī 노 nŏ 하 hā 나 nā

長語頁卆下

Chinese words cited and explained II.

花草 Flowers and grass

Perfume Scent	Fragrance odour	A perfect flower	A blossom A bud	To bloom To open as a flower	Artificial flowers	Centifolia flower clove blossom	Winter fir
芳	香	朶花	英	開	花假	花葉千	栢冬
호 hō 우 oō	고 kŏ 우 oō	과 kwā 다 tā	예 ēy 이 ī	가 kā 이 ī	가 kā 과 kwā	션 seyn 요 yŏ 우 oō 과 kwā	도 tŏ 우 oō 하구 hāk'
곧 kŏt 다 tā 올 ŏr 방 pāng	곧 kŏt 다 tā 올 ŏr 향 hyāng	화 hwā 타 thā	곧 kŏt 부 poō 리 rī 영 yōng	필 p'hoŏr 기 kăī	가 kā 화 hwā	쳔 tshyōn 엽 yōp 화 hwā	동 tŏng 빅 păik
고 kŏ 우 oō 빠 bā 시 sī	고 kŏ 우 oō 빠 bā 시 sī	하 hā 나 nā 노 nŏ 후 hoŏ 사 sā	즈 tsoŏ 뽀 bŏ 미 mī	히 hī 라구 rāk'	즈구 tsoŏk' 리 rī 하 hā 나 nā	야 yā 예 ēy 노 nŏ 하 hā 나 nā	즈 tsŏo 빠 bā 기 kī

To droop To fade	Elegance Beauty	The calyx	The corolla The petals	To fall To drop	A flower pot	Single leafed flower	Cape Jasmine
凋	艷	蔕花	蘂	落	盆花	花葉單	子梔
됴 tyŏ 우 oō	연 ēyn	과 kwā 태 t'hāī 이 ī	스 soŏ 이 ī	라구 lāk'	과 kwā 혼 hŏn	단 tān 요 yŏ 우 oō 과 kwā	시 sī 시 sī
이 ī 올 oōr 죠 tsyŏ	고 kŏ 올 oōr 염 yōm	화 hwā 톄 t'hēy	여 yŏ 히 hăī 예 ēy	질 tsīr 락 rāk	화 hwā 분 poōn	단 tān 엽 yōp 화 hwā	치 tshī 즈 tsā
시 sī 보 pŏ 무 moŏ	우즈 oōts' 구 koō 시 sī	하 hā 나 nā 노 nŏ 시구 zīk'	시 sī 베 pēy	오 ŏ 즈루 tsoŏr'	하 hā 나 nā 바 pā 지 tsī	히 hī 도 tŏ 예 ēy 노 nŏ 하 hā 나 nā	구 koŏ 지 tsī 나 nā 시 sī

86 上

Lin seed Flax	A sedge A rush	Ficus erecta	Ironwort	Plantain	Ginseng	Epidendrum	To become dry. To wither
苧	莞	薜荔	蘇鐵	芭蕉	人蔘	蘭	枯
죠 tsyŏ	관 kwān	헤 hēy 기 ki 레 lēy 이 ı			신 zīn 신 sīn	란 lān	고 kŏ
모 mŏ 시 sī 져 tsyō	요 yŏ 항 hāng 관 kwān	벽 pyŏk 려 ryō	소 sŏ 텰 tshyŏr	파 phā 쵸 ts'hyŏ	인 in 숨 săm	란 lān 초 tshŏ 란 lān	드 tă 롤 roŏr 고 kŏ
오 ŏ	이 i 우 goō 사 sī	즈 tsoŏ 다 tā	소 sŏ 데 tēts' 쯔	매 bā 쇼 syŏ 우 oō	닌 nin 신 zīn	아 ā 라 rā 라 rā 기 gī	가 kā 레 rēyr' 루

Hemp	A grass used for matting	Castoroil seed Palma Christi	Crow's fan	Catstailgrass Typha Lemongrass	A lucky plant	China grass	Grass
麻	茵	蓖麻子	射干	菖蒲	芝	萱	草
마 mā	인 in	히 hi 마 mā 시 sī	샤 syā 간 kān	쇼 syŏ 우 oō 호 hŏ	시 sī	켠 kēyn	소 sŏ 우 oō
삼 sām 마 mā	부 poō 들 toŏr 인 in	피 phi 마 mā ᄌ tsă	샤 syā 간 kān	창 tshyāng 포 p'hŏ	지 tsi 초 tshŏ 지 tsi	훤 hwōn 초 tshŏ 훤 hwōn	플 p'hoŏr 초 tshŏ
아 ā 사 sā	고 kŏ 모 mŏ	도 tŏ 우 oō 고 gŏ 마 mā	가 kā 라 rās' 스 오 ŏ 오 ŏ 기 gi	쇼 syŏ 우 oō 부 poō	무 moō 라 rā 사 sā 기 kī	완 wān 스 soŏ 레 rēy 구 koō 사 sā	구 koō 사 sā

倭語類解 下

雜語

Mixed Words

Luxuriant vegetation	Stalk	Moss	A kind of grass	Artemisia Mugwort	Small garlic	Dolichos hirsutus
蕃	莖	苔	莎	艾	亂	葛
한 hān	계 kēy 이 ī	다 tā 이 ī	샤 syā	가 gā 이 ī	란 lān	갈쓰 kāts'
번 pōn 셩 syōng 홀 hăr 번 pōn	줄 tsoor 기 kī 경 kyōng	잇 it 기 kī 틔 thăī	뙤 ttöī 사 sā	쑥 ssook 애 āī	달 tār 랸 rān	츩 tshŏok 갈 kār
시 sī 계루 gēyr	구 koo 기 kī	고 kŏ 계 kēy	스 soŏ 애 gēy	모 mŏ 오구 goō 사 sā	요 yŏ 시 sī	가 kā ᅀᅩ zŏo 라 rā

A bush	Tendril A vine	Duck-weed	Common grass	Coarse grass	A sort of rush	A flag
叢	蔓	萍	芻	茅	蓬	葦
소 zŏ 우 oō	만 mān	혜 hēy 이 ī	스 soŏ 우 oō	보 bŏ 우 oō	호 hŏ 우 oō	이 ī
피 p'hŏ 기 ki 총 tshŏng	너 nō 출 ts'hoōr 만 mān	평 phyōng 초 ts'hŏ 평 phyōng	싁 skŏr 추 ts'hōo	뙤 stooi 모 mŏ	다 tā 복 pŏk 쑥 ssook 봉 pŏng	갈 kăr 위 oōī
구 koō 사 sā 무 mōo 라 rā / 가 kā 부 poō	즈 tsoŏ 루 roō 오구 goō 사 sā	우 oŏ 기구 kīk' 사 sā	마구 māk' 사 sa / 하 hā 미 mī	지 tsī 가 kā 야 yā	요 yŏ 모 mŏ 에 gī	아 ā 시 sī

87

Integral whole	Many To abound	Coarse	Thick	Long	Broad	Light	Great Big
全	多	麤	厚	長	濶	輕	大
션 seyn	다 tā	소 sŏ	고 kŏ 우 oō	죠 tsyŏ 우 oō	콰 쯔 kwāts'	계 kēy 이 ī	다 tā 이 ī
온 oōn 젼 tsyōn 젼 tsyōn	만 mān 흘 hoōr 다 tā	굴 koōr 굴 koōr 추 tshoō	뚣 toōt 러 rō 올 ŏr 후 hoō	긴 kin 쟝 tsyāng	너 nŏ 롤 roōr 활 hwār	가 kā 븨 pāi 야 yā 올 ŏr 경 kyōng	큰 knoōr 대 tāi
맏 māt 다 tā 구 koō	오 ŏ 우 oō 구 koō	호 hoō 도 tŏ 이 ī	아 ā 즈 tsoŏ 이 ī	나 nā 가 gā 이 ī	히 hī 로 rŏ 이 ī	가 ka 루 roō 이 ī	오 ŏ 오 ŏ 이 ī

倭語類解

Japan… wo… asso… a… expl… Vol…

Half Part	Few	Fine	Thin	Short	Narrow	Heavy	Small Little
半	少	細	薄	短	狹	重	小
한 hān	쇼 syŏ 우 oō	사 sā 이 ī	하 구 hāk	단 tān	고 kŏ 우 oō	쥬 tsyoō 우 oō	쇼 syŏ 우 oō
반 pān 반 pān	자 tsyā 굴 koōr 쇼 syŏ	ᄀ kă 놀 năr 셰 sēy	엷 yōr 올 oōr 박 pāk	져 tsyō 롤 roōr 단 tān	좁 tsŏp 올 oōr 협 hyōp	무 mōo 거 kō 올 ŏr 즁 tsyōong	져 tsyō 굴 koōr 쇼 syŏ
나 nā 가 kā 라 rā / 나 nā 가 kā 바 bā	스 soō 구 koō 시 si	호 hŏ 소 sŏ 이 ī	우 스 oōs' 이 ī	미 mī 시 zī 가 kkā 이 ī	셰 sēy 바 pā 이 ī	오 ŏ 모 mŏ 구 koō	지 tsī 사 sā 이 ī

Replet.	To augment More Increase	Overflowing Superabundant	Full To fill	Wide apart ... apart	Distant Far	Sharp-pointed Conical	A flake A slice Lamina
充	加	餘	盈	疎	遠	尖	片
슈 zyōo 우 oō	가 kā	요 yǒ	예 ēy 이 ī	소 sǒ	연 ēyn	션 sēyn	헌 hēyn
치 tshăi 울 oǒr 즁 tshyōong	더 tō 홀 hăr 가 kā	남 nām 올 oǒr 여 yō	촐 tshăr 영 yōng	성 sōng 길 kwīr 소 sǒ	멀 mōr 원 wōn	샢 spǒ 족 tsyǒk 첨 tshyōm	조 tsǒ 각 kāk 편 phyōn
즈 tsoǒ 메 meyr' 루	구 koō 와 wā 유 yoōr' 루	아 ā 마 mā 리 rī	미 mī 즈 tsoǒr 루	우 oǒ 도 tǒ 기 kī	도 tǒ 우 oō 이 ī	도 tǒ 가 gā 리 rī	가 kā 다 tā 즈 tsǒo 라 rā

Deficient Injured	Less Diminished To abate	To shrive Contracted	Empty void	Close Thick-set	Near Adjacent Contiguous	Circular Round	A lump a clod
損	减	縮	虛	密	近	圓	塊
손 sǒn	갇 kān	슉 syock'	교 kyǒ	미 mits' 쯔	근 kin	연 ēyn	과 kwa 이 ī
손 sǒn 홀 hăr 손 sǒn	덜 tǒr 감 kām	줄 tsoōr 축 tshyoōk	빌 pwīr 허 hó	빅 păik 빅 păik 홀 hăr 길 mīr	갇 kāt 가 kā 올 ǒr 근 koǒn	둥 toōng 굴 koōr 원 wōn	덩 tang 이 ī 괴 kǒi
야 yā 부 poōr' 루	헤 hēyr' 루	지 tsī 시 zī 마 mār 루	아 āk' 구	기 kī 삐 bī 시 sī	지 tsi 가 kā 이 i	마 mā 루 roō 이 ī 마 mā 와 wār' 루	즈 tsoǒ 지 tsī 구 koō 레 rēy

Circumstance Affair Business	Public	Noble Dear	High Honourable	Hanging suspended	Urgent Pressing	To tie round To bind	To add to
事	公	貴	尊	懸	頻	裹	添
시 sī	고 kō 우 oō	기 kī	손 sŏn	현 kēyn	힌 hīn	과 kwā	텬 tēn
일 īr ᄉᆞ să	구 koō 의 wī 공 kŏng	귀 koōī ᄒᆞᆯ hăr 귀 koōī	노 nŏ 플 phooŏr 존 tsoŏn	돌 tăr 현 hyōn	ᄌᆞ tsă 즐 tsoŏr 빈 pīn	ᄊᆞᆯ ssăr 과 kwā	보 pŏ 탤 tēr 렴 ryūm
고 kŏ 도 tŏ	오 ŏ 우 oō 야 yā 케 kēy	메 mēy 즈 tsoō 라 rā 시 sī	다 tā 기 kī 이 ī 닷 tăt 도 tŏ 시 sī	가 kā 케 kēy	사 sā 이 ī 사 sā 이 ī 시 sī 기 kī 리 rī 니 nī	즈 tsoō 즘 tsoom' 무	소 sŏ 예 eyr' 루

Things	Private Particular	Base Abject Cheap	Low Mean	Separated Remote	Careless Remiss	To envelope To close	To make up To repair
物	私	賤	卑	隔	稀	封	補
모 쯔 möts'	시 sī	션 sēyn	히 hī	가 구 kāk'	기 kī	호 hŏ 우 oō	호 hŏ
것 kŏt 믈 moŏr	ᄉᆞ să ᄉᆞ să ᄉᆞ să	쳔 tshyōn ᄒᆞᆯ hăr 쳔 tshyōn	ᄂᆞ nă 즐 tsăr 비 pī	막 măk 힐 hīr 격 kyŏk	드 toŏ 믈 moŏr 희 hwī	봉 pŏng ᄒᆞᆯ hăr 봉 poōng	기 kī 울 ŏr 보 pŏ
모 mŏ 노 nŏ	와 wā 다 구 tāk' 시 sī	이 ī 야 yā 시 sī 이 ī	히 hī 기 kī 시 sī	헤 hēy 다 tā 즈 로 tsoŏr' 헤 hēy 다 tā 다 루 tār'	마 mā 레 rēy	후 hoō 우 oō 스 루 zoŏr'	오 ŏ 에 eī 노 nŏ 우 oō

倭語類解 Japanese words assor... and expl... Vol.

These words … marked II.

韓語

To present / To offer up	To attend on / To wait upon	Double / a pair	An old man	He	Who	Sir	I myself
奉	侍	雙	翁	彼	誰	君	我
호 hŏ 우 oō	시 sĭ	소 sŏ 우 oō	오 ŏ 우 oō	히 hĭ	스 sŏo 이 ĭ	군 koōn	가 gā
받 pāt 들 tŏor 봉 pŏng	뫼 mŏi 실 sĭr 시 sĭ	쌍 ssāng 쌍 ssāng	하 hā 라 ra 비 pi	저 tsyŏ 피 p'hĭ	누 noō 구 koō 슈 syoō	그 koŏ 듸 tăĭ 군 koōn	나 nā 아 ā
다 tā 데 tē 마 mā 즈루 tsoŏr	오 ŏ 도 tŏ 모 mŏ	즈 tsŏo 이 ĭ	오 ŏ 기 kĭ 나 nā	카 kā 래 rēy / 가 kā 노 nō	다 tā 래 rēy	소 sŏ 나 nā 다 tā	와 wā 래 rēy

Inserted Words

To serve	To follow	Single	An old woman	Another	A certain person / Anyone	That person	You / Thou
事	率	隻	嫗	他	某	伊	汝
시 sĭ	소쯔 sŏts'	세 sēy 기 kĭ	오 ŏ 우 oo	다 tā	보 bŏ 우 oō	이 ĭ	죠 zyŏ
섬 syŏm 길 kĭr 사 sā	거 kŏ 느 nă 릴 rĭr 솔 sŏr	짝 tsăk 쳑 tshyŏk	할 hăr 미 mĭ 오 ŏ	다 tā 룰 roōr 타 thā	아 ā 모 mŏ 모 mŏ	저 tsŏ 이 ĭ	너 nŏ 여 yŏ
즈 tsoŏ 가 kā 에 ēy 루 roō	즈 tsoŏ 래 rēy 노 nŏ 우 oō	소 sŏ 우 oō	바 bā 바 bā	요 yŏ 노 nŏ	나 nā 니 nĭ 가 gā 시 sĭ	소 sŏ 노 nŏ 미 mĭ	소 sŏ 지 tsĭ / 나 na 시 zĭ / 소 sŏ 노 nŏ 호 hŏ 우 oō

89

Peaceful Quiet	Flourishing Plentiful	Auspicious Lucky	Misery	Glory	Grace Bounty	Amicable Harmonious	To console To comfort
安	盛	吉	禍	榮	恩	睦	慰
안 ān	세 sēy 이 ı	기 굣 kits'	과 kwā	에 gi 이 ī	온 oŏn	맥 구 bŏk'	이 ī
평 phyong 안 ān 안 ān	셩 syōng 홀 hăr 셩 syōng	길 kir 홀 hăr 길 kir	지 tsāi 화 hwā 화 hwā	영 yōng 화 hwā 영 yōng	은 oŏn 헤 hēy 은 oŏn	화 hwā 목 mŏk 목 mŏk	위 oōi 로 rŏ 위 oōi
야 yā 스 soŏ 이 ī	시 sī 가 kā 에 ēy 루 roō	요 yŏ 시 sī	와 wā 사 zā 와 wā 이 ī	에 ēy 이 ī 과 kwā	메 mēy 구 gōo 무 moō	와 wā 맥 구 bŏk'	나 nā 구 gōo 사 sā 미 mī

Hazardous Dangerous	Decrepid Decaying	Inauspicious Unlucky	Happiness	Disgrace	Favour	To nourish To bring up	To guard To defend
危	衰	凶	福	辱	寵	養	護
기 kī	스 sōo 이 ī	교 kyŏ 우 oō	후 구 hŏk'	쇼 구 zyŏk'	쇼 syŏ 우 oō	요 yŏ 우 oō	고 gŏ
위 oōī 틔 thāi 위 oōi	쇠 sōi 홀 hăr 쇠 sōi	흉 hyōong 홀 hăr 흉 hyōong	복 pŏk 복 pŏk	욕 yŏk 홀 hăr 욕 yŏk	툐 kŏ 일 ir 춍 tshyŏng	칠 tshir 양 yāng	구 koō 호 hŏ 호 hŏ
아 ā 바 boō 나 nā 이 ī, 아 ā 야 yā 우 oo 기 kī	오 ŏ 로 rŏ 로 rŏ 에 ēy	아 ā 시 sī	사 sā 이 ī 와 wā 이 ī	지 tsī 쇼 구 zyŏk' 하 hā 시 zī	죠 tsyŏ 우 oō 아 ā 이 ī	야 yā 시 sī 노 nŏ 우 oō	도 tŏ 리 rī 모 又 mŏts'

倭語類解 大

Japanese Words Explained II.

雜語 Mixed Words

Fallacious Deceitful	True	Excelling Abundant	Diverse Different	Crooked	Aright Right It is	To possess To have	To obtain To get To acquire
誤	真	優	異	曲	是	有	得
괴 gŏ	신 sīn	이 ī 우 oō	이 ī	교 구 kyŏk'	시 si	이 ī 우 oō	도 구 tŏk'
그 koŏ 른 roōt 홀 hăr 오 ŏ	춤 tshăm 진 tsīn	나 nā 올 oŏr 우 oō	다 tā 롤 roŏr 이 ī.	구 koō 볼 poŏr 픽 kyŏk	올 ŏr 홀 hoŏr 시 sī	이 ī 실 sir 유 yoō	어 ō 돌 toŏr 득 toŏk
오 ŏ 로 rŏ 이 ī	마 mā 고 kŏ 도 tŏ 니 nī	유 yoō 다 tā 가 kā 나 루 nār'	고 kŏ 도 tŏ 나 nā 루 roō	마 mā 가 gā 루 roō	나 nā 가 kā 나 nā 가 kā	아 ā 루 roō	여 ĕy 데 de

Disorderly Corrupt	False	Inadequate Deficient	The same Similar Alike	Straight Downright	Amiss Wrong It is not	To be without Not to have	To lose To miss
妄	僞	劣	同	直	非	無	失
모 mō 우 oō	긔 gī	레 쯔 lyts'	도 tŏ 우 oō	쇼 구 tsyŏk'	히 hī	므 boō	시 쯔 sits'
90 망 māng 녕 tōng 될 tŏir 망 māng	거 kŏ 즛 tsoŏt 위 oōī	용 yŏng 렬 ryŏr 렬 ryōr	흔 hān 가 kā 지 tsī 동 tŏng	고 kŏ 돌 toŏr 직 tsīk	그 koŏ 롤 roŏr 리 rī	엽 ōp 술 săr 무 moō	일 īr 홀 hoŏr 실 sir
보 bŏ 우 oō 갸 구 kyăk	이 ī 즈 tsoŏ 와 wā 리 rī	오 ŏ 도 tŏ 루 roō	오 ŏ 나 nā 시 구 zīk'	스 soŏ 구 goō 니 nī	아 ā 야 yā 마 mā 리 rī	나 nā 이 ī	우 oō 시 sī 나 nā 이 ī

Tardy	Difficult Hard	Long (in time)	Slow Late	Commencement	Beginning Origin	New Fresh	Ancient Of old
緩	難	久	遲	初	始	新	古
관 kwān	난 nān	규 kyoō 우 oō	지 tsi	쇼 zyǒ	시 sī	신 sān	고 kǒ
늑 nǎk 올 oǒr 완 wān	어 ǒ 려 ryǒ 올 ǒr 난 nān	오 ǒ 랠 rér 구 koō	더 tō 듸 twir 지 tsi	처 tshō 음 oǒm 초 tshǒ	비 pī 로 rǒ 솔 sǎr 시 sī	새 sāi 신 sīn	데 te 고 kǒ
유 yǒo 루 roō 이 ī / 유 yōo 루 rōo 야 yā 가 kā	무 mōo 즈 tsoǒ 까 kkā 시 sī	히 hī 사 sā 시 sī 이 ī	오 ǒ 소 sǒ 시 sī	하 hā 시 zī 메 mē	하 hā 시 zī 예 ēy 데 te / 하 hā 시 zī 말 mā 루 roō	아 ā 다 tā 라 rā 시 sī	이 ī 니 nī 시 sī 예 ēy
Swift Hasty	Easy	Short (in time) A little while	Speedy Quick	Termination Extremity	End Conclusion	Old	Modern New
急	易	暫	速	末	終	舊	今
규 kyōo 우 oō	이 ī	산 sān	소 구 sǒk	마 쪼 mǎtǎ	시 sī 우 oō	규 kyōo 우 oō	금 kin
급 koǒp 홀 hǎr 급 koǒp	쉬 soǒī 올 ǒr 이 ī	잠 tsām 샌 sēn 잠 tsām	섈 spǎ 룰 rǎr 속 sǒk	끋 skoǒt 말 mǎr	무 mǎ 춤 tshǎm 종 tsyoǒng	데 te 구 koǒ	이 ī 직 tsǐk 금 koǒm
이 ī 소 sǒ 구 goǒ	야 yā 스 soǒ 이 ī	시 sī 비 pī 락 구 rāk / 좃 tyǒt 도 tǒ	스 soǒ 미 mī 야 ā 가 kā	스 soǒ 예 ēy / 사 sā 기 kī	오 ǒ 와 wā 루 roō / 시 sī 아 ā 우 ǒo	무 moō 가 kā 시 sī	이 ī 마 mā

下 II. 雜語

Luxurious Fond	To envy Jealous	To terrify To threaten	Crafty Cunning	To insult To affront	To cheat To deceive To feign	To dislike To loathe	To hesitate To distrust
耽	妬	嚇	猥	侮	欺	忌	嫌
단 tān	도 tŏ	갸 kyā	와 wā 이 ī	뫄 boō	기 ki	기 ki	견 kēyn
즐 tsoŏr 긜 kīr 탐 thām	루 roō 긔 kwi 투 thoō	쟈 tsō 칠 hīr 햐 hyā	외 ŏī 람 rām 외 oōī	엄 ōm 슈 syoō 이 ī 너 nō 길 kīr 모 mō	소 sŏ 길 kīr 긔 kwī	시 ski 릴 rir 긔 kwi	함 hām 의 oăī 혐 hyōm
스 soŏ 기 ki	대 tē 마 mā 무 mōo	오 ŏ 도 dŏ 로 rŏk' 구	미 mī 다 dā 리 ri	나 nā 이 ī 가 gā 시 sīr' 루	아 ā 자 zā 무 mōok' 구	이 ī 무 mōo	기 kī 로 rŏ 우 oō

Mixed Words

Eagerly Desirous	To injure To hurt Damage	Respectful Devout	Contemp- tuous	To be proud Pride	To doubt Suspicious	To shun To avoid	To guess
羨	害	虔	傲	驕	疑	諱	猜
	가 ka 이 ī	견 kēyn	오 gŏ 우 oō	교 kyŏ 우 oō	이 gi	기 ki	사 sā 이 ī
부 poō 러 rō 홀 hăr 선 syōn	해 hāī 홀 hăr 해 hāī	전 tsōt 소 sā 올 ŏr 권 kōn	거 kō 오 ŏ 오 ŏ	교 kyŏ 만 mān 교 kyŏ	의 wī 심 sim 의 wī	긔 kwi 일 ir 회 hoōī	싀 swi 긔 kwi 싀 swi
우 oō 라 rā 아 ā 마 mā 시 sī 이 ī	소 sŏ 고 kŏ 노 nŏ 우 oō	하 hā 바 pā 가 kā 리 rī	아 ā 나 nā 도 dŏr' 루	오 ŏ 오 gŏ 루 roō	우 oō 다 tā 가 gā 이 ī	이 ī 이 ī 시 si	소 sŏ 비 pī 우 oō

91 九十一

To annul / To abolish	To abandon / To reject	To meet / To assemble	To resist / Contrary	To imitate / Effect / Result	To play / To sport	Mysterious	Trouble-some
廢	棄	會	逆	效	翫	秘	煩
하 hā 이 ī	기 kī	과 kwā 이 ī	예 ěy 기 kī	고 kŏ 우 oō	관 kwān	히 hī	한 hān
폐 phěy 할 hăr 폐 p'hěy	브 pĭ 릴 rīr 기 kī	모 mŏ 돌 toŏr 회 hwī	거 kō 스 sā 릴 rīr 역 yŏk	본 pōn 바 pā 돌 toŏr 효 hyŏ	구 koō 경 kyŏng 완 wān	숨 soēm 길 kīr 비 pī	번 pōn 거 kī 린 rin
하 hā 이 ī 스 루 soor'	스 soō 테 루 tēr	아 ā 즈 tsoŏ 마 루 mār'	사 sā 고 kŏ 우 oō	시 sī 루 roō 사 sī	겐 kēyn 뽀 boō 즈 tsōo	히 hī 소 sŏ 까 kkā	고 kŏ 도 tŏ 시 sī 께 gēy 시 sī

To place / To set up	To take	To unite / To agree / To combine	To oppose	To fulfil	To prove / To try / To attempt	Strange / Wonderful	Miserable / Wretched
置	取	合	違	驗	試	怪	苦
지 tsī	슈 syōo	고 kŏ 우 oō	이 ī	겐 kēyn	시 sī	과 kwā 이 ī	구 koō
둘 toŏr 치 tshī	취 tshyōoi 할 hăr 취 tshyōoi	함 hām 할 hăr 함 hām	어 ō 길 kwīr 위 oōī	효 hyŏ 험 hōm 험 hōm	사 sī 험 hōm 시 sī	괴 kŏī 이 ī 할 hăr 괴 kŏī	과 kwā 로 rŏ 올 ŏr 고 kŏ
오 구 ŏk'	도 루 tŏr	아 ā 와 wā 세 sēy	지 tsī 가 gā 이 ī	시 sī 가 kā 이 ī 미 루 mīr	고 kŏ 고 kŏ 로 rŏ 미 루 mīr'	아 ā 야 yā 시 sī 무 moō	구 koō 르 rŏō 우 oō

倭語類解

Japanese wo[rds] associa[ted] an[d] expla[ined] Vol. I

倭語類解下

II. 雜語 Mixed words

To loose To untie	To bind	To connect To join	To succeed to To receive	To receive To accept	To beg To intreat	To give To communicate	To transmit
解	維	連	承	受	求	給	遞
가 kā 이 ī	유 yoō 이 ī	련 lēyn	쇼 syŏ 우 oō	시 sī 우 oō	규 kyoō 우 oō	규 kyoō 우 oō	데 tēy 이 ī
풀 p'hoor 희 hăī	얼 ŏr 굴 koōr 유 yoō	련 lyŏn 홀 hăr 련 lyōn	니 nī 을 oŏr 승 soŏng	바 pā 돌 toōr 슈 syōo	구 koō 홀 hăr 구 koō	줄 tsōor 급 koŏp	갈 kăr 례 rēy
도 tŏ 케 kēy	구 koō 우 goō 루 roō	즈 tsoŏ ᅀ zoŏ 케 kēy	우 oŏ 케 kēy 다 tā 마 mā 와 wā 리 rī	우 oō 구루 koōr'	모 mŏ 도 tŏ 메 mēy	다 tā 모 mŏ 우 oō 야루 yār	가 kā 와 wā 루 roō

To tie	To join in succession	To cut off	To fail To want	To give To deliver to	To promise To consent To acquiesce	To snatch To bereave	To hand down
結	續	絶	乏	授	許	奪	傳
게쪼 kēyts'	소구 sŏk'	세쪼 zēyts	보 pŏ 우 oō	시 sī 우 oō	교 kyŏ	다또 tāte'	뎐 tēn
92 맺 mäĭt 결 kyōr	나 nā 을 oŏr 쇽 syŏk	ᄭᅳᆫ skoŏn 홀 hoŏr 졀 tsyōr	곱 kŏĭp 진 tsīn 홀 hăr 핍 kŏĭp	맛 māt 질 tsīr 슈 syoō	허 hō 홀 hăr 허 hō	아 ā 슬 soŏr 랄 răr	젼 tsyōn 홀 hăr 젼 tsyōn
무 moō 스뼈 soŏb'	즈 tsoŏ ᅀ zoŏ 케 kēy 즈 tsoŏ ᅀ구 zoŏk'	기 kī 레루 rēyr'	즈 tsoŏ 기루 kīr'	아 ā ᅀ zoŏ 케루 kēyr'	유 yoō 루 roō 스 soŏ 교 kyŏ 다구 dāk'	우 oō 바 pā 이 ī 도루 tŏr'	즈 tsoŏ 다 tā 에 ōy

To disperse To scatter	To change	To ruin	To incline Aslant	More & more	To heap up	Stiff Firm	Hard Callous
散	變	獘	傾	彌	疊	堅	硬
산 sān	혠 hēyn	혜 hey 이 ī	계 kēy 이 ī	비 bī	됴 tyŏ 우 oō	견 kēyn	고 kŏ 우 oō
흣 hoŏt 르 roŏr 산 sān	변 pyōn 홀 hăr 변 pyōn	흐 hă 야 yă 질 tsīr 폐 p'hēy	기 ki 우 oō 러 rō 질 tsīr 경 kyōng	ㄱ kă 독 tăk 미 mī	포 phŏ 필 p'hīr 텹 t'hyŏp	구 koō 들 toŏr 견 kyōn	셜 sēr 경 kyōng
지 tsī 라 rā 셰 sēy 지루 tsir'	혠 hēyn 쪼 tsoŏ	소 sŏ 우 oō 시 sī	가 kā 다 tā 무구 mōok'	이 ī 요 yŏ 이 ī 요 yŏ	가 kā 사 sā 나 nā 리 rī	가 kā 다구 tăk'	가 kā 다 tā 이 ī

To remove	To alter	To do an injury To cut short	Tottering Upset	Again & again To repeat	To pile up To accumulate	Broken to pieces	Soft
移	改	虧	頹	重	累	殘	軟
이 ī	가 kā 이 ī	기 kī	다 tā 이 ī	죠 tsyŏ 우 oō	루 loō 이 ī	산 zān	션 sēyn
옴 ŏm 길 kīr 이 ī	고 kŏ 칠 ts'hīr 기 kăī	이 ī 즈 tsoŏ 러 rō 질 tsīr 휴 hyoŏ	문 moōn 허 hō 질 tsīr 리 roōī	겸 kyōm 즁 tsyōong	여 yō 러 rō 루 roō	잔 tsān 홀 hăr 잔 tsān	연 yōn 홀 hăr 연 yōn
우 oō 즈루 tsoŏr'	아 ā 라 rā 다 tā 메 mēy	가구 kāk' 루 roō	구 koō 스 soō 레 rēy	가 kā 사 sā 누루 noōr'	아 ā 마 mā 다 tā	노 nŏ 고 kŏ 리 rī	아 ā 와 wā 라구 rāg'

倭語類解

Japanese words assorted and explained Vol.

倭語類解下 These words explained II.

雜語 Mixed Words

Level Plain	To exhaust	To move abruptly	To unsew To open a seam	Abundant Forest-like	To float in the wind	To hang down	Transverse Athwart
均	盡	衝	綻	森	飄	垂	橫
긴 kīn	신 zīn	쇼 syŏ 우 ōō	단 thān	신 sīn	효 hyŏ 우 ōō	스 soŏ 이 ī	고 kŏ 우 ōō
고 kŏ 루 roŏr 균 kyoōn	다 tā 홀 hăr 진 tsīn	질 tsīr 을 oŏr 츙 tshyōng	터 thō 질 tsīr 탄 thān	븩 pwik 븩 pwik 홀 hăr 숨 săm	블 pōor 릴 rīr 표 phyŏ	드 toŏ 리 rī 울 oŏr 슈 syoō	빗 pīt 길 kīr 횡 hwīng
무 moō 라 rā 모 mŏ 노 nŏ 우 ōō / 히 hī 도 tŏ 시 sī 이 ī	즈 tsoŏ 구 스 koōs'	사 스 sās'	호 hŏ 고 kŏ 로 rŏ 비 bī	모 mŏ 리 rī	히 hī 사 sā 오 gŏ	다 tā 루 루 roōr'	요 yŏ 고 kŏ 이 ī

Even Equal Parallel	Altogether Entirely	To perforate To thread	To tear To rip open	To arrange	To soar	To screen To shelter	Slanting Oblique
平	悉	貫	裂	列	翻	翳	斜
헤 hē 이 ī	시 쯔 sits	관 kwān	레 쯔 lēyts'	레 쯔 lēyts'	혼 hoōn	에 ēy 이 ī	샤 syā
평 phyŭng 홀 hăr 평 phyōng	다 tā 실 sīr	쏄 skōoer 관 kwān	쏄 stewir 렬 ryōr	벌 pōr 렬 ryōr	번 pōn 드 toŏ 길 kīr 번 pōn	ᄀ kă 리 rī 울 oōr 예 ēy	빗 pīt 길 kīr 샤 syā
다 tā 이 ī 라 rā 가 kā	고 kŏ 도 tŏ 오 gŏ 도 tŏ 구 koō	즈 tsoŏ 라 rā 누 noō 기 kī	사 구 sāk'	나 nā 리 rī 베 bēy / 즈 tsoō 라 rā 날 nār'	히 hī 루 roō 아 gā 기 루 gīr	사 sā 에 ēy 이 루 gīr'	나 nā 나 nā 메 mēy

93 ㄴ三

To avoid	Occult Hidden	Calamity Adversity	Influence	To endeavour To apply the mind	To follow after To pursue	To fix To appoint	To choose To select
避	幽	灾	權	務	趣	定	擇
히 hī	이 ī 우 oō	사 sā 이 ī	견 kēyn	뮈 boō	진 tsīn	데 tē 이 ī	다 구 tāk'
피 p'hī 흘 hăr 피 p'hī	그 koŏ 옥 oŏk 유 yoō	지 tsăī 화 hwā 지 tsăī	권 kwōn 셰 sēy 권 kwōn	힘 hm 쓸 ssoŏr 무 moō	ᄯ stă 롤 răr 진 tsīn	뎡 tyōng 홀 hăr 뎡 tyōng	골 kăr 힐 hīr 릭 răīk
노 nŏ 가 루 găr'	가 kā 스 soŏ 카 kkā	와 wā 자 zā 와 wā 이 ī	곤 kŏn 셰 sēy 이 ī	즈 tsoŏ 도 무 tŏm	옫 ŏt 데 tē	사 sā 마 mā 메 mēy 데 tē	예 ēy 라 rā 뫼 boō

To shun To flee	Retired Concealed	Straits Distress	Power Authority	To instruct	To reach to To attain	To order A messenger	To send.
逃	隱	厄	勢	示	及	使	差
도 to 우 oā	인 īn			ᄉ zī	규 kyōo 우 oō	시 sī	사 sā 이 ī
모 mŏ 망 māng 도 tŏ	숨 soōm 올 oŏr 은 oŏn	지 tsăī 익 ăīk 익 ăīk	형 hyōng 셰 sēy 셰 sēy	뵐 păīr 시 sī	미 mī 출 tshoŏr 급 koŏp	브 poŏ 릴 rīr 시 sī	치 tshăī 송 sŏng 치 tshăī
니 nī 게 gēy	가 kā 구 koō 스 soŏ	야 구 yāk'	셰 sēy 이 ī	시 sī 메 스 mēys	오 ŏ 요 부 yŏb'	즈 tsoŏ 가 kā 이 ī	사 sā 시 sī 소 sŏ 에 루 ēyr'

To pluck To pick	To fathom	To fish	Leasure	To measure	To hear	A class A series	Service
採	探	漁	閑	量	聞	科	役
사 sā 이 ī	단 tān	어 gyŏ	간 kān	료 lyŏ 우 ōō	뿐 boōn	과 kwā	에 ēy 기 kī
캘 khăir 채 tshăi	더 tŏ 듬 toŏm 올 oŏr 람 răm	고 kŏ 기 kī 잡 tsăp 을 oŏr 어 ŏ	한 hān 가 kā 한 hān	헤 hēy 아 ā 릴 rīr 량 lyāng	드 toŏ 를 roŏr 문 moŏn	과 kwā 기 kī 과 kwā	역 yŏk 亽 să 역 yŏk
도루 tŏr'	사 sā 구 gōōr'	스 soŏ 나 nā 도 dŏ 리 rī	간 kān 교 kyŏ 우 ōō	하 hā 가 kā 로 rŏ 우 ōō	기구 kik'	규 kyoē 우 ōō 다 dā 이 ī	구 kŏō 야구 yăk'

To break off	To dig To scoop out To excavate	To chase To hunt	Ease	To be aware of	To know	Merit	Patrimony Estate
折	掘	獵	暇	覺	知	功	業
세쯔 sēyts'	구쯔 koōts'	료 lyŏ 우 ōō	가 kā	가구 kāk'	지 tsī		요 gyŏ 우 ōō
머 mŏ 골 kŏr 절 tsyŏr	팔 phăir 굴 koōr	산 săn 힝 hăing 렵 lyŏp	결 kyŏr 을 oŏr 가 kā	서 skăi 다 tă 를 roŏr 각 kāk	알 ăr 지 tsī	공 kŏng 공 kŏng	업 ŏp 업 ŏp
오 ŏ 리 rī	호 hŏ 리 rī	가 kā 리 rī	이 ī 도 tŏ 마 mā	사 sā 메 mēy	시루 sīr	고 kŏ 우 ōō	와 wā 사 zā

To wait	To unite To comprise	To conduct To lead	To carry on the back	To revolve To turn round	To cover To hide	To hang To suspend	To catch
等	兼	引	負	繞	掩	掛	捕
도 tō 우 oo	켠 keyn	인 in	후 hoō 우 oō	뇨 nyŏ 우 oō	연 eyn	가 kā 이 ī	호 hŏ
무 moō 리 ri 등 toǎng	겸 kyōm ᄒᆞᆯ hăr 겸 kyōm	힐 hīr 인 īn	질 tsīr 무 moō	두 toō 를 roŏr 요 yŏ	ᄀᆞ kă 리 ri 올 oōr 엄 ōm	걸 kŏr 괘 kwāi	잡 tsām 올 oōr 포 p'hŏ
라 rā	가 kā 네 nē 데 tē	히 hī 기 kī	오 ŏ 우 oō	메 mēy 구 루 goōr'	오 ŏ 오 ŏ 우 oō	가 kā 게 루 kēyr'	도 tŏ 라 rā 유 yoō 루 roō

To tarry	To mix To compound	To take hold of	To carry on the head	To brush away	To drag To sport	To fling To throw To cast	To squeeze under the arm
待	糝	執	戴	撲	搆	[illegible]	挾
다 tā 이 ī	산 sām	시 sī 우 oō	다 tā 이 ī	보 구 pŏk'	고 kŏ 우 oō	데 tē 기 ī	교 kyŏ 우 oō
기 kī 드 tă 릴 rir ᄃᆡ tăi	참 tshām 예 ēy 참 tshām	잡 tsăp 을 oŏr 집 tsīp	닐 nīr ᄃᆡ tăi	부 poō 되 twī 칠 tshīr 박 pāk	얼 ŏr 글 koŏr 구 koō	더 tŏ 질 tsir 척 tshyŏk	ᄭᅵᆯ skīr 협 hyōp
마 mā 지 tsī	마 mā 이 ī 리 rī	도 루 tŏr'	이 ī 다 tā 따 dā 기 kī	하 hā 라 rā 후 hoō	다 tā 와 wā 무 루 moŏr'	나 nā 게 gēy 우 oō 즈 tsoŏ	하 hā 사 sā 무 moō

倭語類解

Japan[ese] wo[rds] assor[ted] an[d] explai[ned] Vol.I

To bequeath A bequest	To confer To distribute	A corner An edge	Condition State	Connected series	Fringe	A single one One of a thing	A measure of 10 feet A length
遺	頒	稜	際	秩	組	枚	丈
이 ī	한 hān	료 lyo 우 oō	셰 sēy 이 ī	지 쯔 tsīts'	소 sŏ		쟈 tsyŏ 우 oō
기 kī 칠 tsīr 유 yoō	반 pān 포 phŏ 반 pān	모 mŏ 롱 loōng	즈 tsoō 음 oōm 제 tsēy	太 tshă 례 rēy 질 tsīr	인 īn 신 skīn 조 tsŏ	낟 nāt 매 māī	길 kīr 쟝 tsyāng
노 nŏ 고 kŏ 리 rī	이 ī 이 ī 후 hoō 라ㅅ rās'	가 kā 도 tŏ	하 hā 스 zoō 기 kī 와 wā	이 ī 지 tsī ᄲᅮ boō	구 koō 미 mī	마 mā 이 ī	냐 nā 가 gā 시 sī

A bribe To bribe	To remunerate To reward	Leisure Avoid	A limit Boundary To define	A case A casket	A line	An article	An order A series
賂	賞	隙	限	匣	条	件	級
로 lŏ	쇼 syŏ 우 oō	계 kēy 기 kī	근 kōn	교 kŏ 우 oō	됴 tyŏ 우 oō	견 kēyn	규 kyŏ 우 oō
션 syŏn 물 moōr 뢰 lŏ	샹 syāng 츌 tshoōr 샹 syāng	틈 thoōm 극 koōk	한 hăn 할 hăr 한 hān	겁 kōp 질 tsīr 갑 kāp	오 ŏ 리 rī 됴 tyŭ	벌 pŏr 건 kŏn	드 toō 름 roōm 급 koōp
미 mī 아 a 애 gey [illegible]	호 hŏ 우 oō 비 pī	스 soō 기 kī 히 hī 마 mā	가 kā 기 gī 리 rī	혼 hŏn 배 bā 교 kŏ	스 sōo 시 zī	구 koō 단 tān	렌 lēyn

To cultivate To adorn	Constant Often	To admit To allow	To associate To exchange	To build To erect	To cause To occasion	A sign A token	To bestow
修	常	容	交	建	致	標	賑
시 sī 우 oō	쇼 zyō 우 oō	요 yō 우 oō	교 kō 우 oō	견 kēyn	지 tsī	효 hyō 우 oō	신 sīn
닷 tāt 글 kōar 슈 syoō	덛 tōt 덛 tōt 샹 syāng	용 yōng 납 nāp 홀 hār 용 yōng	사 sā 괼 p'hīr 교 kyō	셰 sēy 올 oōr 건 kōn	니 nī 뢸 rwīr 치 ts'hī	표 p'hyō 홀 hār 표 p'hyō	진 tsīn 홀 hoōr 진 tsīn
미 mī 가 gā 기 kī	즈 tsöo 네 nē	이 ī 루 roōr 루	교 kyō 이 ī 예 ēy	다 tā 즈 tsoō 루 roō	이 ī 다 tā 스 soō	시 sī 루 roō 시 sī	니 nī 기 gī 와 wā 라 rā

To practice	Common	Opposite	Together with	A joint Economy	A despatch A document	To display Manifest	Poor Destitute
行	俗	對	與	節	檄	顯	窮
교 kō 우 oō	소 구 zōk'		요 yō	셰 쯔 sēyts	게 sēy 기 kī	견 kēyn	규 kyoō 우 oō
힝 hāing 홀 hār 힝 hāing	풍 phoōng 쇽 syōk 쇽 syōk	디 tāi 홀 hār 디 tāi	더 tō 블 poōr 여 yō	므 mā 디 tāi 졀 tsyōr	격 kyōk 셔 syō 격 kyōk	남 nām 라 rā 날 nār 현 hyōn	궁 koōng 홀 hār 궁 koōng
오 ōk' 구 느 nō 우 oō	후 hoō 우 oō 소 zōk'	다 tā 이 ī	즈 tsoō 레 rēy 데 tē	후 hoō 시 sī	후 hoō 다 dā	아 ā 라 rā 와 wā 레 rēy	기 kī 와 wā 마 mār

倭語類解 / Japan[ese] wo[rds] assort[ed] an[d] expl[ained] Vol I

倭語類解 下 雜語

Desire	To drive a carriage	Expence / To waste / To consume	To do / To make	To be, To do / To commit / To act	To celebrate / To extol / To speak of	A principal	Ahead / Paramount
欲	御	費	作	爲	稱	正	魁
욕 yŏk'	교 gyŏ	히 hī	삭 sak'	이 ī	쇼 syŏ 우 oō	쇼 syŏ 우 oō	과 kwā 이 ī
호 hă 고 kŏ 져 tsyŏ 홀 hăr 욕 yŏk	어 ō 거 kŏ 어 ŏ	허 hŏ 비 pi 비 pi	지 tsī 을 oŏr 작 tsāk	위 ooī 홀 hăr 위 ooī	일 ir 콧 k'hă 롤 roor 칭 tshing	바 pā 롤 rŏr 정 tsyŏng	괴 kwī 슈 syŏŏ 괴 kwī
다 tā 이 ī	히 hī 기 kī 마 mā 와스 wās'	즈 tsoo 이 ī 예 ēy	즈구 tsook' 루 roo	다 tā 메 mēy	나비구 nā pīk' / 호메루 hŏ mēyr	마 mā 사 sā / 다 tā 다 tā 시 sī	도 tŏ 오 ŏ 도 dŏ 리 ri

96

To recompense	An enemy / A foe	Abundant / Affluent	A stranger / A guest	To help / An assistant / Coadjutor	To thank	A deputy / A second	An origin
報	仇	饒	旅	輔	謝	副	元
호 hŏ 우 oō	규 kyŏŏ 우 oō	쇼 zyŏ 우 oō	료 lyŏ	호 hŏ	샤 syā	후 hoō 우 oō	겐 gēyn
갑 kāp 홀 hŏŏr 보 pŏ	원 wŏn 슈 syŏŏ 구 koō	넉 nŏk 넉 nŏk 홀 hăr 요 yŏ	나 nā 그 koŏ 내 nāī 려 lyŏ	도 tŏ 올 ŏr 보 pŏ	샤 syā 례 rēy 샤 syā	버 pŏ 금 kŏŏm 부 poō	으 ŏŏt 뜸 stŏŏm 원 wŏn
호 hŏ 오 ŏ 즈루 zŏŏr	아 ā 다 da	유 yoō 다 tā 가 kā	다 tā 비 pi	다 tā 스 sŏo 계 kēy	샤 zyā 스루 sŏŏr	소 sŏ 이 ī	모 mŏ 도 tŏ

A requital / To requite	To provide All / To comprise	Urgent	Busy / Hurried	To stop / To leave off	To stand on tiptoe	To arrive at / To set against	Preparation / To prepare
報	具	緊	忙	止	企	抵	預
호 hŏ 우 oō	구 goō	긴 kīn	망 bŏ 우 oō	시 sī	기 kī	데 tē 이 ī	요 yĕ
보 pŏ 흘 hăr 보 pŏ	ㄱ kă 출 tshoŏr 구 koō	긴 kīn 흘 hăr 긴 kīn	밧 pāt 블 poŏr 망 māng	그 koŏ 칠 tshir 지 tsī	져 tsyō 기 kī 드 toŏ 될 twir 기 kī	다 tā 도 tă 를 roŏr 뎌 tyō	긔 kwī 리 rī 예 ēy
쥬 tsyoo 우 oō 신 sīn	소 sŏ 로 rŏ 예 루 ēyr'	간 kān 요 yŏ 우 oō	이 ī 소 sŏ 가 gā 시 sī	야 yā 무 moō	구 koō 와 wā 따 즈 dāts'	이 ī 다 tā 루 roo / 오 ŏ 이 ī 데 tē	가 kā 네 nē 데 tē / 아 ā 즈 tsoŏ 가 kă 리 rī

To present up	From	Extreme / Intense	Very	To receive / To connect	To go to / To arrive at	To pass by / To transgress	Before / Formerly
呈	由	切	甚	接	至	過	先
데 tē 이 ī	이 ī 우 oō	세 쯔 sēyts	신 zīn	쇼 syŏ 우 oō	시 sī	과 kwā	션 sēyn
뎡 tyōng 흘 har 뎡 tyōng	말 mār 미 māi 유 yoû	일 ir 졀 tsyŏr 졀 tsyŏr	심 sīm 흘 hăr 심 sīm	부 poō 칠 tshir 졉 tsyŏp	니 nī 르 rā 지 tsī	지 tsī 날 nŏr 과 kwā	몬 mŏn 져 tsyŏ 션 syŏn
사 sā 사 sā 게 gēy	히 hī 마 mā 도 dŏ 리 rī	잇 it 셋 sēyt 즈 tsoō	하 hā 나 nā 하 hā 다 da	즈 tsoō 게 kēy	이 ī 다 루 tār'	스 soō 구 구 goor'	사 sā 기 kī 니 ni / 마 mā 즈 tsoŏ

Pervading Ample Spread abroad	Violent Forcible	To dry Dry	To slant To swerve	A prospect A landscape	Leisurely Tranquil	To meet	To approach To come
普	强	乾	欹	景	徐	逢	臨
후 hoō	교 kyŏ 우 oō	간 kān	기 kī		쇼 zyŏ	호 hŏ 우 oo	린 lin
두 toō 로 rŏ 보 pŏ	강 kāng 잉 ing 홀 hăr 강 kāng	므 mā 롤 kŏr 간 kān	기 kī 울 oōr. 긔 kwī	볃 pyŏt 경 kyŏng	나 nā 로 rŏ 여 yŏ 셔 syŏ	만 mān 날 năr 봉 pŏng	림 līm 홀 hăr 림 līm
히 hī 로구 rŏk'	시 sī 기 kī 리 ri 니 nī	가 kī 와 wā 고 kkoā	유 yoō 가무 gām'	계 kēy 이 ī	소 sŏ 로 rŏ 소 sŏ 로 rŏ	오 ŏ 우 oō	노 nŏ 소 sŏ 미 mī
To depend on	To avoid To escape	Dangerous	To recline To rely on	A place	To go towards over against	An appointed time	Ready Convenient
賴	免	險	倚	處	向	期	便
다 lā 이 ī	면 mēyn	겐 kēyn	이 ī	쇼 syŏ	교 kyŏ 우 oō	기 kī	벤 pēyn
힘 hīm 닙 nīp 올 oŏr' 뢰 lŏī	면 myōn 홀 hăr 면 myōn	험 hōm 홀 hăr 험 hōm	의 wī 지 tsī 홀 hăr 외 wī	곧 kŏt 처 tshyō	향 hyāng 홀 hăr 향 hyāng	긔 kwī 약 yāk 긔 kwī	인 in 편 p'hyōn 편 p'hyōn
고 kŏ 우 oō 무루 moōr'	마 mā 누 noō 가 kā 레 rēy	게 kēy 와 wā 시 sī	요 yŏ 리 rī 가 kā 가루 kār'	도 tŏ 고 kŏ 로 rŏ	무 moō 고 kŏ 우 oō	기 kī 야구 yāk	다 tā 요 yŏ 리 rī

To repress To press down	To saunter	To draw on one To provoke	Usurping Dissolute	Seasonable Exactly	To compare To resemble To liken	Altogether Complete	In company with
壓	迸	惹	僭	恰	比	齊	共
오 ŏ 우 oō	호 hō 우 oō	샤 zyā	신 sin	됴 .. 우 oō	히 hī	세 sēy 이 ī	교 kyŏ 우 oō
누 noō 를 roŏr 압 āp	비 pō 들 toŏr 병 pyōng	읻 it 글 koor 야 yā	춤 tshăm 람 rām 춤 tshăm	마 mā 치 tshī 홉 hoop	견 kyon 졸 tsŏr 비 pī	フ kā 쪽 tsoŏk 졔 tsēy	흔 hăn 가 kā 지 tsī 공 kŏng
오 ŏ 소 sŏ 우 oō	호 hŏ 도 dŏ 바 pā 시 sīr' 루	히 hī 기 kī 이 ī 다 dās' 스	호 hŏ 시 sī 이 ī 마 mā 마 mā	죠 tsyŏ 우 oō 도 dŏ	구 koō 라 rā 부 poor' 루 다 tā 구 koō 라 rā 부 boō	도 tŏ 도 tŏ 노 nŏ 에 ēy	도 tŏ 모 mŏ 니 nī

To break in pieces	To set To suppose	To confuse Confusion	To mix To mingle	Resembling	Like as	Accompanying	Mutually
碎	設	擾	雜	似	如	偕	相
사 sā 이 ī	세 sēyts' 쯔	요 yŏ 우 oō	소 zŏ 우 oō	시 zī	쇼 zyŏ	가 kā 이 ī	쇼 syŏ 우 oō
바 pă 아 ā 질 tsīr 쇄 swāi	베 pē 플 p'hoŏr 셜 syŏr	요 yŏ 란 rān 요 yŏ	섣 sōt 긜 kīr 잡 tsāp	フ kă 툴 thăr 亽 să	フ kă 툴 t'hăr 여 yō	홈 hăm 쉬 skwī 히 hăī	서 sō 릭 rā 상 syāng
구 koō 다 dāk' 구	호 hŏ 도 dŏ 꼬 kkŏ 시 sī 모 mŏ 우 oō 굴 koŏr' 루	미 mi 다 dā 레 rēy	마 mā 시 zī 에 ēyr 루	니 nī 다 tā 리 rī	고 gō 도 tŏk' 구	이 ī 지 tsi 도 dŏ 니 nī	다 tā 가 gā 이 ī 아 ā 이 ī

倭語類解

Javan[ese] word[s] assort[ed] and explain[ed]

Vol I

Mi...
Wo...

9

九十七

Restingon According to	Scarcely Just enough	Many Accompany A group	A herd A flock	To perforate	To bear	Not yet	No
憑	僅	夥	群	慣	堪	未	不
효 hyŏ 우 oō	긴 kīn	과 kwā	군 goōn	관 kwān	간 kān	미 mi	후쯔 hoots
빙 ping 교 kŏ 빙 ping	벼 kyō 요 yŏ 군 koŏn	만 mān 올 oŏr 화 hwā	물 moŏr 군 koōn	니 nī 굴 koŏr 관 kwān	견 kyŏn 딜 tăir 감 kām	아 ā 닐 nir 미 mī	못 mŏt 홀 hăr 불 poŏr
쇼 syŏ 우 oō 고 gŏ	요 yŏ 우 oō 요 yŏ 우 oō 와 wā 스 zoŏ 기 ki	오 ŏ 비 pi 다 tā 시 sī 기 kī	도 tŏ 모 mŏ 아 ga 라 rā	고 kŏ 우 oŏ 샤 syā	고 kŏ 다 tā 예 ëyr' 루 다 tā 예 ēyr 다 tā 리 ri	아 ā 라 rāz' 스	마 mā 이 i 센 sēyn

98

To exhaust To examine	To use To employ	Sufficient Enough Adequate	Fine Subtile	To pervade Through	To sustain To suffer	To interdict	Do not
究	用	足	精	通	當	没	勿
규 kyōo 우 oō	요 yŏ 우 oō	소구 sŏk'	세 sēy 이 ī	쯔 tsoŏ 우 oō	도 tŏ 우 oō	보쯔 bŏts'	모쯔 mŏts'
궁 koōng 구 koō 홀 hăr 구 koō	쓰 psŏ 용 yŏng	죡 tsyok 홀 hăr 죡 tsyŏk	졍 tsyōng 홀 hăr 졍 tsyōng	사 să 마 mă 출 tshăr 통 thŏng	당 tāng 홀 hăr 당 tāng	몰 mŏr 홀 hăr 몰 mŏr	말 măr 문 moōn
기 kī 와 wā 무 mŏ	쯔 tsoŏ 고 kŏ 우 oō 모 mŏ 지 tsī 유 yoō	다루 tār'	구 koō 와 wā 시구 sīk'	도 tŏ 우루 oōr'	아 ā 다루 tār'	볻 bŏt 스루 soŏr'	나 na 가 kā 레 rēy

To pick To pluck	To sweep	To engrave	To clip To cut with shears	To allow To grant To permit	Near At hand	An order Next in order	To arrange To put in order
摘	摟	彫	剪	准	親	次	排
다구 tâk	시 si 우 oō	됴 tyŏ 우 oō		쥰 zyoon	신 sin	시 sī	하 hā 이 ī
ᄯᆞᆯ stăr 뎍 tyŏk	뒬 twïr 수 soo	아 ā 로 rŏ 사 sā 길 kïr 됴 tyŏ	갈 kar 길 kïr 젼 tsyon	쥰 tsyoon 홀 hăr 쥰 tsyoon	친 ts'hin 이 ī 홀 hăr 친 ts'hin	버 pō 금 koŏm ᄎᆞ ts'hă	버 pō 릴 rïr 비 păr
즈 tsŏo 무 mōo	시 sā 아가스 gās'	호루 hŏr'	기루 kïr'	나 nā 소 zŏ 라 rā 우 oō	시 zi 기 kī 니 nī	즈 tsoŏ 이 gī	나 nā 라 ra 베루 pēyr' 소 sŏ 나 nā 예루 ēyr'

To disclose To display	To search	To cut	To dissect To cleave asunder	To sort To arrange	Clandestine Deceitful	A series	A row
發	尋	刻	剖	檢	竊	第	行
바쯔 pats'	신 zin	고구 kŏk'	호 hŏ 우 oō	겐 kēyn	세쯔 sēyts'	데 tē 이 ī	고 kŏ 우 oō
발 pār 홀 hăr 발 pār	ᄎᆞ ts'hă 즐 tsoŏr 심 sim	사 sā 길 kïr 각 kăk	쯰 skăi 힐 hir 부 poō	검 kōm 찰 ts'här 검 kōm	그 koŏ 윽 oŏk 절 tsyŏr	ᄎᆞ ts'hă 례 rēy 데 tēy	줄 tsoŏr 항 hāng
아 ā 라 rā 와루 wār'	다 tā 즈 tsoŏ 네 nē	기 kī 시무 zīm	와루 wār'	사 sā 시 sī 스 zoŏ	히 hī 소 sŏ 카 kkā 니 nī	신 sin 다 tā 이 ī	군 koōn 다 tā 리 rī

倭語類解

Javar...
wo...
assor...
an...
expla...
Vol.

Mi...
W...

太...

99

Yesterday and to-day	In front	Previously A foretime	Thus In this way	Generally speaking		To arrange together To compose	To belong
今昨	前在	者嚮	斯如	槩大	二字類	編	屬
삭 sāk' 긴 kīn		교 kyŏ 우 oō 샤 syā	죠 zyŏ 시 sī			헌 hēyn	쇽 zŏk'
작 tsāk 금 koōm	재 tsāi 젼 tsyŏn	향 hyang 쟈 tsyā	여 yŏ ᄉᆞ sa	대 tāi 개 kāi	Phrases	엮 yŏk 슬 skoōr 편 phyŏn	부 pōo 릴 rīr 쇽 syŏk
기 ki 노 nŏ 우 oō 교 kyŏ 우 oō 삭 sāk 곤 kŏn	사 sā 이 ī 셴 sēyn	사 sā 기 kī 에 gŏ 로 tŏ 셰 sēy 도 dŏ	각구 kāk 노 nŏ 에 gŏ 도 tŏ 시 sī	다 tā 이 ī 야 gā 이 ī		아 ā 무 moō	쇼구 syŏk' 스 soŏ 조구 tsoŏk

Presently Just now	Nearabouts Almost	Suddenly Rashly	Thus or thus only	In the beginning		To perform To accomplish	A kind A tribe
今卽	間近	者俄	已而	初當		成	類
소구 sók' [illegible]	긴 kīn 간 kān	야 gā 샤 syā	시 zī 이 ī	도 tŏ 우 oō 죠 zyŏ		셰 sēy 이 ī	루 loō 이 ī
즉 tsoŏk 금 koōm	근 koōn 간 kān	아 ā 쟈 tsyā	이 ī 이 ī	당 tāng 초 ts'hŏ		일 īr 올 ŏr 셩 syŏng	동 tŏng 류 lyoō 류 lyoō
다 tā 다 dā 이 ī 마 mā	고 kŏ 노 nŏ 에 gŏ 로 rŏ	니 nī 와 wā 가 kkā	노 nŏ 미 mī	소 sŏ 노 nŏ 도 tŏ ㅣ kī		나 nā 스 soŏ	다 tā 구 goō 이 ī

To glitter	Fame Reputation	Ornamental	Clear Intelligible	To make a light To cut a figure	Dismal Dull the moonset	Easy and light	A short time An instant
煌輝	聲名	彩文	白明	光生	朧朦	緲縹	刻頃
기 kī 고 kǒ 우 oo	메 mēy 이 i 세 sēy 이 ī	뿐 bōōn 사 sā 이 ī		쇼 syǒ 우 oō 고 kǒ 우 oō	모 mǒ 우 oō 로 lǒ 우 oō	효 hyǒ 우 oō 뾰 byǒ 우 oō	케 kēy 이 āi 고구 kǒk'
휘 hōoi 황 hwāng	명 myōng 셩 syōng	문 moōn 채 tshāi	명 myūng 백 pāik	싱 sāing 광 kwāng	몽 mōng 롱 lōng	표 p'hyǒ 묘 myǒ	경 kyūng 각 kāk
가 kā 야 gā 야구 yāk'	사 sā 다 tā	사 sā 이 ī 와 gwā	메 mēy 이 i 하구 hāk'	히 hī 가 kā 리 rī 니 nī 나루 nār'	오 ǒ 뽀 bǒ 로 lǒ	하루 hār' 빠루 bār' / 보 pyǒ 우 oō 묘 myǒ 우 oō	산 zān 시 zī

Gaiety Show	Cast away Ruined	Luminous Resplendent	Blithe Hearty Cheerful	Virtuous appearance	Seeming Appearing as if	Vague and uncertain	A little while By and bye
華繁	藉狼	爛燦	快爽	色德	俙依	茫蒼	臾須
			소 sǒ 우 oō 콰 kwā 이 ī	도구 tōk' 쇼구 syǒk'	이 i 기 kī		슈 syōō 유 yoō
번 pān 화 hwā	랑 lāng 쟈 tsyā	찬 tshān 란 lān	상 sāng 쾌 khwāi	덕 tǒk 색 sāik	의 wi 희 hwī	창 tshāng 망 māng	슈 syōō 유 yoō
한 hān 과 kwā	로 lǒ 우 oō 샤 syā	산 sān 란 lān	기 kī 산 sān 시 zī 나 nā	기 kī 보 pǒ	다 tā 시 sī 가 kā 나 nā 라스 rāz'	소 sǒ 우 oō 뽀 bǒ 우 oō	시 sī 바 pā 라구 rāk'

To go out to walk	Embarrased Irresolute	To linger about	An opportunity	To run away To flee	Diligent Attentive	To be disappointed	Indistinct Unsettled
行出	躇躕	遛逗	會機	走奔	懃慇	悵怊	惚恍
슈쓰 syoots' 고 kŏ 우 oō	쥬 tsyoō 쇼 syŏ			훈 hoōn 소 sŏ 우 oŏ		됴 tyŏ 우 oō 쥬 tsyŏ 우 oō	교 kyŏ 우 oō 고쓰 kŏts'
츌 tshyoon 힝 hing	쥬 tsyoō 져 tsyŏ	두 toō 류 lyoō	긔 kwi 회 hŏi	분 poōn 주 tsoō	은 oōn 근 koōn	죠 tsyŏ 챵 tshāng	홍 hŏng 홀 hŏr
가 kā 도 tŏ 이 ī 데 tē	후 hoō 미 mī 마 mā 요 yŏ 우 oō	도 tŏ 우 oō 리 lī 우 oō	기 kī 과 kwā 이 ī	가 kā 케 kēy 마 mā 와루 wār 도 tŏ 리 rī 와 gŏ 미 mī	인 īn 긴 gīn	이 ī 다 tā 와 wā 시 zi	아 goō 도 tŏ 즈구 tsoōk'

To meet accidentally	Impediment in walking	Dilatory Delaying	Extended Displayed	Confused Sunk	Irregular Incoherent	Magnanimous Generous	Tinkling Sound of gems
逅邂	趄赼	滯遲	大張	沒汨	齬齟	慨慷	瓏玲
가 kā 이 ī 고 kŏ 우 oō	시 sī 쇼 syŏ	지 tsī 데 tē 이 ī	죠 tsyŏ 우 oŏ 다 tā 이 ī	고쓰 kŏts' 보쓰 bŏts'			레 lēy 이 ī 로 lŏ 우 oō
히 hăi 후 hoō	자 tsă 져 tsyŏ	지 tsī 쳬 ts'hēy	쟝 tsyāng 대 tāī	골 kŏr 몰 mŏr	서 sō 어 ō	강 kāng 개 kāī	령 lyōng 롱 lōng
다 tā 마 mā 다 tā 마 mā 오 ŏ 우 oō	무 goō 시 zī 즈구 tsoōk'	도 tŏ 도 dŏ 고 kŏ 오 ŏ 리 rī	고 kŏ 모 mŏ 오 ŏ 오 ŏ 고스 kŏs'	이 ī 소 sŏ 가 ka 시 sī	소 sŏ 고 gŏ	고 kŏ 우 oō 가 kā 이 ī	스 soō 기 kī 도 tŏ 우루 oōr'

Certainly	Confused	Copious Rainy	Totally wholly	Originally	This person	We, us.	Separated Asunder
然自	然恍	然沛	然全	來原	漢這	等我	別離
	교 kyŏ 우 oo 센 zēyn		센 sēyn 센 zēyn		쇼 syō 간 kān	애 gā 도 tŏ 우 oō	
자 tsă 연 yōn	황 hwāng 연 yōn	패 p'hāi 연 yān	전 tsyon 연 yōn	원 wōn 릐 lāi	져 tsyō 한 hān	아 ā 둥 tōong	리 lī 별 pyōr
시 sī 세 zēyn	히 hī 레 rēy 야 yā 가 kā	하 ha 이 ī 센 zēyn	네 nē 가 kā 라 rā	앤 gēyn 라 lā	고 kū 야 yā 조 tsoō	와 wă 래 rēy 라 rā	라 lī 뻬 pēyts 쯔

倭語類

Javar wor assor an explai Vol.

Suddenly Accidentally	Suitable Corresponding	Verily Indeed	Remote Distant	In future Time to come	That person	You, Ye	United Met together
然偶	然依	然果	然逈	來將	漢那	等汝	會和
교 gō 우 oō 센 zēyn	이 ī 센 zēyn	과 kwā 센 zēyn	계 kēy 이 ī 센 zēyn	쇼 syŏ 우 oō 라 lā 이 ī	나 nā 간 kān	쇼 syō 도 tŏ 우 oo	과 kwā 과이 kwāi
우 oō 연 yōn	의 wī 연 yōn	과 kwā 연 yōn	형 hyōng 연 yōn	장 tsyāng 릐 lāi	나 nā 한 hān	여 yŏ 동 tŏng	화 hwā 화 hwā
다 tā 마 mā 사 sā 가 kā	아 ā 다 tā 까 kka 모 mŏ	애 gēy 니 nī 모 mŏ	고 kŏ 도 tŏ 노 nŏ 호 hŏ 가 kā	사 sā 기 kī 사 zā 기 kī	아 ā 야 yā 조 tsoō	난 nān 시 zī 라 rā	나 nā 가 kā 나 nā 오 ŏ 시 sī

倭語類解 下

Japanese words collected and explained. II.

二字類 Phrases

To prevent egress	A map	Your noble country	To diverge / To separate	Exhausted	To esteem / important	Happy	Defective
出攔	圖地	國貴	離支	屈窮	重珍	福有	然缺
란 lān 슈 syōots 쯔	지 tsi 도 tŏ		시 sī 리 lī			이 ī 우 oō 후 구 hook	케 쯔 kēyts 젠 zēyn
란 lān 츌 tshyoor	디 tī 도 tŏ	귀 kwi 국 kook	지 tsī 리 lī	궁 kyoong 굴 koor	진 tsin 듕 tsyoong	유 yoo 복 pŏk	결 kyŏr 연 yŏn
사 sā 가 kā 이 i 오 ŏ 고 kŏ 에 즈 ēyz'	예 ēy 조 tsōo	기 kī 고 구 kŏk'	나 nā 아 gā 힉 hīk' / 구 koo 리 rī 타 kā 에 ēys'	규 kyŏ 우 oō 구 쯔 koots'	진 tsīn 쥬 tsyŏ 우 oŏ	콰 kwā 호 hŏ 우 oō	노 nŏ 고 kŏ 리 rī 오 ŏ 오 ŏ 이 ī

To divulge / To disclose	A journey	A lodging place	To delay / To procrastinate	To slip / To stumble	Rare / special	Very lucky	Publicly
出露	程路	所館	延遷	跎蹉	特奇	幸多	然公
로 lŏ 슈 쯔 syōots	로 lŏ 데 tē 이 i		셴 sēyn 엔 ēyn	사 sā 다 tā			고 kŏ 우 oŏ 셴 syēyn
로 lŏ 츌 tshyoor	로 lŏ 뎡 tsyōng	관 kwān 소 sŏ	쳔 tshyŏn 연 yŏn	차 tshā 타 t'hā	긔 kwi 특 thook	다 tā 힝 hīng	공 kōng 연 yŏn
로 lŏ 켄 kēyn	로 lŏ 시 sī	관 kwān 쇼 syŏ	오 ŏ 소 sŏ 나 nā 오 ŏ 리 rī	고 kŏ 고 kŏ 로 rŏ 도 tŏ 케 kēyz	기 kī 도 구 tŏk'	다 tā 고 kŏ 우 oo	무 mōo 나 nā 시 구 sīk'

101

101 엽

To impede To embarrass	Dull indistinct	To appear [illegible]	Vulgar and common	To scheme To contrive	A good appearance	Lucky influences	[illegible] arrange
掣肘	朦昧	抑勒	野俗	圖謀	好樣	祥瑞	進排
셰 sēyts 즈 쥬 tsyoō 우 oō	아 ā 이 ī 바 bā 이 ī	요 yŏk' 구 로 lŏk' 구	야 yā 소 zŏk' 구	도 tŏ boŏ bŏ 우 oō	고 kŏ 우 oō 요 yŏ 우 oō	죠 syŏ 우 oō 스 zoŏ 이 ī	신 sīn 하 nā 이 ī
쳘 tshyŏn 쥬 tsyoō	이 ĭi [illegible] tăi	억 ŏk 득 thoŏk	야 yā 속 syŏk	도 tŏ 모 mŏ	호 hŏ 양 yāng	샹 syāng 셔 syō	진 tsīn 빈 pāi
무 moō 즈 tsoŏ 카 kkā 시 sī 우 oō	무 moō 시 sits' 즈	오 ŏ 시 sī 데 tē	사 sā 무 moō 시 sī 이 ī	하 hā 가 kā 라 ra 우 oō	요 yŏ 이 ī 요 yŏ 우 oō	메 mēy 데 tē 다 tā 이 ī	사 sā 시 sī 아 ā 게 gēy

Japa[…] w[…] asso[…] a[…] expla[…] Vo[…]

Ruined	To wipe off a reproach	To chew To bite and gnaw	Violent Overbearing	To plot To conspire	To correspond to each other	Omens and causes	To go out and collect
狼狽	雪耻	齮齕	強愆	謀害	符作	兆朕	出斂
로 lŏ 우 oō 배 bā 이 ī	셰 sēyts 즈 디 tsī	기 kī 끄 kŏts' 즈	고 kŏ 우 oō 신 zin	뽀 bŏ 우 oō 가 kā 이 ī	후 hoō 사 sāk' 구	됴 tyŏ 우 oō 진 tsīn	슈 syoōts' 쯔 렌 lēyn
랑 lāng 패 phāi	셜 syŏr 치 tshi	긔 kwī 홀 hoŏr	강 kāng 인 in	모 mŏ 해 hāi	부 poō 작 tsāk	죠 tsyŏ 진 tsīn	츌 tshyŏr 렴 lyŏm
도 tŏ 모 mŏ 야 yā 뿌 boō 레 rēy	하 hā 시 zī 오 ŏ 소 soŏ 스 soŏg' 구	이 ī 꺼 kēy 즈 tsoŏ 고 kŏ 로 rŏ 시 sīts' 즈	즈 tsoŏ 요 yŏk' 구 시 si 노 nŏ 뿌 boō	오 ŏ 도 tŏ 시 si 이 ī 루	마 mā 시 zī 나 nā 이 ī	기 kī 사 zā 시 sī	다 dā 시 sī 아 ā 와 wā 셰 sēy

倭語類解 下 | ...ese ...rds ...ted ...d ...ined II.

二字類 | ...hrases

To esteem To admire	Piebald	To ooze or leak out	Easy Uncon-strained	Slightly Disturbed	One and the same	Profitable	Thin & insipid Trifling
尚崇	駁斑	漏滲	容從	迷熹	般一	益有	薄淡
소 sŏ 우 oō 쇼 syŏ 우 oō	한 hān 하구 hāk'	신 sin 로 lŏ 우 oō	쇼 syŏ 우 oō 요 yŏ 우 oō	기 kī 뻬 bēy 이 ī	이쯔 its' 한 hān	이 ī 우 oō 예 ēy 기 kī	단 tān 하구 hāk'
숭 syoōng 상 syāng	반 pān 박 pāk	삼 sām 루 loō	죵 tsyŏng 용 yŏng	희 hwī 미 mī	일 ir 반 pān	유 yoō 익 ik	담 tām 박 pāk
닫 tāt 모 mŏ 뻬 bī	시 sī 와 wā 계루 kēyr'	메 mēy 모 mŏ 리 rī	유 yoō 루 roō 리 rī 또 ttŏ	기 kī 미 mī	또 dŏ 우 oō 셴 sēyn	예 ēy 기 kī 아 gā 아루 ār'	유 yoō 이 ī 하 hā 로 rŏ 우 oō

Merit	Uneven Long & short	The flowing of water	Cool	Scarce	Of one sort	Unprofitable	Carelessly
業功	差參	湲潺	凉凄	罕稀	樣一	益無	且苟
	신 sin 시 sī	산 sān 관 kwān		기 kī 관 kān	이쯔 its 요 yŏ 우 oō	부 boō 예 ēy 기 kī	고 kŏ 우 oō 샤 syā
공 kŏng 업 ŏp	참 ts'hăm 치 ts'hī	잔 tsān 원 wōn	처 ts'hyō 량 lyāng	희 hwī 한 hān	일 ir 양 yāng	무 moō 익 ik	구 koō 차 tshyā
고 kŏ 우 oō 괴 gyŏ 우 oō	가 kā 다 tā 다 tā 가 gā 이 ī	야 yā 리 rī 미즈 miz'	세 sēy 이 ī 료 lyŏ 우 oō	마 mā 레 rēy 모 mŏ 노 nŏ	이 ī 치 tsī 요 yoō 우 oō	에 ēy 기 kī 나 na 이 ī	후 hoō 지 zī 유 yoō 우 oō

102

께

倭語類解

Japanese words associated and explained Vol.I

Certain sure	To break an agreement	To anticipate	Urgent Pressing	In haste In a hurry	To circulate To go round	A bad beginning	Separated Divided
當的	約背	望顒	迫切	卒倉	旋周	端獘	揀分
테 tēy 기 kī 도 tŏ 우 oō	하 hā 이 ī 야구 yāk'	교 kyo 우 oō 뽀 bŏ 우 oō	세쯔 sēyts' 하구 hāk'	소 sŏ 우 oō 슈쯔 syoots	시 sī 우 oō 셴 sēyn		분 poon 간 kān
뎍 tyŏk 당 tāng	배 pāi 약 yāk	옹 ŏng 망 māng	절 tsyŏr 박 pāk	창 tshāng 졸 tsŏr	쥬 tsyoō 션 syŏn	폐 phēy 단 tān	분 poon 간 kān
몯 mŏt 도 tŏ 모 mŏ	야구 yāk' 오 ŏ 소 sŏ 무구 mook	아 ā 지 tsī 와 wā 즈 zŏo 로 rŏ 우 oō	사 sā 시 sī 즈 tsŏo 가 kā 에 ēy	데 tē 바 pā 시 sī 고 kŏ 이 ī	슈 syoō 우 oō 셴 sēyn / 가 kā 이 ī 호 hŏ 우 oō	혜 hēy 이 ī 단 tān	와 wā 계루 kēyr'

Arranged Settled	To look narrowly	To believe & obey	Not content	Miserable Wretched	Close-wove	Mixed in confusion	The dregs of wine
當停	視蔑	聽信	安未	苦辛	縫彌	雜亂	粕糟
테 tē 이 ī 모 mŏ 우 oō	베쯔 pēyts' 시 sī	신 sīn 데 tē 이 ī	미 mī 안 ān		비 bī 호 hŏ 우 oō	란 lān 소 zŏ 우 oō	소 sŏ 우 oō 하구 hāk'
뎡 tyŏng 당 tāng	멸 myŏr 시 sī	신 sīn 텽 thyŏng	미 mī 안 ān	신 sīn 고 kŏ	미 mī 봉 pŏng	란 lān 잡 tsāp	조 tsŏ 박 pāk
기 kī 와 wā 메 mēy	나 nā 이 ī 가 gā 시 sī 로 rŏ	신 sīn 요 yŏ 우 oō	야 yā 스 sōo 가 kā 라스 rāz	신 sīn 구 koō	고 kŏ 도 tŏ 유 yoō 에 ēy 나 nā 시 sī	란 lān 사즈 zāts'	아 ā 라 rā 가 kā 다 tā

II.

二字類

Phrases

103

Just like Like as	Uncommon	Alas! Pitiable	News Tidings	Bent Crooked	Common Usual	To inculcate To charge	To pledge
他效	常非	惜可	息消	折曲	常尋	嚀叮	當支
교 kŏ 우 ōō 다 tā	히 hī 쇼 zyŏ 우 ōō	가 kā 세 sēy 기 kī	쇼 syŏ 우 ōō 소구 sŏk	교구 kyŏk' 세쪼 sēyts	신 sīn 쇼 zyŏ 우 ōō		시 sī 도 tŏ 우 ōō
효 hyŏ 타 thā	비 pī 샹 syāng	가 kā 셕 syŏk	쇼 syŏ 식 sīk	곡 kŏk 졀 tsym	심 sīm 샹 syāng	뎡 tyŏng 녕 nyŏng	지 tsī 당 tāng
마 mā 네 nē	조 tsoŏ 네 nē 나 nā 라스 rāz	오 ŏ 시 sī 이 ī	오 ŏ 도 tŏ 스 zŏ 레 rēy	와 wā 게 kēy 아 ā 이 ī	요 yŏ 노 nŏ 조 tsoŏ 네 nē / 우 ōō 갸 kā 도 tŏ	데 tē 이 ī 네 nē 이 ī	고 kŏ 다 tā 에루 ēyr

To put on an under garment	Important serious	Miserable	Connected	Exceedingly Excessive	A cause A reason	To charge	To stand alone
着襯	輕非	憐可	絡連	過太	故緣	囑咐	當獨
신 sīn 사구 zāk'	히 hī 게 kēy 이 ī	가 kā 렌 lēyn	렌 lēyn 라구 lāk'	다 tā 이 ī 과 kwā	엔 ēyn 고 kŏ	후 hoō 쇼구 syŏk'	도구 tŏk' 도 tŏ 우 ōō
츤 ts'hoōn 착 tshyak	비 pī 경 kyŏng	가 kā 련 lyŏn	련 lyŏn 락 lāk	태 t'hāi 과 kwā	연 yŏn 고 kŏ	부 poō 쵹 tshyŏk	독 tŏk 당 tāng
조 tsoŏ 요 gŏ 우 ōō 시 sī 다 tā	가 kā 루 roŏ 가 kā 라스 rāz	미 mī 렌 lēyn	우 ōō 지 tsī 조 tsoŏ 소 zŏ 기 kī	호 hŏ 우 ōō 라스 rāz'	사 sā 시 sī 아 ā 이 ī	소 sŏ 우 ōō / 구 koō 요 yŏ 리 rī	미 mī 니 nī 우 ōō 게루 kēyr'

애

Importunate	Do not	To reject roguery	According to Circumstances	Certainly	A bother A myriad sounds	A fisherman's light	To sport
促催	可不	奸攘	道權	定一	籟萬	火漁	弄戲
	훗 hoots' 쯔 가 kā	데 tē 기 ki 간 kān	켄 kēyn 도 tŏ 우 ŏo	이 its' 쯔 데 tē 이 ī	빤 bān 라 lā 이 ī	교 kyŏ 과 kwā	기 ki 로 lŏ 우 ŏo
최 tshŏi 쵹 tshŏk	불 poor 가 kā	쳑 tshyŏk 간 kān	권 kwŏn 도 tŏ	일 ir 뎡 tyŏng	만 mān 뢰 lŏi	어 ŏ 화 hwā	희 hŏi 롱 lŏng
사 sā 이 i 소 구 sŏk	요 yŏ 로 rŏ 시 si 가 kā 라 스 rāz'	켄 kēyn 미 mī	미 mī 하 hā 가 kā 로 rŏ 우 ŏo	이 ī 지 tsī 됴 tyŏ 우 ŏo	요 yo 로 lŏ 스 zŏo 노 nŏ 고 kŏ 예 ēy	이 ī 사 zā 리 rī 히 hī	다 tā 와 wā 무 mŏo 레 rēy
Wrong	Severe Rigid Austere	About to stretch wider	How	Because	Silent Still	Clear	Very laughable
錯差	肅嚴	張方	何如	緣因	寞寂	明分	倒絶
시 i 사 sāk' 구			쇼 syŏ 가 kā	인 in 엔 ēyn		분 poon 메 mēy 이 i	메 mēyts 쯔 도 tŏ 우 ŏo
차 tshā 착 tshak	엄 ŏm 슉 syŏck	방 pāng 쟝 tsyāng	여 yŏ 하 hā	인 in 연 yŏn	젹 tsyŏk 막 māk	분 pŏon 명 myŏng	절 tsyŏr 도 tŏ
마 mā 지 tsi 가 gā 이 i 노 nŏ 하 hā 시 si	겐 gēyn 슈 구 syŏck	호 hŏ 우 ŏo	이 ī 가 kā 하 gā	요 yŏ 리 rī	세 sēy 기 kī 빠 구 bāk'	훈 hŏon 묘 myŏ 우 ŏo	오 ŏ 가 kā 시 sī 이 ī

倭語類解 Japanese words associated and explained Vol.

倭語類解 下

Chinese words ... II

二字類

To gratify desire To indulge self	To imitate exactly	All one's life long	A coop A cage A spittal	Cross Practices	Undecided	To calculate beforehand	Hung up by the heels
意任	效卽	生平	穽檻	行橫	豫猶	度預	懸倒
신 zin 이 i	소구 sŏk' 고 kŏ 우 oō	혜 hēy 이 i 쇼 syŏ 우 oō	간 kan 세 sēy 이 i	고 kŏ 우 oō 고 kŏ 우 oō	이 i 우 oō 요 yŏ	요 yŏ 다구 tāk	도 tŏ 우 oō 겐 kēyn
임 im 와 wā	죽 tsoōk 효 hyŏ	평 phyong 싱 sāing	함 hām 졍 tsyong	횡 hōing 힝 hāing	유 yoō 예 ēy	예 ēy 탁 thāk	도 tō 현 hyon
고 kŏ 고 kŏ 로 rŏ 마 mā 마 mā	속 sŏk 고 kŏ 우 oō	혜 hēy 이 ī 세 zēy 이 i	간 kān 데 tē 이 ī	오 ŏ 우 oō 고 kŏ 우 oō	후 hoō 게 kēy 조 tsoō 쇼 zyŏ 우 oō	가 kā 네 pi 데 tē 하 hā 가루 kār	혠 hēyn 아 gā 예루 eyr

Phrases

10A

To convert To change thoroughly	To adjust exactly	To be thought unskilful To be slighted	Unlucky Unhappy	In what place	To stop and cease	Nearabouts	To scour with sand
通變	節撙	拙見	幸不	處何	止停	介幾	汰沙
	손 sŏn 세쯔 sēyts'	겐 kēyn 세쯔 sēyts'	후쯔 hoōts' 고 kŏ 우 oō	가 kā 쇼 syŏ	데 tē 이 ī 시 si	기 kī 가 kā 이 ī	샤 syā 다 tā 이 ī
변 pyon 통 thōng	존 tsŏn 졀 tsyŏr	견 kyōn 졸 tsŏr	불 pōor 힝 hāing	하 hā 쳐 tshyō	뎡 tyōng 지 tsī	긔 kwi 개 kāi	사 sā 태 thāi
헨 hēyn 즈 tsoō 우 oō	호 hŏ 도 tŏ 요 yŏ 우 oō	사 sā 애 gēy 시 sī 무 moō	후 hoō 시 si 아 ā 와 wā 세 sēy	이 i 스구 zoōk'	됴 tyŏ 우 oō 지 tsī	남 nām 보 pŏ 까 kkā	사 sā 다 tā 야 yā 마 mā 시 si 오 ŏ

以

倭語類

Japanese words associated and explained Vol. I

疊字類 Double Characters

Again & again Repeated	Troubled A little clear	Inexhaustible Infinite	Since Very soon	To fall down & leak out	Given up to rule	Wonderful Doctrine
重重	耿耿	窮無	已業	漏落	主專	理妙
죠 tsyŏ 우 oō 죠 tsyŏ 우 oō		무 boō 규 kyoū 우 oō	교 gyŏ 우 oō 이 ī	라구 lāk' 로 lŏ 우 oō	션 sēyn 슈 syoō	
즁 tsyoōng 즁 tsyoōng	경 kyŏng 경 kyŏng	무 mōo 궁 koōng	업 ŏp 이 ī	락 lāk 루 loō	젼 tsyŏn 쥬 tsyoō	묘 myŏ 리 lī
가 kā 사 sā 비 pī 야 yā 사 sā 비 pī	교 kŏ 우 oō 교 kŏ 우 oō	기 ki 와 wā 마 mā 리 ri 이 ī 나 nā 이 ī	스 soŏ 데 dē 니 nī 모 mŏ 하 hā 야 yā	오 ŏ 도 스 tŏs'	몯 mŏt 바 bā 라 rā 즈 tsoŏ 가 kā 살 sa 돌 tŏr'	묘 myŏ 우 oō 리 lī

Layer on layer	Dejection Melancholy	Conclusion of a business	To get one's living	How much	To alter one's choice	Raw and Unacquainted
層層	蕭蕭	役畢	營經	何幾	撰改	疎生
			계 kēy 이 ī 에 ēy 이 ī	기 kī 가 kā		쇼 syŏ 우 oō 소 sŏ
층 tshoōng 층 tshoōng	쇼 syŏ 쇼 syŏ	필 p'hĭr 역 yŏk	경 kyŏng 영 yŏng	긔 kwi 하 hā	기 kī 찬 tshān	싱 sing 소 sŏ
소 zŏ 우 oō 소 zŏ 우 oō	쇼 syŏ 우 oō 쇼 syŏ 우 oō	이 쯔 hits' 예 ēy 기 ki	이 ī 도 tŏ 나 nā 미 mi	이 ī 구 koō 라 rā	가 kā 이 ī 센 sēyn	후 hoō 교 kŏ 우 oō

倭語類解下

(…hese …ords …ted …d …ined II.)

疊字類

Borrowed Imitative	Elegant Well adjusted, neat	Vexed Harrassed	Dark and gloomy	White and clean	Recondite Minute	Hastily Rapidly	Piled one on another
藉藉	彬彬	欝欝	冥冥	皓皓	隱隱	倐倐	壘壘
						구 koots' 쯔 구 koots' 쯔	됴 tyŏ 우 oo 됴 tyŏ 우 oo
자 tsyā 자 tsyā	빈 pin 빈 pin	울 oor 울 oor	명 myong 명 myong	호 hŏ 호 hŏ	은 ŏn 은 ŏn	훌 hoor 훌 hoor	텹 thyŏp 텹 thyŏp
샤 syā 샤 syā	힌 hin 멘 bin	우 oots' 쯔 우 oots' 쯔	메 mey 이 i 메 mey 이 i	고 kŏ 우 oo 고 kŏ 우 oo	인 in 인 in	슈 syo k' 구 슈 syook' 구	아 ā 맏 māt 다 tā 아 ā 맏 māt 다 tā

(…oub. …mac)

Silent still	Spread out Extended	Small Fine	Obscure Dim	Brilliant Luminous	Floating in the wind	Hurried	Reiterated
寂寂	揚揚	細細	昏昏	皎皎	飄飄	忩忩	縷縷
105 적 tsyŏk 적 tsyŏk	양 yāng 양 yāng	셰 sey 셰 sey	혼 hŏn 혼 hŏn	교 kyŏ 교 kyŏ	표 phyŏ 표 phyŏ	총 tshŏng 총 tshŏng	루 loo 루 loo
셰 sey 기 kī 셰 sey 기 kī	요 yŏ 우 oo 요 yŏ 우 oo	사 sā 이 ī 사 sa 이 ī	곤 kŏn 곤 kŏn	교 kyŏ 우 oo 교 kyŏ 우 oo	효 hyŏ 우 oo 효 hyŏ 우 oo	소 sŏ 우 oo 소 sŏ 우 oo	루 loo 루 loo

Complete Abundant	Delicate Feeble	Hurried Precipitate	Unsettled Incessant	Falling to ruins	Vast Vague Uncertain	Abundant over whelming	Distant Remote
藹藹	嫋嫋	遑遑	憧憧	落落	茫茫	蒼蒼	悠悠
	됴 dyŏ 우 oō 됴 dyŏ 우 oō	교 kŏ 우 oō 교 kŏ 우 oō					
애 āi 애 āi	뇨 nyŏ 뇨 nyŏ	황 hwāng 황 hwáng	동 tŏng 동 tŏng	락 lāk 락 lāk	망 māng 망 māng	창 tshāng 창 tshāng	유 yoō 유 yoō
아 ā 이 ī 아 ā 이 ī	가 kā 루 roō 이 ī 가 kā 루 roō 이 ī	도구 tŏk' 도구 tŏk'	도 tŏ 우 oō 도 tŏ 우 oō	라구 lāk' 라구 lāk'	보 bŏ 우 oō 보 bŏ 우 oō	소 sŏ 우 oō 소 sŏ 우 oō	이 ī 우 oō 이 ī 우 oō

Dry and Careless	High, Lofty	Uninterrupted continuous	The noise of a carriage	Exuberant	Disregarded	Expanded as water	Solitary Deserted
漠漠	峨峨	綿綿	轔轔	萋萋	忽忽	渺渺	寥寥
			린 līn 린 līn	세 sēy 이 ī 세 sēy 이 ī			
막 māk 막 mak	아 ā 아 ā	면 myōn 면 myōn	린 līn 린 līn	처 tshyŏ 처 tshyŏ	홀 hŏr 홀 hŏr	묘 myŏ 묘 myŏ	료 lyŏ 료 lyŏ
바구 bāk' 바구 bāk	가 gā 가 gā	멘 mēyn 멘 mēyn	지 tsī 루 roō 이 ī 지 tsī 루 roō 이 ī	무 moō 라 rā 무 moō 라 rā	고쯔 kŏts' 고쯔 kŏts'	뵤 byŏ 우 oō 뵤 byŏ 우 oō	료 lyŏ 우 oō 료 lyŏ 우 oō

倭語類解

Japanese words associated and explained Vol.

倭語類解 下

Chinese words repeated and explained XII.

疊字類

Doub. charac.

The noise of a stream	The rippling sound of water	Cold Frigid	Drizzling Foggy	Confused	Arranged Retired	The sound of hewing timber	Drifting snow
潺潺	渢渢	泠泠	濛濛	紛紛	歷歷	丁丁	霏霏
산 sān 산 sān				훈 hoōn 훈 hoōn			히 hī 히 hī
잔 tsān 잔 tsān	풍 phoōng 풍 phoōng	령 lyōng 령 lyōng	몽 mŏng 몽 mŏng	분 poōn 분 poōn	력 lyŏk 력 lyŏk	뎡 tyōng 뎡 tyōng	비 pī 비 pī
유 yoō 루 roō 리 rī 유 루 yoō 리 rī	후 hoō 우 oō 후 hoō 우 oō	레 lēy 이 ī 레 lēy 이 ī	모 mŏ 우 oō 모 mŏ 우 oō	미 mī 다 dā 레 rēy 미 mī 다 dā 레 rēy	레 lēy 기 kī 레 lēy 기 kī	데 tē 이 ī 데 tē 이 ī	도 tŏ ᄢᅵ bī 도 tŏ ᄢᅵ bī

Fast Quick	Bubbling up Rolling along	Flowing rapidly	The noise of water flowing	Gently flowing	A sudden gust of wind	Gradually	A small stream
快快	汹汹	滾滾	淙淙	溶溶	颯颯	漸漸	涓涓
과 kwā 이 ī 과 kwā 이 ī		곤 kŏn 곤 kŏn			소 sŏ 우 oō 소 sŏ 우 oō	셴 zēyn 셴 zēyn	켄 kēyn 켄 zēyn
쾌 kwāī 쾌 kwāī	흉 hyoōng 흉 hyoōng	곤 kŏn 곤 kŏn	종 tsŏng 종 tsŏng	용 yŏng 용 yŏng	삽 sāp 삽 sāp	졈 tsyŏm 졈 tsyŏm	연 yŏn 연 yŏn
삿 sāt 바 pā 라 rā	교 kyŏ 우 oō 교 kyŏ 우 oō	혼 hŏn 혼 hŏn	소 sŏ 우 oō 소 sŏ 우 oō	요 yŏ 우 oō 요 yŏ 우 oō	삳 āt 사 즈 sāts	시 sī 다 dā 이 ī 시 sī 다 dā 이 ī	소 sŏ 로 rŏ 리 rī 소 sŏ 로 rŏ 리 rī

106

이

Trivial Trifling Petty	Grieved wounded
區區	慽慽
구 koō 구 koō	
구 koō 구 koō	쳑 ts'hyŏk 쳑 ts'hyŏk
마 mā 지 tsī 마 mā 자 tsī	셰 sēy 기 ki 셰 sēy 기 ki

Retired sombre	Cold & stern
闇闇	凜凜
암 ām 암 ām	름 loŏm 름 loŏm
안 ān 안 ān	린 līn 린 līn

	and the notes	The intercalary	The Autumn	The Cold	the stars	the sun	the canopy	Heaven
	律 법 pŏp 측 ts'hŏok 뉼 nyŏor	閏 부 poō 룰 răr 윤 yoōn	秋 가 kă 올 ăr 추 ts'hyōo	寒 출 ts'hăr 한 hān	辰 별 pyŏ 신 sin	日 날 năr 일 ir	宇 집 tsip 우 oō	天 하 hā 놀 năr 텬 t'hyōn
	of the gamut	super-fluities	is for ingathering	comes	and constellations	and Moon	of the Universe	and Earth
	呂 법 pōp 측 ts'hōok 녀 nyō	餘 나 nā 몰 măr 여 yō	收 거 kō 들 toor 슈 syoō	來 올 ŏr 릭 lăi	宿 잘 tsār 슉 syoōk	月 돌 tăr 월 wōr	宙 집 tsip 듀 tyoō	地 따 ttā 디 tī
The 1000 char classic	adjust	complete	and the winter	and the heat	arranged	full	wide	black
	調 고 kŏ 롤 răr 됴 tyŏ	成 이 ī 룰 răr 셩 syōng	冬 겨 kyō 으 ŏō 동 tōng	暑 더 tŏ 울 oōr 셔 syō	列 벌 pōr 렬 ryōr	盈 졸 ts'hăr 영 yōng	洪 너 nō 불 poŏr 홍 hŏng	玄 가 kā 물 moŏr 현 hyōn
107	the superior principle of nature	the year	for hoarding up.	goes,	and spread out	and waning,	and waste;	and yellow,
일	陽 볃 pyŏt 양 yāng	歲 히 hăis 셰 sēy	藏 갈 kār 몰 măr 장 tsāng	往 갈 kār 왕 wāng	張 베 pē 풀 tyoŏr 장 tsyāng	昃 기 ki 울 oōr 측 ts'hăik	荒 거 kō 출 ts'hoōr 황 hwāng	黃 누 noō 룰 roōr 황 hwāng

and of vegetables 菜 나 nă 물 măr 채 tshăi	Of fruits 果 여 yō 름 roōm 과 kwā	Of pearls 珠 구 koō 슬 săr 쥬 tsyoō	Of swords 劒 칼 kār 검 kōm	Gems 玉 구 koō 슬 soŏr 옥 ŏk	Gold 金 쇠 swī 금 koŏm	when the dews 露 이 ī 슬 săr 로 lŏ	When the clouds 雲 구 koō 름 roōm 운 oōn
the most important 重 므 mŏo 거 kō 올 oōr 듕 tyoōng	the most precious 珍 보 pŏ 븨 păi 딘 tin	the most celebrated 稱 일 ir 킈 khă 를 rŏr 칭 tshing	the most distinguished 號 일 ir 훔 hoōm 호 hŏ	come from 出 날 nār 츌 tshyoor	is produced 生 날 nār 싱 săing	concrete 結 밋 măit 결 kyōr	ascend on high 騰 놀 năr 등 toōng
are the mustard plant 芥 계 kēy 즈 tsă 개 kāi	are the damson 李 외 wī 얏 yās 니 nī	is the "Night 夜 바 pā 야 yā	is the "Great 巨 클 k'hoŏr 거 kō	the "Kwănlun 崑 뫼 mwo 곤 kŏn	at the graceful 麗 빗 pīs 날 nār 려 lyō	they become 爲 할 hăr 위 ooī	they occasion 致 닐 nīr 올 ooīr 티 tō
and ginger. 薑 싱 săing 강 kāng 강 kāng	and plum: 柰 엇 ŏt 너 nāi	splendor;" 光 빗 pīt 광 kwāng	chamber;" 闕 집 tsip 궐 kwŏr	hill." 岡 뫼 mois 부 poō 리 lī 강 kāng	water," 水 물 moŏr 슈 syoō	hoarfrost: 霜 서 sō 리 lī 상 sāng	rain, 雨 비 pī 우 oō

The 1000 char. clas-sic.

108

were 有 아 ī 실 sīr 유 yoo	but they who resigned 推 밀 mīr 츄 tshyoo	then 乃 사 sā 나 nāi	At that early period 始 비 pī 로 roo 술 soor 시 si	while birds were the mark of 鳥 새 sāi 됴 tyo	The dragon designat[illegible] 龍 미 mi 르 roo 룡 lyŏng	The scaly [illegible] 鱗 비 pī 느 när 린 lin	[illegible] 海 바 pā 다 tā 해 hăi
the royal Yu. 虞 해 hē 아 ā 릴 rīr 우 oo	their dignity 位 벼 pyŏ 슬 soor 위 ooi	were worn 服 니 nī 블 poor 복 pook	were invented 制 지 tsī 울 oor 제 tsēy	offices 官 구 koo 의 wī 관 kwan	a teacher 師 스 soo 승 soong 스 sā	plunge deep 潛 줌 tsăm 길 kīr 줌 tsăm	is saltish 鹹 쯘 tshär 함 hăm
and the potter 陶 딜 tīr 것 kŏs 도 tŏ	and yielded up 讓 스 sā 양 yāng 양 yāng	clothes 衣 옷 ŏs 의 wī	litera-ture 文 글 koor 월 wŏr 문 moon	under the Human 人 사 sā 룸 rām 언 ŏn	(in the time of) the Fire 火 블 poor 화 hwā	but the feathered 羽 짓 tsit 우 oo	and the river water 河 ㄱ kā 룸 răm 하 hā
Tang. 唐 대 tāi 광 kwāng 당 tāng	a kingdom, 國 나 nā 라 rā 국 kook	and garments: 裳 치 tshi 마 mā 샹 syāng	and learning 字 글 koor 월 wŏr ᄌᆞ tsā	sovereign" 皇 님 nīm 굼 koom 황 hwāng	Emperor, 帝 님 nim 굼 koom 뎨 tēy	soar high 翔 늘 năr 샹 syāng	fresh 淡 물 măr 골 kăr 담 tām

while they led 率 드 tă 릴 rir 솔 sŏr	the distant 遐 멀 mŏr 하 hā	and to subjects 臣 신 sin 하 hā 신 sin	they loved 愛 스 să 랑 rāng 이 ăi	they let fall 垂 드 tŏo 리 ri 울 oŏr 슈 syoō	they sat 坐 안 ān 즐 tsăr 좌 tsŏa	were of the Chow dynasty 周 무 moŏ 무 moŏ. 쥬 tsyoō	They who consoled 弔 됴 tyŏ 문 moŏn 됴 tyŏ
strangers 賓 손 sŏn 빈 pin	and near 邇 갓 kās 까 skā 울 oŏr 이 i	reduced 伏 굿 koŏs 샐 spoŏr 복 pŏk	and cherished 育 칠 tshir 육 yoŏk	their folded hands 拱 고 kŏ 즐 tsăr 공 kŏng	in their court 朝 아 ā 춤 tshăm 됴 tyŏ	the Emperor Hwat 發 배 paī 풀 phoŏr 발 pār	the people 民 뵉 păik 셩 syŏng 민 min
to revert to 歸 도 tŏ 라 rā 갈 kār 귀 kwi	(became) one 壹 혼 hăn 일 ir	the northern 戎 되 tŏi 융 yoong	the black 黎 가 kā 몰 măr 려 lyŏ	and tranquillized 平 평 phyŏng 홀 hăr 평 phyŏng	and asked after 問 무 moŏ 롤 răr 문 moŏm	and of the Yin dynasty 殷 만 mān 홀 hăr 은 oŏn	and punished 伐 베 pŏi 힐 hir 벌 pŏr
the great King 王 님 nim 굼 koŏm 왕 wāng	body 體 몸 mŏm 톄 thēy	and western hordes 羌 되 tŏi 강 kāng	headed (people), 首 마 mā 리 ri 슈 syoō	the whole body: 章 글 koŏr 월 wŏr 장 tsyāng	the right way; 道 도 tŏ 리 ri 도 tŏ	the emperor Thang: 湯 끌 skoŏr 홀 hoŏr 탕 thāng	crime; 罪 허 hŏ 물 moŏr 죄 tsŏi

朝鮮千字文

109 汝

how	(we should therefore) respect	(dwells under the) four	Now	and the support	therefore	and the white	(In their day) the crowing
豈	恭	四	蓋	賴	化	白	鳴
엇 ōs 시녀 snyō 기 kwi	온 ŏn 공 kŏng 공 kŏng	넉 nŏk ᄾ sǎ	두 toō 풀 phoŏr 개 kāi	힘 him 니 nī 불 poŏr 뢰 lŏi	될 twir 화 hwā	힌 hāin 빅 pāik	울 oŏr 명 myōng
dare we	that which	great (powers)	this	extended	overspread	colt	phoenix
敢	惟	大	此	及	被	駒	鳳
구 koō 틀 t'hir 감 kām	오 ŏ 직 tsik 유 yōo	큰 k'hoŏn 대 tāi	이 i ᄎ tshǎ	미 mī ᄎᆞᆯ tshǎr 급 koŏp	니 nī 불 poŏr 피 p'hī	ᄆᆡ māi 아 yā 지 tsī 구 koō	봉 pŏng 황 hwāng 봉 pŏng
destroy	(our mother) has nourished	(and is influenced by) the five	body	to a myriad	the grass	grazed	perched
毁	鞠	五	身	萬	草	食	在
헐 hŏr 훼 hwē	칠 tshir 국 kook	다 tā ᄉᆞᆺ sǎs 오 ŏ	몸 mŏm 신 sin	일 ir 만 mān 만 mān	플 p'hoŏr 초 ts'hŏ	ᄆᆡ mō 글 koŏr 식 sik	이 ĭ 슬 sir 지 tsāi
or injure it.	(and our father) supported	constant (virtues)	and its hairs	regions,	and trees,	in the mead:	on the tree,
傷	養	常	髮	方	木	場	樹
헐 hor 상 syāng	칠 tshir 양 yāng	상 syāng 녯 neys 상 syāng	터 t'hō 럭 rŏk 발 pār	모 mŏ 방 pāng	나 nā 모 mŏ 목 mŏk	빝 pāt 장 tsyāng	나 nā 모 mŏ 슈 syoō

朝鮮千字文

but capacities	let engagements	and cease	For bear	obtaining	Knowing	while men	Females
器	信	靡	罔	得	知	男	女
그kŭn 릇roos 긔kwī	미mī 돌tăr 신sĭn	아ā 닐nĭr 미mī	업ŏp 술sŏŏr 망măng	어ŏ 돌tŏŏr 득tŏŏk	알ăr 디tī	아ā 돌măr 남nām	계kēy 집tsĭp 녀nyŏ
and desires	be rendered	to presume on	to prate about	abilities	a fault	should emulate	should aspire after
欲	使	恃	談	能	過	效	慕
하hă 고kŏ 져tsŏ 홀hăr 욕yŏk	브pŏŏ 릴rĭr 사să	미mī 돌tăr 시sĭ	말măr 솜săm 담tām	잘tsăr 홀hăr 능noong	디tī 날năr 과kwá	본pŏn 볼pŏr 효hyŏ	스sŭ 모mŏ 모mŏ
are with difficulty	so that they can	your own	another's	do not	you should	talent	chastity
難	可	己	彼	莫	必	才	貞
어ŏ 려ryŏ 울oor 난rān	올ŏr 홀hăr 가kā	몸mŏm 긔kwī	더tŏ 피p'hī	말măr 막măk	반pān 득tŏŏk 필p'hĭr	재tsăi 조tsŏ 재tsăi	고kŏ 돌tăr 뎡tyŏng
measured	be repeated,	superiority;	deficiencies,	neglect them	amend it,	and goodness:	and constancy:
量	覆	長	短	忘	改	良	烈
혜hěy 아ā 릴rĭr 량lyāng	다tā 시sĭ 복pŏk	긴kĭn 댱tyăng	뎌tyŏ 롤răr 단tān	니nĭ 줄tsăr 망măng	고kŏ 칠tshĭr 개kăi	어ŏ 딜tĭr 냥nyăng	미măi 몰mŏr 렬lyŭr

The 1000 char. classic.

110

and in the vacant 虛 빌 poōir 허 hō	then even to the empty 空 빌 pwir 공 kōng	when a man's form 形 얼 ōr 굴 koōr 형 hyōng	when virtue 德 큰 k'hoōn 덕 tōk	subdue 剋 이 ī 길 kwir 극 koōk	Illumine 景 볏 pyōt 경 kyōng	while of odes 詩 글 koōr 월 wōr 시 sī	what Mih-tsze 墨 먹 mōk 묵 moōk
hall 堂 집 tsīp 당 tāng	valley 谷 골 kōr 곡 kōk	is exact 端 끗 koōt 단 tān	is built up 建 셀 sēyr 건 kōn	your thoughts 念 념 nyōm 홀 hār 념 nyōm	your practice 行 녈 nēyr 힝 hāing	the most to be praised 讚 기 kī 릴 rir 찬 ts'hān	most regretted was 悲 슬 soōr 홀 hōr 비 pi
it will be repeatedly 習 니 nī 길 kir 습 soōp	will be handed down 傳 옴 ōm 길 kir 뎐 tyōn	his exterior 表 밧 pāt 표 p'hyō	a man's name 名 일 ir 홈 hoōm 명 myōng	and you will become 作 지 tsi 을 oōr 작 tsāk	and you will be 維 얼 ōr 굴 koōr 유 yoo	is the "lamb 羔 염 yōm 고 kō	that the silky threads 絲 실 sir 사 sā
heard. 聽 드 toō 를 roōr 텽 t'hyōng	his fame, 聲 소 sō 릐 rāi 셩 syōng	will be correct: 正 졍 tsyōng 홀 hār 졍 tsyōng	is established, 立 셜 syōr 닙 nip	a sage 聖 셔 syō 인 in 셩 syōng	a philosopher, 賢 어 ō 딜 tir 현 hyōn	and sheep" ditty, 羊 양 yāng 양 yāng	were defiled, 染 믈 moōr 들 toōr 염 yōm

[illegible] to our prince 忠 튱 t'hyōng 셩 syong 튱 t'hyoong	[illegible] piety 孝 효 hyŏ 도 tŏ 효 hyŏ	are required 曰 ᄀᆞᆯ kăr 왈 wăr	In aiding 資 ᄌᆞ tsă 뢰 rwī ᄌᆞ tsă	but an inch length 寸 ᄆᆞ mă 듸 tăi 촌 tshŏn	An foot's length of 尺 자 tsā 쳑 tshyŏk	happiness 福 복 pŏk 복 pŏk	Misery 禍 ᄌᆡ tsāi 화 hwā 화 hwā
then let us 則 법 pŏp 측 tshŏŏk 측 tshŏŏk	we ought 當 맛 pās 샹 stāng 당 tāng	strictness 嚴 싁 swik 싁 swik ᄒᆞᆯ hăr 엄 yom	a father 父 아 ā 비 pī 부 pŏŏ	of time 陰 그 koŏ 늘 nŏŏr 음 ŏŏm	a gem 壁 구 koŏ 슬 sŏŏr 벽 pyŏk	on account of 緣 ᄆᆞᆯ măr 미 măi 연 yŏn	because of 因 지 tsī ᄌᆡᆯ tsăir 연 yŏn
exhaust 盡 다 tā ᄋᆞᆯ ăr 진 tsīn	to exert to the utmost 竭 다 tā ᄋᆞᆯ ăr 갈 kār	with 與 더 tŏ 불 pŏŏr 여 yŏ	observing 事 셤 syŏm 길 kĭr ᄉᆞ să	this is to be 是 잇 is 시 sī	is not 非 아 ā 닐 nir 비 pī	virtue 善 어 ŏ 딜 tĭr 션 syŏn	vice 惡 모 mŏ 딜 tĭr 악 āk
our lives. 命 목 mŏk 숨 sŏŏm 명 myŏng	our strength, 力 심 sĭm 력 ryŏk	respect. 敬 공 kŏng 경 kyŏng 경 kyŏng	a prince 君 님 nīm 금 koŏm 군 koŏn	carefully guarded. 競 ᄃᆞ tă 톨 toŏr 경 kyŏng	so precious. 寶 보 pŏ ᄇᆡ păi 보 pŏ	becomes our congratulation 慶 경 kyŏng 하 hā 경 kyŏng	accumulates 積 사 să ᄒᆞᆯ hăr 뎍 tyŏk

and your words 言 말 măr 슴 săm 언 ŏn	Let your carriage 容 즛 tsoŏs 용 yŏng	or as the settled pool 淵 못 mŏs 연 yŏn	as the stream 川 내 nāī 쳔 tshyŏn	and resemble 如 가 kā 틀 thăr 여 yŏ	(then should we be) like 似 가 kā 틀 thăr ᄉᆞ să	early in the morning 夙 마 mā 눌 năr 슉 syoŏk	As in approaching 臨 니 nī 놀 năr 림 lim
and expressions 辭 말 măr 슴 săm ᄉᆞ să	and demeanour 止 그 koŏ 출 tshoŏr 지 tsī	so clear 澄 몱 măr 글 kăr 딩 tīng	flowing 流 흐 hoŏ 롤 răr 류 lyoŏ	the pine tree 松 솔 sŏr 숑 syŏng	the epidendrum 蘭 난 nān 초 tshŏ 난 nān	we should rise 興 닐 nīr 흥 hoŏng	a deep (ravine) 深 기 kī 플 kŏr 심 sīm
be fixed 安 편 phyŏn 안 ān 안 ān	be as it were 若 가 kă 틀 thăr 약 yăk	that it may be taken 取 다 ā 올 ăr 취 tshyoŏi	without 不 아 ā 닐 nīr 불 poŏr	in its 之 갈 kăr 지 tsī	for its 斯 이 ī ᄉᆞ să	(to see that our parents) are warm 溫 드 tă 술 săr 온 ŏn	or in treading on 履 볼 păr 올 ŏr 리 lī
and settled: 定 알 īr 뎡 tyŏng 뎡 tyŏng	reflected on, 思 ᄉᆞ să 링 răing ᄉᆞ să	for a mirror. 暎 비 pī 췰 tshoŏir 명 myong	cessation, 息 쉴 swir 식 sik	exuberance: 盛 셩 syŏng 홀 hăr 셩 syŏng	fragrance, 馨 곳 kŏs 다 tă 올 ŏr 형 hyŏng	or cool: 淸 시 sī 글 koŏr 졍 tsyŏng	thin (ice); 薄 열 yŏr 올 oŏr 박 pak

and at our departure 去 갈 kăr 거 kŏ	then our fame will be retained 存 이 ĭ 실 sĭr 존 tsŏn	take charge of 攝 자 tsă 볼 poŏr 섭 syŏp	when in learning 學 배 păi 홀 hŏr 학 hăk	the records of whose fame 籍 글 koor 월 wŏr 적 tsyŏk	this is the most glorious 榮 영 yŏng 화 hwă 영 yŏng	and care 愼 삼 săm 갈 kăr 신 sĭn	Earnest attention (to learning) 篤 도 tŏ 타 thă 올 ŏr 독 tŏk
still 而 말 măr 리 rĭ 올 oŏr 이 ĭ	as the 以 써 psŏ 이 ĭ	business 職 벼 pyŏ 슬 săr 직 tsik	we excel, 優 나 nă 올 oŏr 우 oŏ	will be exceeding great 甚 심 sĭm 할 hăr 심 sĭm	occupation 業 업 ŏp 업 ŏp	about the conclusion 終 모 mă 참 tshăm 종 tsyong	at the commencement 初 저 tsŏ 엇 ŏt 초 tshŏ
there will be an increased 益 더 tŏ 올 oŏr 익 ik	sweet 甘 들 tăr 감 kăm	and attend to 從 조 tsŏ 출 tshăr 종 tsyŏng	we mount high 登 오 ŏ 를 răr 등 toŏng	without 無 업 ŏp 슬 soŏr 무 moŏ	which has ever been 所 바 pă 소 sŏ	ought to be 宜 맛 măs 당 stang 의 wĭ	is really 誠 정 tsyŏng 셩 syŏng 셩 syŏng
celebration of it 詠 으 oŏ 플 phoor 영 yŏng	peartree, 棠 아 ă 가 kă 외 ŏi 당 tăng	the affairs of government 政 졍 tsyŏng 亽 să 졍 tsyŏng	in office, 仕 벼 pyĕ 슬 soŏr 亽 să	bounds. 竟 모 mă 참 tshăm 경 kyŏng	founded, 基 터 thŏ 긔 kwĭ	medicated 令 어 ŏ 딜 tĭr 령 lyŏng	beautiful 美 아 ă 롬 lăm 다 tă 올 ŏr 미 mĭ

The 1000 char- clas- sic.

(and treat your nephews) as	(respect, all	at home (young women)	abroad (young men)	when the husband	superiors	ceremony	Music
猶 가 kă ᄐᆞᆯ thăr 유 yoō	諸 모 mŏ ᄃᆞᆯ tăr 졔 tsěy	入 들 toōr 입 ip	外 밧 pās 외 ōi	夫 짓 tsis 아 ā 비 pi 부 poō	上 웃 oōs 샹 syāng	禮 녜 něy 도 tŏ 녜 něy	樂 풍 p'hoōng 류 nyoō 악 āk
sons	your aunts	should obey	should receive	sings	should be harmonious	distinguishes	differs
子 아 ā ᄃᆞᆯ tăr ᄌᆞ tsă	姑 ᄒᆞᆯ hăr 미 mī 고 kŏ	奉 받 pāt 들 toōr 봉 pŏng	受 바 pā 들 toōr 슈 syoō	唱 브 poō 를 rŏr 챵 ts'hyāng	和 고 kŏ ᄅᆞᆯ răr 화 hwā	別 다 tā ᄂᆞᆯ năr 별 pyŏr	殊 다 tā ᄂᆞᆯ năr 슈 syoō
and equal to	with your senior	a mother's	the teachers	the wife	and inferiors	between honorable	when used by noble
比 견 kyŏn 줄 tsoōr 비 pī	伯 ᄆᆞᆮ măt ᄇᆡᆨ pāik	母 어 ŏ 미 mī 모 mŏ	傅 스 soō 승 soōng 부 poō	婦 며 myŏ ᄂᆞ nă 리 lī 부 poō	下 아 ā 래 lāi 하 hā	尊 노 nŏ ᄑᆞᆯ p'hăr 존 tsŏn	貴 구 koō ᄒᆞᆯ hăr 귀 kwī
your children;	and junior uncles	rules:	instructions	should accord to it	amicable	and base;	and mean persons,
兒 아 ā ᄒᆡ hāi ᄋᆞ ā	叔 아 ā ᄌᆞ tsā 비 pī 슉 syoōk	儀 거 kŏ 동 tŏng 의 ik	訓 가 kă ᄅᆞ lā 칠 tshir 훈 hoōn	隨 조 tsŏ ᄎᆞᆯ ts'hăr 슈 syoō	睦 화 hwā 목 mŏk 목 mŏk	卑 ᄂᆞ nă ᄌᆞᆯ tsăr 비 pī	賤 쳔 tshyŏn ᄒᆞᆯ hăr 쳔 tshyŏn

112

even when subverted 顛 엎 op 더 tŏ 질 tīr 뎐 tyŏn	Economy 節 마 mă 듸 tăi 졀 tsyŭr	even in 造 지 tsī 을 ŏŏr 조 tshŏ	Benevolence 仁 클 k'hŏŏr 인 īn	slitting 切 그 kŏŏ 츨 tshŏŏr 졀 tsyŭr	In associating 交 사 să 필 p'hīr 교 kyŏ	who are of the same 同 오 ŏ 한 hīn 동 tŏng	ardently 孔 구 kŏŏ 무 mŏŏ 공 kŏng
and prostrate 沛 잣 tsyŏs 싸 spa 질 tīr 패 p'hāi	rectitude 義 올 ŏr 흘 hăr 의 ik	a hurry 次 ᄁᆞ kă 옴 ăm 차 ts'hă	tenderness 慈 즈 tsă 빋 pit 즈 tsă	and grinding 磨 갈 kăr 마 mă	with friends, 友 벋 pŏt 우 ŏŏ	spirit 氣 긔 kwi 운 ŏŏn 긔 kwi	embrace 懷 푸 p'hŏŏ 물 mŏŏr 회 hŏi
do not 匪 아 ă 닐 nīr 비 pī	purity 廉 졍 tsyŏng 렴 lyŏm 렴 lyŏm	do not 弗 말 măr 불 pŏŏr	commiseration 隱 수 sŏŏ 흘 hŏŏr 은 ŏŏn	probing 箴 경 kyŏng 계 kĕy 잠 tsăm	cast in with those 投 더 tŏ 질 tsīr 투 t'hŏŏ	and connected 連 나 nă 을 ŏŏr 련 lyŏn	your elder 兄 몯 măt 형 hyŏng
come short in 虧 이 ī 즐 tsăr 휴 hyŏŏ	and a retiring disposition 退 므 mŏŏ 룰 lŏŏr 퇴 t'hŏi	relinquish 離 여 yŏ 흴 hŏir 리 lī	and feeling 惻 슬 sŏŏr 흘 hŏŏr 측 ts'hŏŏk	and rounding off their excrescencies 規 법 pŏp 식 sik 규 kyŏŏ	who may share your affections 分 는 năn 홀 hŏr 분 pŏŏn	branches: (with yourself) 枝 가 kă 지 tsi 지 tsi	and younger brothers, 弟 아 ă ᄋᆞ ă 뎨 tĕy

The 000 char classic.

113

are the eastern 東 동 tŏug 녁 nyŏk 동 tŏng	The metropolitan 都 모 mŏ 돌 tŏr 도 tŏ	and a good 好 됴 tyŏ 홀 hăr 호 hŏ	Firmly 堅 구 koō 들 tŏŏr 견 kyŏn	but if you drive after 逐 뽀 ptsŏ 찰 tshăr 튝 thyŏŏk	Maintain 守 닥 tăk 킐 khwĭr 슈 syŏŏ	when the mind 心 ᄆᆞ mă 음 ăm 심 sĭm	when the disposition 性 셩 syŏng 셩 syŏng
and western 西 서 syŏ 녁 nyŏk 서 syŏ	cities 邑 고 koŏ 올 ŏr 읍 oŏp	degree of nobility 爵 벼 pyŏ 슬 săr 쟉 tsyăk	grasp 持 가 kă 질 tsĭr 디 tĭ	foreign things 物 것 kŏs 믈 mŏŏr	the truth 眞 참 tshăm 진 tsĭn	is agitated 動 뮐 mŏŏir 동 tŏng	is still 靜 고 kŏ 요 yŏ 홀 hăr 졍 tsyŏng
two 二 두 tŏŏ 이 ĭ	of the Flowery 華 빗 pĭt 날 năr 화 hwă	will certainly 自 스 sŏŏ 스 sŏŏ 리 lĭ 자 tsă	some excellent 雅 몰 mă 골 kăr 아 ă	your intentions 意 뜯 ptŏŏt 의 wĭ	and your designs 志 뜯 ptŏŏt 지 tsĭ	the spirits 神 신 sĭn 령 lyŏng 신 sĭn	the affections 情 뜯 ptŏŏt 졍 tsyŏng
capitals 京 서 syŏ 울 oŏr 경 kyŏng	summer (i.e. China) 夏 녀 nyŏ 롬 lăm 하 hă	be annexed 縻 어 ŏ 굴 koor 미 mĭ	purpose, 操 자 tsă 볼 păr 조 tso	will vacillate 移 옴 ŏm 길 kir 이 ĭ	will be fulfilled 滿 찰 tshăr 만 măn	will be harrassed 疲 곳 kăs 볼 păr 피 p'hĭ	will be tranquil 逸 편 p'hyŏn 안 ăn 홀 hăr 일 ir

and the expanded	there are the splendid	painted	there are delineations	while the galleries	the palaces	with the floating	Backed by
甲 갑 kap 갑 kap	丙 남 nām 녁 nyok 병 pyong	畫 그 kŏŏ 림 lim 화 hwā	圖 그 kŏŏ 림 līm 도 tŏ	樓 다 tā 락 lak 누 nŏŏ	宮 집 tsip 궁 koong	浮 뜰 ptŏŏr 부 poo	背 등 toong 븨 pāi
pavilions	edifices	and ornamented	and descriptions	and prospects	and halls	Wei river	the Măng hill
帳 댱 tyang 댱 tyang	舍 집 tsip 샤 syā	綵 치 tshăi 식 saik 치 tshăi	寫 슬 sŏŏr 샤 syā	觀 볼 pŏr 관 kwān	殿 집 tsip 뎐 tyŏn	渭 위 ŏŏi 슈 syŏŏ 위 ŏŏi	邙 뎌 thŏ 망 mang
facing	on all sides	like fairies	of birds	are flying high	(appear) winding	and the meandering	and faced by
對 되 tăi 홀 hăr 되 tăi	傍 겻 kyŏs 방 pāng	仙 션 syŏn 인 in 션 syŏn	禽 새 săi 금 kŏŏm	飛 놀 năr 비 pi	盤 서 sŏ 릴 rir 반 pān	據 루 lŏŏ 를 rŏŏr 거 kŏ	面 낫 nās 면 myŏn
the pillars	opened,	or sprites	and beasts,	and alarmingly lofty:	and curving	King stream.	the Lŏh river
楹 기 ki 동 tŏng 영 yŏng	啓 열 yŏr 계 key	靈 녕 nyŏng 홀 hăr 녕 nyŏng	獸 즘 tsoong 승 sŏŏng 슈 syŏŏ	驚 놀 nŏr 날 năr 경 kyŏng	鬱 덥 tŏp 거 kŏ 출 tshŏŏr 울 ŏŏr	涇 경 kyŏng 슈 syŏŏ 경 kyŏng	洛 낙 nāk 슈 syŏŏ 낙 nāk

The 1000 char classic.

they also	Having already	on the left	on the right	when the caps of office	They ascend	while they drum upon	There they spread out
亦	既	左	右	弁	陞	鼓	肆
또 stŏ 역 yŏk	이 ī 믜 mwī 긔 kwī	왼 ŏĭr 자 tsā	올 ŏr 흘 hăr 우 oŏ	곳 kŏs 갈 kăr 변 pyŏn	오 ŏ 를 rā 승 soŏng	갓 kās 붑 poŏp 고 kŏ	베 pē 플 phŏor 亽 să
assemble	collected	is the thoroughfare	you go through	revolve	the steps	the guitar	the carpet
聚	集	達	通	轉	階	瑟	筵
모 mŏ 돌 tăr 취 tshyoŏi	모 mŏ 돌 tăr 집 tsip	亽 să 뭇 mă 출 tshăr 달 tăr	亽 să 뭇 mă 출 tshăr 통 thŏng	구 koŏ 을 oŏr 뎐 tyŏn	드 tă 리 lī 계 kēy	비 pī 화 hwā 슬 sŏr	디 tī 의 wī 연 yŏn
the host of	the ancient books	to the entertain	to the broad	like as if were	and are received on	and blow	and arrange
群	墳	承	廣	疑	納	吹	設
물 moŏr 군 koŏn	무 moŏ 덤 tŏm 분 poŏn	니 nī 올 ăr 승 sŏŏng	너 nŏ 블 poŏr 광 kwāng	의 wī 심 sīm 의 wī	드 toŏ 릴 rīr 납 năp	불 poŏr 취 tshyoŏi	베 pē 플 phŏor 셜 syŏr
geniuses	and records	with splendour (chamber)	interior (hall)	the stars	the stairs	the flageolet	the entertainment
英	典	明	內	星	陛	笙	席
곳 kŏs 부 spoŏ 리 lī 영 ŏng	법 pīp 뎐 tyŏn	블 păr 갈 kăr 명 myŏng	안 ān 닉 năi	별 pyŏr 셩 syŏng	셤 sŏm 페 phēy	뎌 tyŏ 싱 săing	돗 tŏs 셕 syŏk

14

and driving 驅 몰 mŏr 구 koo	with their high 高 노 nŏ 폴 p'hŏor 고 kŏ	and their houses 家 집 tsip 가 kā	their families 戶 지 tsī 게 kěy 호 hŏ	and along the roads 路 길 kĭr 로 lŏ	In the mansions 府 마 mā 올 ăr 부 pōo	with the varnished 漆 옷 ŏs 칠 ts'hĭl	There were specimens of Mr. Thoo's 杜 마 mā 글 koŏr 두 toō
their carriages 轂 술 sŏor 위 ooī 곡 kok 가 kā	hats 冠 고 kŏ 갈 kār 관 kwan	are gifted 給 줄 tsoŏr 급 koŏp	are promoted 封 봉 pŏng 할 hăr 봉 pŏng	are ranged side by side 俠 낄 skĭr 엽 yŏp	are entertained 羅 벌 pŏr 라 rā	books 書 글 koŏr 월 wŏr 셔 syō	running hand 藁 딥 tĭp 고 kŏ
they shake 振 떨 ptŏr 진 tsin	they attend upon 陪 뫼 mŏī 실 sĭr 배 pāī	with a thousand 千 일 ĭr 쳔 ts'hyōn 쳔 ts'hyōn	over eight 八 여 yŏ 덟 tărp 팔 p'hăr	the lignum vitae 槐 괴 kŏī 화 hwā 괴 kŏī	the generals 將 쟝 tsyang 슈 syoō 쟝 tsyang	and the wainscoted 壁 바 pă 람 lăm 벽 pyŏk	and of Mr. Chung's 鍾 죵 tsyŏng 쟈 tsă 죵 tsyŏng
their tassels 纓 긴 kīn 영 yōng	the Imperial chariot 輦 년 nyŏn 년 nyŏn	soldiers; 兵 병 pyŏng 마 mā 병 pyŏng	districts, 縣 고 kŏ 올 ăr 현 hyŏn	nobles: 卿 벼 pyŏ 슬 sŏor 경 kyŏng	and prime ministers, 相 서 săī 로 loŭ 상 syāng	classics. 經 글 koŏr 월 wŏr 경 kyŏng	correct writing 隷 글 koŏr 시 sī 메 mēy

The good char. classic

	if it had not been 微 쟈 tsyā 굴 koŏr 미 mī	To make a shelter 奄 문 moŏn 득 toŏk 엄 ŏm	aiding their (princes) 佐 도 tŏ 올 ăr 자 tsā	The stony 磻 돌 tŏr 반 pan	they will be carved 勒 굴 koŏr 에 ē 륵 loŏk	when their schemes 策 막 măk 대 tāī 착 tshăk	and their carriages 車 술 soŏr 위 ooi 거 kō	with their hereditary 世 인 in 간 kān 셰 sēy
	for Mr Tan 旦 아 ā 참 tshăn 단 tăn	and a dwelling place 宅 집 tsip 틧 thīt	at that period 時 시 sī 절 tsōr 시 si	rivulet (teacher) 溪 시 sī 내 nāī 계 kēy	on stone tablets 碑 빗 pis 비 pī	and deserts 功 공 kŏng 공 kŏng	and studs 駕 멍 mōng 에 ē 가 kā	emoluments 祿 녹 nŏk 녹 nŏk
	who could 孰 누 noō 구 koō 슉 syoōk	at the crooked 曲 고 kŏ 볼 păr 곡 kŏk	(rose to the office of) "a 阿 두 toō 던 tōn 아 ā	with Mr. E. 伊 저 tsō 이 ī	and engraven 刻 사 sā 길 kīr 각 kak	are fertile 茂 거 kō 츌 tshoŏr 무 moō	are fat 肥 살 săr 질 tsir 비 pī	they become extravagantly 侈 샤 syā 치 tshī 치 tshī
115	have accomplished it 營 지 tsī 올 oŏr 영 yōng	mound 阜 두 toō 던 tōn 부 poō	balance," 衡 서 sō 올 oōr 새 stāī 형 hōng	Yin 尹 못 măt 윤 yoōn	on metal plates 銘 조 tsŏ 글 koŏr 영 yōng	and real 實 엳 yōt 몰 măr 실 sir	and light 輕 가 kā 비 păī 야 yā 올 ŏr 경 kyōng	rich 富 가 kā 아 ă 멸 myōr 부 poō

in the time of the Teaou 趙 됴 tyŏ 국 kook 됴 tyŏ	The Tsin 晋 진 tsin 국 kook 진 tsin	and having many 多 할 hār 다 tā	Men of talent 俊 미 măi 올 ŏr 쥰 tsyoon	(the clever) Yŭĕh 說 니 nī 놀 năr 셜 syōr	(The virtuous) Ke 綺 깁 kīp 긔 kwī	helping 濟 피 p'hī 딜 tīr 졔 tsēy	Hwan 桓 재 tsăi 와 wā 돌 tăr 환 hwān
and Gwuy states 魏 위 oōi 국 kook 위 ooī	and Ch'hoo countries 楚 초 tshŏ 국 kook 쵸 tshŏ	sholars 士 셔 syō 비 păi ᄉᆞ să	regulated 乂 어 ō 딜 tīr 예 ēy	was moved by 感 늗 noot 길 kīr 감 kām	brought back 囬 도 tŏ 라 lā 올 ŏr 회 hŏī	the infirmities 弱 약 yāk 홀 hăr 약 yāk	the duke 公 구 kōo 의 wī 공 kŏng
(the empire) was disordered 困 잇 is 블 poŏr 곤 kŏn	altered (the form of government) 更 공 kŏng 틸 thīr 굉 kŏing	(the prince) was truly 寔 잇 is 식 sīk	the secret 宻 븩 pwik 븩 pwīk 밀 mīr 밀 mīr	(the virtue) of Woo 武 미 măi 믈 moŏr 무 moō	(the prince) Han 漢 한 hān 슈 syoō 한 hān	and upholding 扶 붇 poōr 들 toŏr 부 poō	rectified 匡 고 kŏ 길 kīr 광 kwāng
and perverse 橫 빗 pis 긜 skīr 훵 hŏing	to tyranny 霸 읏 oŏs 듬 toŏm 패 phāi	safe. 寧 편 p'hyōn 홀 hăr 녕 nyūng	forbidden (palace) 勿 말 mār 물 moŏr	Ting 丁 쟝 tsāng 뎡 tyōng 뎡 tyōng	Hwuy 惠 은 oōn 혜 hēy 혜 hēy	the falling (house of Chow) 傾 기 kī 올 oōr 경 kyōng	and united (the empire) 合 모 mŏ 돌 tăr 합 hāp

and gallopped	they proclaimed	in employing	The General's Ke "arise"	while the magistrate Han	The statesman Ho	and at "tread"	They borrowed
馳 돌 tăr 일 īr 티 t'hī	宣 배 pāi 풀 p'hoor 션 syōn	用 쓰 psō 용 oōng	起 닐 nīr 긔 kwī	韓 한 hān 국 kook 한 hān	何 엇 ōs 되 tāi 하 hā	踐 볼 păr 올 ŏr 쳔 tshyōn	假 빌 pīr 가 kā
their praise	their dignity	their troops	Tsëen "clip"	ruined all	complied with	the ground district	a road
譽 기 kī 릴 rīr 예 ey	威 위 oōī 엄 ōm 위 oōī	軍 군 koōn 군 koōn	翦 술 kăr 길 kīr 젼 tsyōn	弊 하 hā 여 yō 딜 tīr 폐 p'hey	遵 조 tsō 출 tshăr 쥰 tsyoōn	土 흙 hărk 토 thŏ	途 길 kīr 도 tŏ
to the red	at the sandy	were very	P'ho "little"	by his vexatious	the covenanted	they assembled	to exterminate
丹 불 poor 글 koor 단 tān	沙 몰 mŏr 애 ăi 사 sā	最 ㄱ kă 장 tsang 최 tshŏi	頗 ᄌ tsă 므 mă 파 p'hā	煩 이 ī 조 tsoo 러 lō 울 oor 빈 pīn	約 언 ōn 약 yāk 약 yāk	會 모 mŏ 돌 tăr 회 hŏi	滅 ᄡ psōr 멸 myūr
azure country	desert,	clever;	and Mok "pasture"	punishments.	laws:	and made a confederacy	the Keih country
青 프 p'hoo 를 roor 쳥 tshōng	漠 아 ā 독 tăk 홀 hăr 막 māk	精 졍 tsyōng 홀 hăr 졍 tsyōng	牧 칠 tshīr 목 mŏk	刑 형 hyōng 벌 pōr 형 hyōng	法 법 pōp 법 pōp	盟 밍 māing 셔 syō 밍 māing	虢 괵 kōik 국 kook 괵 kŏik

九	百	嶽	禪	鴈	雞	昆	鉅
The nine 아 ā 홉 hŏp 구 koō	while the hundred 온 ŏn 빅 pāik	Of mountain 뫼 mōis 무 moō 리 lī 악 āk	Of sacred places 터 t'hō 닷 tās 글 koŏr 션 syōn	There is the "wild goose 그 koŏ 려 lyō 기 kī 안 ān	there is also "the fowl 닭 tārk 계 kēy	likewise "the brother 므 măt 곤 kŏn	with the "wide 듬 t'huoŏp 거 kō
州 provinces 고 kŏ 올 ăr 쥬 tsyoō	**郡** districts 고 kŏ 올 ăr 군 koōn	**宗** the most honoured 므 mă 르 lă 종 tsŏng	**主** the principal 님 nīm 군 koōn 쥬 tsyoō	**門** door" district 오 ŏ 대 t'hāi 문 moōn	**田** field" 받 pāt 뎐 tyōn	**池** pool" 못 mŏt 디 tī	**野** desert" district 들 toŏr 야 yā
禹 (marked) Yu's 님 nīm 군 koōn 우 oō	**秦** (were the effect of) Tsin's 진 tsīn 국 kŏok 진 tsīn	**恒** is the everduring 샹 syāng 녜 ney 항 hāng	**云** is the "speaking 니 nī 놀 năr 운 oōn	**紫** and the redearth 블 poŏr 글 koŏr 즈 tsă	**赤** and the carnation 블 poŏr 글 koŏr 적 tsyŏk	**碣** and the "rocky 돌 tŏr 갈 kār	**洞** and the "cavern 골 kŏr 동 tŏng
跡 foot steps 자 tsā 최 tshŏi 적 tsyŏk	**幷** associa-tions 아 ā 올 ŏr 병 pyŏng	**岱** Tae hill 뫼 mŏis 디 tāi	**亭** pavilion" 뎡 tyōng 즈 tsă 뎡 tyŏng	**塞** "obstruction country 마 mā 글 koŏr 식 sāik	**城** city," 잣 tsās 셩 syōng	**石** stone," 돌 tŏr 셕 syŏk	**庭** court" lake 블 ptoŏr 뎡 tyōng

	(and accor-ding as they have) urged 勸 권kwŏn 할hăr 권kwŏn	The rent (is paid) 稅 낙năk 세sĕy	I 我 나na 아ā	(You) begin 俶 비pī 릇lă 살săr 쇽syŏok	apply the mind 務 힘him 쓸psŏŏr 무mŏŏ	Put in order 治 다tā 사să 리rī 티thi	full of grottoes 巖 바pā 회hŏī 암ām	(in the prospect we see) the outstretched 曠 너nō 를rŏŏr 광kwāng
	and encouraged (the work) 賞 상syāng 할hăr 상syang	in ripe (corn) 熟 니nī 글kŏŏr 쇽syŏok	will plant 藝 시sī 믈măr 예ēy	to carry on (the work) 載 시sī 롤rār 지tsăī	to this (namely) 玆 이ī 즈tsă	the main thing 本 믿mit 본pŏn	and dells 峀 뫼mŏīs 부spoŏ 디tī 슈syŏo	and distant (hills) 遠 멀mōr 원wŏn
The 1000 char clas-sic	(will the officers be) degraded 黜 내năī 틸thīr 튤thyŏor	the tribute 貢 바pā 틸thīr 공kŏng	common millet 黍 기kī 장tsāng 셔syŏ	at the southern 南 앏ārp 남nām	sowing 稼 곡kŏk 식sik 시sī 믈mŏŏr 가kā	in attending to 於 늘nŏor 어ŏ	and sombre 杳 마mā 득tăk 할hăr 묘myŏ	connected in a chain 緜 소sŏ 옵ŏŏp 면myŏn
117	or elevated 陟 오ŏ 롤răr 텩thyŏk	in new (grain) 新 새săī 시sī	and Barbarians millet 稷 피phī 직tsik	acre 畝 이ī 럼rŏm 묘myŏ	and in-gathering 穡 곡kŏk 식sik 거kŏ 둘tŏŏr 석săĭk	husbandry 農 녀nyŏ 름rŏŏm 지tsī 을ŏŏr 롱lŏng	and dark waters 冥 아ā 득tăk 할hăr 명myŏng	remote space 邈 멀mŏr 막măk

and encourage	Hand down to posterity	inspect	Listen to	being laborious	they were near	the historian	The philosopher Măng
勉 힘 hĭm 쓸 psoor 면 myŏn	貽 줄 tsŏŏr 이 i	鑑 거 kō 울 moŏr 감 kām	聆 드 toŏ 를 răr 령 lyōng	勞 잇 īs 슬 smoŏr 로 roŏ	庶 물 moŏr 셔 syō	史 ᄉᆞ să 긔 kwi ᄉᆞ să	孟 맛 măt 맹 măng
them	your	the countenance	sounds	humble	within an ace of	Yu	Ko
其 그 koŏ 기 kī	厥 그 koŏ 궐 kwŏr	貌 양 yāng ᄌᆞᆺ tsăt 모 mŏ	音 소 sŏ 리 lăī 음 ŏŏm	謙 겸 kyōm 손 sŏn 겸 skyōm	幾 거 kō 의 oŏī 긔 kwi	魚 고 kŏ 기 kī 어 ō	軻 술 soŏr 위 oŏī 가 kā
respect	excellent	and distinguish	and examine	careful	the due medium	grasped firmly	was liberal (in his attention)
祗 공 kong 경 kyong 지 tsī	嘉 아 ā 름 lăm 다 tā 올 ŏr 가 kā	辨 골 kar 힐 hăir 변 pyŏn	察 ᄉᆞᆯ săr 필 phīr 찰 tshār	謹 삼 sām 갈 kăr 근 koŏn	中 가 kā 온 ŏn 대 tāī 듕 tyŏong	秉 자 tsā 불 poŏr 병 pyōng	敦 두 toŏ 터 thō 울 oŏr 돈 tŏn
planting	plans	colours	principles	and correct	and the common rule	uprightness	to his original duties
植 심 tsī 물 moŏr 식 sīk	猷 ᄭᅬ skăi 유 yoŏ	色 빗 pīs 색 săik	理 더 tō ᄉᆞ să 릴 rīr 리 lī	勅 셩 tsyōng 히 hī 골 hăr 틱 t'hik	庸 샹 syāng 녜 nēy 용 yŏng	直 고 kŏ 돈 tăn 딕 tīk	素 힐 hīr 소 sŏ

The 1000 char classic.

118

sink deep 沉 드 tă 몰 măr 틈 thĭm	seek to 索 노 nŏ 삭 săk	and stripping off 解 고 koŏ 를 răr 히 hăi	Both the 两 두 toō 냥 nyāng	then to the woods 林 수 soō 플 phoŏr 림 lĭm	when on the verge 殆 바 pā 드 toŏ 라 ra 올 ŏr 틔 thăi	when favours 寵 괼 kŏir 툥 thyŏng	Examine 省 슬 săr 필 phīr 셩 syōng
in meditation 默 좀 tsăm 좀 tsăm 묵 moŏk	dwell in 居 살 sār 거 kō	their fringe of office 組 인 in 긴 kin 조 tsŏ	Drs. Soo 疏 소 sŏ 통 thŏng 홀 hăr 소 sŏ	and mounds 睪 두 toō 던 tŏn 고 kŏ	of disgrace 辱 욕 yŏk 홀 hăr 욕 yŏk	increase 增 더 tŏ 을 oŏr 증 tsoŏng	yourself 躬 몸 mŏm 궁 koong
in stillness 寂 괴 kŏi 오 ŏ 적 tsyŏk	a leisure 閑 겨 kyŏng 를 rā 한 hān	who could 誰 누 noō 구 koō 슈 syoō	observed 見 볼 poŏr 견 kyŏn	it will be fortunate 幸 힝 hăing 혀 hyō 힝 hăing	and near 近 갓 kās 사 sta 올 ŏr 근 koŏn	the elevation 抗 결 kyōr 울 oor 항 hang	with care 譏 긔 kwi 롱 long 긔 kwi
and solitude 寥 괴 kŏi 오 ŏ 료 lyŏ	place, 處 곧 kŏt 처 tshyŏ	push them out of place 逼 갓 khās 쉬 syoōi 믈 moŏr 핍 phip	the springs of action 機 틀 thoŏr 긔 kwi	to betake one's self 卽 즉 tsoŏk 재 tsē 즉 tsoŏk	to shame 恥 붓 poŏs 그 koŏ 리 rir 티 thi	may be too extreme 極 가 kă 재 tsăi 극 koŏk	and caution 誡 경 kyŏng 겟 keys 계 key

the trumpet 梧 머 mŏ 귀 kwī 모 mŏ	the Mespilus 枇 나 nā 모 mo 비 pī	in the garden 園 동 tŏng 산 sān 원 wŏn	In the pools 渠 몯 mŏt 거 kŏ	(when the prince) is vexed 慼 슬 sŏor 플 p'hŏŏr 쳑 tshyŏk	when (ministers) please 欣 깃 kīs 슬 skoor 흔 hŏŏn	in order to disperse 散 흗 hŏŏt 틀 thŏŏr 산 sān	Explore 求 구 koō 할 hăr 구 koō
flower tree 桐 머 mŏ 귀 kwī 동 tŏng	Japonica 杷 나 nā 모 mŏ 파 p'hā	the China grass 莽 플 phŏr 망 māng	the water lily 荷 련 nyŏn 하 hā	he dismisses them 謝 샤 syā 례 rēy 샤 syā	they are advanced 奏 솔 săr 올 oŏr 주 tsoō	anxious thoughts 慮 ㅅ sā 념 nyōm 녀 nyō	the ancients 古 데 tē 고 kŏ
is early 早 이 ī 놀 năr 조 tsŏ	is late 晩 느 nŏŏ 즐 tsŏŏr 만 mān	is drawn out 抽 쌔 spā 일 īr 튜 t'hyoō	drips 的 마 mā 잘 tsăr 뎍 tyōk	when delighted 歡 즐 tsoor 길 kīr 환 hwān	when involved 累 더 tŏ 러 rō 일 īr 류 lyōo	and promote ease 逍 노 nŏ 닐 nīr 쇼 syŏ	and search into 尋 츠 tshă 잘 tshăr 심 sim
in letting fall the leaf 彫 벼 pnyŏ 러 lō 딜 tīr 됴 tyŏ	in becoming green 翠 프 p'hoō 늘 noŏr 취 tshyoōi	in lengths, 條 올 ŏr 됴 tyŏ	and passes by 歷 디 tī 날 nār 력 lyŏk	he summons them 招 브 pŏŏ 를 rōŏr 툐 thyŏ	they are sent away 遣 보 pŏ 낼 nāir 견 kyŏn	and sauntering 遙 노 nŏ 닐 nīr 요 yŏ	deliberations 論 의 wī 논 nŏn 논 nŏn

	since there is what belongs 屬 브 poō 틀 thūr 속 syŏk	Even in easy 易 밧 pās 굴 kŏr 역 ŏk	and when he rested 寓 브 poō 틀 thūr 우 oō	There was one excessively fond 耽 즐 tsoōr 길 kūr 탐 thām	(when it mounts) is frozen 凌 모 mŏ 롤 răr 릉 loōng	The rambling 遊 노 nŏ 늘 nīr 유 yoō	the falling 落 덜 tir 낙 nāk	when the spreading 陳 무 moō 글 koŏr 딘 tin
	to the ear 耳 귀 koōi 이 ī	and light circumstances 輶 가 kā 비 pāi 야 kya 올 ŏr 유 yoō	his eyes (on books) 目 눈 noōn 목 mŏk	of reading 讀 닑 nīr 글 koŏr 독 tŏk	and rubs against 摩 문 mān 질 tsir 마 mā	albitross 鯤 새 sai 곤 kŏn	leaf 葉 닙 nip 엽 yŏp	roots 根 불 poŏr 휘 hoōi 근 koōn
The 1000 char. classic	even without fences 垣 담 tām 원 wŏn	we should have that which 攸 바 pā 유 yoō	he sacked 囊 드 tă 못 măs 낭 nāng	so that he played on it 翫 구 koō 경 kyŏng 완 wān	the red 絳 불 poŏr 글 koŏr 강 kāng	alone 獨 홀 hoŏr 독 tŏk	floats lightly 飄 부 poō 칠 tshūr 표 phyŏ	are bent down 委 브 pă 릴 rīr 위 oōi
119	and walls, 牆 담 tām 장 tsyāng	we may dread 畏 저 tsyŏ 홀 hoor 외 ŏi	and bagged them. 箱 상 syāng 자 tsā 상 syāng	in the market place 市 저 tsyŏ 제 tsē 시 sī	vault of heaven 霄 하 hā 날 năr 쇼 syŏ	sailing (about the ocean) 運 옴 ŏm 길 kūr 운 oōn	in the wind 颻 부 poō 칠 tshūr 요 yŏ	and obscured 翳 가 ka 릴 rīr 예 ēy

朝鮮千字文

and wait 侍 뫼 mŏi 실 sĭr 시 sī	wives and concubines 妾 쳡 tshyŏp 쳡 tshyŏp	and between old 老 늘 nŏor 글 koŏr 로 lŏ	Even among relatives 親 친 tshin 할 hăr 친 tshĭn	but the hungry 饑 주 tsoō 릴 rĭr 긔 kwī	He that is fed to the full 飽 비 păĭ 브 pŏo 를 răr 포 phŏ	then you may suit 適 마 mā 즐 tsăr 뎍 tyŏk	Carefully provide 具 가 kă 졸 tsăr 구 koō
napkin in hand 巾 수 syeō 건 kōn 건 kōn	should attend to 御 뫼 mŏi 실 sir 어 ŏ	and young people 少 져 tsyŏ 믈 mŏŏr 쇼 syŏ	and connections 戚 아 ā 흠 ăm 쳑 tshyŏk	will be satisfied with 厭 슬 sŏŏr 흘 hăr 염 yŏm	will loathe 飫 슬 sŏŏr 뮐 wăr 어 ŏ	your palate 口 입 ip 구 koō	food 膳 차 tshă 반 pān 션 syŏn
in the curtained 帷 댱 tyāng 유 yoō	spinning 績 질 tsĭr 삼 sām 뎍 tsyŏk	make some difference 異 다 tă 룰 răr 이 ī	(think of) friends 故 놀 năr 글 koŏr 고 kŏ	grains 糟 지 tsăi 강 kāng 조 tsŏ	roast meat 烹 술 săr 믈 măr 팽 phăng	and fill 充 촐 tshar 츙 tshyoōng	for a meal's 飡 밥 pāp 손 sŏn
chamber 房 방 pāng 방 pāng	and making thread, 紡 질 tshĭr 삼 sām 방 pāng	in their provisions 糧 냥 nyāng 식 sik 냥 nyāng	and former acquaintances, 舊 뎨 tey 구 koō	and chaff. 糠 겨 kyō 강 kāng	and slaughtered oxen, 宰 버 pō 힐 hĭr 재 tsăī	your belly 腸 애 āi 댱 tāng	meat, 飯 밥 pāp 반 pān

The 1000 char. clas-sic.

	we are pleased 悅 깃 kĭs 슬 skŏŏr 열 yŏr	stretching out 矯 들 tŏŏr 교 kyŏ	we receive 接 브 pŏŏ 를 rŏŏr 졉 tshyŏp	with stringed instruments 絃 시 sĭ 울 ŏŏr 현 hyŏn	on the blue 藍 족 tsŏk 남 nām	In the day-time 晝 낫 nās 듀 tyŏŏ	like the silver 銀 은 ŏŏn 은 ŏŏn	with silken 紈 깁 kīp 환 hwān
	and delighted 豫 즐 tsŏŏr 길 kĭr 예 ēy	the hands 手 손 sŏn 슈 tsyŏŏ	the cups 杯 잔 tsān 빈 pāĭ	and songs 歌 놀 nŏr 애 āĭ 가 kā	mats 筍 듀 tyŏŏ 슌 syŏŏn	we recline 眠 조 tsŏ 올 ăr 면 myŏn	candle (moon) 燭 쵸 tsnyŏ 쵹 tshyŏk	fans 扇 부 pŏŏ 체 tshē 션 syŏn
	and also 且 또 stŏ 차 tshyā	and bending 頓 구 kŏŏ 를 rŏŏr 돈 tŏn	and raise 擧 들 tŏŏr 거 kŏ	with wine 酒 술 kŏŏr 쥬 tsyŏŏ	and ivory 象 고 kŏ 키 khĭr 리 rĭ 샹 syāng	and in the evening 夕 나 nā 조 tsŏ 셕 syŏk	splendid 煒 빗 pĭs 날 nār 위 ŏŏĭ	round 圓 두 tŏŏ 원 wŏn
120	at ease 康 편 phyŏn 안 ān 강 kāng	the feet 足 발 pār 족 syŏk	the bowls 觴 잔 tsān 샹 syāng	and entertainments 讌 이 ī 바 pā 지 tsī 연 yŏn	bedsteads; 床 상 sāng 상 sang	slumber, 寐 잘 tsār 미 maī	and luminous. 煌 빗 pĭs 황 hwāng	and clean, 潔 조 tsŏ 할 hăr 결 kyŏr

and when we get hold of	when our bones	and in favours	In epistles	with dread	then bowing down	(presenting the spring) Sacrifice	The son of the principal wife
執	骸	顧	牋	悚	稽	祭	嫡
자 tsa 블 pǎr 집 tsip	뼈 spyo 히 hǎi	돌 tör 볼 poǒr 고 kǒ	죠 tsyǒ 히 hǎi 젼 tsyon	두 toō 릴 rīr 송 sǒng	조 tsǒ 을 ǎr 계 kěy	졔 tsěy ᄉᆞ sǎ 졔 tsěy	뎍 tyǒk 실 sīr 뎍 tyǒk
any thing hot	are scurfy	and replies	and letters	and awe	his forehead	(the summer) offering	after one's demise
熱	垢	答	牒	懼	顙	祀	後
더 tō 올 oōr 열 yōr	때 ptǎi 구 koō	디 tǎi 답 tāp 답 tāp	글 koǒr 월 wōr 졉 tsyōp	두 toō 릴 rīr 구 koō	니 nī 마 mā 상 syang	졔 tsěy ᄉᆞ sǎ ᄉᆞ sà	뒤 toōi 후 hoō
we wish for	we think of	we should use judgment	we should be concise	fear	he repeatedly	(the autumn) stew	inherits the property
願	想	審	簡	恐	再	烝	嗣
원 wǒn 할 hǒr 원 wǒn	ᄉᆞ soō 칠 tshīr 샹 syāng	살 sǎr 필 p'hīr 심 sīm	갈 kār 략 lyāk 간 kān	저 tsǒ 홀 hoǒr 공 kǒng	두 toō 지 tsāi	찔 ptīr 증 tsoǒng	니 nī 을 oǒr ᄉᆞ sǎ
cold water	bathing	and accuracy	and weighty	and trepidation	makes obeisance	(and the winter) tasting	and connects the succession,
凉	浴	詳	要	惶	拜	嘗	續
서 sǒ 늘 noǒr 량 lyāng	약 yāk 마 māk 약 yāk	ᄌᆞ tsā 셰 sěy 샹 syāng	중 tsoǒng 요 yǒ 요 yǒ	저 tsǒ 홀 hoǒr 황 hwāng	절 tsǒr 비 pǎi	맛 mās 볼 poǒr 샹 syāng	나 nǎ 을 ǎr 쇽 syǒk

The 1000 char. classic.

one Kin 鈞 므 moŏ 거 kō 울 oŏr 균 kyoŏn	Mr. Théen 恬 안 ān 졍 tsyōng 텸 thĭm	the musician Khe 嵇 헤 hăi 가 kā 헤 hăi	The general Poo 布 뵈 pŏi 포 p'hŏ	catch 捕 잡 tsā 볼 poŏr 포 phŏ	Punish 誅 버 pō 힐 hĭr 듀 tyoŏ	when frightened 駭 놀 nŏr 랄 rār 해 hăi	Asses 驢 나 nā 귀 kwi 려 lyō
was clever as a carpenter 巧 공 kōng 교 kyŏ 교 kyŏ	invented the pencil 筆 붓 poŏt 필 phĭr	for playing on the harp, 琴 거 kō 문 moŏn 고 kŏ 금 koŏm	was famous for archery, 射 쏠 psŏr 샤 syā	and apprehend 獲 어 ō 들 toŏr 획 hwik	and behead 斬 버 pō 힐 hĭr 참 tshām	dance about 躍 뛸 ptoŏr 약 yāk	and mules 騾 로 rō 새 sāi 라 lā
and square Jin 任 맛 mās 들 toŏr 임 ĭm	and Mr. Lun 倫 몰 moŏr 륜 lyoŏn	and the piper Yuen 阮 완 wan 가 kā 완 wān	the wrestler Leaou 遼 멀 mŏr 료 lyŏ	rebels 叛 배 păi 반 pān 반 pān	thieves 賊 도 tŏ 조 tsŏ 적 tsŏk	leap 超 뛸 ptoŏr 툐 t'hyŏ	calves 犢 쇠 syŏi 야 yā 지 tsi 독 tŏk
was a good angler, 釣 랏 las 실 skăr 됴 tyŏ	paper, 紙 죠 tsyŏ 희 hăi 지 tsi	for blowing the flute 嘯 프 phă 람 lām 쇼 syŏ	for tossing up balls 丸 탄 t'hăn 자 tsă 환 hwān	and deserters, 亡 업 ŏp 슬 soŏr 망 māng	and robbers, 盜 도 tŏ 적 tsăr 도 tŏ	and run. 驤 달 tăr 일 ĭr 양 yāng	and cows. 特 쇼 syŏ 특 thŏk

shew the waning 晦 그koŏ 뭄meom 회hoöi	The quadrants 璇 구koŏ 술soor 션syōn	while the light 曦 희hāis 수kwī 휘hwī	The years 年 희hăī 년nyŏn	they worked up 工 바pá 치tshī 공kŏng	Mrs. Mo 毛 터t'hō 럭lōk 모mŏ	were together 並 골kăr- 올ŏr 병pyōng	(These eight persons in) unravelling 釋 그koŏ 롤răr 셕syŏk
and waxing of the moon 魄 딕tīk 빅păĭk	and astronomical instruments 璣 구koō 술soŏr 긔kwī	glare the sun 暉 힛hāĭs 귀kwī 휘hoōī	like arrows (fly away 矢 살sār 시sī	their smiles 嚬 빙psĭng 길kwĭr 빔pīm	and Mrs. She 施 베pé 풀phoŏr 시sī	all 皆 다tā 개kăĭ	difficulties 紛 어ō 조tsoŏ 리li 울ōor 분poon
with their revolutions 環 골kōr 회hōĭ 환hwān	suspended 懸 돌tăr 현hyōn	is bright 朗 볼păr 골kăr 랑ring	every one 每 미măĭ 양yāng 미măĭ	and made pretty 姸 고kŏ 올ăr 연yōn	were cleanly 淑 몰măr 굴koŏr 슉syoōk	excellent 佳 아ā 름lăm 다tă 올oŏr 가kā	and in benefiting 利 니nī 홀hăr 리ri
and reflection 照 비pī 췰tshwĭr 죠tsyŏ	and revolving 斡 돌tŏr 알ār	and shining 曜 비pī 췰tshwĭr 요yŏ	pressing on after the other, 催 뵈pŏĭ 알ār 죄tsŏī	their laugh, 笑 우oŏ 움ōom 쇼syŏ	and handsome 姿 잉ĭng 즈tsă 즈tsă	and wonderful 妙 묘myŏ 홀hăr 묘myŏ	the manners of the age 俗 풍phoong 쇽syŏk 쇽syŏk

The 1000 char. clas-sic.

122

even the stupid	Being destitute	and walking backwards	they should bind on	and in looking down	Courtiers should square	eternal	Point to (virtue)
愚 어 ō 릴 rīr 우 oō	孤 외 ŏī 로 rŏ 을 ŭr 교 kŏ	徘 머 mō 몰 moŏr 비 pī	束 뭇 moŏs 셜 skoŏr 속 sŏk	俯 구 koō 볼 poŏr 부 poŏ	矩 모 mŏ 날 nār 구 koō	永 긘 kīn 영 yŏng	指 ᄀ kă ᄅ rā 칠 tshĭr 지 tsī
and dull	and vulgar	and forwards	their girdles	or looking up	their steps	tranquility	as the fuel (is supplied to the fire)
蒙 니 nĭr 불 poŏr 몽 mŏng	陋 더 tŏ 더 tŏ 움 oōm 루 loō	徊 머 mō 몰 moŏr 회 hŏī	帶 씌 stwi 디 tăi	仰 울 ŏor 얼 ŏr 앙 ăng	步 거 kŏ 름 room 보 pŏ	綏 편 p'hyŏn 안 ăn 유 yoō	薪 셥 tsŏm 신 sīn
&c.	and of small	they should look up	with reverence	think of the chambers	and stretch forth	and good luck	and cultivate
等 골 kăr 올 ŏr 등 toŏng	寡 쟈 tsyā 쿨 koŏr 과 kwā	瞻 볼 pŏr 쳠 tshyŏm	矜 쟈 tsyā 랑 lyāng 긍 koŏng	廊 힝 hăing 낭 năng 낭 năng	引 혈 hyŏr 인 in	吉 길 kĭr 홀 hăr 길 kĭr	脩 닷 tăs 셜 skăr 슈 syoŏ
will censure me.	information.	and look out	and sedateness,	and the temple	their necks,	should be the end of exertions.	happiness
誚 구 koō 지 tsī 즐 tsăr 초 ts'hyŏ	聞 도 toŏ 롤 roŏr 문 moŏn	眺 볼 pŏr 됴 tyŏ	莊 츰 tshăm 될 twĭr 장 tsăng	廟 종 tsŏng 묘 myŏ 묘 myŏ	領 녕 nyŏng 향 t'hyăng	邵 노 nŏ 폴 p'hăr 쇼 tsyŏ	祜 복 pŏk 우 oŏ

In uttering	謂	니 nī ᄂᆞᆯ năr 위 oōī
words	語	말 măr ᄉᆞᆷ săm 어 ō
helps	助	ᄃᆞ tă ᄋᆞᆯ ăr 조 tsŏ
and such like	者	놈 nōm 쟈 tsyā
we may use "how"	焉	입 īp 계 kēy 언 ōn
"indeed"	哉	입 īp 계 kēy 재 tsāī
"Is it so?"	乎	온 ŏn 호 hoŏ
and "yes."	也	입 īp 계 kēy 야 yā

全本漢字依部目録第一 二数目乃遞 頁行数

一部

一 自 般 様 定 ○二 丁
欞 ○七 皇 月 夕 ○三 皇 月
瞧 韓 升 青 ○上 弦 営 建 宴 盤 宴
○下 弦 人 盤 帯 ○丙 ○丑
時 ○不 實 可 幸 ○丈 ○且 苟
○丘 ○世 ○丞 相 ○並

全本字依部目録 一丨丶丿

亅部

了 鬐 ○中 伏 資 今 媒 宴 嵐 ○事

講 款 通 錄 ○串

丶部

丸 鉄 ○月 黄 楓 壯 仙 ○主 公

人 專

丿部

之 鑽 盡 鑽 ○乃 ○乂 ○及 ○久

○乏 ○乘

乙部

乙 ○九 ○乞 ○也 ○乳

○乾 ○亂

二部

二 ○云 ○井

亠部

漢字依部目錄 乙二亠人

亠 ○交 ○亦 ○亥時

○京 ○享宴 ○亭

人部

人 耆老 定 倫 品 常 才 指揮 主

證 參 ○仁 ○介紹 幾 ○仇 ○

今 年 月 日 夕 昨 即 ○付 當 分 言語 ○仕

○令 守 傳 號 ○他 款 交 ○仙 人

神 鳳 ○以 ○任 意 ○企 ○

伊 ○伏 初 兵 ○件 記 ○仰

伐 ○何 時 如 處

以 幾 ○佩 ○似 ○位 方 ○作

○但 ○伯 ○修 ○俗

○伸 ○佐 ○佛 ○來 年 月 員 將 原 ○

使 全 府 御 勅 信 酒 ○舍 廊 ○命

○依 稀 然 ○供 ○佳 ○侍

○俙 依 ○俄 ○便 ○俎 ○侮 ○促

傕 ○ 倫 ○ 信 ○ 使 標 听 ○ 俟

語 ○ 俊 ○ 俠 ○ 侵 ○ 保 ○ 候 時 ○ 倨

慢 ○ 俯 ○ 倒 絶 懸 ○ 倉 船

許 辛 ○ 借 ○ 倍 ○ 倣 ○ 傀 假 托 ○

健 ○ 偏 辟 ○ 偷 ○ 倚 ○ 偶 然 ○ 側 ○

偕 ○ 貪 ○ 傍 ○ 禽 ○ 僅 ○ 備 官 差

武 ○ 傘 雨 敉 ○ 傲 ○ 傳 ○ 停 止 ○ 傷

寒 ○ 傳 唱 令 ○ 傑 豪 ○ 傾 ○ 催

倢 ○ 債 ○ 偺 ○ 僧 僧 ○ 僕 ○ 儀

○ 僻 偏 ○ 儉 ○ 億 ○ 價 ○ 儒 ○ 償

○ 優

儿部

元 ○ 兄 弟 嫂 從弟 ○ 光 生 ○ 充

○ 兆 朕 ○ 先 ○ 兎 ○ 免 ○ 兒 孩 幼

○ 羗 ○ 競

入部

入 ○ 内 大 ○ 全 兪 然 ○ 兩

八部

八 貝 方 字 ○ 公 正 論

主 式 屬 然 ○ 六 月 貝 脯 ○ 共

○ 兵 起 伏 符 ○ 其 時 ○ 具

器 ○ 典 當 ○ 兼

冂部

冊 ○ 再 冒 ○ 冐 段

冖部 冠 鶤 冤 ○ 冪

冫部

冬 貫 冱 査 柏 ○ 冲 杜 況 ○ 決 斷

○ 冶 匠 ○ 冷 ○ 凈 ○ 凉 凄 ○ 凋

○ 凌 ○ 凍 ○ 凊 ○ 准 ○ 飡

○ 減 ○ 凘 ○ 凝 ○ 凜

几部 几 ○ 凡 ○ 凰

凵部

凶 牟 ○ 出 船 行 露 欄 歛 ○ 凸

○ 凹

刀部

刀 利 挾 研 ○ 刃 ○ 刈 ○ 分 付

執 揀 明 ○ 刑 獄 ○ 列 ○ 判 ○

利 興 ○ 別 差 幅 離 ○ 刻

墳 ○ 剎 寺 ○ 刷 推 羽 ○ 前 在 ○ 則

○ 刨 ○ 制 ○ 刺 ○ 剖 ○ 剛 ○ 剃 頭 ○

剪 ○ 副 ○ 劍 劈

力部

力 ○ 功 名 業 ○ 加 ○ 劣 ○ 劭

劤 ○ 助 ○ 勅 使 ○ 勇 ○ 勉 ○ 勤 鬚

勑 ○ 動 ○ 勒 ○ 勤 ○ 勞 ○ 勝

○ 勢 ○ 勸

勹部

勺 ○ 勿

匕部

化 ○ 比 ○ 北 嵐 南 狄 匙

力勹匕匚二十

匚部 巨 ○ 匝 ○ 匡 ○ 匠人 ○ 匣

○ 匪

匸部 區

十部

十 月 ○ 千 廚 鏡 花 ○ 午 端 時

飯 ○ 升 三升 ○ 平 明 地 太 生 ○

半 行 ○ 卓子 ○ 卒 倉 ○ 南 風 北 安

○ 率

劈 ○ 副 ○ 劍 竇

力部

力 ㅣ ○ 功 ㅣ 名 業 ○ 加 ○ 劣 ○ 劭

○ 助 ○ 勅 使 ○ 勇 ○ 勉 ○ 勤 鬚

抑 ○ 動 ㅣ ㅣ ○ 勤 ○ 勞 ㅣ ○ 勝

○ 勢 ○ 勸 ㅣ ㅣ

勹部

勺 ○ 勿 ㅣ

匕部

化 ○ 比 ○ 北 嵐 南 ㅣ 秋 匙

漢字依部目錄

匚部 巨 ○ 匝 ○ 匪 ○ 匠 人 鑄 ○ 匣

○ 匯

匸部 區

十部

十 月 ○ 千 眼 醫 鏡 葉花 ○ 午 端 時

賣 飯 ○ 升 三升 ○ 平 明 地 太 生 ○

半 行 ○ 卓 子 ○ 卒 倉 ○ 南 風 北 安

蠻 ○ 率

卜部

卜 音 物

卩部

卯 時 ○ 危 ○ 印 ○ 卵 ○ 巻 ○ 卽

日 質 今 敎 效 ○ 卿

厂部

厄 ○ 原 來 ○ 厚 ○ 厠 ○ 厨 ○ 厥

○ 厩 ○ 厭 ○ 厲 ○ 廳

厶部

去 年 月 ○ 參 皇 差

又部

又 ○ 叉夜 ○ 友朋 ○ 叔 母父 ○ 取

○ 受 ○ 叛 背 敗

口部

口 開 箇 銀魚 大魚 ○ 右 ○ 可

吉 惜 憐 不 ○ 史 ○ 司監 ○ 台 三星 貞 ○ 叮嚀

○ 古 蒙 道 薫 乾魚 ○ 叭 喇 ○ 叱 ○

名 白 貧 字 無 指 功 聾 宮 大 ○ 各 ○ 吏 書

漢字依部目錄

卄一張五行 ○后皇ㅣ卄張二行 ○吉說ㅣ二行 ○同年ㅣ十行 生 婿ㅣ十七張二行 謀

十三張 ○吊卄七張五行 ○吐卄六張五行 ○舌十八張 ○合卄七張ㅣ ○哭十八張 ○呑

卄九張二行 ○呂十二張三行 ○吮卄九張二行 ○君卄七張二行 指子卄九張五行 大卄八張 ○向卄七張三行 ○

告卄八張六行 ○吹卄九張 螺十九張 ○呈卄七張 ○含卄八張 ○谷三行 ○吝

卄八張 ○吸呼ㅣ二行 ○否可ㅣ二行 ○味十行 ○和ㅣ二行 瞳ㅣ

十三行 親ㅣ會ㅣ二行 ○咄卄八張 ○呼卄八張 吸ㅣ二行 ○吟卄八張 ○咐囑ㅣ二行

○周卄九張 牟ㅣ二行 旋ㅣ十行 ○咂口卄七張 ○吳卄九張 ○尚

索ㅣ二行 ○呵欠ㅣ二行 ○咽喉ㅣ 塞ㅣ二行 ○品ㅣ二行 人ㅣ二行 ○哭ㅣ五行

唇 鈌 啄 ○ 唐 ○ 問 ○ 嚳 情 ○ 商

嗇 舶 ○ 噐 輪 ○ 啟 闡 ○ 唱 ○ 喉

喟 乾 ○ 善 ○ 喜 ○ 唱 傳 ○ 唾 ○

喧 ○ 喇 叭 ○ 喘 ○ 噬 嘔 ○ 喪 祭 ○ 嗆 ○

○ 啞 ○ 嗜 ○ 單 子 衣 囊 花 ○ 嗅 ○

嗣 ○ 嘔 噬 ○ 器 軍 樂 具 ○ 嚮 着 ○

鳴 自鳴鐘 ○ 噴 ○ 嘲 弄 ○ 嘗 ○ 嘶 ○

嘴 ○ 嘯 洞 ○ 噬 ○ 噪 ○ 嚇 ○ 囈 ○

嚬 빈 〇 嚴 엄 ㅣ 肅 〇 囊 낭 〇 囑

口部

四 사 自 面 盤 囚 〇 回 〇 因 ㅣ

〇 困 ㅣ 〇 固 執 〇 國 ㅣ 貴 〇 園

ㅣ 〇 圓 ㅣ 圍 〇 圖 書 地 ㅣ 謀 〇 團

ㅣ 領

土部

土 ㅣ 〇 切 ㅣ 迫 〇 地 ㅣ 理 平 ㅣ 衣 圖 〇

在 前 ○ 寺 剎 ○ 坑 ○ 均 ○ 坎 ○ 坐

丨 ○ 城 郭 ○ 垢 丨 鉎 ○ 垂 丨 ○

垣 ○ 埋 ○ 堅 丨 ○ 埃 塵 ○ 培 ○ 執

丨 固 丨 分 政 ○ 堗 ○ 堂 上官 嗣 ○ 基

丨 ○ 堤 ○ 塗 滌 ○ 塊 ○ 堪 填 ○

堞 ○ 堠 ○ 塔 ○ 塲 牧 戰 ○ 報 丨

丨 儺 ○ 塞 豎 ○ 塵 埃 境 ○ 墨 水 ○ 墓

丨 ○ 增 ○ 墩 ○ 墳 ○ 壓 車 ○ 壁 丨

總 四十張一以下 ○ 墻 卅二張十行 一 卅張三行 ○ 壁 廿三張 ○ 壇 卅一張二行

士部

士 以下 卅四張 隱烈 一以下 五行 道 以下 ○ 壬 三張一行 ○ 壯 卅三張 ○ 壹 卅四張

嘉 卅四張 ○ 壽 卅 行

夂部

夆 卅四張 二行

夊部

夏 三張 一 卅一張一行 一 卅一張三行

夕部

夕 七十張二行 御除七 一 三行 陽 五張 昨 今十行 飯 以下 ○ 外 十 一 卅一張五行 罔 十 方 三行 慮

夘 四十張二行 ○ 多 三十張 一 以下 幸 十一張二行 ○ 夙 卅一張行 ○ 夜 以下 十一張 月 達 五張 二行 又 卅一張三行 ○ 夢

○影

大部

大 內 君 紅 船 白魚 張

○天 文 ○夫 婦 妹 樵 工 ○夭 ○

太 息 字 辛 過 ○失 音 ○奉

○奄 ○奔走 ○奇特 ○奕 ○契書 ○

奏 ○泰 ○ ○莫 ○奢 ○奧 奪

夊部

女 織 貞 息 烈 處 男 ○ 奴 ○ 好 樣

○ 如 倘 ○ 妄 發 ○ 奸 擲 ○ 妙

理 ○ 姍 ○ 姓 字 ○ 妓 女 ○ 姤

○ 姊 妹 ○ 妹 姊 ○ 姑 ○ 妯 娌

○ 妻 ○ 妾 ○ 始 ○ 妻 知 ○

妣 祖 ○ 姻 婚 ○ 姪 女 ○ 姿 ○ 姦 ○

娘 ○ 娌 妯 ○ 娶 婚 ○ 婦 夫 ○ 婚

家 娶 姻 ○ 婆 牙 ○ 婢 ○ 娼 ○ 嫡 室

女子

○媒中○婿同○媪○嫌○嫁○嫂

兄弟○嫺○嬌

子部

子時養孳孝戲章板大世閑單彈

膩靴帽矮縫柑柚葉許箱鎖簇灑

鐘剪艘轎松楂蕈○孔鼻無

雀○孕○字八二○存○孝

字○孤○孟○孩○孫曾○孰

十四張 二行 ○學 十二張 文 十三張 二行 ○孼 子 十二張 三行

宀部

安 十一張 一 十二張 二行 南 十五張 二行 未 十二張 ○守 十六張 一 十三張 三行 令 十五張 十行 ○宇 二張 三行 ○宅

十四張 二行 ○宋 十七張 ○定 十一張 二行 一 十二張 ○宗 十二張 水 四行 貢 廟 十五張 室 十六張 二行

○宙 二張 三行 ○官 十五張 一 十二張 十一行 同 一 十二張 職 十五張 一行 接慰 堂上 員 美備 軍 ○宜 十五張 一

十四張 十行 ○客 十七張 二行 ○宣 十四張 二行 ○室 後 十二張 十一行 嫡 十二張 三行 宮 十五張 五行 宗 十五張 二行 ○容 十四張 二行

○宮 十五張 一 十四張 十 室 闕 十五張 二行 ○密 十二張 四行 一 十六張 十 ○宰 十四張 十 相 十五張 五行 ○宴 進上

十五張 三行 ○寘 十四張 三行 十六張 二行 ○害 二十四張 三行 謀 十二張 十 ○家 十五張 一 十四張 十 貫 十六張 三行 婚 一 十二張

漢字依部目錄

[illegible] ○ 宿 ○ 寄 ○ 寅 ○ 寧 ○ 寂

寞 ○ 寃 ○ 寒 ○ 食 傷 ○ 富 ○

寓 ○ 寐 ○ 察 ○ 寬 ○ 寓 ○ 塞

咽 ○ 賓 ○ 寞寂 ○ 寥 ○ 寧 ○ 寡

審 ○ 實 確 不 梅 豫 ○ 寶

劍

寸部

寸 ○ 耐 ○ 專 主 ○ 冠 ○ 射

[illegible] ○ 封 [illegible] ○ 尋 [illegible] 常 [illegible] ○ 將 [illegible] 大

[illegible] 乘 來 [illegible] ○ 尊 [illegible] ○ 對 [illegible] 敵 [illegible]

小部

小 [illegible] 人 [illegible] 指 [illegible] 心 [illegible] 船 [illegible] 轎 [illegible] ○ 少 [illegible]

[illegible] ○ 尖 [illegible]

尸部

尸 [illegible] ○ 尺 [illegible] 銅 [illegible] ○ 尼 [illegible] ○ 尹 [illegible] ○ 尻 [illegible] ○ 尿

[illegible] 臭 [illegible] ○ 屎 [illegible] ○ 局 [illegible] ○ 尾 [illegible] ○ 居 [illegible] ○ 屈 [illegible] 窮

小尸山巛

音行 ○ 屛·㕀 ○ 屋·茅 ○ 屑 ○ 犀 ○ 屐

○ 履 ○ 層·檻 ○ 屬 公

山部

山 禿·麓 椒 獺·猪 暎花 ○ 岸 岱 ○ 岫 ○ 炭

幕 ○ 峯 ○ 峴 ○ 峨 ○ 崇·尙 ○ 崗 ○

崎·嶇 ○ 嵐 ○ 崑 ○ 嵇 琴 ○ 島 ○ 嶇·崎

○ 嶺 ○ 嶽 ○ 巖

巛部

川 椒 ○ 州

工部

工 雇 夫 沙 ○ 左 ○ 巧

○ 巫 ○ 差 別 參 錯

己部

己 貞 業 ○ 已 而 ○ 巳 時 貞

巾部

巾 頭 ○ 布 瀑 帛 潤 黑 ○ 市

人 直 ○ 帆 ○ 帒 ○ 帖 法 ○ 帝 皇

○ 帶 下 腰 海 肚 胸 ○ 師 鷹

○ 帷 ○ 帽 子 僧 ○ 帳 蚊 ○ 常

丨人 ○ 幅 ○ 帳 ○ 幕

干部

干 支 欄 射 ○ 平 ○ 年 當 明

今 去 朞 ○ 幸 丨 多 不 ○ 拜

丨

幺部

幻 術 ○ 幼 兒 ○ 幽 ○ 幾 丨

白 介 何

广部

床 丨 繩 ○ 庚 ○ 底 ○ 府 丨 ○ 店

○度 預 ○席 ○庫 ○庭 ○

唐 ○廊 ○舍 ○庶 ○蓆 ○庸 ○康 ○廉

○廣 織 魚 廟 宗 ○廢

廴部

廷 ○迫 逼 延 遷 ○建

廾部

弁 ○弄 嘲 談 戲 ○弊 端

弋部

式

弓部

弓 强 ○引 ○弟 ○弗 ○弱

○弟 兄 覺 ○弦 上下 ○强 盜 木

弓 愁 ○張 大 京 ○號 别 令 ○彈

子 ○彌 ○彎 路

彡部

形 ○修 理 ○彩色 文

○彫 ○影 日

彳部

役 畢 ○彼 ○往 ○律 ○待 接

○後 明日 堂 ○徐 ○徑路 ○徒 ○

徊 三十行 徘 三十一行 ○ 得 二十一行 一行 十一 ○ 從 兄弟 四十一行 容 四行 ○ 徘

三行 徊 三行 ○ 御 二十行 史 二十一 十一 ○ 徹 二十行 ○ 徵 推 三十行 ○ 德 二十行

十行 色 十一

心部

心 三十一行 十行 小 十一行 ○ 必 二十行 十一 ○ 志 十一行 十行 ○ 忌 十一行 日

十一 ○ 怯 十一 ○ 忘 十一 十一 ○ 忍 十一 發 十一行 強 十一 ○ 快 十一行 船

十一 爽 十一 二十行 ○ 念 十一 十行 ○ 忠 二十行 十一 怎 十行 ○ 忽 十行

十行 ○ 忿 十行 ○ 忿 十行 ○ 怪 十行 右 二十行 ○ 急 十一 風 雨 行 ○ 思 十行

丨 怊悵 ○ 性 丨 ○ 怒 ○ 恐 ○ 恭 ○

恬 ○ 恩 ○ 恰 ○ 息 氣 女 本 消 ○

恣 ○ 恕 ○ 恚 ○ 恨 ○ 悋 ○ 恍惚 然

○ 悶 ○ 悅 丨 ○ 悟 頹 ○ 悖 惡 ○ 悔

○ 悠悠 ○ 悉 ○ 悚 ○ 惟 丨 ○ 惜 可

○ 情 丨 間 ○ 悲 ○ 惠 ○ 悴 憔 ○ 惑

○ 惚恍 ○ 惻 ○ 悵 怊 ○ 惱 肉 ○ 惡 丨

姦 悖 ○ 意 丨 任 ○ 惹 ○ 感 外 ○

惻 ○ 惶 ○ 想 ○ 愚 ○ 慈 ○ 愎 ○

愛 ○ 愁 ○ 態 ○ 慎 ○ 慕 ○ 慰

接官 問官 ○ 憑 ○ 慷慨 ○ 慨慷 ○ 慇懃 ○ 憂

○ 慾 ○ 慢倨 ○ 慶 ○ 慽慽 ○ 感 ○ 慮

○ 慧 ○ 慣 ○ 懃懇 ○ 憔悴 ○ 憧憧 ○ 憎

○ 應 ○ 憐 ○ 懷 ○ 懸 板 倒

○ 懶 ○ 懼 ○ 戀

戈部

戈 ○ 戊 ○ 戌 時 ○ 成 ○ 我

○ 我 等 ○ 或 ○ 威 ○ 哉 ○

戚 親 ○ 戲 子 枝 弄 ○ 戰 場 桃 ○ 戴

戶部

戶 獵 ○ 房 艙 ○ 扉

○ 扇 ○ 扈 工 馬

手部

手 指 掌 背 腕 本 ○ 才 輕 馬 ○ 打 ○ 扣 ○ 托

假 ○ 抛 碇 ○ 技 雜 ○ 折 曲 ○ 抑 勒 ○

抖 ○ 扯 ○ 扶 ○ 抗 ○ 承 ○ 抵

○ 擑 見 ○ 抅 ○ 投 ○ 掛 指 ○ 拜

○ 抱 ○ 拂 ○ 抹 樓 ○ 拍 ○ 招 搽 ○

抽 ○ 拔 ○ 挑 戦 灯 ○ 梅 荷 ○ 拳

○ 拭 ○ 拾 ○ 持 ○ 拱 ○ 拿 ○

拯 ○ 掐 ○ 掛 長 ○ 揮 角 環 ○ 挾

扐 ○ 捕 ○ 捫 ○ 振 ○ 探 ○ 捧 ○

掠 ○ 授 ○ 掘 ○ 採 ○ 掩 ○ 掌 申

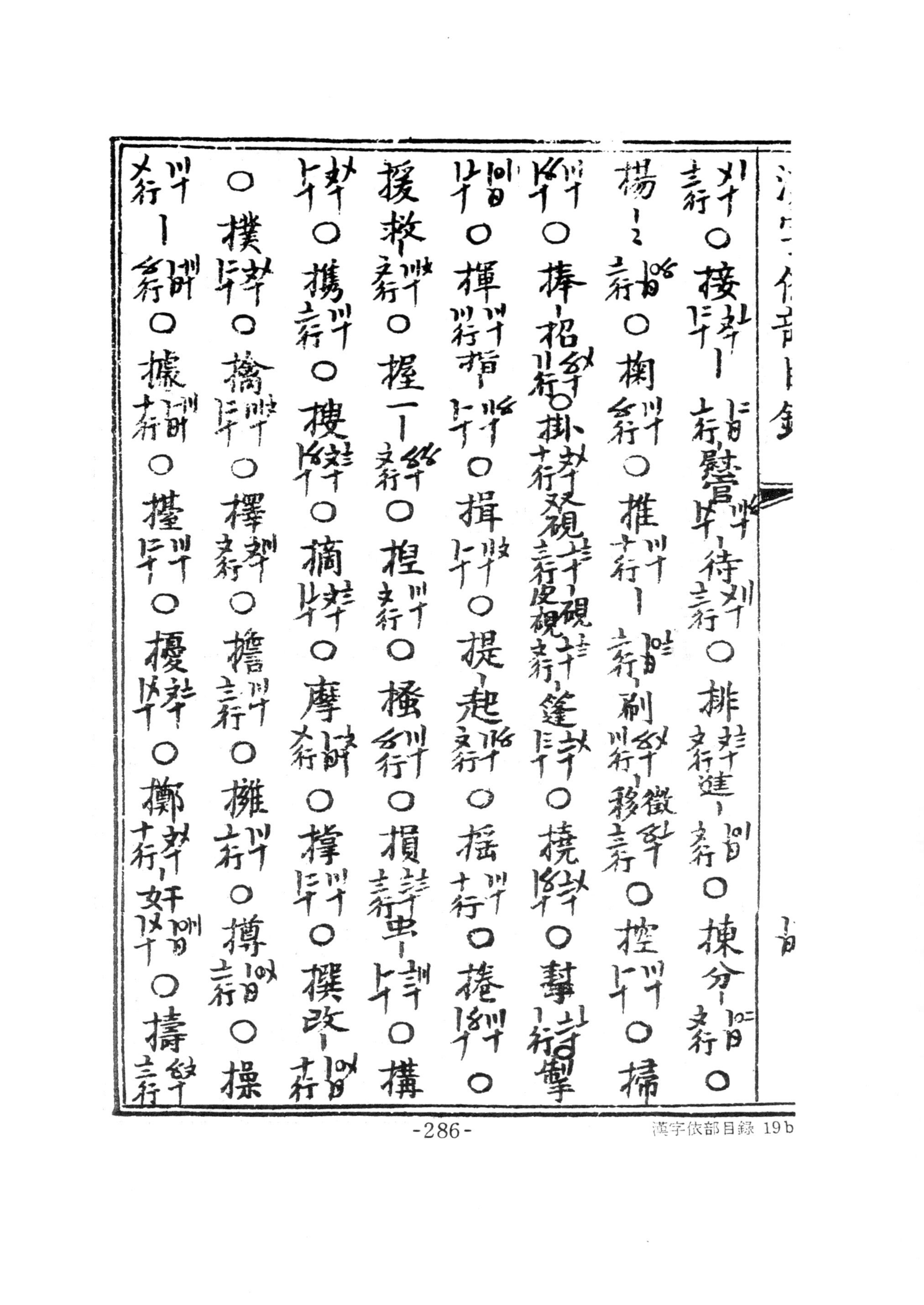

行 ○ 接 行 讋 待 行 ○ 排 行 進 行 ○ 揀 分 行 ○

揚 行 ○ 掬 行 ○ 推 行 刷 行 移 徵 行 ○ 控 ○ 掃

○ 捧 招 行 ○ 掛 行 覘 硯 行 覘 行 篷 ○ 撓 ○ 摯 行 擊

○ 揮 行 指 ○ 揖 ○ 提 起 行 ○ 搖 行 ○ 捲 ○

援 救 行 ○ 握 一 行 ○ 揑 行 ○ 搔 行 ○ 損 行 害 ○ 搆

○ 携 行 ○ 搜 ○ 摘 ○ 摩 行 ○ 撐 ○ 撰 改 行

○ 撲 ○ 擒 ○ 擇 行 ○ 擔 行 ○ 攤 行 ○ 撙 行 ○ 操

行 ○ 據 行 ○ 擡 ○ 擾 ○ 擲 行 奸 ○ 擣 行

○攀 ○攜 ○攔 ○攝 ○攫

支部

支 離 當

攴部

收 ○改 擾 ○攸 ○放 砲 ○

故 鄉 緣 ○政 ○效 他

卽 ○致 ○敏 ○教 ○救 援 病 ○

赦 ○敗 ○敢 ○散 ○敦 ○敬

○數 籌 ○敵 對 ○整 齊

文部

文 天 孝 諺 明 彩 ○ 斑

兩 駁

斗部

斗 水 鬱 ○ 斜 路 眼 斡

斤部

斤 ○ 所 館 ○ 欣 ○ 斧 鉞 ○ 斫 刀

○ 斬 ○ 新 ○ 斯 如 斷決

方部

方 四 外 邊 物 紬 席 位 張 ○ 於

ㅣ ○ 施 ○ 族 ㅣ 水 ㅣ ○ 旋 風 ㅣ 周 ㅣ ○ 旗

旡部

旣 ㅣ

日部

日 餂 暈 名 ㅣ 明 習 ㅣ 幾 終 ㅣ 影 記 忌 ㅣ 本 ㅣ 遮 ㅣ 傘

○ 旦 ○ 早 ㅣ 飯 ○ 旬 ○ 旱 ○ 明

ㅣ 年 ㅣ 白 ㅣ 舊 平 ㅣ 聰 ㅣ 發 ㅣ ㅣ 白 今 ㅣ ○ 昊

○ 易 ㅣ ㅣ ○ 昏 ○ 昔 ○ 昆

虫 ○ 是 ㅣ ㅣ ○ 映 ○ 昨 ㅣ 日 夕 ㅣ 今

行 ○星 三台 老人 織女 ○春 立 ○時 候 節

其 此 何 病 ○晋 ○晦 ○晝 ○晶

○景 ○暑 處 ○晩 ○智

○普 ○晴 ○晷 短 ○曉 ○暗 ○暄 和

○暎 花 ○暈 月 日 眩 船 ○暇 ○暉 ○

暴 風 ○暫 ○暮 ○曀 ○曆 書 ○曝 ○

曜 ○曦

曰部

日 ○曲 ○更 ○曳

○書 吏 簡 契 圖 曆 棄 鎮 ○曹 ○晝 ○最

○曾 ○會 和

月部

月 貢正 貢令 貢當 夜 風 ○有 福

○朋 友 ○青 ○服 飾 ○朔

○朗 ○望 顛 ○朞 年 ○期 ○朝

廷 鮮 ○滕 ○謄

木部

木　强　漱　麻　灰　綿　槌　樹　蘇　柴

○桊　手　刀　日　○末　伏　○未　時　牘

安　○朱　砂　紅　○朴　純　○朽　○朶　○杜

○条　約　○村　○材　○杞　○東

○杏　銀　○李　○杉　○杵　○杯

○杖　○柾　○枚　○松　魚　甕

○杷　鉄　○板　字　懸　船　字　○林

檎 ○杳 ○杖 ○枝 ○東風
西宮 ○相 宰 ○果 審 然
○枕 ○查蘡 ○其 ○枯 ○柑子 ○柚
○柿乾 ○柰 ○林 ○柄 ○枳 ○染
柔 ○架 ○柱 ○枇 ○柁 ○梆
梁 ○根 ○栽 ○核 ○栗黄 ○格
○桂 ○栢子 側冬 ○條 ○桓 ○
梳頭洗 箸貼 ○桁 ○柴扉 未 ○株 ○桃

胡樓 紅 黃 ○ 桑 ○ 梁鼻 ○ 案書 ○ 桐
梧 ○ 梅 寔 ○ 梟 示 ○ 梲 ○ 械 ○ 梧
桐 ○ 渠 ○ 梨 ○ 棱 ○ 桶 水 碁 ○ 梢
船 魚 尺 ○ 棺 ○ 棚 ○ 梯 ○ 椅 ○
椒 湖山 ○ 集 ○ 植 ○ 極 ○ 棠
○ 椎 ○ 棲 ○ 棕 ○ 楮 ○ 槐子 ○ 森
○ 椽 ○ 業 功 已 ○ 棨 ○ 楚 園
○ 楧 ○ 極 層 ○ 槐 ○ 楪 ○ 榆 ○ 楸

○椵 ○楓 丹 ○楂 ○棄 ○椸 ○樵

○椒 石 ○榛 ○椋 酒 ○槌 木 ○櫜 ○槎

○樹 木 ○槐 ○槿 花 ○榮

○榤 ○櫨 ○檣 ○標 信 ○樸 好

○樂 ○横 器 ○横 行 ○樓

○榊 林 ○鐘 ○機 ○會 ○縣 大 ○櫨

○檜 ○榛 ○樺 ○橘 柑 ○橡 寔 ○

○橙 丁 ○樵 夫 ○橋 ○檎 林 ○樻 ○檀

漢字依部目錄 木 欠 止

○檢 검 三行 ㅣ 上 ○ 檄 격 七行 ○ 檣 장 五行 ○ 檻 함 穽 정 五行 ○ 櫳 롱 五行 櫽 은 三行

○ 櫚 려 一行 ㅣ 棕 종 一行 ○ 櫛 즐 八行 ○ 櫓 로 六行 ○ 欄 란 四 ○ 櫻 앵 ㅣ 桃 도 一行 ○ 權 권 上

道 도 上 ○ 欞 령 窓 창 上

欠部

欠 呵 가 六行 ○ 次 차 十行 ㅣ 四 韻 운 四 路 로 宴 연 行 ○ 欲 욕 三行 ㅣ 上 ○ 欸 애 誠

上 ○ 歆 흠 六行 ○ 欺 기 八行 ○ 歌 가 上 ㅣ 二行 ○ 歎 탄 四 ○ 歛 렴 出 출 又行 歔 허 二

止部

止 지 上 ㅣ 六行 風 풍 十行 停 정 十行 ○ 正 정 十行 ㅣ 六行 月 월 三行 端 단 十行 公 공 五行 書

一行 ○ 此 ○ 時 ○ 步 ○ 行 ○ 武 ○ 備

○ 歲 ○ 歷 ○ 歸

歹部

死 ○ 殊 ○ 殘 ○ 風 ○ 恐

殳部

殳 ○ 段 ○ 縕 ○ 悄 ○ 閔 ○ 殺 ○ 殷

殿 ○ 毀

毋部

毋 ○ 祖父 ○ 叔 ○ 乳 ○ 每 ○ 毒 ○ 蛇

比部

比

毛部

毛 ○ 毬 ○ 氈 ○ 氊

氏部 氏 ○民 魚

气部 氣 瑞 息 絶

水部

水 路 鈴 臺 經 熟 銀 晶 風

斗 桶 獺 族 ○氷 ○永 ○求 ○

汀 ○汎 濫 ○江 湖 ○池 ○汐 ○汝

○汗 衫 ○沒 泪 ○汨 沒 ○汲

○沙 綱 瀰 工 汰 ○沐 浴 ○沉

香一行 ○ 汰沙一行 ○ 沐朧二行 ○ 泄漏夢一行 ○ 法十行一三行

帖三行 ○ 畓 ○ 泥海一頁 ○ 泗三行 ○ 油蠟十行衫

綠一 ○ 冷二行 ○ 泊漂一行 ○ 河一頁一行 ○ 一十行銀頁十行

○ 沛二行一 然 ○ 泉頁二行 ○ 泒頁 ○ 波頁二行 ○ 泡十頁十行 ○

注頁 ○ 治一三行 ○ 洪三行 魚三行 ○ 流二行 順 逆一 十頁十行 ○ 洞二頁三行

一 嘯 ○ 淵二頁 ○ 涜二行 梳 ○ 洛 ○ 津二頁 液二行

○ 滋二 二行 ○ 消二 一行 ○ 浮十頁 文行一 十行 ○ 涇十行 ○ 海頁三行一

行 帶 衣 參 棠花二行 ○ 涓三行 渴十行 息二行 ○ 浦文頁文行 漢

漢字之部目錄 水

녀行 ○ 涎 流ㅣ 니行 ○ 洛 낙沐ㅣ 쇠行 ○ 涯 生ㅣ 애 ○ 淙 ㅣㅣ 솜行 ○ 渠

렴 績ㅣ 림 ○ 淑 슉行 ○ 酒 쥬行 使酌ㅣ쇠 淸ㅣ 쇠 搾 쟈 ○ 淡 담ㅣ 담行

ㅣ 압行 薄 ○ 深 심行ㅣ 심行 ○ 添 텀行 ○ 清 청行ㅣ 酒 醬 쟝行 ○

渚 뎌 ○ 淺 쳔行 ○ 液 津ㅣ 익行 ○ 淚 루行 ○ 涕 鼻 뎨 ○ 渴 갈行 消ㅣ

온行 ○ 溫 온行ㅣ 井 졍 ○ 湯 탕行ㅣ 탕 ○ 淵 연行ㅣ 연行 ○ 渭

도行 ○ 渡 도 ○ 迷 미行 ○ 濩 漯 탕行 ○ 滚 ㅣㅣ 곤行 ○ 渢 ㅣㅣ 풍行 ○

湖 江ㅣ 호行 ○ 湧 용行 ○ 淫 음 ○ 淘 도 ○ 滛 亂 음 ○ 滅 멸ㅣ

ㅣ行 灯 ○ 渺 ㅣㅣ 묘行 ○ 溶 ㅣㅣ 용行 ○ 源 원行 ○ 溪 계ㅣ 계行 ○

滋十頁一行○滑八行○滓六行○滯遲二行○漢八行丨○南丨二行這那

溢十一頁二行○溺十一頁○澄二行○漆丨十行蠶三行塗○漏

十二頁罷六行十二頁落泄滲二行○滴十三頁硯十行○激丨太三行○漉

行○潤布一行○漂風泊一行漁六行翁六行船八行火十行○滲漏

行○漠三○漸三八行○潦十三頁一行○潺湲六行三二行○潰

十三頁一行○灘語一行○潔六行丨一行○潚八行○潛八行○潙泄六行

○潮十三頁八行○濟六行丨十行○潤丨迈八行○濁十三頁六行酒八行○澤

十三頁六行○潭十三頁三行○濫泥八行○濛三六行○海泥十三頁○瀑十三頁三行○

濵○濠○濕○灘○灑○灣

火部

火 藥 繩 鐵 漁○灰○炎○災○

炊○灸○炒○炬○烈 士 女 炭○烝

○烟 鑽○烏 銅○烙 鉄○倏○烹

○焄○焇 熖○烽 燧○焉○黒 麻布

○無○窩 盔 窮○然 迴 全 果

悅 自 鉄○爲○煑○焚

火瓜父爻片牙牛

○煙ㅣ竹연行 燻훈行 ○煎전行 酒子쟌 鉄잔行 ○煩번ㅣ번行 ○燁

엽 煌황 煌ㅣ황行 煇휘ㅣ휘 ○照죠ㅣ조 ○燧슈 烽ㅣ봉 ○燒쇼 ㅣ酒쇼行

○煖난 煖난行 ○熊웅行 ○煒위行 ○熄식行 ○熘류 熘ㅣ류行 ○熨울ㅣ울

탕 ○熄 熱열ㅣ열行 ○熱열 熄ㅣ열行 ○熟슉 ㅣ슉行 ㅣ水슉 鰻

탕 ○熏훈 迷ㅣ미行 ○燈등 行 ㅣ火 ㅣ挑도行 ○燕연行 ○燭쵹ㅣ쵹行

○臺대行 ○點뎜 ㅣ船뎜行 ○營영 經ㅣ영行 ○燦찬 ㅣ爛란行 ○爐로 煙ㅣ로行 ○

爛란行 燦찬ㅣ란行 ○爐로 行 神ㅣ로 風ㅣ로行 香ㅣ로行 水ㅣ로行 ○爨찬ㅣ찬

瓜部

瓜과行 ○爭쟁 ㅣ쟁行 ○爵쟉 ㅣ쟉行

父部 父 祖 爹 伯 叔

爻部 爻 爾

片部 片 ○ 牌 ○ 牋 ○ 牒

牙部 牙 婆

牛部

牛 牽星 ○ 牡丹 ○ 物 ○ 陽 礼 方 貨

○ 牧 塲 ○ 特 奇 ○ 犀 ○ 犂

○ 牽 牛星 ○ 犢

犬部

犯[illegible] ○ 狄北[illegible]十行 ○ 狃[illegible]行 ○ 狂[illegible] ○ 狐[illegible]行 ○ 狁[illegible] ○ 狗

[illegible] ○ 狠[illegible]行 藉[illegible] 狽[illegible] ○ 狽狼[illegible] ○ 狔[illegible] ○ 狹[illegible] ○ 狸

[illegible]行 ○ 猿[illegible]行 ○ 猪[illegible]山[illegible] ○ 猜[illegible]行 ○ 猛[illegible] ○ 猯[illegible]行 ○ 猫

[illegible] ○ 猥[illegible]行 ○ 獅[illegible]行 ○ 猶[illegible]行 豫[illegible]行 ○ 獐[illegible]行 ○ 獄刑

[illegible]行 ○ 獵[illegible]行[illegible] ○ 㺚子[illegible]行 ○ 獨[illegible]行 當[illegible]行 ○ 獸[illegible]行

[illegible] ○ 獺[illegible]行 ○ 獾[illegible]行

玉部

王 ○ 玉 ○ 珍 寶 珠 重

○ 玲瓏 ○ 玳瑁 ○ 珊瑚 ○ 琉球 璃 ○ 珠

璽 珍 ○ 璽 ○ 珥 ○ 球琉 ○ 理 瑪 修

調 妙 ○ 琥珀 ○ 瑙馬 ○ 瑁玳 ○ 瑞氣

祥 ○ 瑚珊 ○ 琴瑟 瑟 ○ 瑟琴

○ 琵琶 ○ 琶琵 ○ 瑪瑙 ○ 璃琉 ○ 環

指 ○ 璇 ○ 璣 ○ 璧 ○ 瓏玲

玄部

玄 ○ 玆 ○ 率

瓜部

瓜 ○ 瓠 ○ 瓢

瓦部

瓦 ○ 瓮 ○ 瓶 ○ 甓 ○ 甑

甘部

甘 醬 甚 ○ 甞

生部

生 同 儒 涯 銅 布 鰒 寄

光 平 疎 ○ 產 財 ○ 甦 ○ 甥 外

用部

用

田部

田 夫 ○由 ○申 時 甲 掌

○男 ○町 ○畢 ○畝 ○

畏 ○留 ○異 離 ○畢 役 ○富

○當 年 月 貨 付 典 初 的 支 獨 ○畫

○畫 貞 瓶 ○暢 ○疊 衣 席

疋部

疋 ○疏 ○疑

疒部

疥 ○ 病 疾 時 ○ 疾病 痢 ○ 瘧 ○ 痲

疹 痘 痳 ○ 疣 ○ 疸 黄 ○ 疿 ○ 痊 ○

痕 ○ 痛 頭 ○ 痢 疾 ○ 痘 疹 ○ 痣 ○ 痰

病 ○ 瘧 疾 ○ 瘡 ○ 瘐 ○ 癩 疾 ○ 瘰 癧

○ 癘 ○ 瘴 ○ 瘕 癡 ○ 癧 瘰 ○ 癢 ○ 癩

○ 癬

癶部

癸 ○ 祭 喪 ○ 登 ○ 發

皆 宴 明

白部

白　髮　鬠　蟣　鷺　馬　明　○百

濟　種　貝　○的　當　○皇　帝　后　○皎

○皓　○魄

皮部

皮　籠　韉　○皺　○皷　長

皿部

皿　○盆　花　○盃　○盒　有無　○盒

香　○蓋　之　○盛　○盜

強ㅣ ○監 ○盟 約 ○盐 ○盡 ㅣ ○

盤 ○盤罱 ○盪 ○盥 ○盬

目部

目 ㅣ 錄 ㅣ ○直 ㅣ 純 ○首

○眉 ○省 ○眞 ㅣ 旅 紅 ○眄

○眠 ㅣ ○眛 瞍 ○眩 暈 ○眼 膜 龍 ㅣ 廚

鏡 叔 ○眹 兆 ○睁 ○眺 ○睛 白 ○睦

ㅣ ○瞋 ○瞥 ○瞭 失 ○瞳 ○瞬 ○瞍

眛매평 ○ 瞻쳠평행 ○ 瞽고상 ○ 矌광거행

矛部

矜긍평행ㅣ근평행 ○ 務무거ㅣ모거행

矢部

矢시상ㅣ시평 ○ 知지평행ㅣ지거 ○ 矮와상 ○ 矩구상행 ○

短단상ㅣ단거 暑? ㅣ행 ○ 矮왜상 ○ 矯교상행

石部

石셕입ㅣ셕행ㅣ셕ㅣ셕입 怪괴거행 薄박입행 磬경거행 磁ㅣ자평행 魚어평행 花화평

筰작입 ○ 矼강평행 ○ 砂사평행 糖당평 硼붕평행 冬동평 ○ 斫작입행 ○ 砧침평

○ 砒비 礵상평행 ○ 破파거 船션평행 ○ 砲포 放방ㅣ거행 ○ 硫류 黃황평행 ○ 研연평

○硬 ○硯、滴 十行 掛、 三行 掛 行 ○碇 二行、纜 二行 ○硼、砂 行 ○

碓 行 ○碎 ○碑 ○碁 子、楠 假 行 ○磁、石

行 ○碣 ○磑 ○磧 三行 ○磵 ○確 寔 行 ○磬石

行 ○磨 ○磻 行 ○礎 行 ○礪 行 ○礫 三行 ○礬

行 ○礌砒 行

示部

示 十行 ○礼 行 ○社 稷 ○祀 十行 ○祈 行 雨 二行

○祜 行 ○祠堂 ○祗 ○神 行 精 行 主 仙 行 ○

石 示 内 禾

祖ㅣ父母 行 ○ 視 蔑 ○ 補 行 ○ 禍 ㅣ 行 ○ 祿 行 ㅣ

行 ○ 禀 行 ○ 福 ㅣ 行 有 行 ○ 禮 行 單 ○ 禪

内部

禹 行 ○ 禽 飛 行

禾部

禾 行 ○ 禿頭 行 ○ 私 ○ 秀 行 ○ 秉 行 ○ 秋 行 ㅣ 行

ㅣ夕 行 ○ 科 行 ○ 秦 行 ○ 秘 行 ○ 秩 行 ○ 移 ㅣ 行

稚 行 ○ 黍 行 ○ 稃 ○ 稅 行 ㅣ 行 ○ 稀 行 ○ 程

路 行 ○ 稱 行 ㅣ 行 ㅣ 自 行 ○ 稜 行 ○ 稚 ○ 種 ㅣ 行

百 ○穀 ○稷 ○稼 ○稻 ○積

穉 ○稽 ○穗 穡

穴部

穴 ○究 ○空 ○言 ○穽 檻 ○容

窺 從 ○窓 樓 ○窟 ○窖 ○窺 ○窮

屈 ○竈 ○竊

立部

立 ○春 ○站 ○竟 ○章 ○竭

端 正 弊 ○ 競

竹部

竹 煙 篩 花 ○ 竿 ○ 笏 ○ 笑

○ 笋 ○ 筐 ○ 符兵 作 ○ 筬 ○ 筍

○ 笛口 ○ 笳 ○ 笠簑 ○ 筥 ○ 箴 ○ 筐

○ 筏 ○ 答 ○ 筆 能 ○ 等

○ 第 ○ 筋 ○ 筈 ○ 筵 策 ○ 箏 ○

箕 箸 ○ 篇 ○ 箭葦 ○ 篙 ○ 箱 硯 子

行○節 時 簣傳 行○箕 行○筲 行 梳 行○筬

○簩 ○策 ○篤 ○簇子 ○籦 ○篩 行

行○篙 ○篷 掛 ○簡 書 行○蓑衣 ○簣

○簪 ○簷 行○簾 行 草 行○籔 ○簞 行○簽 行

○籌員 行 數 ○籍 文 行○籟 ○籠 行 皮 行○

籬

米部

米 行○粉 行 葛 行○粕 糟 行○粧 行○粳 行○

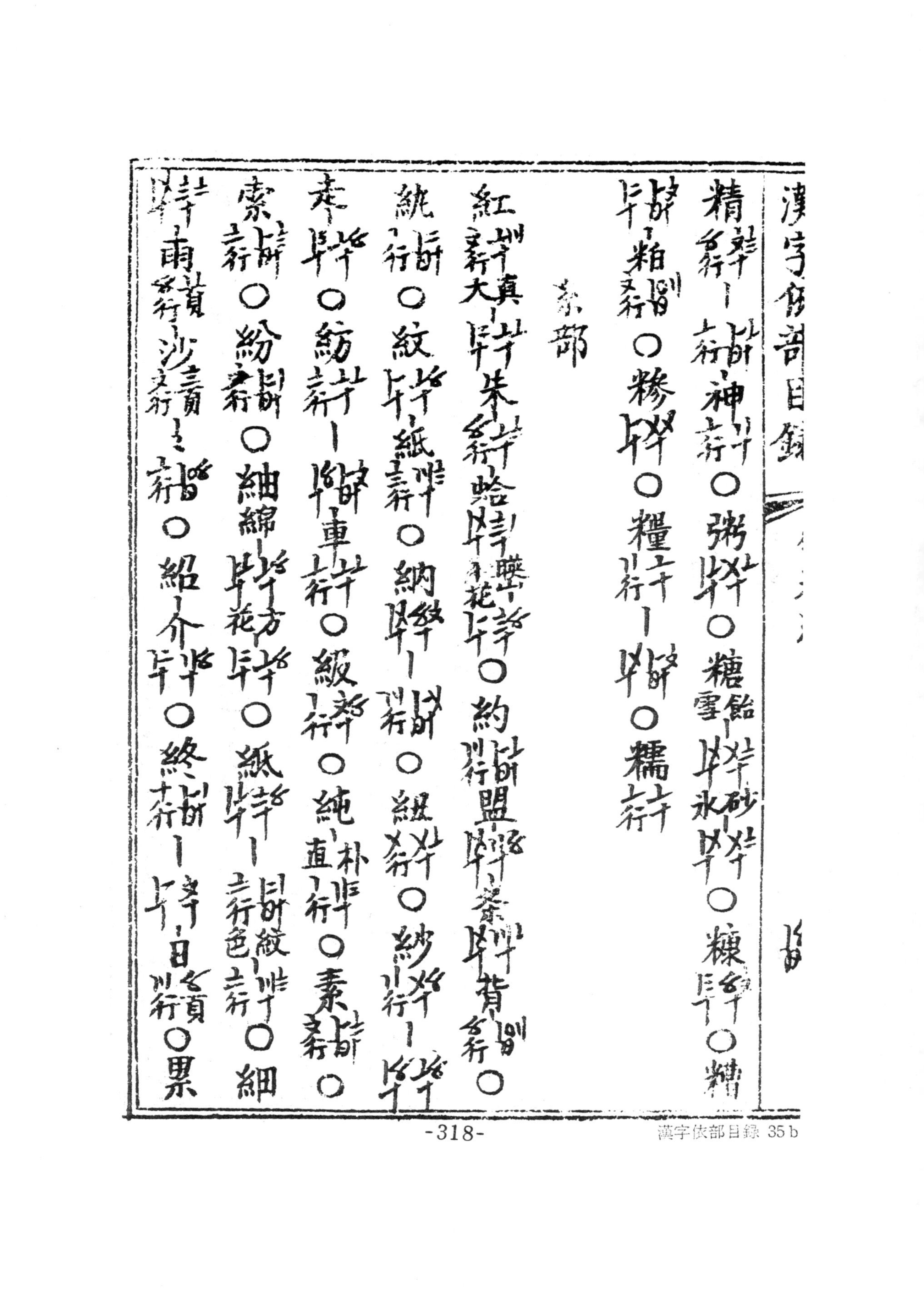

精 神 ○ 粥 ○ 糖 飴 雪 砂 冰 ○ 糠 ○ 糟

粕 ○ 糁 ○ 糧 ○ 糯

糸部

紅 大 真 朱 蛤 櫻 花 ○ 約 盟 茶 背 ○

紞 ○ 紋 紙 ○ 納 ○ 紐 ○ 紗 ○

紡 ○ 紡 車 ○ 綴 ○ 純 直 朴 ○ 素 ○

索 ○ 紛 ○ 紬 綿 方 花 ○ 紙 紋 色 ○ 細

雨 沙 ○ 紹 介 ○ 終 日 ○ 累

ㅣ行 ○ 組 ㅣ行 ○ 紘 ㅣ ○ 結 ㅣ十行 縛

寔 ○ 紫 ㅣ 芝 ○ 絕 壁 貢 島 賓 氣 倒

○ 給 ㅣ ○ 絡 連 ○ 絞 ○ 緣 ㅣ ○ 經 十行

ㅣ 十行 永 營 ○ 絳 ○ 綏 ○ 綺 ○ 緣 ○ 維

ㅣ ○ 綿 紬 木 ㅣ行 ○ 網 ○ 綱 ○ 繩

火 床 龍 ○ 綻 ○ 綉 ○ 綾 ○ 縈 ○

綠 銅 油 豆 草 ○ 緜 ○ 緣 故 因 ○ 縇 段 ○

緞 ○ 線 金 十行 ○ 緪 ○ 緩 ○ 繞 ○ 編 ○ 繇

넉 ○ 緯위 ○ 縿縹표行 ○ 縛박 結결行 ○ 縮숙行 脚각 ○ 縹표 縿

조行 ○ 繁번 ○ 縫봉行 ○ 縆 ○ 縷루行 ○ 縻미行 ○ 績

넉 ○ 纖섬行 ○ 織직行 廣광 交 ○ 繪회行 ○ 繝 縫봉行 ○

纜 碇정行 ○ 續속行 ○ 纏전行 ○ 纓영行 ○ 纛독行

○ 縳잔行

缶部

缸항行 ○ 缺결 磨마 然연行 ○ 罇준行 ○ 罐관行

网部

罕한 稀희行 ○ 罔망 ○ 罪죄 ○ 罝저 ○

罰벌 罷파 濡유行 熊웅行 羅라 罽계行 杭항 膺응行

羊部

羊 ○ 美 ○ 羔 ○ 羖 ○ 羌 ○ 群 ○ 義 ○ 羹 ○ 羶

羽部

羽 ○ 扇 ○ 翁 ○ 翌 ○ 習 ○ 翔 ○ 翡 ○ 翠 ○ 翫 ○ 翦 ○ 翼 ○ 翻 ○ 翳

老部

老 ○ 考 ○ 者

長 … 衡 … 行 …

而部

而 … 耐 …

耒部

耒 ○ 耘 ○ 耕 ○ 耞

耳部

耳 … 付語 … 十 ○ 耻 … 雪 … ○ 耿 … ○

聊 … ○ 聆 … ○ 耽 … ○ 聖 … 人 … ○ 聞 …

啓 … ○ 聰 … 明 … ○ 聒 … ○ 聲 … 名 … ○ 聽 … 信 …

… ○ 職 … ○ 聾 …

聿部　肄行○肅嚴

肉部

肉○腦○肌○肝○肘○肁○肚蔕○

肩○肥○育○背○手○叛龜約

○肴○胡桃椒鷰○胸襟○肺○

胃○脉○胄○胎○胱膀○能○

筆○脩茸○脊痛精○脂○脊

○脚飛麻緇○脛○脘○腋○腑

聿肉至自

○脾○脹○腐豆-○腕手-○腎○
腸○腰-○腥○腫○腹鳴-痛
○膀胱○腸蟬-○腿○膜眼-○膠阿-
○膝○膩子-○膳退-○膾○膲○膂
○臍○臀○臆○臏赤-○朦朧○臘
臂○臓○膩脂○朧朦-

臣部

臣 忠- 使-○臥-○臨-

自部

自-○稱-○嗚-然○臭腐-

[illegible]○皐[illegible]

至部

至[illegible]冬[illegible]○臺[illegible]墩[illegible]灼[illegible]

臼部

臼[illegible]○臾須[illegible]○舂[illegible]○與[illegible]○興[illegible]

[illegible]利[illegible]○舅[illegible]○舉[illegible]舊[illegible]親[illegible]

舌部

舐[illegible]○舘[illegible]所[illegible]守[illegible]

舛部

舞[illegible]

舟部

身신訓부○般一ㅣ반音기行○船선訓부大小快ㅣ부ㅣ艄기行頭두艣로出ㅣ부破ㅣ기行倉창暈ㅣ漁商ㅣ艭

여부下ㄱ行上宴ㅅ行○艙ㅣ房방三行

良部

良량音十行

色部

色색부ㅣ紙ㅣ三行茶ㅣ沉香ㅣ松花ㅣ藍草ㄱ行彩ㅣ行德ㅣ부○艷十行

艸部

艾애부ㅣ行○芋우부○芒ㅣ魚ㅣ行○芝지十行紫ㅣ부○芍藥부十行○花

階ㅅ行五糖ㅣ부ㅣ細ㅣ부ㅣ靈ㅣ부石ㅣ行草ㅣ行蓮ㅣ行梅ㅣ行蔾ㅣ行海藻ㅣ行辛夷ㅣ鳳仙ㅣ

紅ㅣ雞冠ㅣ蓼ㅣ千葉ㅣ盆ㅣ金錢ㅣ石부ㅣ槿부ㅣ萬葉ㅣ行茶ㅣ行○芥ㅣ부ㅣ○芹ㅣ行○芰

芳蘛 ○ 芼 ○ 芙蓉 ○ 芭蕉 ○ 芳 ○ 菌 ○

茨 真 西 ○ 茄 ○ 茉 ○ 苜蓿 ○ 苔 甘 ○

苧 布 ○ 芽 麦 ○ 苡 ○ 英 雄 ○

茅 屋 ○ 苦 辛 ○ 若 ○ 苟 且

○ 茂 ○ 茵 ○ 茶 色 ○ 荅 狀 ○ 荒

○ 菩 ○ 荏 ○ 荆 ○ 荔支 ○ 莽 ○ 茫

蒼 ○ 草 書 記 鞋 綠 簾 花 ○

茱萸 ○ 莓 莊 ○ 萊 ○ 荷 葉

搭 ○莧 ○蕫 ○蕙華花 ○莘蕙花 ○莞 ○
蔣 ○莖 ○華繁 ○葅 ○菴 ○菩薩
○著暮襯 ○菖蒲 ○菁 ○蕊紫野 ○
菘 ○萵 ○菌 ○菱 ○菊 ○華摩 ○蕳
○萍 ○萋 ○菉豆 ○葛粉 ○蕈
○葬 ○萸茱 ○蒸 ○萬 籍 ○落
○葉 荷 單花 ○葵
○葡萄 ○萄葡 ○萌 ○葦修 ○萱 ○蒼

茫十行三十行 ○ 蔓泄 ○ 蒙行古行 ○ 蔡十行 ○ 蒜行 ○
蔕花行 ○ 蒔繪行 ○ 蓉芙 ○ 幕炭行 ○ 蒲菖
○ 葦行箔行 ○ 蔑視 ○ 蔘海人 ○ 蓼行花
○ 蓬行 ○ 蓮行 ○ 蔓行 ○ 蕃行 ○ 董行｜ ○ 蕉
芭 ○ 藏｜行 ○ 蕨行 ○ 蘭行 ○ 蘚行 ○ 蕎 ○
蔔 ○ 薏 ○ 蔬 ○ 薙行 ○ 薺行 ○ 薔薇行 ○ 薪
｜行 ○ 薜荔 ○ 叢行 ○ 薄｜行石行淡行 ○
薦擧行 ○ 薩菩行 ○ 蕿行 ○ 藍｜行 ○ 藉狼

漢字依部目錄

行○蕭○藜○藤○薇○藁○

蓺行○藺○藪○藥○蘆

○藟○蘿○蘇○蘖○蘭

○藹○蘗○蘿

虍部

虎○虔○虛○處

何○虧○虞○號

虫部

虫倒ㅣ 蝗ㅣ 臭ㅣ 損ㅣ ○ 虹 ○ 蚩 ○ 蛷蠼 ○
蛟 帳 ○ 蛇 毒ㅣ ○ 蚣 蜈 ○ 蚤 ○ 蚪 蝌ㅣ
○ 蚑 ○ 蚱 ○ 蛞 ○ 蚯 蚓 ○ 蚓 蚯ㅣ ○ 蛆
○ 蛭ㅣ ○ 蛟 龍 ○ 蛤 紅 ○ 蛩 ○ 蛛
○ 蛙 ○ 蜀 ○ 蜜 果 蜾 蠟 ○ 蜂 ○ 蜓
○ 蜋 螳ㅣ ○ 蜉 蝣 ○ 蜍 蟾ㅣ ○ 蝣 蜉ㅣ ○ 蝇 ○
蝸 ○ 蜈 蚣 ○ 蝙 蝠 ○ 蝠 蝙 ○ 蝟 ○ 蝘
○ 蝨 ○ 蝗 虫 ○ 蝦 蟆 ○ 蝌 蚪 ○ 蟒 ○ 蝶

훈 行 ○ 螢 훈 行 ○ 蜺 훈 行 ○ 螺 훈 吹 훈 鈿 훈 行 ○ 蟆 蝦 훈 行 ○ 蝗

蜋 훈 ○ 蜷 蜂 훈 ○ 蟀 蟋 훈 ○ 蟠 훈 十行 ○ 蟲 훈 行 ○ 蠛 훈 ㄨ行 ○

蟹 훈 行 ○ 蟶 蝪 훈 行 ○ 蟬 훈 行 ○ 蟻 훈 ○ 蟾 훈 行 蜍 훈 行 ○ 蠐 훈 行

○ 蠟 油 훈 十行 蠶 훈 行 白 훈 ㄨ行 ○ 蠢 훈 行 ○ 蠹 훈 行 ○ 蠻 南 훈 行 ○ 蠼

蛜 훈 行 ○ 蠶 훈 行

血部

血 훈

行部

行 훈 行 훈 行 훈 훈 行 훈 步 훈 行 半 훈 行 纏

훈 行 横 훈 ㄨ行 奉 훈 ○ 衛 훈 十行 紹 훈 行 ○ 街 훈 行 ○ 衝 馬 훈 行 ○ 衙 훈 行

○衛 ○衛

衣部

衣 氅 單 海 地 ○初 伏 當 ○

表 衣 ○衫 油 長衫 ○衰 ○衷 ○

衲 ○被 ○裂 ○袍 ○袖 ○衾 ○袈裟

○衹 ○裁 ○袒 ○補 ○褏 ○裡 ○

裘 ○裴 ○裟 袈 ○裳 ○褒貶 ○褓

襍 ○褌 ○褙 ○袴 ○襪 ○襁褓 ○褉

三行 ○ 襞 二行 ○ 襪 三行 ○ 襯 著 三行 ○ 囊 二行 陰 一行 ○ 襲 三行 ○ 襻 五行

西部

西 二行 覈 東 覆 ○ 要 ○ 覆 ○ 覈 查 七行

見部

見 一行 規 五行 觀 十行 ○ 規 ○ 覗 十行 ○ 親 ○ 覓 五行 舊 十行 和 二行 ○ 覺 五行 ○ 觀

角部

角 十行 七行 指 三行 梳 六行 黃 十行 犀 四 盤 ○

解 ○ 觴 ○ 觸

言部

言 語 空 ○ 訓 導 ○ 記 件 錄 草 ○

訖 ○ 訟 ○ 訢 ○ 訥 ○ 設 ○ 許

諾 字 ○ 証 ○ 詳 試 誠 歎

○ 詁 ○ 詩 ○ 詠 ○ 誚 ○ 語 言 譜

○ 雜 ○ 誡 ○ 誦 ○ 說 ○ 誰 ○

論 公 ○ 誤 ○ 調 曲 理 ○ 誘 ○ 請

漢字依部目錄

○諸져ㅣ二行 ○侯ᄉᆡᆼ八行 ○談담 閑ㅣ부 ○諾 許ㅣ부 ○謀 同ㅣ

紅ㅣ 圖ㅣ 害ㅣ부 ○諫간二行 ○謂위 幺行 ○諭유 開ㅣ 二行 ○諛유 八行 ○諺언 文 八行 ○

諢 二行 ○謙겸 八行ㅣ부 ○謊황 八行 ○講강 十行ㅣ부 ○謹근 부 ○謝

辭ㅣ부 ○讁젹 六行 ○證증 八行 ○譏긔 八行ㅣ ○議의 六行 ○譖 語

行 ○譽예ㅣ 二行 ○護호 文行 ○變변 適 二行 ○讀독ㅣ 八行 ○

讚찬 二行 ○讎슈 報ㅣ 行 ○讓양 十行ㅣ 二行 ○讌연 八行

谷部 谷곡 讀 二行

豆部 豆두 腐 六行 大 小 文行 綠ㅣ부 ○豈긔 三行 ○豐풍 年 二行 賀

豕部　象○豪○豫

豸部　豹○豺○貂○貌

貝部

貝○負○貞○員○貢

財○貶○貨○販○貴

貸○買○賣○貽○貫○買

貼○賊○買○賃○賂

貧○費○資○賑○賢○賭

○賤 行 ○賞 行 ○賣買 ○質 行 ○賴 行

○寶 勉 行

赤部

赤

走部

走 歡 行 奔 行 ○起 提 行 兵 ○趄 趔

行 ○赴 趨 行 ○超 行 ○越 ○趣 ○趙

足部

足 行 掌 背 行 ○跑 蹉 行 ○距 行 ○路 斜 彎 行 水 行

䗪(?)程 ○ 跟 ○ 跡 ○ 跪 ○ 踈
○ 踣 踌 ○ 踐 ○ 蹄 ○ 踶 ○ 蹈 ○ 踰 ○
蹉 跎 ○ 蹇 ○ 躕 躇 ○ 躇 躅 ○ 蹶 ○ 蹴
○ 躅 躑 ○ 躁 ○ 蹲 踞 ○ 躍 ○ 躑 躅

身部

身 ○ 躬 ○ 體

車部

車 轣 轆 身 軍 官 器 ○ 軟
○ 軻 ○ 載 ○ 輕 才人 非 ○ 輔

○輪 ○輦 ○輸 ○轂 ○轉 ○輶 ○轎 ○轔 ○轡 ○鞍

辛部

辛 ○辦 ○辭 ○辯

辰部

辰 ○時 ○辱 ○農

辵部

适 ○返 ○近 ○間 ○逆 ○迫 ○切 ○迷 ○逃 ○送 ○迴 ○然 ○遂 ○逆

颩流 ○退 膳 ○送 ○逮 遲 ○

連 絡 ○逅 邂 ○通 事 變 ○

這 漢 ○逢 ○逐 ○造 ○途 ○逍

○逗 遛 ○進 宴 排 ○遠 ○達

○逸 ○道 權 ○過

太 ○遂 ○遑 ○逼 迫 遊 ○遐

○遙 ○運 ○遣 ○遲 滯 ○違 ○遡

○遮 陽 面 ○適 ○還 ○遼

○遺 二十行 ○遷ㅣ延 四十行 ○避 ○邂ㅣ逅 三十行 ○遵 川行 ○邇

○邊ㅣ 十行 ㅣ方 三十行 ○邈 ㅣ行

邑部

邑 四十行ㅣ 三十行 ○邛 六十行 ○邪ㅣ漢 ○郊ㅣ行 ○郡 四十行ㅣ 十行 ○

部 ○逢 ○都ㅣ 三十行 ○鄕 故ㅣ 六十行 ○郭 城 ○鄭 六十行

酉部

酉ㅣ時 ㅣ行 ○配 ○酌ㅣ酒 ○酢 酬ㅣ 三十行 ○酏ㅣ酪 六十行 ○醂

酢 三十行 ○酪 酡ㅣ 六十行 ○猷 ○酸 ○醋 ○醉 ○醒

○醎함○醜츄○醫의員 三行○醬쟝清 二行○釀냥 五行

釆部

釋셕 二行

里部

里리 千鏡 三行○重듕 十行 | 즁 | 뎡 陽 十行 珍 二行 | 뎡 | 량○野야 三行
| 량 | 뎡 俗 | 량○董소 | 냥○量량 五行 | 뎡

金部

金금 三行 | 뎡 泥 | 뎡 線 十行 錢花 | 금○釜부 五行○釘뎡 三行 蛭 | 뎡 三行○釪
| 뎡○鈞균 | 뎡 三行○釧쳔 | 뎡○鉅거 五行 | 뎡○鈍둔 三行 | 뎡 三行○

釪○鈞○鉛○鉢砂ㅣ○鉗○鉋○鉤○鈴水ㅣ○銃烏ㅣ○鉦○鈿螺ㅣ○鉒○銀ㅣ杏ㅣ河水ㅣ白魚○銅烏ㅣ○緣○銘○鉞斧○鋪○鉀○鋤○銲○錢ㅣ金花○錄事ㅣ記ㅣ○錫○合○錦○錡○錐○錯差ㅣ○錙○鍼○鍾○鍮○鍊○錘○鐃○鎭書○鏃○鎌○鎖烟ㅣ○鎔○鏊○鏟

鏡 重 魚 ○ 鏝 ○ 鐙子 鐵 九 火
煎 椎 杷 烙 蘇 ○ 鐘 樓 自鳴 ○ 鐥
○ 鐝 ○ 鑑 ○ 鑯 鑄 匠 ○ 鑰 ○ 鑽 之
鑢 ○ 鑿

長部

長 者 指 威 鼓 老 衫

門部

門 蓋 陰 段 ○ 閉 ○ 開 論
○ 閑 談 ○ 間 近 ○ 閏 月 貫 ○ 閨

丨 ○閨 ○閭丨閶 ○闓 ○闕丨子 ○闠闤丨

○闇丨： ○關 丨 ○闘

阜部

阜 ○阮 ○防 ○阿丨膠 ○限 ○陋丨

○除丨攵 ○降丨 ○陣 ○陳 丨 丨

○陸丨路 ○陛丨 ○陟 ○陪 ○階丨花丨

○陶丨 ○隋 ○際 ○隔 ○隅 ○陽

丨 重丨夕丨物丨遮 ○陰丨 丨門丨囊 ○隔

○隙 ○障 子 ○隱 ○險 ○

隨 ○隣

隶部

隸

隹部

隻 ○雄 英 ○雀 孔 [?] ○雉

○雅 ○雌 石黃 ○雞[?] ○雖 ○離 異

別 支 ○雜 技 語 亂 ○雞[?] ○難

○雙 [?]

雨部

雨 비우 〥行 細ㅣ 急ㅣ 〢頁 〦行 析 驟ㅣ 〢頁 〦行 ㅣ裝 ㅣ傘 〢行 ○ 雪 〢頁 十行 ㅣ糖 ㅣ恥 ○ 雲 〢頁 川行

ㅣ 〥行 ○ 雷 〢頁 川行 ○ 電 〢頁 〤行 雹 〢頁 ○ 霄 〤行 ○ 霍ㅣ 亂 〤行 ○ 霖ㅣ 雨

〢頁 〦行 ○ 霜 〢頁 ㅣ 十行 ○ 霞 〢頁 ○ 霧 〢頁 ○ 霰 〢頁 十行 ○ 露 〢頁 ㅣ 十行

ㅣ 出 〦行 ○ 霹 靂 〢頁 〤行 ○ 霸 ○ 靂 霹ㅣ 〢頁 〤行 ○ 霾ㅣ 花 ○ 靄 〢頁

○ 靈 〢行 ㅣ

青部

青 鴉ㅣ 二 〣ㅣ 十行 花ㅣ 回ㅣ ○ 靜 ㅣ 〡行 動

非部

非 〢行 ㅣ 常ㅣ 輕 〦行

面部　面　四　麻　遲

革部

革　貫　○勤　○靴　子　○䩞　○鞍　轡　馱　○
鞋　草　○鞘　○鞠　○鞦　韆　○鞭　○鞲
○韂　○韁　○韉　○韆　鞦

韋部　韓

非部

音部　音　失　○韻　次　○響

頁部

頃 ○ 頂 ○ 項 ○ 須 ○ 順 [illegible] 流 ○ 預 ○ 頒 ○ 頌 ○ 頗 ○ 頓 ○ 領 ○ 頭 [illegible] ○ 頹 ○ 賴 ○ 頻 ○ 顆 ○ 頻 ○ 顒 ○ 類 ○ 額 ○ 顏 ○ 顯 ○ 題 ○ 願 ○ 顙 ○ 顛 ○ 顧 ○ 顯 ○ 顱 ○ 顰

風部

風 東ㅣ南ㅣ西ㅣ北ㅣ 白ㅣ 中ㅣ 頭ㅣ 屛ㅣ 水ㅣ ○ 飌 ○

飄 風ㅣ

飛部

飛 脚ㅣ 船ㅣ 禽ㅣ

食部

食 寒ㅣ 歡ㅣ 飮ㅣ ○ 飢 ○ 飮 食ㅣ ○ 飯

早ㅣ 午ㅣ 夕ㅣ ○ 飫 ○ 飽 ○ 飯 ○ 飴 糖ㅣ ○ 餂

日ㅣ 月ㅣ ○ 餅 ○ 養 父ㅣ 母ㅣ 子ㅣ ○ 餌 魚ㅣ ○ 餉

○ 餘 ○ 餙 服ㅣ ○ 餞 ○ 饒 ○ 饅

○饌 찬

首部

首 슈

香部

香 향 三行 況 황 盒 文行 ○馨 형 四行

馬部

馬 마 理 四行 才 文行 駙 三行 衡 三行 雇 驄 駿 ○騆 三行 ○馳 三行

三行 ○馱 鞍 文行 十行 ○駁 班 三行 ○駙 篤 三行 ○駝 ○

騮 四行 ○駕 三行 ○駭 四行 ○駿 ○騅 馬 ○騎 三行

馬 ○騙 馬 ○騰 文行 ○騾 行 行 ○驅 三行

○驚 ○騐 ○驕 ○驟雨 ○驢

○驥

骨部 骨 髓 ○骸 ○髓骨 ○髏 ○體

高部 高 麗

髟部 髢 ○髮 白 ○髯 ○髻 ○鬚

勃 ○鬑 ○鬟

門部 鬪

鬯部 鬱

鬼部

鬼귀十三行○魂、魄귀十二行○魄魂ㅣ귀十二行○魁괴ㅣ行○魏

위ㅣ외

魚部

魚어三十ㅣ十行 魴방 鰹ㅣ어三十 鱷악三十 雞家ㅣ사 庚ㅣ洪홍三十 芒行、餌이三十行○魯로三十三行○鮀河ㅣ타三十上行○

魴방三十○鮎ㅣ魚점三十上行○鮒ㅣ魚부三十ㄱ行○鮪ㅣ魚유三十ㄱ行○鯊ㅣ魚사三十○鰥

ㅣ魚리三十上行○鯉ㅣ魚리三十○鯔ㅣ魚치三十○鯖ㅣ魚청三十又行○鯨ㅣ魚경三十○鰍

魚추三十三行○鰕하三十ㄱ行○鰒全生ㅣ복三十十行熟ㅣ숙三十○鰱ㅣ魚련三十○鰾ㅣ魚표三十○

鰥ㅣ夫환三十○鱖ㅣ魚궐三十ㄱ行○鱗린三十十行ㅣ앙ㄱ行○鱣ㅣ魚전三十又行○鱸ㅣ魚로三十

鳥部

鳥 二十 二行 一 乂行 統 二十 刂行 餌 二十 亠行 ○ 烏 二十 ○ 梟 二十 三行 ○ 鳳 二十 三行 一 一行 鶵

○ 鳩 二十 ○ 鳴 二十 刂行 ○ 鳰 二十 三行 ○ 鴦 二十 刂行 ○ 鴦 鴦 二十 十行 ○ 鴈 二十 一

○ 鴦 鴦 二十 十行 ○ 鴣 鷓 二十 刂行 ○ 鴿 鸛 二十 行 ○ 鴨 二十 刂行 ○ 鴉 青 二十

○ 鵂 鶹 二十 刂行 ○ 鵑 杜 二十 行 杜 花 二十 十行 ○ 鴷 二十 十行 ○ 鵝 二十 亠行 ○ 鵲 二十 ○

鵬 二十 ○ 鵡 鸚 二十 ○ 鶖 二十 ○ 鷓 鴿 二十 乂行 ○ 鵲 二十 ○ 鶉 二十 ○

鵙 二十 刂行 ○ 鶼 鶼 二十 ○ 鶻 二十 一行 ○ 鷄 家 魚 三十 鬥 雞 二十 ○ 鸂 鶒 二十 刂行 ○ 鷗

鵂 二十 刂行 ○ 鶴 鷓 二十 乂行 ○ 鶴 二十 行 ○ 鷗 二十 ○ 鷹 二十 師 二十 乂行 ○ 鸕 鵜

○鷹○鵂鶹○鶖鶬○鸛鶴○鸜○

鶺○鷺○鷀○鸂○鶩胡○鷯○

鸚鵡○鸕○鸞○鸑

鹿部

鹿○麒麟○麗高○麝○麟

麒○麤

麥部

麥○麰○麴○麵

麻部

麻 面 脚 疹 布 卑子○麾

黃部

黃 疸 芪 角 栗 硫 漆 丹

卄三行

黍部

黍 丄十三行

黑部

黙 卝十三行｜丄十三行○黠 卝十｜更｜頁三行○黜 卌十三行｜丄十三行○

黽部

黥 卌十三行○黶 卌十三行

黽部

鼈 丄十三行

鼎部

鼎 三十 乂行

鼠部

鼠 丄十○鼢 丄十○鼯 丄十

鼻部

鼻｜梁 卜十 孔十行｜洟 丄十○鼾 丄十

齊部 齊졔卆 一 齎재十行 䪫졔卆 ○ 齋재卆

齒部 齒치門粤卆 ○ 齔친卆 ○ 齕흘卆 ○ 齡령卆 ○ 齠툐 齟져卆

○ 齟져 齬어 三行 ○ 齦은卆 ○ 齬 齟져 三行 ○ 齮 齕흘卆

龍部 龍룡 十行 一 三行 龍방 龐방 文行 繩승 三行 蛟교 十行

龜部 龜귀 卄 貴귀 卄

漢字目録終

국어국문학총서 87

朝鮮偉國字彙

2018년 9월 15일 초판 1쇄 발행

저　자 : 메드허스트
펴낸이 : 김병환
펴낸곳 : 학자원
주　소 : 134-814 서울시 강동구 천호대로 1121
전　화 : 02) 6403-1000
팩　스 : 02) 6338-1001
E-mail : hakjaone@daum.net
등　록 : 2011년 3월 24일 제324-2011-14호

HAKJAONE Publishing Co.
1121 Cheonho-Daero Kangdong-Gu Seoul

ISBN : 979-11-6247-056-5 93810

값 45,000원

國語國文學叢書 087

朝鮮偉國字彙

학자원